Plastering

NVQ and Technical Certificate **Level 2**

Series Editor: **Arthur Watkins**

Contributing authors:

Kevin Jarvis
Eddie Gallagher
Mike Gashe

www.heinemann.co.uk

✓ Free online support
✓ Useful weblinks
✓ 24 hour online ordering

01865 888118

Heinemann

Heinemann is an imprint of Pearson Education Limited, a company incorporated in England and Wales, having its registered office at Edinburgh Gate, Harlow, Essex, CM20 2JE. Registered company number: 872828

www.heinemann.co.uk

Heinemann is a registered trademark of Pearson Education Limited

Text Chapters 1, 2, 3 and 5 © Carillion Construction Limited, Chapters 4, 6, 7, 8, 9, 10, 11 and 12 © Harcourt Education Limited.

First published 2007

12 11 10 09 08
10 9 8 7 6 5 4 3 2

British Library Cataloguing in Publication Data is available from the British Library on request.

ISBN 978 0 435449 45 2

Designed and typeset by HL studios
Produced by HL studios
Original illustrations © Harcourt Education Ltd 2007
Illustrated by HL studios

Cover design by GD Associates
Cover photo/illustration © Harcourt Education Ltd/Gareth Boden and Corbis
Printed in China (CTPS/02)

Websites

There are links to relevant websites in this book. In order to ensure that the links are up-to-date, that the links work, and that the sites are not inadvertently linked to sites that could be considered offensive, we have made the links available on the Heinemann website at www.heinemann.co.uk/hotlinks. When you access the site, the express code is 9522P.

The information and activities in this book have been prepared according to the standards reasonably to be expected of a competent trainer in the relevant subject matter. However, you should be aware that errors and omissions can be made and that different employers may adopt different standards and practices over time. Therefore, before doing any practical activity, you should always carry out your own Risk Assessment and make your own enquiries and investigations into appropriate standards and practices to be observed.

Contents

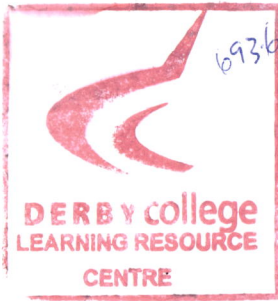

Introduction

The art of the plasterer combines many different practical and visual skills with knowledge of plastering materials and techniques. The information contained in these pages covers the plastering trade as a whole and in particular the knowledge and skills needed by the internal plasterer, the external plasterer and the fibrous plasterer. This book has been written based on a concept used within Carillion Training Centres for many years. That concept is about providing learners with the necessary information they need to support their studies and at the same time ensuring it is presented in a style which is both manageable and relevant.

This book has been produced to help the learner build a sound knowledge and understanding of all aspects of the NVQ and Technical Certificate requirements associated with plastering. It has also been designed to provide assistance when revising for Technical Certificate end tests and NVQ job knowledge tests.

Each chapter of this book relates closely to a particular unit of the NVQ or Technical Certificate and aims to provide the right level of information needed to form the required knowledge and understanding of that subject area.

This book provides a basic introduction to the tools, materials and methods of work required to complete work activities effectively and productively. Upon completion of your studies, this book will remain a valuable source of information and support when carrying out your work activities.

For further information on how the content of this student book matches to the unit requirements of the NVQ and Intermediate Construction Award, please visit www.heinemann.co.uk and follow the FE and Vocational link, followed by the Construction link, where a detailed mapping document is available for download.

Acknowledgments

The publishers would like to thank the author team for their contributions to this book: Arthur Watkins, Eddie Gallagher, Mike Gashe and Kevin Jarvis. In particular we would like to thank Arthur Watkins for his fine efforts as lead author and series editor for plastering.

We would also like to thank Dennis Crook, Steve Finch, Ryan Maher, Darren Maher, David Maguire and Rob Wilson, from Accrington and Rossendale College for their expert help and assistance at the photo shoot as plasterers and models, and Ian Pollitt for his role as technical adviser.

Photos

Alamy Images/Adrian Sheratt, p27, p168; Alamy Images/Creon Co. Ltd, p182; Alamy Images/Manor Photography, p40, p180; Art Directors and TRIP/Helene Rogers, p155; constructionphotography. com/Chris Henderson, p183; constructionphotography.com/Damien Gillie, p269; constructionphotography.com/David Potter, p131; constructionphotography.com/DIY Photolibrary, p149; Corbis, p37, p58, p59, p67, p125, p129; Getty Images/PhotoDisc, p1, p7, p11, p15, p17, p19, p31, p46, p48, p115, p127; Pearson Education Ltd, p3, p60, p61; Pearson Education Ltd/Chris Honeywell, p59; Pearson Education Ltd/Gareth Boden, p33, p50, p52, p52, p52, p52, p52, p54, p55, p55, p55, p97, p99, p101, p102, p102, p98, p101, p104, p106, p107, p107, p95, p104, p107, p111, p231, p231, p232; iStockPhoto.com/Guy Erwood, p130; iStockPhoto. com/Stan Rohrer, p148; Jupiter Images/Photos.com, p121; Maria Joannou, p104; Photographers Direct/Douglas Neil Photography, p150; Shout, p55; Toolbank, p59, p61.

All other photographs copyright Pearson Education Ltd/Jules Selmes.

How this book can help you

You will discover a variety of features throughout this book, each of which have been designed and written to increase and improve your knowledge and understanding. These features are:

- Photographs – many photographs that appear in this book are specially taken and will help you to follow a step-by-step procedure or identify a tool or material.

- Illustrations – clear and colourful drawings will give you more information about a concept or procedure.

- Definitions – new or difficult words are picked out in bold in the text and defined in the margin

- Remember – key concepts or facts are highlighted in these margin boxes to help you work safely.

- FAQs – frequently asked questions appear in all chapters along with informative answers from the experts.

- On the job scenarios – read about a real-life situation and answer the questions at the end. What would you do? (Answers can be found in the Tutor Resource Disc that accompanies this book.)

- End of chapter knowledge checks – test your understanding and recall of a topic by completing these questions.

- Glossary – at the end of this book you will find a comprehensive glossary that defines all the bold words and phrases found in the text. A great quick reference tool.

- Links to useful websites – any websites referred to in this book can be found at www.heinemann.co.uk/hotlinks. Just enter the express code 9452P to access the links.

chapter 1

The construction industry

OVERVIEW

Construction means creating buildings and services. These might be houses, hospitals, schools, offices, roads, bridges, museums, prisons, train stations, airports, monuments – and anything else you can think of that needs designing and building! What about an Olympic stadium? The 2012 London games will bring a wealth of construction opportunity to the UK, and so it is an exciting time to be getting involved.

In the UK, 2.2 million people work in the construction industry – more than in any other – and it is constantly expanding and developing. There are more choices and opportunities than ever before, and pay and conditions are improving all the time. Your career doesn't have to end in the UK either – what about taking your skills and experience abroad? Construction is a career you can take with you wherever you go. There's always going to be something that needs building!

This chapter will cover the following:

- Understanding the industry
- Communication
- Getting involved in the construction industry
- Sources of information and advice

Understanding the industry

The construction industry is made up of countless companies and businesses that all provide different services and materials. An easy way to divide these companies into categories is according to their size.

- A small company is defined as having between 1 and 49 members of staff.

- A medium company consists of between 50 and 249 members of staff.

- A large company has 250 or more people working for it.

A business might consist of only one member of staff (a sole trader).

The different types of construction work

There are four main types of construction work.

1. New work – this refers to a building that is about to be or has just been built.

2. Maintenance work – this is when an existing building is kept up to an acceptable standard by fixing anything that is damaged so that it does not fall into disrepair.

3. Refurbishment/renovation work – this generally refers to an existing building that has fallen into a state of disrepair and is then brought up to standard by repair. It also refers to an existing building that is to be used for a different purpose – for example, changing an old bank into a pub.

4. Restoration work – this refers to an existing building that has fallen into a state of disrepair and is then brought back to its original condition or use.

Find out

Think of an example of a small, a medium and a large construction company. Do you know of any construction companies that have only one member of staff?

New work is just one type of construction area

These four types of work can fall into one of two categories depending upon who is paying for the work.

1. Public – the government pays for the work, as is the case with most schools and hospitals, for example.

2. Private – work is paid for by a private client, and can range from extensions on an existing house to new houses or buildings.

Jobs and careers

Jobs and careers in the construction industry fall mainly into one of four categories:

1. building

2. civil engineering

3. electrical engineering

4. mechanical engineering.

Building involves the physical construction (making) of a structure. It also involves the maintenance, restoration and refurbishment of structures.

Civil engineering involves the construction and maintenance of work such as roads, railways and bridges.

Electrical engineering involves the installation and maintenance of electrical systems and devices such as lights, power sockets and electrical appliances.

Mechanical engineering involves the installation and maintenance of things such as heating, ventilation and lifts.

The category that is the most relevant to your course is building.

Plasterers are building craft workers

Job types

The construction industry employs people in four specific areas:

1. professionals

2. technicians

3. building craft workers

4. building operatives.

Professionals

Professionals are generally of graduate level (i.e. people who have a degree from a university), and may have one of the following types of job in the construction industry:

- architect – someone who designs and draws the building or structure; the head of the team

- structural engineer – someone who oversees the strength and structure of the building

- surveyor – someone who checks the land for suitability to build on

- service engineer – someone who plans the services needed within the building, for example, gas, electricity and water supplies.

Technicians

Technicians link professional workers with craft workers. This group is made up of the following people:

- architectural technician – someone who looks at the architect's information and makes drawings that can be used by the builder

- building technician – someone who is responsible for estimating the cost of the work and materials, and general site management

- quantity surveyor – someone who calculates ongoing costs and payment for work done.

Building craft workers

Building craft workers are the skilled people who work with materials to physically construct the building. The following jobs fall into this category:

- carpenter or joiner – someone who works with wood but also other construction materials such as plastic and iron. A carpenter works primarily on site whereas a joiner usually works off site, producing components such as windows, stairs, doors, kitchens and **trusses**, which the carpenter then fits into the building

- bricklayer – someone who works with bricks, blocks and cement to build the structure of the building

- plasterer – someone who adds finish to the internal walls and ceilings by applying a **plaster skim**. They also make and fix plaster **covings** and plaster decorations

- painter and decorator – someone who uses paint and paper to decorate the internal plaster and timberwork such as walls, ceilings, windows and doors, as well as **architraves** and **skirtings**

Definition

Truss – a prefabricated component of a roof that spreads the load of a roof over the outer walls and forms its shape

Plaster skim – a thin layer of plaster that is put onto walls to give a smooth and even finish

Coving – a decorative moulding that is fitted to the top of a wall where it meets the ceiling

Architrave – a decorative moulding, usually made from timber, that is fitted around door and window frames to hide the gap between the frame and the wall

Skirting – a decorative moulding that is fitted at the bottom of a wall to hide the gap between the wall and the floor

- electrician – someone who fits all electrical systems and fittings within a building, including power supplies, lights and power sockets

- plumber – someone who fits all water services within a building, including sinks, boilers, water tanks, radiators, toilets and baths. The plumber also deals with lead work and rainwater fittings such as guttering

- slater and tiler – someone who fits tiles on to the roof of a building, ensuring that the building is watertight

- woodworking machinist – someone who works in a machine shop, converting timber into joinery components such as window sections, spindles for stairs, architraves and skirting boards, among other things. They use a variety of machines such as lathes, bench saws, planers and sanders.

Building operatives

There are two different types of building operative working on a construction site:

1. specialist building operative – someone who carries out specialist operations such as dry wall lining, asphalting, scaffolding, floor and wall tiling or glazing

2. general building operative – someone who carries out non-specialist operations such as kerb laying, concreting, path laying and drainage. These operatives also support other craft workers and do general labouring. They use a variety of hand tools and power tools as well as **plant**, such as dumper trucks and JCBs.

Definition

Plant – in the context of the construction industry, industrial machinery

The building team

Constructing a building or structure is a huge task, which needs to be done by a team of people, who all need to work together towards the same goal. This group is often known as the building team. It is made up of the following people.

Client

The client is the person who requires the building or refurbishment. This person is the most important in the building team, because they finance the project, and without the client there is no work. The client can be a single person or an organisation.

Architect

The architect works closely with the client, interpreting their requirements to produce the building design and contract documents that enable the client's wishes to be realised.

Clerk of works

Selected by the architect or client to oversee the actual building process, the clerk of works ensures that construction sticks to agreed deadlines. They also monitor the quality of workmanship.

The building team is made up of many different people

Local authority

The local authority is responsible for ensuring that construction projects meet relevant planning and building legislation. Planning and building control officers inspect and approve building work.

Quantity surveyor

The quantity surveyor works closely with the architect and the client, acting as an accountant for the job. They are responsible for the ongoing evaluation of cost and interim payments from the client, establishing whether or not the contract is within budget. The quantity surveyor will prepare and sign off final accounts when the contract is complete.

Specialist engineers

Specialist engineers assist the architect in specialist areas, such as civil engineering, structural engineering and service engineering.

Health and safety inspectors

Employed by the Health and Safety Executive (HSE), health and safety inspectors ensure that the building contractor fully implements and complies with government health and safety legislation. For more information on health and safety in the construction industry, see Chapter 2 (page 37–66).

Building contractors

The building contractor agrees to carry out building work for the client. Contractors will employ the required workforce based on the size of the contract.

Estimator

The estimator works with the contractor on the cost of carrying out the building contract, listing each item in the bill of quantities (e.g. materials, labour and plant). They calculate the overall cost for the contractor to complete the contract, including further costs as overheads, such as site offices, management administration and pay, and not forgetting profit.

Site agent

The site agent works for the building contractor and is responsible for the day-to-day running of the site, such as organising deliveries.

Suppliers

The suppliers work with the contractor and estimator to arrange the materials that are needed on site and to ensure that they are delivered on time and in good condition.

General foreman

The general foreman works for the site manager and is responsible for coordinating the work of the ganger (see below), craft foreman and subcontractors. He or she may also be responsible for the hiring and firing of site operatives. The general foreman also liaises with the clerk of works.

Ganger

The ganger supervises the general building operatives.

Craft foreman

Each craft foreman works for the general foreman, organising and supervising the work of a particular craft. For example, the plastering craft foreman will be responsible for all plasterers on site.

Chargehand

A chargehand is normally only employed on large building projects, and is responsible for various craftworkers and working with joiners, bricklayers and plasterers.

Operatives

Operatives are the workers who carry out the building work. They are divided into three subsections.

1. Craft operatives are skilled tradesmen such as joiners, plasterers and bricklayers.

2. Building operatives are general building personnel who are responsible for drain laying, mixing concrete, unloading materials and keeping the site clean.

3. Specialist operatives include tilers, pavers, glaziers, scaffolders and plant operators.

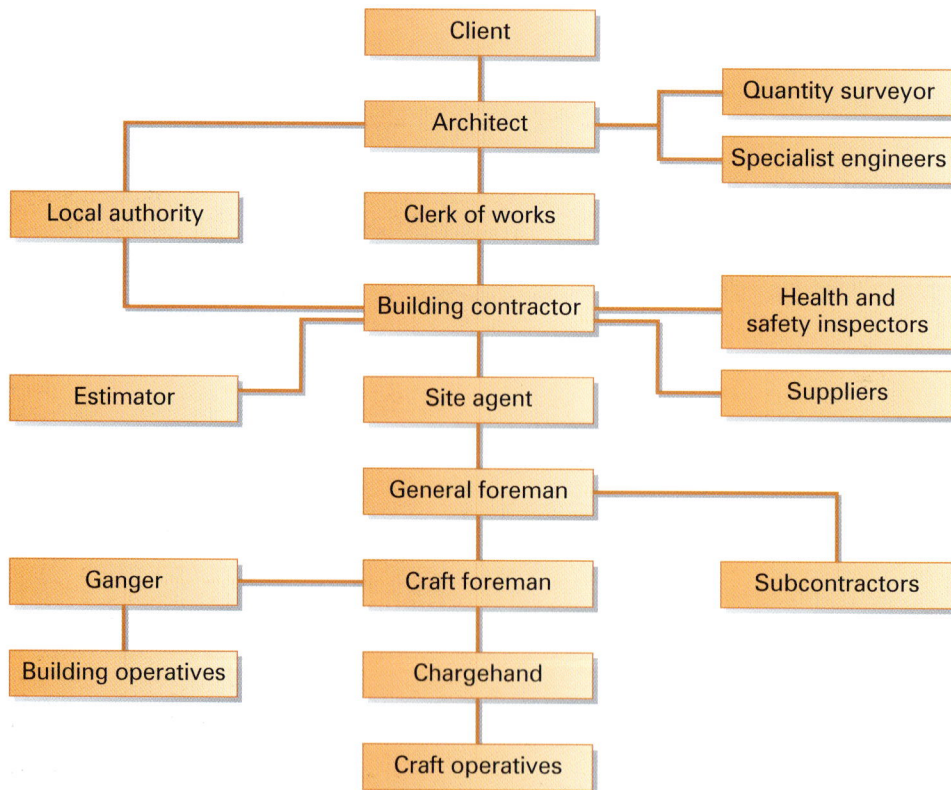

Figure 1.1 The building team

The different types of building

There are, of course, lots of very different types of building, but the main types are:

- residential – houses, flats or similar

- commercial – shops, supermarkets or similar

- industrial – warehouses, factories or similar.

These types of building can be further broken down by their height or the number of storeys that they have (one storey being the level from floor to ceiling):

- low rise – a building with one to three storeys

- medium rise – a building with four to seven storeys

- high rise – a building with more than seven storeys.

A low rise residential building

Buildings can also be categorised according to the number of other buildings they are attached to:

- detached – a building that stands alone and is not connected to any other building

- semi-detached – a building that is joined to one other building and shares a dividing wall, called a party wall

- terraced – a row of three or more buildings that are joined together, of which the inner buildings will share two party walls.

Building requirements

Every building must meet the minimum requirements of the Building Regulations, which were first introduced in 1961 and then updated in 1985. The purpose of Building Regulations is to ensure that safe and healthy buildings are constructed for the public, and that **conservation** is taken into account when they are being constructed. Building Regulations enforce a minimum standard of building work, and ensure that the materials used are of a good standard and fit for purpose.

What makes a good building?

When a building is designed, there are certain things that need to be taken into consideration, such as:

- security

- safety

- privacy

- warmth

- light

- ventilation.

A well-designed building will meet the minimum standards for all of the considerations above, and will also be built in line with Building Regulations.

The different parts of a building

All buildings consist of the following two main parts:

1. the substructure
2. the superstructure.

The substructure consists of all building work below ground level, including the foundations, up to the **damp proof course**. The purpose of the substructure is to spread the load of the building.

The superstructure consists of all the building work above the substructure; its purpose is to provide shelter and to divide the space.

The things that make up the substructure or superstructure can be divided into four different sections.

1. Primary elements – these include the main parts of the building that provide support, protection, floor-to-floor access and the division of space. Examples of primary elements are foundations, walls, floors, roofs and stairs.

2. Secondary elements – these include the non-essential and non-load-bearing parts that are used to close off openings or to provide a finish. Examples of secondary elements are doors, windows, skirtings and architraves.

3. Finishing elements – these include the final parts required to complete a component; they can be superficial or necessary to complete the job. Examples of finishing elements are paint, wallpaper, plaster or face brickwork.

4. Services – these are the electrical, mechanical and specialist installations that are normally piped or wired into the building. Examples of services are running water and electricity.

Definition

Damp proof course – a waterproof layer placed above ground level in a brick, block or stone wall to stop moisture coming up into the building

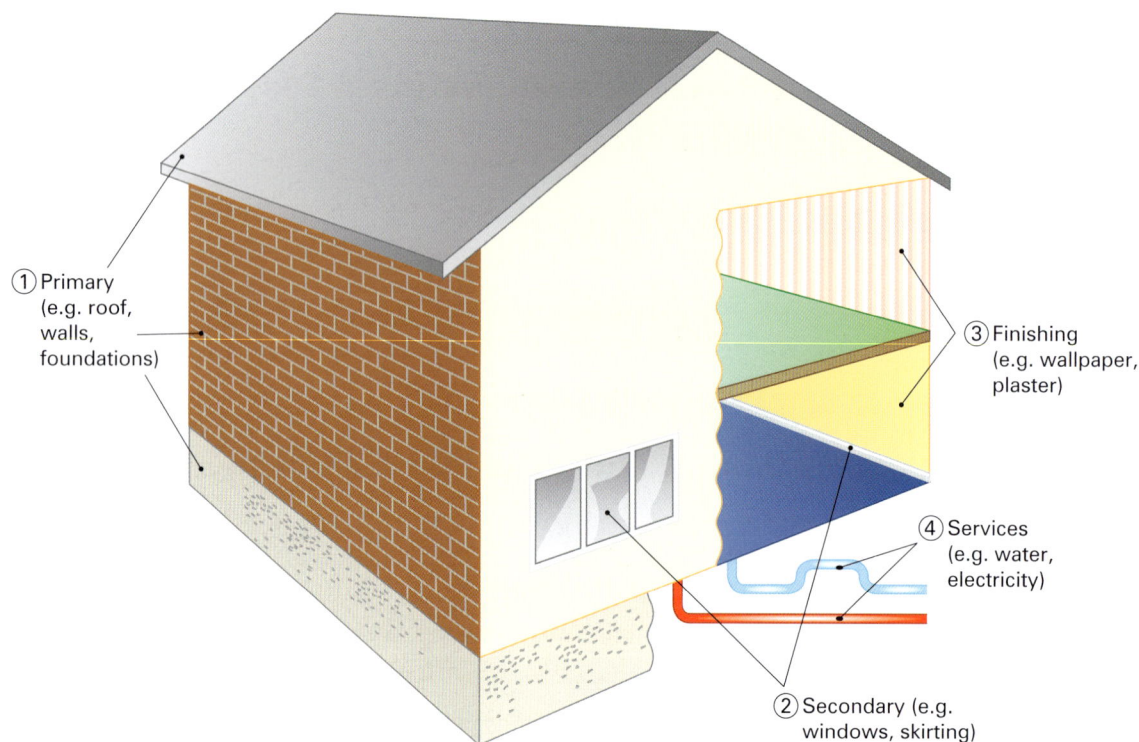

Figure 1.2 The four elements of a building

Communication

Communication, in the simplest of terms, means a way or means of passing on information from one person to another. Communication is very important in all areas of life, and we often do it without even thinking about it. You will need to communicate well when you are at work, no matter what job you do. What would happen if someone couldn't understand something you had written or said? If we don't communicate well, how will other people know what we want or need, and how will we know what other people want?

Companies that do not establish good methods of communicating with their workforce, or with other companies, will not function properly, and will end up with bad working relationships. Good working relationships can *only* be achieved with cooperation and good communication.

Methods of communication

There are many different ways of communicating with others, but they all generally fit into one of these three categories:

1. speaking (verbal communication), for example talking face to face or over the telephone

2. writing, for example sending a letter or taking a message

3. body language, for example the way we stand or our facial expressions.

Each method of communicating has good points (advantages) and bad points (disadvantages).

Verbal communication

Verbal communication is the most common method that we use to communicate with each other. If two people don't speak the same language, or if someone speaks very quietly or not very clearly, verbal communication cannot be effective. Working in the construction industry you may communicate verbally with other people face to face, over the telephone or by radio/walkie-talkie.

Advantages

Verbal communication is instant, easy and can be repeated or rephrased until the message is understood.

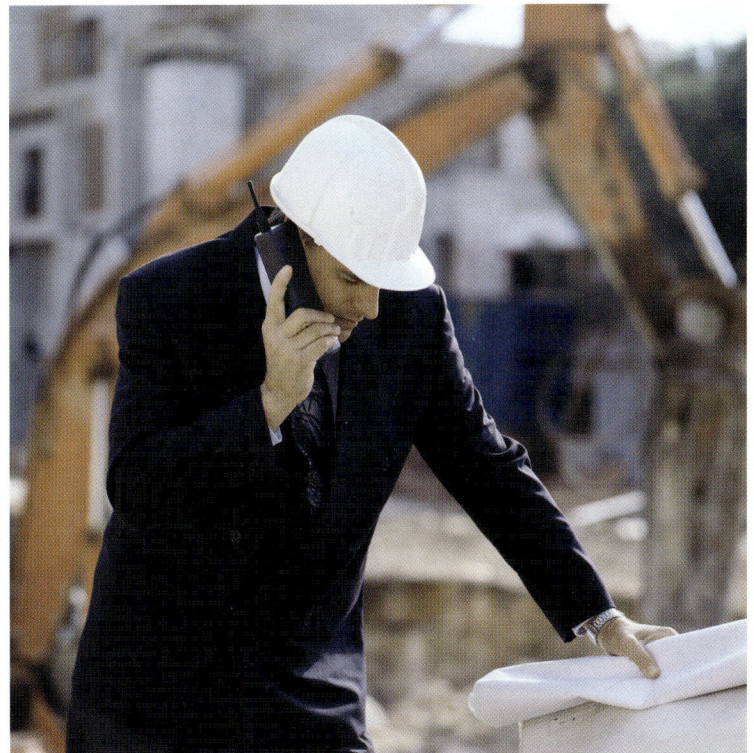

Verbal communication is probably the method you will use most

Disadvantages

Verbal communication can easily be forgotten as there is no physical evidence of the message. Because of this, it can be easily changed if passed on to other people. Someone's accent, or their use of slang words, can sometimes make it difficult to understand what they are saying.

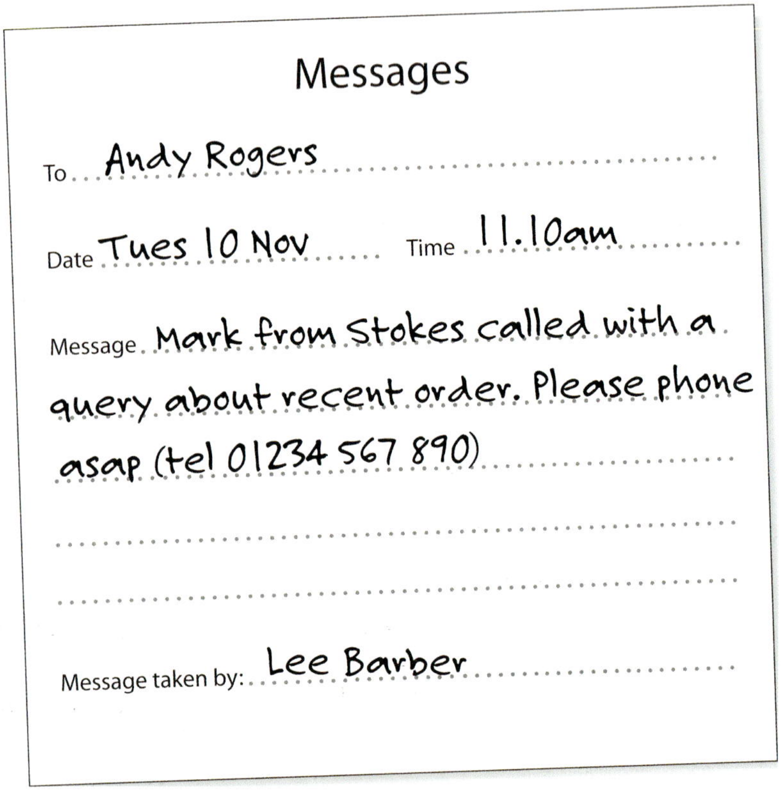

> ### Messages
>
> To Andy Rogers
>
> Date Tues 10 Nov   Time 11.10am
>
> Message Mark from Stokes called with a query about recent order. Please phone asap (tel 01234 567 890)
>
> Message taken by: Lee Barber

Figure 1.3 A message slip is a form of written communication

Written communication

Written communication can take the form of letters, faxes, messages, notes, instruction leaflets, text messages, drawings and emails, among others.

Advantages

There is physical evidence of the communication, and the message can be passed on to another person without it being changed. It can also be read again if it is not understood.

Disadvantages

Written communication takes longer to arrive and understand than verbal communication and body language. It can also be misunderstood or lost. If it is handwritten, the reader may not be able to read the writing if it is messy.

Body language

It is said that, when we are talking to someone face to face, only 10 per cent of the communication is verbal; the rest of the communication is body language and facial expression. This form of communication can be as simple as the shaking of a head from left to right to mean 'no', or as complex as the way someone's face changes when they are happy or sad, or the signs given in body language when someone is lying.

We often use hand gestures as well as words to get across what we are saying, to emphasise a point or to give a direction. Some people are able to communicate entirely through a form of body language called sign language.

Advantages

If you are aware of your own body language and know how to use it effectively, you can add extra meaning to what you say, for example when you are talking to a client or a work colleague. Even if the words you are using are friendly and polite, if your body language is negative or unfriendly, the message that you are giving out could be misunderstood. Simply by maintaining eye contact, smiling and not folding your arms, you can make sure that the person you are communicating with has not got a mixed or confused message.

Try to be aware of your body language

Body language is quick and effective. A wave from a distance can pass on a greeting without being close, and using hand signals to direct a lorry or a load from a crane is instant and doesn't require any equipment such as radios.

Disadvantages

Some gestures can be misunderstood, especially if they are given from very far away, and gestures that have one meaning in one country or culture can have a completely different meaning in another.

Which type of communication should I use?

Of the many different types of communication, the type you should use will depend upon the situation. If someone needs to be told something formally, then written communication is generally the best way. If the message is informal, then verbal communication is usually acceptable.

The way that you communicate will also be affected by who it is you are communicating with. You should, of course, always communicate in a polite and respectful manner with anyone you have contact with, but you need also to be aware of the need to alter the style of your communication sometimes. For example, when speaking to a friend, it may be fine to talk in a very informal way and use slang words, but in a work situation, with a client or a colleague, it is best to alter your communication to a more formal style in order to show professionalism. In the same way, it may be fine to leave a message or send a text to a friend that says 'C U @ 8 4 work', but if you wrote this down for a work colleague or a client to read, it would not look very professional, and they might not understand it.

Communicating with other trades

Communicating with other trades is vital, because they need to know what you are doing and when, and you need to know the same information from them. Poor communication can lead to delays and mistakes, which can both be costly. It is quite possible for poor communication to result in work having to be stopped or redone. Say you are plastering a room in a new building. You are just about to finish when you find out that the electrician, plumber or carpenter has to finish off some work under the plaster. This information didn't reach you, and now you will have to hack the new plaster off and do it again once the other work has been finished. What a waste of time and money! A situation like this can be avoided with good communication between the trades.

You will work with people from other trades

Common methods of communicating in the construction industry

A career in construction means that you will often have to use written documents such as drawings, specifications and schedules. These documents can be very large and seem very complicated but, if you understand what they are used for and how they work, using such documents will soon become second nature.

For more detailed information, see Chapter 3, 'Drawings' (pages 67–86).

Drawings

Drawings are done by the architect, and are used to pass on the client's wishes to the building contractor. Drawings are usually done to scale, because it would be impossible to draw a full-sized version of the project. A common scale is 1:10, which means that a line 10 mm long on the drawing represents 100 mm in real life. Drawings often contain symbols instead of written words to get the maximum amount of information across without cluttering the page.

Specifications

Specifications accompany a drawing and give you the sizes that are not available on the drawing, as well as telling you the type of material to be used and the quality to which the work has to be finished.

Schedules

A schedule is a list of repeated design information used on large building sites when there are several types of similar room or house. For example, a schedule will tell you what type of door must be used and where. Another form of schedule used on building sites contains a detailed list of dates by which work must be carried out, or materials delivered.

Other documents

As well as drawings, specifications and schedules there are some other important types of document you will come across that are not specifically about the building or structure that you are working on. Rather, they are about your day-to-day tasks and your job. We will now look at a selection of these documents.

Timesheet

A timesheet is used to record the hours you have worked and where the work was carried out. Failure to complete your timesheet accurately and submit it on time may result in a loss of wages.

P. Gresford Building Contractors

Timesheet _____

Employee _____   **Project/site** _____

Date	Job no.	Start time	Finish time	Total time	Travel time	Expenses
M						
Tu						
W						
Th						
F						
Sa						
Su						
Totals						

Employee's signature _____

Supervisor's signature _____

Date _____

Figure 1.4 A typical timesheet

Job sheet/daywork sheet

A job sheet is also used to record work you have done but includes the materials used, what plant was used and what hours were spent on a specific task. A daywork sheet is used to record work done that wasn't originally planned.

P. Gresford Building Contractors

Job sheet

Customer   Chris MacFarlane

Address   1 High Street

Any Town

Any County

Work to be carried out

Hang internal door in kitchen

Special conditions/instructions

Fit with door closer

3 × 75mm butt hinges

Figure 1.5 A typical job sheet

P. Gresford Building Contractors

Daywork sheet _____

Customer _____ **Date** _____

Description of work being carried out _____

_____

_____

Labour	Craft	Hours	Gross rate	TOTALS
Materials	Quantity	Rate	% addition	
Plant	Hours	Rate	% addition	

Comments

Signed _____ **Date** _____

Site manager/foreman signature _____

Figure 1.6 A typical daywork sheet

Requisition form

A requisition form (also known as an order form) is used when you require plant, materials or equipment. Once you have worked out what you need, and how much of it you need, a requisition form can then be filled in and sent to the relevant supplier.

Figure 1.7 A typical requisition form (order form)

P. Gresford Building Contractors

Requisition form

Supplier _____   Order no. _____

_____   Serial no. _____

Tel no. _____   Contact _____

Fax no. _____   Our ref _____

Contract/Delivery address/Invoice address   Statements/applications

_____   for payments to be sent to

_____   _____

Tel no. _____   _____

Fax no. _____   _____

Item no.	Quantity	Unit	Description	Unit price	Amount

Total £ _____

Payment terms _____   Date _____

Originated by _____

Authorised by _____

Remember

Make sure you have all the tools and equipment you need before you go to do a job. You will need to plan ahead and fill in a requisition form early!

Delivery note

A delivery note is sent by a supplier along with an order. It lists the materials delivered and the quantity. If you receive a delivery, you must check the delivery note against the tools, equipment or materials delivered. If everything matches, then you can sign the note. If anything is missing or damaged, you should not sign the note, but inform your supervisor.

Delivery Note

Bailey & Sons Ltd

Building materials supplier

Tel: 01234 567890

Your ref: AB00671

Our ref: CT020   **Date:** 17 Jul 2006

Order no: 67440387

Invoice address:
Carillion Training Centre,
Deptford Terrace, Sunderland

Delivery address:
Same as invoice

Description of goods	Quantity	Catalogue no.
OPC 25kg	10	OPC1.1

Comments:

Date and time of receiving goods:

Name of recipient (caps):

Signature:

Figure 1.8 A typical delivery note

Work programme

A work programme is a method of showing very easily what work is being carried out on a building and when. Used by many site agents or supervisors, a work programme is a bar chart that lists the tasks that need to be done down the left side and shows a timeline across the top (see Figure 1.9). A work programme is used to make sure that the relevant trade is on site at the correct time and that materials are delivered when needed. A site agent or supervisor can quickly tell from looking at the chart whether work is keeping to schedule or falling behind.

		Time in days						
		1	2	3	4	5	6	7
Activity	A	■						
	B	■	■	■				
	C		■	■				
	D			■	■	■		
	E		■	■	■	■	■	■
	F				■	■	■	■
	G						■	■

Figure 1.9 A work programme

Getting involved in the construction industry

There are many ways of entering the construction industry, but the most common way is as an apprentice.

Apprenticeships

You can become an apprentice by:

- being employed directly by a construction company, which will send you to college
- being employed by a training provider, such as Carillion, which combines construction training with practical work experience.

On 1 August 2002, the construction industry introduced a mandatory induction programme for all apprentices joining the industry. The programme has four distinct areas:

1. apprenticeship framework requirements

2. the construction industry

3. employment

4. health and safety.

An apprenticeship will give you on-the-job training and experience

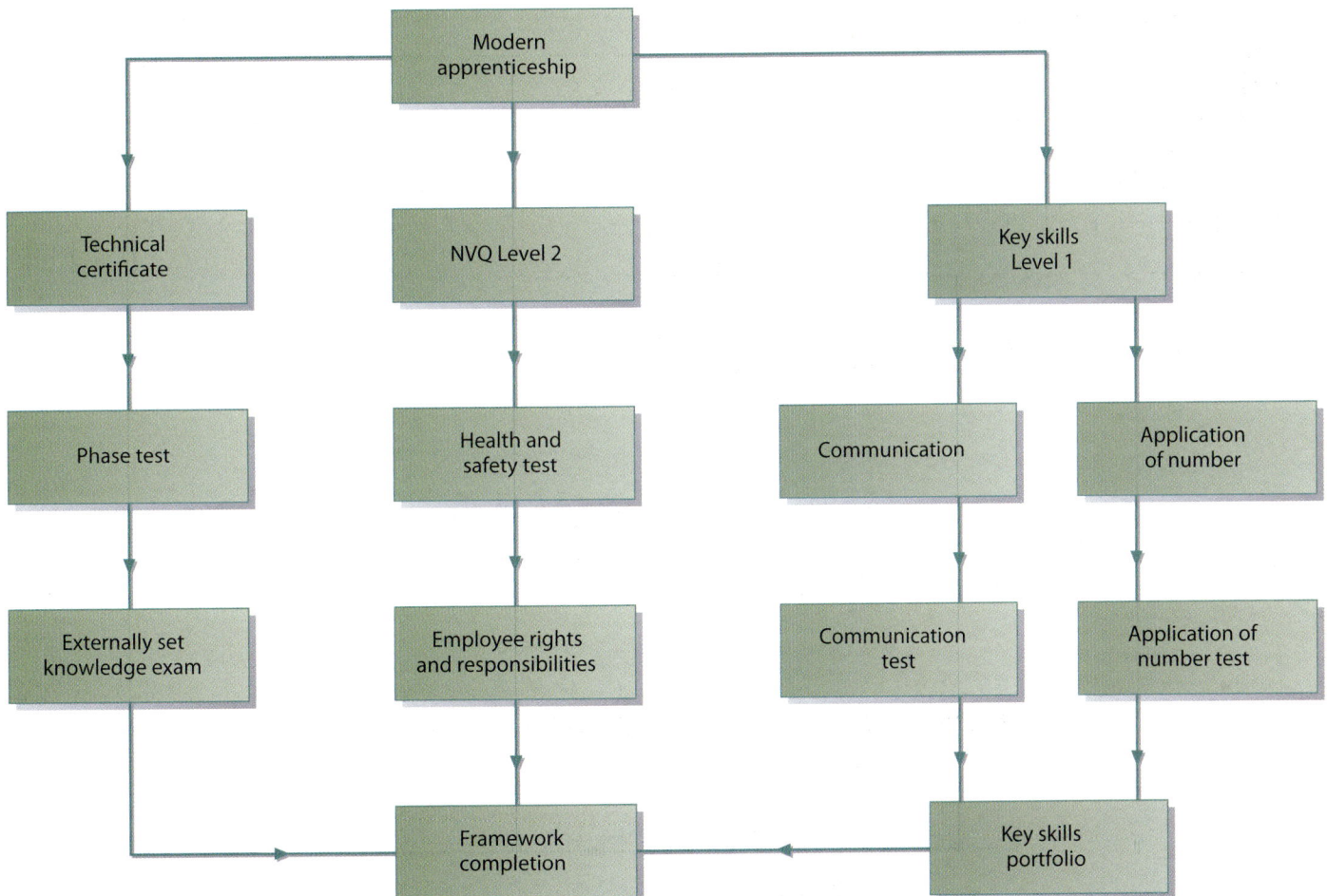

Figure 1.10 Apprenticeship framework

Apprenticeship frameworks are based on a number of components designed to prepare people for work in a particular construction occupation.

Construction frameworks are made up of the following mandatory components:

- NVQs

- technical certificates (construction awards)

- key skills.

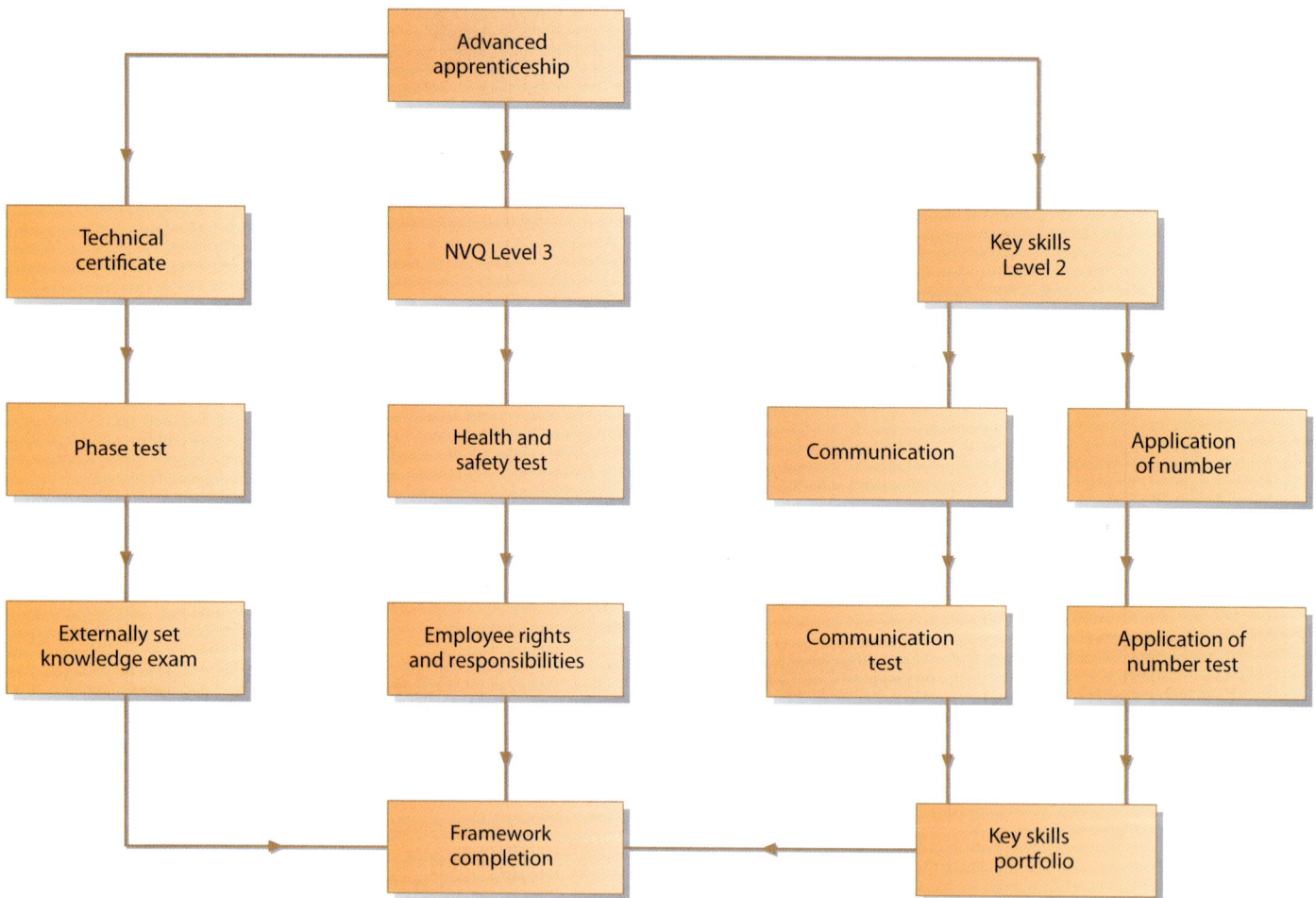

Figure 1.11 Advanced apprenticeship framework

However, certain trades require additional components. Bricklaying, for example, requires abrasive wheels certification.

National Vocational Qualifications (NVQs)

NVQs are available to anyone, with no restrictions on age, length or type of training, although learners below a certain age can only perform certain tasks. There are several levels of NVQ (1, 2, 3, etc.), which in turn are broken down into units of competence. NVQs are not like traditional examinations in which someone sits an exam paper. An NVQ is a 'doing' qualification, which means it lets the industry know that you have the knowledge, skills and ability to actually 'do' something.

The Construction Industry Training Board (CITB) is the national training organisation for construction in the UK, and is responsible for setting training standards. NVQs are made up of both mandatory and optional units, and the number of units that you need to complete for an NVQ depends on the level and the occupation.

NVQs are assessed in the workplace, and several types of evidence are used.

- Witness testimony consists of evidence provided by various individuals who have first-hand knowledge of your work and performance relating to the NVQ. Work colleagues, supervisors and even customers can provide evidence of your performance.

- Your actual performance can be observed a number of times in the workplace while you are carrying out work-related activities.

- The use of historical evidence means that you can use evidence of past achievement or experience, if it is directly related to the NVQ.

- Assignments or projects can be used to assess your knowledge and understanding of a subject.

- Photographic evidence showing you performing various tasks in the workplace can be used, provided it is authenticated by your supervisor.

Technical certificates

Technical certificates are often related to NVQs. A certificate provides evidence that you have the underpinning knowledge and understanding required to complete a particular task. An off-the-job training programme, either in a college or with a training provider, may deliver technical certificates. You generally have to sit an end-of-programme exam to achieve the full certificate.

Key skills

Some students have key skills development needs, so learners and apprentices must achieve key skills at Level 1 or 2 in both Communications and Application of number. Key skills are signposted in each level of the NVQ and are assessed independently, so you will need to be released from your training to attend a key skills test.

Employment

Conditions of employment are controlled by legislation and regulations. The Department for Business, Enterprise and Regulatory Reform (formerly the Department of Trade and Industry, DTI) publishes most of this legislation. To find out more about your working rights, visit their website. A quick link has been made available at www.heinemann.co.uk/hotlinks – just enter the express code 9522P.

These are the main pieces of legislation that will apply to you.

- The Employment Act 2002 gives extra rights to working parents, and gives guidance on resolving disputes, among other things.

- The Employment Relations Act 1999 covers areas such as trades union membership and disciplinary and grievance proceedings.

- The Employment Rights Act 1996 details the rights an employee has by law, including the right to have time off work and the right to be given notice if being dismissed.

- The Sex Discrimination Acts of 1975 and 1986 state that it is illegal for an employee to be treated less favourably because of their sex, for example paying a man more than a woman or offering a woman more holiday than a man, even though they do the same job.

- The Race Relations Act 1976 states that it is against the law for someone to be treated less favourably because of their race, nationality or ethnic origin.

The Race Relations Act protects people of all races and nationalities

- The Disability Discrimination Act 1995 makes it illegal for someone to be treated less favourably just because they have a physical or mental disability.

- The National Minimum Wage Act 1998 aims to make sure that everyone in the UK is paid at least a minimum rate. How much you must be paid depends on how old you are and whether or not you are on an apprenticeship scheme. The national minimum wage is periodically assessed and increased, so it is a good idea to make sure you know what it

Find out

What is the national minimum wage at the moment? You can find out from lots of different places, including the DTI website. You can find a link to the site at www.heinemann.co.uk/hotlinks – just enter the express code 9552P

is. At the time of writing, under 18s and those on apprenticeship schemes do not qualify for the minimum wage. As of 1 October 1997, for those aged 18–21, the minimum wage is £4.60 per hour; and for adult workers aged 22 or over, the minimum wage is £5.52 per hour.

Contract of employment

Within two months of starting a new job, your employer must give you a contract of employment. This will tell you the terms of your employment, and should include the following information:

- job title
- place of work
- hours of work
- rates of pay
- holiday pay
- overtime rates
- statutory sick pay
- pension scheme
- disciplinary procedure
- termination of employment
- dispute procedure.

If you have any questions about information contained within your contract of employment, you should talk to your supervisor before you sign it.

When you start a new job, you should also receive a copy of the company's safety policy and an employee handbook containing details of the company's general policy, procedures and disciplinary rules.

Discrimination in the workplace

Discrimination means treating someone unjustly, and in the workplace it can range from bullying, intimidation or harassment to paying someone less money or not giving them a job. Discriminating against people within the working environment is against the law. This includes discrimination on the grounds of:

- sex, gender or sexual orientation

- race, colour, nationality or ethnic origin

- religious beliefs

- disability.

The law states that employment, training and promotion should be open to all employees regardless of any of the above. Pay should be equal for men and women if they are required to do the same job.

Men and women must be treated equally at work

Sources of information and advice

There are many places you can go to get information and advice about a career in the construction industry. If you are already studying, you can speak to your tutor or your school or college careers advisor, or you can get in touch with Connexions for careers advice especially for young people. Visit www.heinemann.co.uk/hotlinks and enter the express code 9552P for a link to the Connexions website. You can also find their telephone number in your local phonebook.

Organisations such as those listed below are very good sources of careers advice specific to the construction industry.

- CITB (Construction Industry Training Board) – the industry's national training organisation
- City and Guilds – a provider of recognised vocational qualifications
- The Chartered Institution of Building Services Engineers
- The Institution of Civil Engineers
- Trades unions such as GMB (Britain's General Union), UCATT (Union of Construction, Allied Trades and Technicians), UNISON (the public services union), Amicus (the manufacturing union, previously MSF).

Links to all these organisations' websites can be found by visiting www.heinemann.co.uk/hotlinks and entering the express code 9552P.

FAQ

Why do I need to learn about different trades?

It is very important that you have some basic knowledge of what other trades do. This is because you will often work with people from other trades, and their work will affect yours and vice versa.

What options do I have once I have gained my NVQ Level 2 qualification?

Once you are qualified, there is a wide range of career opportunities available to you. For example, you could progress from a tradesperson to a foreman and then to a site agent. There may also be the opportunity to become a clerk of works, an architect or a college lecturer. Some tradespeople are happy to continue as they are, and some start up their own businesses. You may wish to progress onto NVQ Level 3, which can offer a better route into work as an architect or as a college or university lecturer.

Knowledge check

1. How many members of staff are there in a small company, a medium company and a large company?

2. Give an example of a public construction project. Who pays for public work?

3. Name a job in each of the four construction employment areas: professional; technician; building craft worker; building operative.

4. Why is the client the most important member of the building team?

5. Explain the meaning of the following building types: residential; low rise; semi-detached.

6. What is the substructure of a building?

7. What are the three different methods of communication?

8. What information might a schedule give you?

9. What does NVQ stand for?

10. What information must be in your contract of employment?

chapter 2

Health and safety

OVERVIEW

Every year in the construction industry over 100 people are killed and thousands more are seriously injured in the course of the work that they do. There are thousands more who suffer from health problems, such as dermatitis, asbestosis, industrial asthma, vibration white finger and deafness. You can therefore see why it is essential to learn as much as you can about health and safety.

This chapter will cover:

- Health and safety legislation
- Health and welfare in the construction industry
- Manual handling
- Fire and fire-fighting equipment
- Safety signs
- Personal protective equipment (PPE)
- Reporting accidents
- Risk assessments

Health and safety legislation

While you are at work, in whatever location or environment that may be (e.g. on a building site or in a client's home), you need to be aware of some important laws that are there to protect you from harm. The laws state how you should be protected and what your **employer** has to do to keep you safe, i.e. their responsibilities.

Health and safety legislation not only protects you, but also states what your responsibilities are in order to keep others safe. It is very important that you follow any guidance given to you regarding health and safety, and that you know what your responsibilities are.

What is legislation?

The word 'legislation' generally refers to a law that is made by Parliament, and is often called an Act. For our purposes, Health and Safety Acts state what should and shouldn't be done by employers and employees in order to keep workplaces safe. If an employer or an employee does something they shouldn't or, just as importantly, doesn't do something they should, they could face paying a large fine or may even receive a prison sentence.

Health and safety legislation you need to be aware of

There are a lot of different pieces of legislation and regulations that affect the construction industry. Over the next few pages are just a few of those that you need to be aware of. The day-to-day effects of these are covered in this chapter.

Health and Safety at Work Act 1974

The Health and Safety at Work Act 1974 applies to all places of work, not just construction environments. It protects not only employers and employees but also any member of the public who might be affected by the work being done. The Act outlines what must be done by employers and employees to ensure that the work they do is safe.

The main objectives of the Health and Safety at Work Act are:

- to ensure the health, safety and welfare of all persons at work

- to protect the general public from work activities

- to control the use, handling, storage and transportation of explosives and highly flammable substances

- to control the release of **noxious** or offensive substances into the atmosphere.

The Health and Safety at Work Act is **enforced** by the Health and Safety Executive (HSE). HSE inspectors have the power to:

- enter any premises to carry out investigations

- take statements and check records

- demand seizure of, dismantle, neutralise or destroy anything that is likely to cause immediate serious injury

- issue an improvement notice, which gives a company a certain amount of time to sort out a health and safety problem

- issue a prohibition notice, which stops all work until the situation is made safe

- give guidance and advice on health and safety matters

- **prosecute** people who break the law; this includes employers, employees, the self-employed, manufacturers and suppliers.

As we learnt at the beginning of this chapter, employers and employees have certain responsibilities under health and safety legislation. These are often referred to as 'duties' and are things that should or shouldn't be done by law. If you do not carry out your duties you are breaking the law, and you could be prosecuted.

Definition

Noxious – harmful or poisonous

Enforce – make sure a law is obeyed

Prosecute – accuse someone of committing a crime, which usually results in them being taken to court and, if found guilty, punished

Find out

Will you be working with any highly flammable, explosive or noxious substances? What are they?

Duties of the employer

Under the Health and Safety at Work Act employers must:

- provide a safe entrance and exit to and from the workplace

- provide a safe place to work

- provide and maintain safe machinery and equipment

- provide employees with the necessary training to be able to do their job safely

- have a written safety policy

- ensure safe handling, transportation and storage of machinery, equipment and materials

- provide personal protective equipment (PPE)

- involve trades union safety representatives, where appointed, in all matters relating to health and safety.

You have a legal duty to work safely at all times

Duties of the employee

Under the Health and Safety at Work Act employees must:

- take care at all times and ensure that they do not put themselves or others at risk by their actions

- cooperate with employers with regard to health and safety

- use any equipment and safeguards provided by their employer

- not misuse or interfere with anything that is provided for their safety.

Control of Substances Hazardous to Health (COSHH) Regulations 2002

The COSHH Regulations state how employees and employers should work with, handle, move and dispose safely of potentially dangerous substances. A substance hazardous to health is anything that might negatively affect your health. For example:

- dust or small particles from things such as bricks and wood

- fumes from chemicals

- chemicals in things like paint, **adhesives** and cement

- explosive or flammable chemicals or material.

The main aim of the COSHH Regulations is to ensure that any risks due to working with hazardous substances or being exposed to them are assessed. Action must then be taken to eliminate or control the risks.

There are three different ways in which hazardous substances can enter the body:

1. inhalation – breathing in the dangerous substance

2. absorption – when the hazardous substance enters the body through the skin

3. ingestion – taking in the hazardous substance through the mouth.

The COSHH Regulations are as follows:

1. You should know exactly what products and substances you are using. You should be given this information by your employer.

2. Any hazards to health from using a substance or being exposed to it must be assessed by your employer.

Definition

Adhesive – glue

Find out

Will you be working with any substances hazardous to health? What precautions and safety measures do you think should be taken for each?

Remember

It is not always possible to see a harmful substance so, if you are given any PPE or instructions about how to use/move/dispose of something, be sure to use them. Don't think that just because you can't see a hazardous substance, it isn't there

Safety tip

If you come across a substance that you are unsure about, do not use it. Report it to your supervisor as soon as possible

3. If a substance is associated with any hazards to health, your employer must eliminate or control the hazard, either by using a different substance or by making sure the substance is used according to guidelines (e.g. used outside or used only for short periods of time). Your employer must also provide you with appropriate PPE and make sure that all possible precautions are taken.

4. Your employer must ensure that people are properly trained and informed of any hazards. All staff should be trained to recognise identifiable hazards, and should know the correct precautions to take.

5. In order to make sure precautions are up to date, your employer has to monitor all tasks, and change any control methods when required.

6. In case anyone ever needs to know what happened in the past, a record of all substances used by employees must be kept.

Provision and Use of Work Equipment Regulations 1998 (PUWER)

Under PUWER, all tools and equipment must be regularly serviced and repaired

The PUWER Regulations cover all working equipment such as tools and machinery. Under the PUWER regulations employers must make sure that any tools and equipment they provide are:

- suitable for the job

- maintained (serviced and repaired)

- inspected (a regular check that ensures the piece of equipment and its parts are still in good working condition).

Employers also have to make sure that any risk of harm from using the equipment has been identified, and that all precautions and safety measures have been taken. Employers must also ensure that anyone who uses the equipment has been properly trained and instructed in how to do so.

The Manual Handling Operations Regulations 1992

These regulations cover all work activities in which a person does the lifting instead of a machine. The correct and safe way to lift, which reduces the risk of injury, is covered later on in this chapter (see pages 50–52).

The Control of Noise at Work Regulations 2005

In the course of your career in construction, it is likely that you will be at some time working in a noisy environment. The Control of Noise at Work Regulations are there to protect you against exposure to high levels of noise, which can lead to permanent hearing damage.

Damage to hearing can be caused by:

- the volume of noise (measured in decibels)

- the length of time you are exposed to the noise (over a day, over a lifetime, etc.).

The regulations give guidance on the maximum period of time someone can safely be exposed to a given decibel level, and your employer has to follow it.

If you have access to the internet, you might wish to visit the Health and Safety Executive website to find out what it is like to have hearing loss caused by long-term exposure to noise. A link to the web page has been made available at www.heinemann.co.uk/hotlinks – just enter the express code 9552P.

The Work at Height Regulations 2005

It is not at all unusual for a construction worker to carry out their everyday job high off the ground, for example on scaffolding, on a ladder, or on the roof of a building. The Work at Height Regulations make sure that your employer does all that they can to reduce the risk of injury or death from working at height. Your employer has a duty to:

- avoid work at height where possible
- use equipment that will prevent falls
- use equipment and other methods that will minimise the distance and consequences of a fall.

As an employee, under the regulations you must follow any training that has been given to you, report any hazards to your supervisor, and use any safety equipment that is made available to you.

The Electricity at Work Regulations 1989

The Electricity at Work Regulations cover any work that involves the use of electricity or electrical equipment. Your employer has a duty to make sure that electrical systems that you may come into contact with are safe and regularly maintained. They also have to make sure that they have done everything the law states to reduce the risk of an employee coming into contact with a live electrical connection.

The Personal Protective Equipment at Work Regulations 1992

There are certain situations in which you will need to wear PPE. The Personal Protective Equipment at Work Regulations detail the different types of PPE that are available, and state when they should be worn. Your employer has to ensure appropriate PPE is available for certain tasks (e.g. gloves when working with solvents, face masks when mixing plaster, safety goggles when using a circular saw).

The different types of PPE available are covered in more detail later in this chapter (see pages 58–61).

Reporting of Injuries, Diseases and Dangerous Occurrences Regulations 1995 (RIDDOR)

Employers have duties under RIDDOR to report accidents, diseases or dangerous occurrences. This information is used by the HSE to identify where and how risk arises, and to investigate serious accidents.

Several other regulations exist that cover very specific things such as asbestos, pressure equipment and lead paint. If you want to find out more about these regulations, or any others, ask your tutor or employer for more information, or visit the Health and Safety Executive website (go to www.heinemann.co.uk/hotlinks and enter the express code 9552P for a quick link).

Health and welfare in the construction industry

Jobs in the construction industry have one of the highest injury and accident rates, and as a worker you will be at constant risk unless you adopt a good health and safety attitude. By following the rules and regulations set out to protect you, and by taking reasonable care of yourself and others, you will become a safe worker and thus reduce the chance of injuries or accidents.

The most common risks to a construction worker

What do you think these might be? Think about the construction industry you are working in and the hazards and risks that exist.

Accidents can happen if your work area is untidy

The most common health and safety risks a construction worker faces are:

- accidents
- ill health.

Accidents

We often hear the saying 'accidents will happen', but when working in the construction industry we should not accept that accidents just happen sometimes. When we think of an accident, we quite often think about it as being no one's fault, and something that could not have been avoided. Not so! The truth is that most accidents are caused by human error, which means someone has done something they shouldn't have done or, just as importantly, not done something they should have done.

Accidents often happen when someone is hurrying, not paying enough attention to what they are doing, or have not received the correct training.

If an accident happens, you or the person it happens to may be lucky, and not be injured. More often, an accident will result in an injury, which may be minor (e.g. a cut or a bruise) or possibly major (e.g. loss of a limb). Accidents can also be fatal. The most common causes of fatal accidents in the construction industry are:

- falling from scaffolding

- being hit by falling objects and materials

- falling through fragile roofs

- being hit by forklifts or lorries

- electrocution.

Ill health

While working in the construction industry, you will be exposed to substances or situations that may be harmful to your health. Some of these health risks may not be noticeable straightaway; indeed, it may take years for **symptoms** to be noticed and recognised.

Ill health can result from:

- exposure to dust (such as asbestos), which can cause breathing problems and cancer

- exposure to solvents or chemicals, which can cause **dermatitis** and other skin problems

- lifting heavy or difficult loads, which can cause back injury and pulled muscles

- exposure to loud noise, which can cause hearing problems and deafness

- using vibrating tools, which can cause **vibration white finger** and other problems with the hands.

Everyone has a responsibility for health and safety in the construction industry, but accidents and health problems still happen too often. Make sure you do what you can to prevent them.

Definition

Symptom – a sign of illness or disease (e.g. difficulty in breathing, a sore hand, or a lump under the skin)

Dermatitis – a skin condition where the affected area is red, itchy and sore

Vibration white finger – a condition that can be caused by using vibrating machinery (usually for very long periods of time). The blood supply to the fingers is reduced, which causes pain, tingling and sometimes spasms (shaking)

Staying healthy

As well as keeping an eye out for hazards, you must also make sure that you look after yourself and stay healthy. One of the easiest ways to do this is to wash your hands on a regular basis. By washing your hands you are preventing hazardous substances from entering your body through ingestion (swallowing). You should always wash your hands after going to the toilet and before eating or drinking.

Other precautions that you can take are ensuring that you wear **barrier cream**, use the correct PPE, and only drink water that is labelled as drinking water. Remember that some health problems do not show symptoms straightaway, and that what you do now can affect you much later in life.

Definition

Barrier cream – a cream used to protect the skin from damage or infection

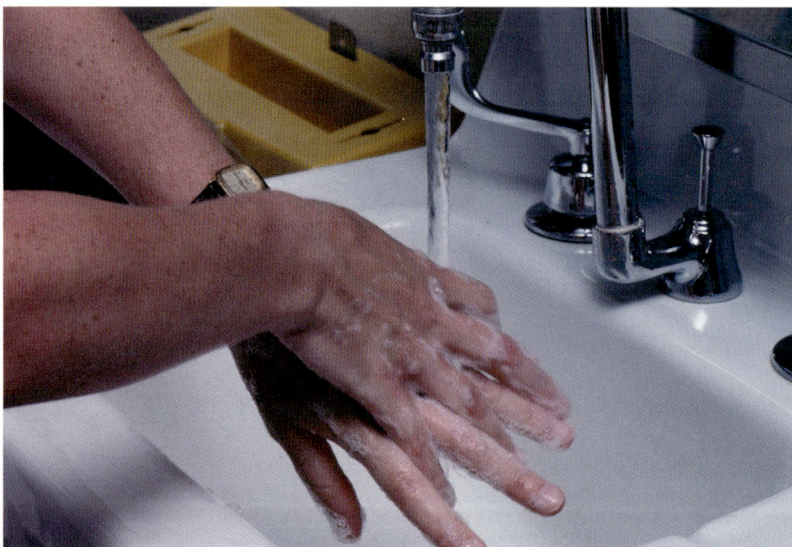

Always wash your hands to prevent ingesting hazardous substances

Welfare facilities

Welfare facilities are things such as toilets, which must be provided by your employer to ensure a safe and healthy workplace. There are several things that your employer must provide to meet welfare standards.

- Toilets – the number of toilets provided depends on the number of people who are intended to use them. Males and females can use the same toilets provided there is a lock on the inside of the door. Toilets should be flushable with water or, if this is not possible, with chemicals.

- Washing facilities – employers must provide a basin large enough to allow people to wash their hands, faces and forearms. Washing facilities must have hot and cold running water as well as soap and a means of drying your hands. Showers may be needed if the work is very dirty or if workers are exposed to **corrosive** or **toxic** substances.

- Drinking water – there should be a supply of clean drinking water available, either from a tap connected to the mains or from bottled water. Taps connected to the mains need to be clearly labelled as drinking water, and bottled drinking water must be stored in a separate area to prevent **contamination**.

- Storage or dry room – every building site must have an area where workers can store the clothes that they do not wear on site, such as coats and motorcycle helmets. If this area is to be used as a drying room, adequate heating must also be provided in order to allow clothes to dry.

- Lunch area – every site must have facilities that can be used for taking breaks and lunch well away from the work area. These facilities must provide shelter from the wind and rain and be heated as required. There should be access to tables and chairs, a kettle or urn for boiling water, and a means of heating food, such as a microwave.

When working in an occupied house, you should make arrangements with the client to use the facilities in their house.

Definition

Corrosive – describes a substance that can damage things it comes into contact with (e.g. material, skin)

Toxic – poisonous

Contamination – when harmful chemicals or substances pollute something (e.g. water)

Safety tip

When placing clothes in a drying room, do not place them directly on heaters as this can lead to fire

On the job: Manual handling

Glynn and Frankie are unloading bags of plaster from a wheelbarrow. While handling a bag of plaster, Glynn gets a sharp pain in his back and drops the bag. Frankie goes and tells their supervisor, who comes over to where Glynn is sitting in a great deal of pain. What do you think should happen next? Do you think this incident could have been prevented?

Manual handling

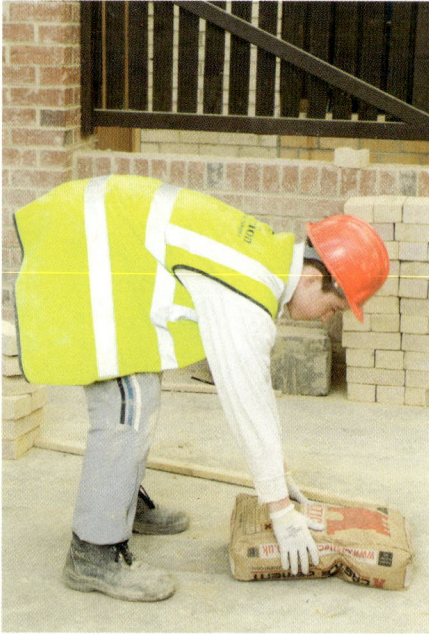

Poor manual handling techniques like this can lead to serious permanent injury

Manual handling means lifting and moving a piece of equipment or material from one place to another without using machinery. Lifting and moving loads by hand is one of the most common causes of injury at work. Most injuries caused by manual handling result from years of lifting items that are too heavy, or are awkward shapes or sizes, or from using the wrong technique. However, it is also possible to cause a lifetime of back pain with just one single lift.

Poor manual handling can cause injuries such as muscle strain, pulled ligaments and hernias. The most common injury by far is spinal injury. Spinal injuries are very serious because there is very little that doctors can do to correct them and, in extreme cases, workers have been left paralysed.

What you can do to avoid injury

The first and most important thing you can do to avoid injury from lifting is to receive proper manual handling training. Kinetic lifting (see opposite) is a way of lifting objects that reduces the chance of injury.

Before you lift anything, you should ask yourself some simple questions:

- Does the object need to be moved?

- Can I use something to help me lift the object? A mechanical aid such as a forklift or crane, or a manual aid such as a wheelbarrow, may be more appropriate than a person.

- Can I reduce the weight by breaking down the load? Breaking down a load into smaller and more manageable weights may mean that more journeys are needed, but it will also reduce the risk of injury.

- Do I need help? Asking for help to lift a load is not a sign of weakness; team lifting will greatly reduce the risk of injury.

- How much can I lift safely? The recommended maximum weight a person should lift is 25 kg, but this is only an average weight, and each person is different. The amount that a person can lift will depend on their physique, age and experience.

- Where is the object going? Make sure that any obstacles in your path are out of the way before you lift. You also need to make sure that there is somewhere to put the object down when you get there.

- Am I trained to lift? The quickest way to receive a manual handling injury is to use the wrong lifting technique.

Lifting correctly (kinetic lifting)

When lifting any load it is important to keep the correct posture and to use the correct technique.

For the correct posture before lifting:

- feet should be shoulder width apart with one foot slightly in front of the other;

- knees should be bent;

- back must be straight;

- arms should be as close to the body as possible; and

- your grip must be firm, using the whole hand and not just the finger tips.

For the correct technique when lifting:

- approach the load squarely, facing the direction of travel;

- adopt the correct posture (as above);

- place hands under the load and pull the load close to your body; and

- lift the load using your legs and not your back.

When lowering a load, you must also adopt the correct posture and technique, as follows:

- bend at the knees, not the back;

- adjust the load to avoid trapping fingers; and

- release the load.

Remember

Even light loads can cause back problems so, when lifting anything, always take care to avoid twisting or stretching

Think before lifting

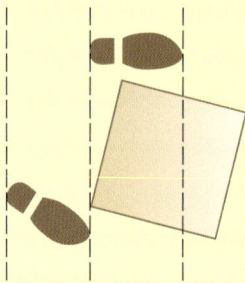

Adopt the correct posture before lifting

Get a good grip on the load

Adopt the correct posture when lifting

Move smoothly with the load

Adopt the correct posture and technique when lowering

Fire and fire-fighting equipment

Fires can start almost anywhere and at any time, but a fire needs three things to burn:

1. fuel

2. heat

3. oxygen.

This can be shown in what is known as the 'triangle of fire'. If any one side of the triangle is removed, the fire cannot burn and it will go out.

Remember:

- remove the fuel and there is nothing to burn, so the fire will go out

- remove the heat and the fire will go out

- remove the oxygen and the fire will go out, as fire needs oxygen to continue burning.

Fires can be classified according to the type of material that is involved:

- Class A – wood, paper, textiles, etc.

- Class B – flammable liquids, petrol, oil, etc.

- Class C – flammable gases, liquefied petroleum gas (LPG), propane, etc.

- Class D – metal, metal powder, etc.

- Class E – electrical equipment.

Figure 2.1 The triangle of fire

Find out

What fire risks are there in the construction industry? Think about some of the materials (fuel) and heat sources that could make up two of the sides of the 'triangle of fire'

Fire-fighting equipment

There are several types of fire-fighting equipment, such as fire blankets and fire extinguishers. Each type is designed to be the most effective at putting out a particular class of fire, and some types should never be used in certain types of fire.

Fire extinguishers

A fire extinguisher is a metal canister containing a substance that can put out a fire. There are several different types, and it is important that you learn which type should be used on specific classes of fire. This is because, if you use the wrong type, you may make the fire worse or risk severely injuring yourself.

Fire extinguishers are now all one colour (red), but they have a band of colour that shows what substance is inside.

Water

The coloured band is red, and this type of extinguisher can be used on Class A fires. Water extinguishers can also be used on Class C fires in order to cool the area down.

A water fire extinguisher should *never* be used to put out an electrical or burning fat/oil fire. This is because electrical current can carry along the jet of water back to the person holding the extinguisher, electrocuting them. Putting water onto burning fat or oil will make the fire worse as the fire will 'explode', potentially causing serious injury.

Water fire extinguisher

Foam

The coloured band is cream, and this type of extinguisher can also be used on Class A fires. A foam extinguisher can also be used on a Class B fire if the liquid is not flowing.

Carbon dioxide (CO_2)

The coloured band is black, and the extinguisher can be used on Class A, B, C and E fires.

Dry powder

The coloured band is blue, and this type of extinguisher can be used on all classes of fire. The powder puts out the fire by smothering the flames.

Foam fire extinguisher

Carbon dioxide (CO_2) extinguisher

Dry powder extinguisher

Fire blankets

Fire blankets are normally found in kitchens or canteens, as they are good at putting out cooking fires. They are made of a fireproof material and work by smothering the fire and stopping any more oxygen from getting to it, thus putting it out. A fire blanket can also be used if a person is on fire.

It is important to remember that, when you put out a fire with a fire blanket, you need to take extra care as you will have to get quite close to the fire.

A fire blanket

What to do in the event of a fire

During **induction** to any workplace, you will be made aware of the fire procedure as well as where to find the fire assembly points (also known as muster points) and what the fire alarm sounds like. On hearing the alarm, you must stop what you are doing and make your way to the nearest muster point. This is so that everyone can be accounted for. If you do not go to the muster point, or if you leave before someone has taken your name, someone may risk their life by going back into the fire to get you.

> ### Definition
>
> **Induction** – a formal introduction you will receive when you start any new job, where you will be shown around, shown where the toilets and canteen, etc. are, and told what to do if there is a fire

When you hear the alarm, you should not stop to gather any belongings, but you must not run. If you discover a fire, you must try to fight it only if it is blocking your exit, or if it is small. Only when you have been given the all-clear can you re-enter the site or building.

Safety signs

Safety signs can be found in many areas of the workplace. They are put up in order to:

- warn of any **hazards**
- prevent accidents
- inform where things are
- tell you what to do in certain areas.

Types of safety sign

There are many different safety signs, but each will usually fit into one of four categories.

1. Prohibition signs – these tell you that something *must not* be done. They always have a white background and a red circle with a red line through it.

2. Mandatory signs – these tell you that something *must* be done. They are also circular but have a white symbol on a blue background.

Figure 2.2 A prohibition sign

Figure 2.3 A mandatory sign

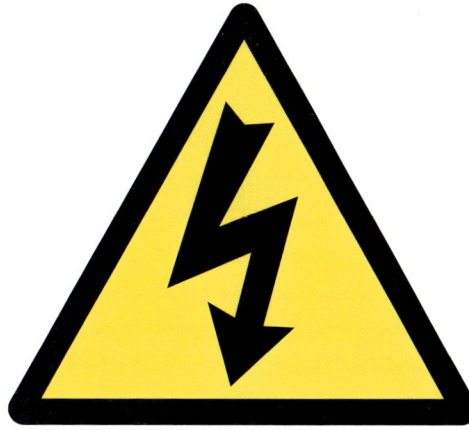

Figure 2.4 A warning sign

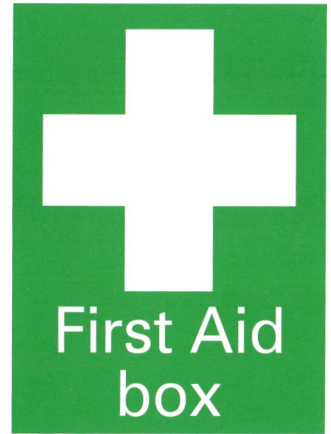
First Aid box

Figure 2.5 An information sign

3. Warning signs – these signs are there to alert you to a specific hazard. They are triangular and have a yellow background and a black border.

4. Information signs – these give you useful information such as the location of things (e.g. a first aid point). They can be square or rectangular and are green with a white symbol.

Most signs only have symbols that let you know what they are saying. Others have some words as well: for example, a no smoking sign might have a cigarette in a red circle, with a red line crossing through the cigarette and the words 'No smoking' underneath.

Remember

Make sure you take notice of safety signs in the workplace – they have been put up for a reason!

Fire exit

Figure 2.6 A safety sign with both symbol and words

Remember

PPE only works properly if it is being used – and used correctly!

Personal protective equipment (PPE)

Personal protective equipment is a form of defence against accidents or injury, and comes in the form of articles of clothing. This is not to say that PPE is the only way of preventing accidents or injury. It should be used together with all the other methods of staying healthy and safe in the workplace (i.e. equipment, training, regulations and laws).

PPE must be supplied by your employer free of charge, and you have responsibility as an employee to look after it and use it whenever it is required.

Types of PPE

There are certain parts of the body that require protection from hazards during work, and each piece of PPE must be suitable for the job and be used properly.

Head protection

A safety helmet

There are several different types of head protection, but the one most commonly used in construction is the safety helmet (or hard hat). This is used to protect the head from falling objects and knocks, and has an adjustable strap to ensure a snug fit. Some safety helmets come with attachments for ear defenders or eye protection. Safety helmets are meant to be worn directly on the head, and must not be worn over any other type of hat.

Eye protection

Eye protection is used to protect the eyes from dust and flying debris. The three main types, all made of a durable plastic, are:

1. safety goggles – used when there is a danger of dust getting into the eyes or a chance of impact injury

2. safety spectacles – give less protection than goggles because they don't fully enclose the eyes and so only protect from flying debris

3. face masks – protect the entire face from flying debris but do not protect the eyes from dust.

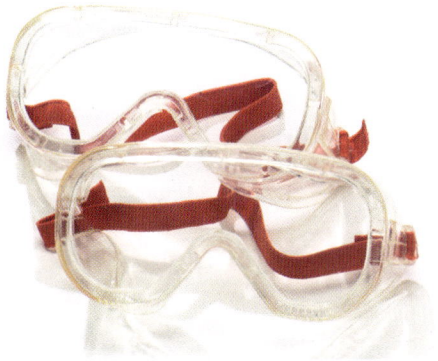

Safety goggles

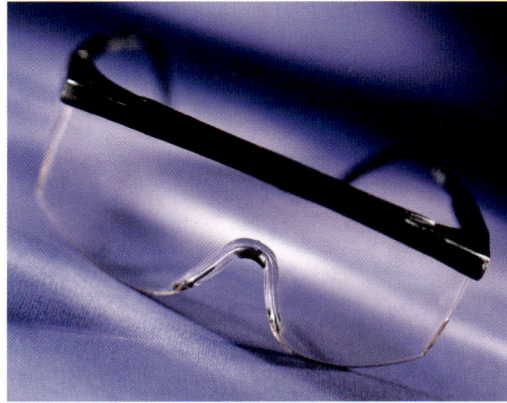

Safety spectacles

Foot protection

Safety boots or shoes are used to protect the feet from falling objects, and to prevent sharp objects such as nails from injuring the foot. Safety boots should have a steel toe-cap and steel mid-sole.

Safety boots

Earplugs

Hearing protection

Hearing protection is used to prevent damage to the ears caused by very loud noises. There are several types of hearing protection available, but the two most common types are:

1. Earplugs – these are small fibre plugs that are inserted into the ear, and used when the noise is not too severe. When using earplugs, make sure that you have clean hands before inserting them, and never use plugs that have been used by somebody else.

2. Ear defenders – these are worn to cover the entire ear, and are connected to a band that fits over the top of the head. They are used when there is excessive noise. They must be cleaned regularly.

Ear defenders

Respiratory protection

Respiratory protection is used to prevent workers from breathing in any dust or fumes that may be hazardous. The main type of respiratory protection is the dust mask.

Dust masks are used when working in a dusty environment, and are lightweight, comfortable and easy to fit. They should be worn by only one person, and must be disposed of at the end of the working day. Dust masks will only offer protection from non-toxic dust so, if the worker is to be exposed to toxic dust or fumes, a full respiratory system should be used.

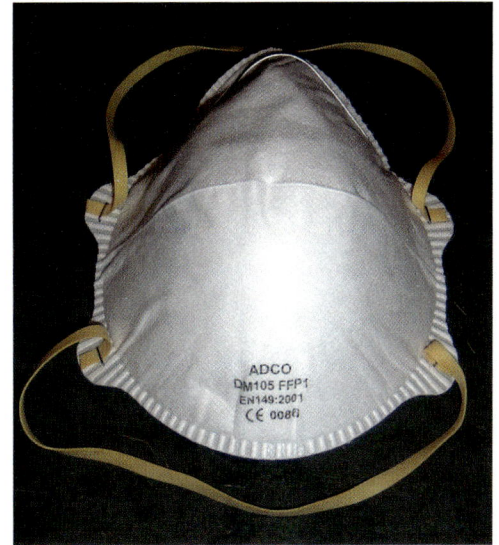

A dust mask

Hand protection

There are several types of hand protection, and each type must be used for the correct task. For example, wearing lightweight rubber gloves to move glass will not offer much protection, so leather gauntlets must be used. Plastic-coated gloves will protect you from certain chemicals, and Kevlar® gloves offer cut resistance. To make sure you are wearing the most suitable type of glove for the task, you need to look first at what is going to be done and then match the type of glove to that task.

Safety gloves

Reporting accidents

When an accident occurs, there are certain things that must be done. All accidents need to be reported and recorded in the accident book (Figure 2.7), and the injured person must report to a trained first aider. Under the Reporting of Injuries, Diseases and Dangerous Occurrences Regulations 1995 (RIDDOR), your employer must report to the HSE any accident that results in:

- death

- major injury

- an injury that means the injured person is not at work for more than three consecutive days.

The accident book is completed by the person who had the accident or, if this is not possible, someone who is representing the injured person.

The accident book will ask for some basic details about the accident, including:

- who was involved

- what happened

- where it happened

- the day and time of the accident

- details of any witnesses to the accident

- the address of the injured person

- what PPE was being worn

- what first aid treatment was given.

As well as reporting accidents, 'near misses' must also be reported. This is because near misses are often the accidents of the future. Reporting near misses might identify a problem, and can prevent the same accidents from happening again. This allows a company to be **proactive** rather than **reactive**.

Definition

Proactive – taking action *before* something happens (e.g. an accident)

Reactive – taking action *after* something happens

Report of an Accident, Dangerous Occurrence or Near Miss

Date of incident _____   **Time of incident** _____

Location of incident _____

Details of person involved in incident

Name _____   Date of birth _____   Sex _____

Address _____

_____

_____   Occupation _____

Date off work (if applicable) _____   **Date returning to work** _____

Nature of injury _____

Management of injury   ☐ First Aid only   ☐ Advised to see doctor

                            ☐ Sent to casualty   ☐ Admitted to hospital

Account of accident, dangerous occurrence or near miss
(Continued on separate sheet if necessary)

[ ]

Witnesses to the incident
(Names, addresses and occupations)

[ ]

Was the injured person wearing PPE? If yes, what PPE? _____

_____

Signature of person completing form _____

Occupation _____   **Date** _____

Figure 2.7 A typical accident book page

Risk assessments

In a risk assessment the dangers of an activity are measured against the likelihood of accidents taking place. People carry out risk assessments hundreds of times each day without even knowing it. For example, every time we cross the road we do a risk assessment without even thinking about it.

In the construction industry, risk assessments are done by experienced people who are able to identify the risks of each task. They are then able to put measures in place to control the risks they have identified. At some point in your career you will have to carry out a risk assessment. You will be given proper training in how to do this but, until then, it is important that you understand how risk assessments work. Below is an example of an everyday situation (crossing the road) and how a risk assessment would be carried out for this.

Step 1

Identify the hazards (the dangers) – in this situation the hazards are vehicles travelling at speed.

Step 2

Identify who will be at risk – the person crossing the road will be at risk, as will any drivers on the road who might have to swerve to avoid that person.

Step 3

Calculate the risk from the hazard against the likelihood of an accident taking place – the risk from the hazard is quite high because, if an accident were to happen, the injury could be very serious. However, the likelihood of an accident happening is low because the chances of the person being hit while crossing are very low.

Step 4

Introduce measures to reduce the risk – in this case, crossing the road at traffic lights or pedestrian crossings reduces the risk.

Step 5

Monitor the risk – changes might need to be made to the risk assessment if there are any changes to the risks involved. In our example, changes might be traffic lights being out of order or an increase in the speed limit on the road.

On the job: Assessing the risk

Vijay and Ralph are working on the second level of some scaffolding, clearing debris. Ralph suggests that, to speed up the task, they should throw the debris over the edge of the scaffolding into a skip below.

The building Vijay and Ralph are working on is on a main road and the skip is not in a closed-off area. What do you think of Ralph's idea?

What are your reasons for this answer?

Knowledge check

1. Name five pieces of health and safety legislation that affect the construction industry.

2. What does HSE stand for? What does it do?

3. What does COSHH stand for?

4. What does RIDDOR stand for?

5. What might happen to you or your employer if a health and safety law is broken?

6. What are the two most common risks to construction workers?

7. State two things that you can do to avoid injury when lifting loads using manual handling techniques.

8. What three elements cause a fire and keep it burning?

9. What class(es) of fire can be put out with a carbon dioxide (CO_2) extinguisher?

10. What does a prohibition sign mean?

11. Describe how you would identify a warning sign.

12. Name the six different types of PPE.

13. Who fills in an accident report form?

14. Why is it important to report 'near misses'?

15. Briefly explain what a risk assessment is.

chapter 3

Drawings

OVERVIEW

Drawings are the best way of communicating detailed and often complex information from the designer to all those concerned with the job or project. They are therefore one of the main methods of communication used in the construction industry.

Drawings are part of the legal contract between client and contractor, and mistakes, either in design or in interpretation of the design, can be costly. Details relating to drawings must follow guidelines by the British Standards Institution: BS 1192 Construction Drawing Practice. This standardises drawings and allows everyone to understand them.

This chapter will help you to understand the basic principles involved in using and reading drawings correctly. You will also be introduced to specifications and numeracy skills that are relevant to plastering.

The following topics will be covered:

- Types of drawing
- Drawing equipment
- Scales, symbols and abbreviations
- Datum lines and points
- Types of projection
- Specifications
- Numeracy skills

Types of drawing

Working drawings

Working drawings are scale drawings showing plans, elevations, sections, details and location of a proposed construction. They can be classified as:

- location drawings
- component range drawings
- assembly or detail drawings.

Location drawings

Location drawings include block plans and site plans.

Block plans identify the proposed site by giving a bird's eye view of the site in relation to the surrounding area. An example is shown in Figure 3.1.

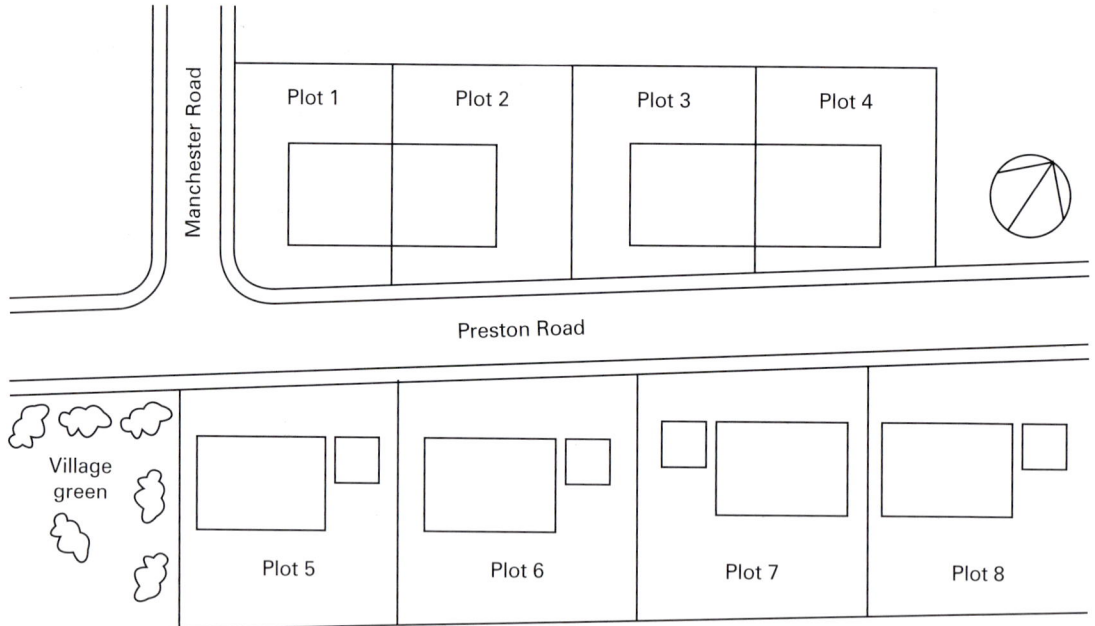

Figure 3.1 Block plan showing location

Site plans give the position of the proposed building and the general layout of the roads, services, drainage, etc. on site. An example is shown in Figure 3.2.

Component range drawings

Component range drawings show the basic sizes and reference system of a standard range of components produced by a manufacturer. This helps in selecting components suitable for a task and available off the shelf. An example is shown in Figure 3.3.

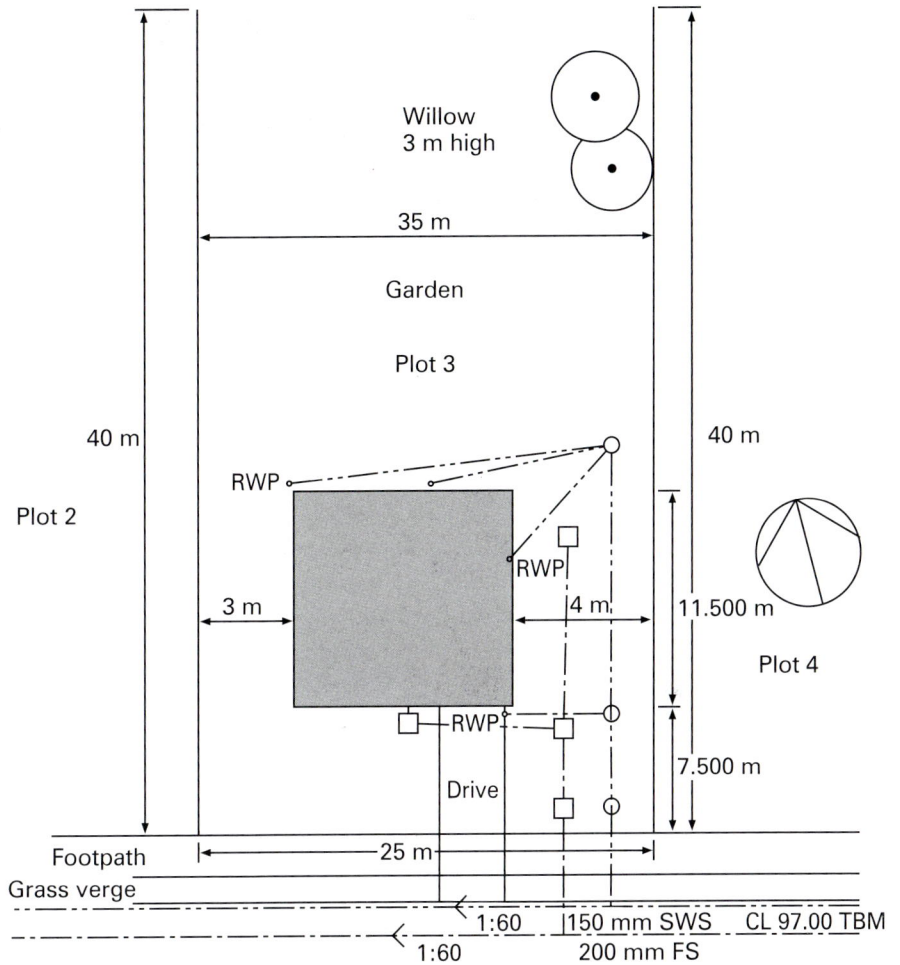

Figure 3.2 Site plan

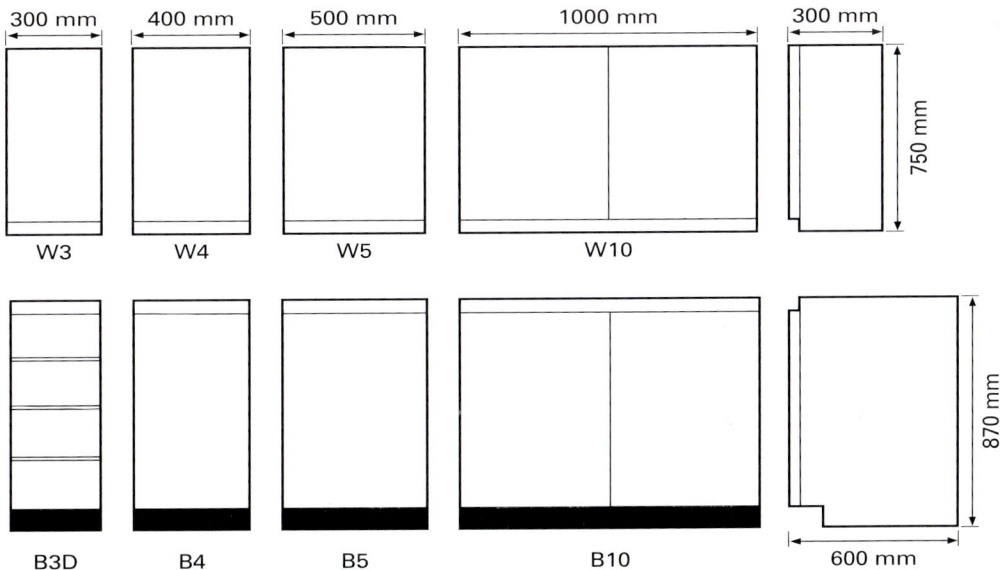

Figure 3.3 Component range drawing

Assembly or detail drawings

Assembly or detail drawings give all the information required to manufacture a given component. They show how things are put together and what the finished item will look like. An example is shown in Figure 3.4.

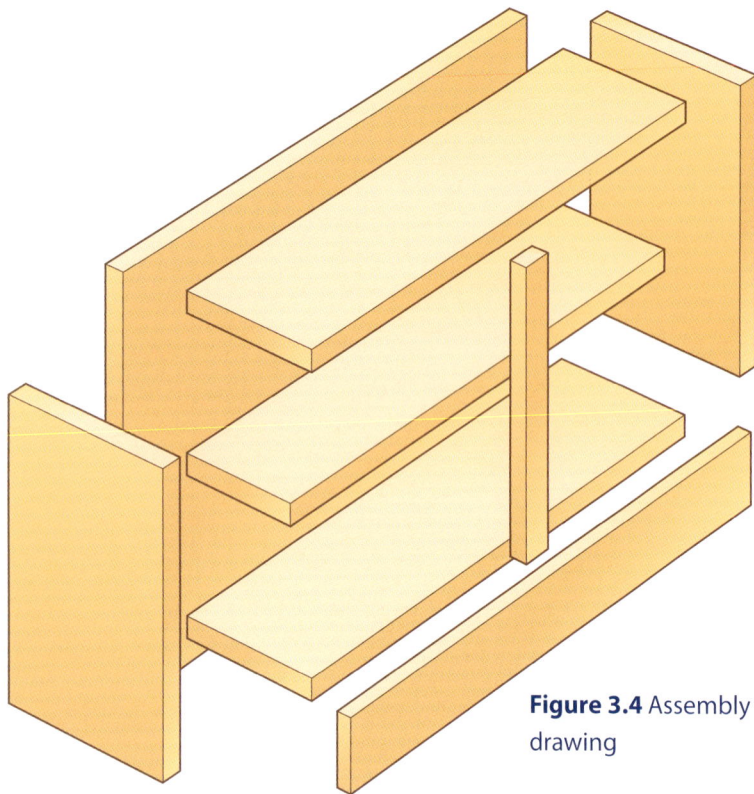

Figure 3.4 Assembly drawing

Title panels

Every drawing must have a title panel, which is normally located in the bottom left-hand corner of each drawing sheet. See Figure 3.5 for an example. The information contained in the panel is relevant to that drawing only and contains such information as:

- drawing title
- scale used
- draughtsperson's name
- drawing number/ project number
- company name
- job/project title
- date of drawing
- revision notes
- projection type.

Remember

It is important to check the date of a drawing to make sure that the most up-to-date version is being used, as revisions to drawings can be frequent

ARCHITECTS Peterson, Thompson Associates 237 Cumberland Way Ipswich IP3 7FT Tel: 01234 567891 Fax: 09876 543210	CLIENT Carillion Development
	JOB TITLE Appleford Drive Felixstowe 4 bed detached
DRAWING TITLE Plan – garage	SCALE: 1:50
	DRAWING NO: 2205-06
DATE: 27.08.2006	DRAWN BY: RW

Figure 3.5 Typical title panel

Drawing equipment

A good quality set of drawing equipment is required when producing drawings. It should include:

- set squares
- protractors
- compasses
- dividers
- scale rule
- pencils
- eraser
- drawing board
- T-square.

Scales, symbols and abbreviations

Scales in common use

In order to draw a building on a drawing sheet, the building must be reduced in size. The result is called a scale drawing.

The preferred scales for use in building drawings are shown in Table 3.1.

Type of drawing	Scales
Block plans	1:2500, 1:1250
Site plans	1:500, 1:200
General location drawings	1:200, 1:100, 1:50
Range drawings	1:100, 1:50, 1:20
Detail drawings	1:10, 1:5, 1:1
Assembly drawings	1:20, 1:10, 1:5

Table 3.1 Preferred scales for building drawings

These scales mean that, for example, on a block plan drawn to 1:2500, one millimetre on the plan would represent 2500 mm (or 2.5 m) on the actual building. Some other examples are:

- On a scale of 1:50, 10 mm represents 500 mm.

- On a scale of 1:100, 10 mm represents 1000 mm (1.0 m).

- On a scale of 1:200, 30 mm represents 6000 mm (6.0 m).

Why not try these for yourself?

- On a scale of 1:50, 40 mm represents: ....

- On a scale of 1:200, 70 mm represents: ....

- On a scale of 1:500, 30 mm represents: ....

The use of scales can be easily mastered with a little practice.

Remember

A scale is merely a convenient way of reducing a drawing in size

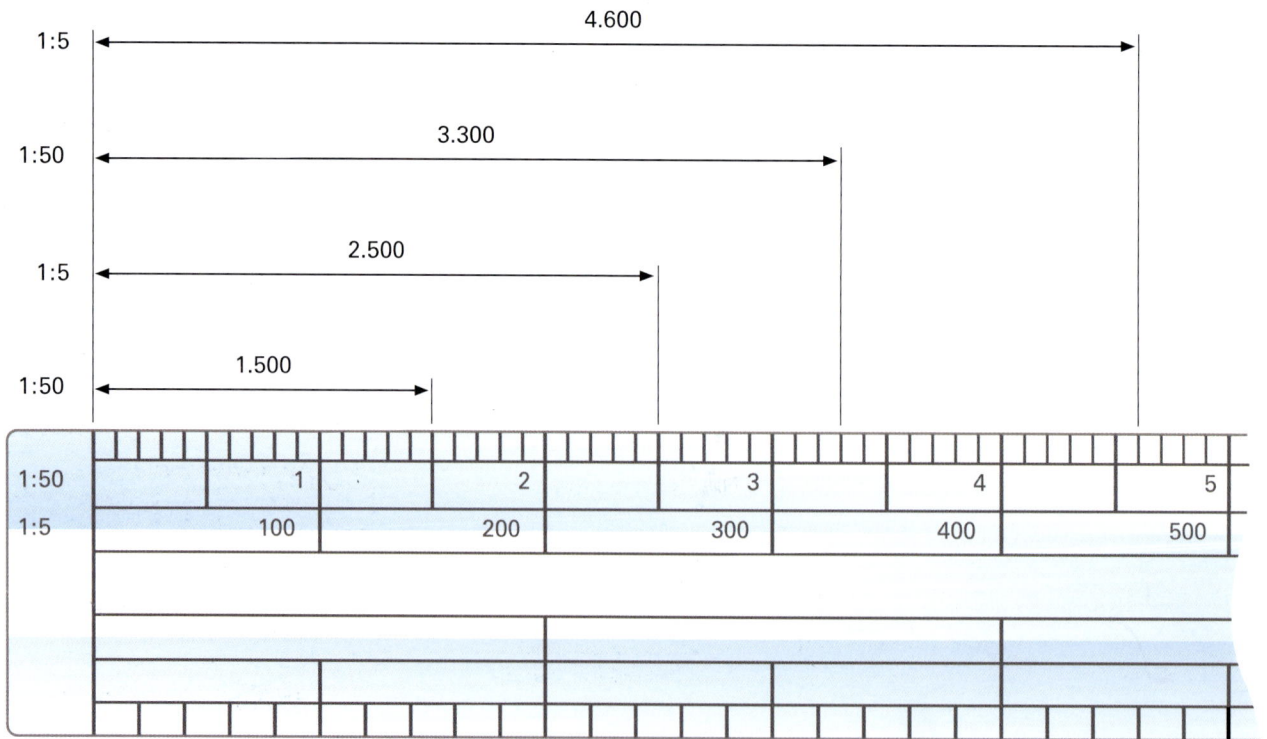

Figure 3.6 Rule with scales for maps and drawings

Variations caused through printing or copying will affect the accuracy of drawings. Hence, although measurements can be read from drawings using a rule with common scales marked, it is recommended that you work to written instructions and measurements wherever possible.

A rule marked with scales used in drawings or maps is illustrated in Figure 3.6. It should not be confused with a 'scale rule', using for measuring lengths, though often the same name is used.

Symbols and abbreviations

The use of symbols and abbreviations in the construction industry enables the maximum amount of information to be included on a drawing sheet in a clear way. Figure 3.7 shows some recommended drawing symbols for a range of building materials.

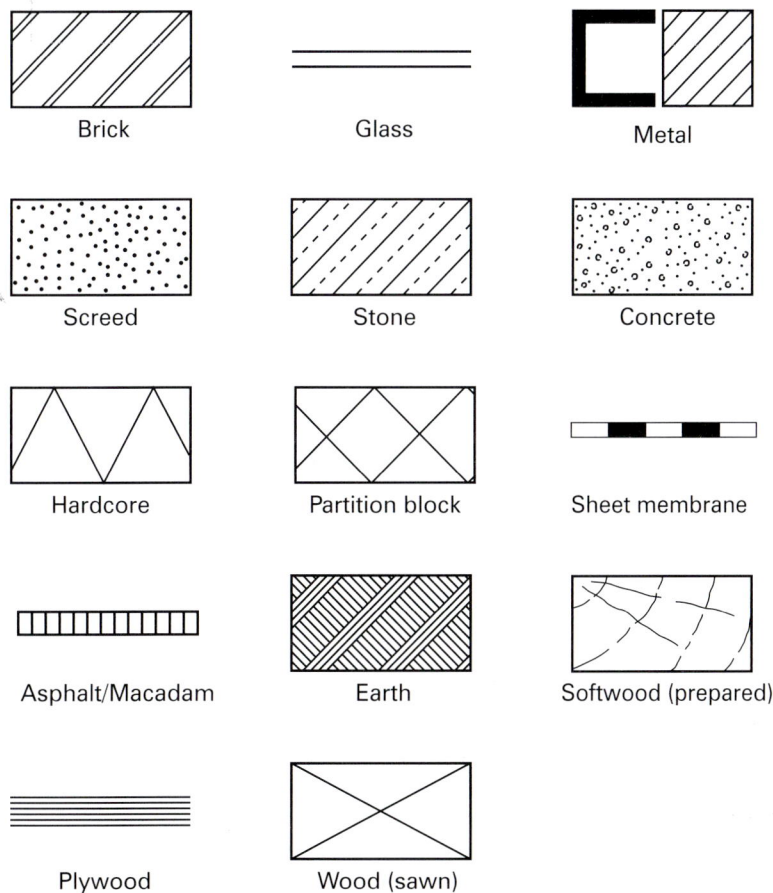

Figure 3.7 Building material symbols

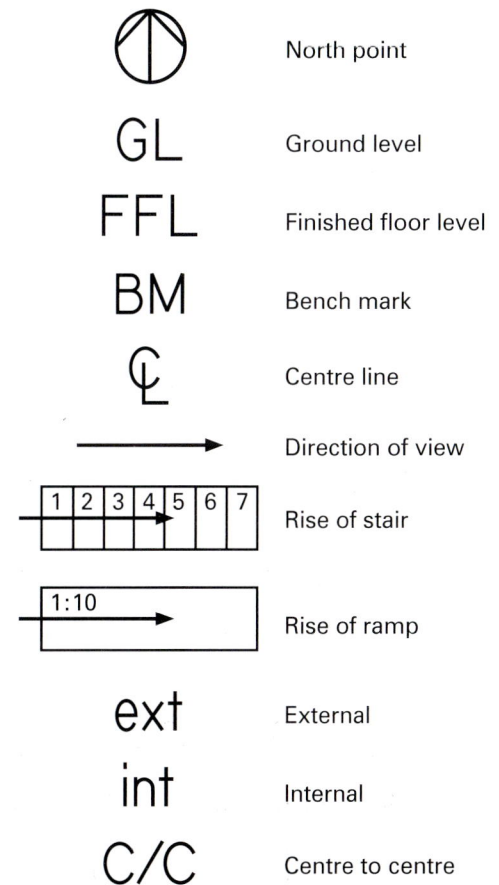

Figure 3.8 Graphical symbols

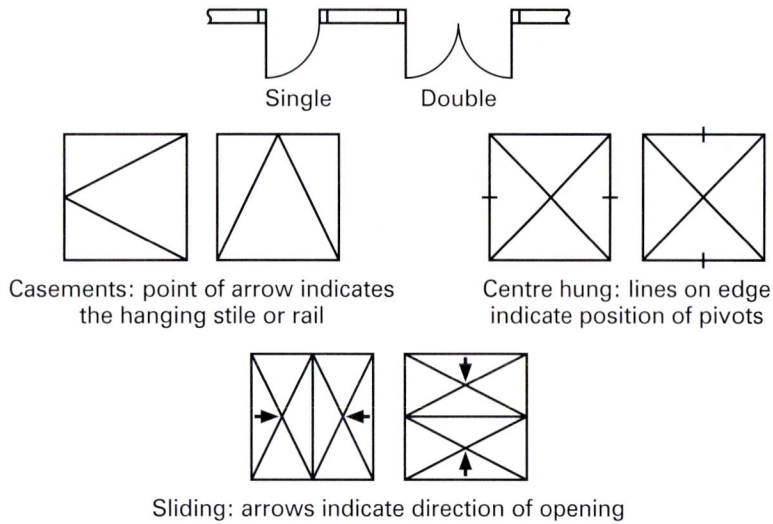

Single   Double

Casements: point of arrow indicates the hanging stile or rail

Centre hung: lines on edge indicate position of pivots

Sliding: arrows indicate direction of opening

Figure 3.9 Doors and windows, type and direction of opening

Figure 3.8 shows some of the most frequently used graphical symbols, which are recommended in the British Standard BS 1192.

Figure 3.9 illustrates the recommended methods for indicating types of doors and windows, and their direction of opening.

Table 3.2 lists some standard abbreviations used on drawings.

Item	Abbreviation	Item	Abbreviation
Airbrick	AB	Hardcore	hc
Asbestos	abs	Hardwood	hwd
Bitumen	bit	Insulation	insul
Boarding	bdg	Joist	jst
Brickwork	bwk	Mild steel	MS
Building	bldg	Plasterboard	pbd
Cast iron	CI	Polyvinyl acetate	PVA
Cement	ct	Polyvinyl chloride	PVC
Column	col	Reinforced concrete	RC
Concrete	conc	Satin anodised aluminium	SAA
Cupboard	cpd	Satin chrome	SC
Damp proof course	DPC	Softwood	swd
Damp proof membrane	DPM	Stainless steel	SS
Drawing	dwg	Tongue and groove	T&G
Foundation	fnd	Wrought iron	WI
Hardboard	hdb		

Table 3.2 Standard abbreviations used on drawings

FAQ

Why not just write the full words on the drawing?

This would take up too much space and clutter the drawing, making it difficult to read.

Datum lines and points

The need to apply levels starts at the beginning of the construction process and continues right up to the completion of the building. The whole country is mapped in detail, and the Ordnance Survey places bench marks at suitable locations from which all other levels can be taken.

Figure 3.10 Ordnance bench mark

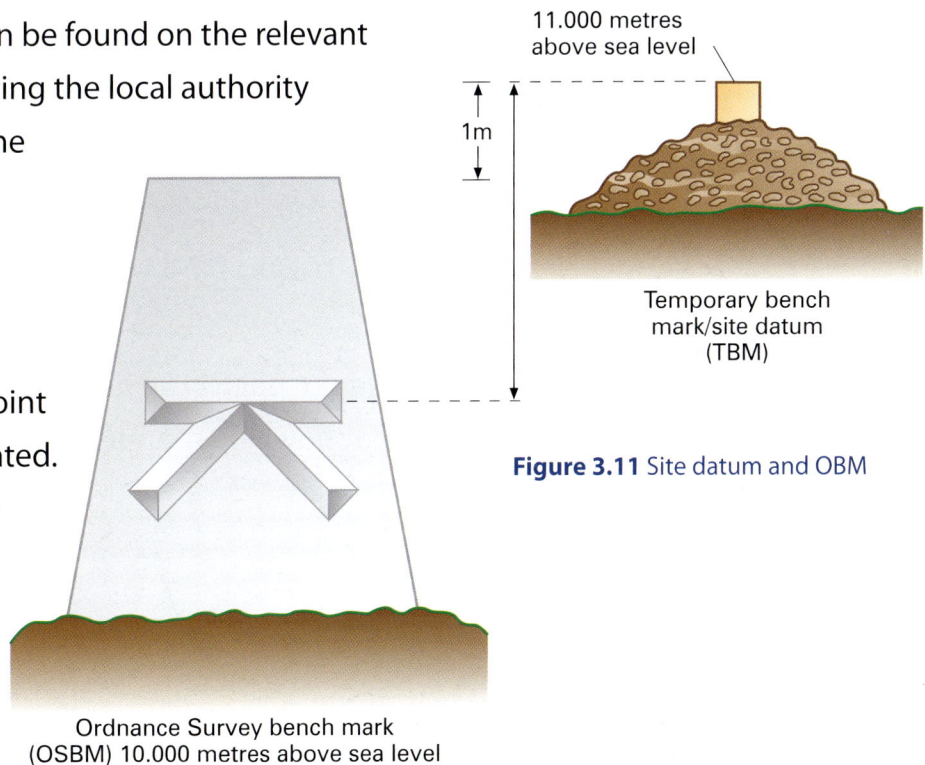

Ordnance bench mark (OBM)

OBMs are found cut into locations such as walls of churches or public buildings. The height of the OBM can be found on the relevant Ordnance Survey map or by contacting the local authority planning office. Figure 3.10 shows the normal symbol used, though it can appear as shown in Figure 3.11.

Site datum

It is necessary to have a reference point on site to which all levels can be related. This is known as the site datum. The site datum is usually positioned at a convenient height, such as finished floor level (FFL).

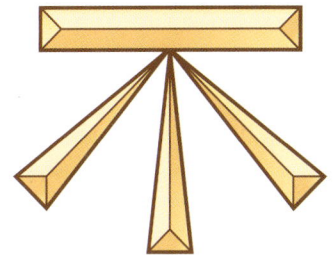

11.000 metres above sea level

1m

Temporary bench mark/site datum (TBM)

Figure 3.11 Site datum and OBM

Ordnance Survey bench mark (OSBM) 10.000 metres above sea level

The site datum itself must be set in relation to some known point, preferably an OBM, and must be positioned where it cannot be moved.

Figure 3.11 shows a site datum and OBM, illustrating the height relationship between them.

If no suitable position can be found, a datum peg may be used, its accurate height transferred by surveyors from an OBM, as with the site datum. It is normally a piece of timber or steel rod positioned accurately to the required level and then set in concrete. However, it must be adequately protected, and is generally surrounded by a small fence for protection, as shown in Figure 3.12.

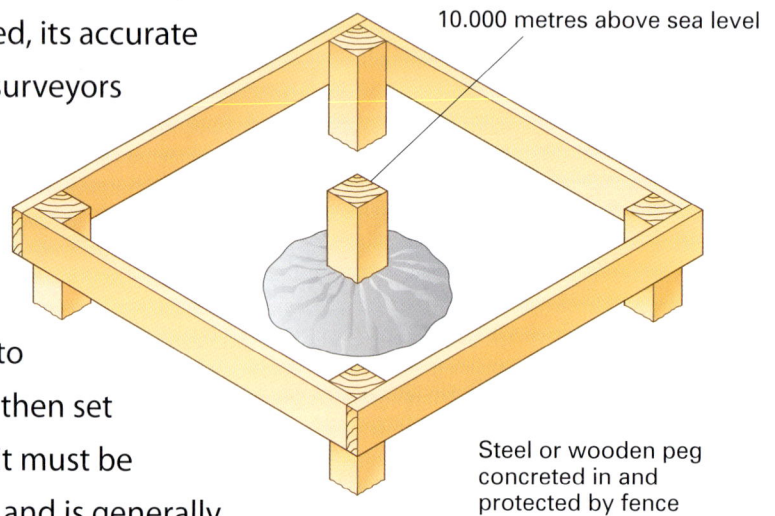

10.000 metres above sea level

Steel or wooden peg concreted in and protected by fence

Figure 3.12 Datum peg suitably protected

Temporary bench mark (TBM)

When an OBM cannot be conveniently found near a site, it is usual for a temporary bench mark (TBM) to be set up at a height suitable for the site. Its accurate height is transferred by surveyors from the nearest convenient OBM.

All other site datum points can now be set up from this TBM using datum lines, which are shown on the site drawings. Figure 3.13 shows datum lines on drawings.

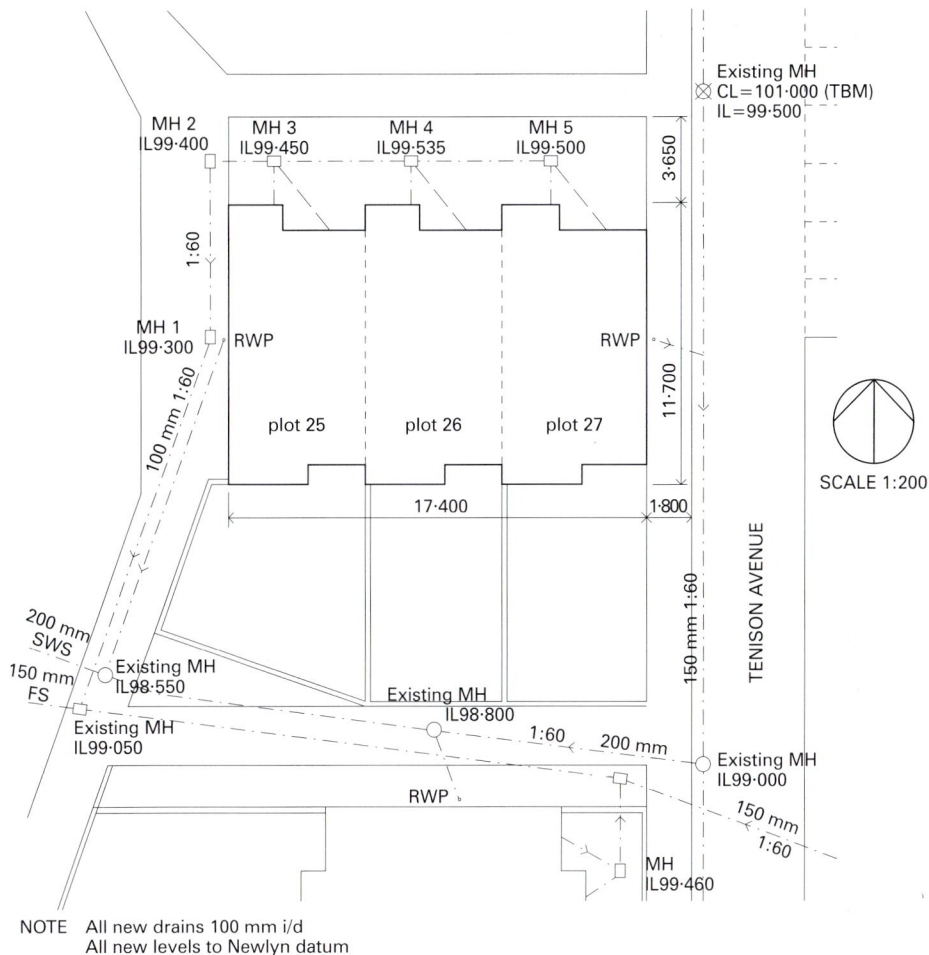

Figure 3.13 Example of datum lines shown on drawings

Types of projection

Building, engineering and similar drawings aim to give as much information as possible in a way that is easy to understand. They frequently combine several views on a single drawing.

These may be elevations (the view we would see if we stood in front or to the side of the finished building) or plan (the view we would have if we were looking down on it). The view we see depends on where we are looking from. There are then different ways of 'projecting' what we would see onto the drawings.

The two main methods of projection, used on standard building drawings, are orthographic and isometric.

Orthographic projection

Orthographic projection works as if parallel lines were drawn from every point on a model of the building onto a sheet of paper held up behind it (an elevation view), or laid out underneath it (plan view).

There are then different ways in which we can display the views on a drawing. The method most commonly used in the construction industry, for detailed construction drawings, is called 'third angle projection'. In this the front elevation is roughly central. The plan view is drawn directly below the front elevation, and all other elevations are drawn in line with the front elevation. An example is shown in Figure 3.14.

End elevation

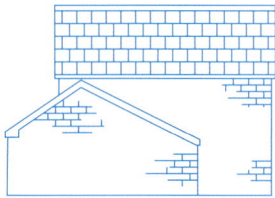

Front elevation

Rear elevation

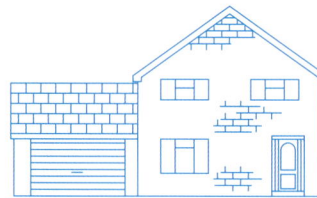

Section

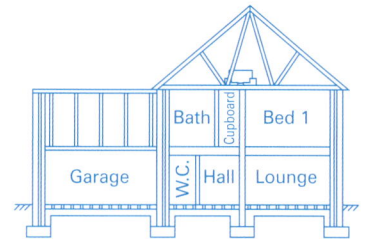

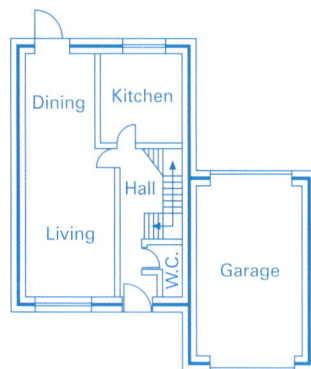

Ground floor plan

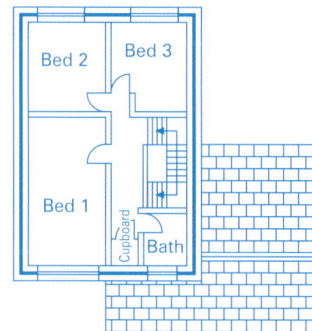

First floor plan

Figure 3.14 Orthographic projection

Isometric projection

In isometric views, the object is drawn at an angle where one corner of the object is closest to the viewer. Vertical lines remain vertical but horizontal lines are drawn at an angle of 30° to the horizontal. This can be seen in Figure 3.15, which shows a simple rectangular box.

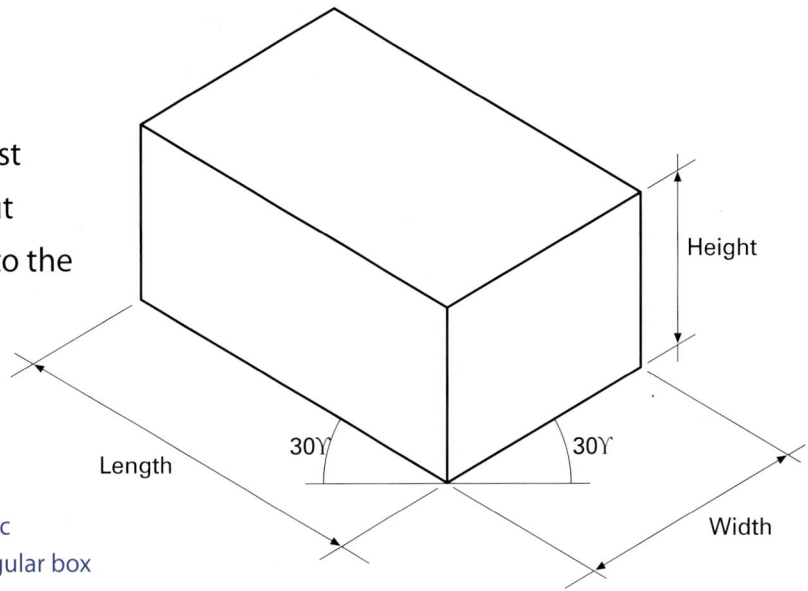

Height

30Ƴ

30Ƴ

Length

Width

Figure 3.15 Isometric projection of rectangular box

Figures 3.16 and 3.17 show the method of drawing these lines using a T-square and set square.

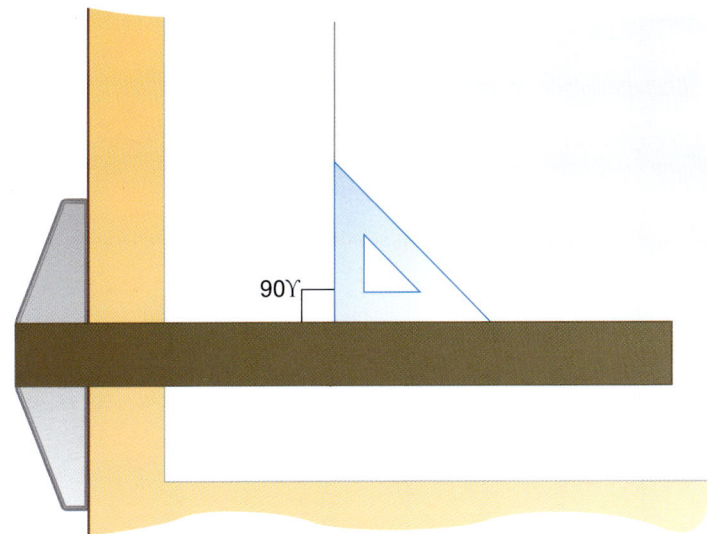

90Ƴ

30Ƴ

Figure 3.16 Drawing vertical lines

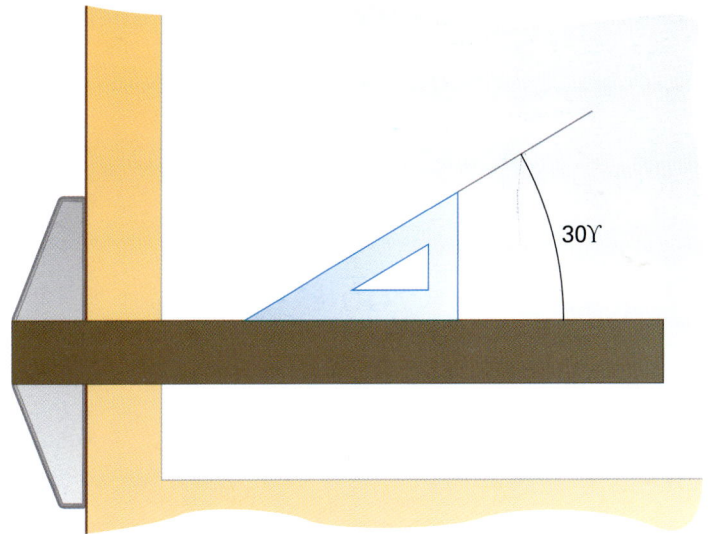

Figure 3.17 Drawing horizontal lines

Specifications

Except for very small building works, drawings cannot contain all the information that the contractor needs – in particular, the standard of materials to be used and the quality of workmanship. For this purpose, the architect will prepare a document called a 'specification' to supplement the working drawings.

The specification is a precise description of all the essential information and job requirements that will affect the price of the work, but cannot be shown on drawings.

Typical items shown on the specification are:

- site description
- restrictions (limited access, working hours)
- services and availability of services (waste, gas, electricity, telephone)
- workmanship (quality, size tolerances, finishing requirements)
- other information (nominated suppliers, subcontractors, site clearance).

Numeracy skills

Units of area

Area is measured in square units such as mm^2, cm^2, m^2.

The area of this square is 1 cm^2 or $10 \times 10 = 100$ mm^2

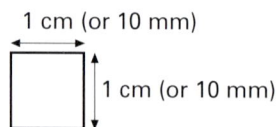

1 cm (or 10 mm)

1 cm (or 10 mm)

The area of this square is 1 m^2 or 100 × 100 = 10,000 cm^2

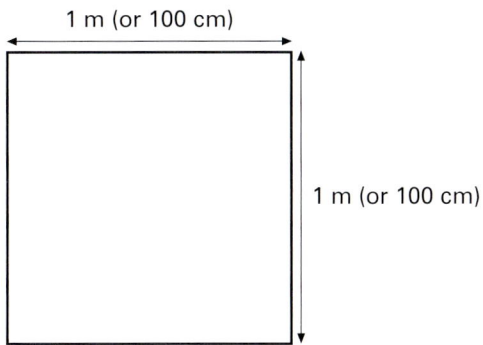

1 m (or 100 cm)

1 m (or 100 cm)

We can work out the area of the rectangle below

(a) in cm^2

(b) in m^2

124 cm

65 cm

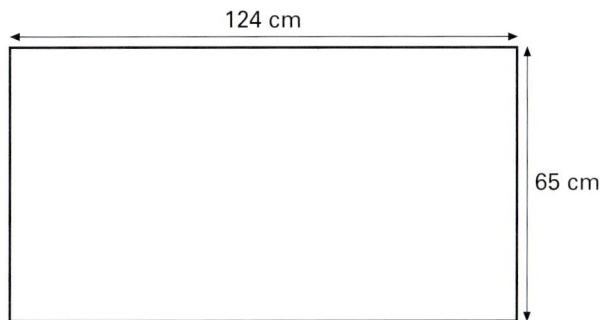

(a) $A = l \times w = 124 \times 65 = 8060$ cm^2

(b) $8060 \div 10,000 = 0.806$ m^2

Areas of composite shapes

Composite shapes are made up of simple shapes such as rectangles and squares. To find the area, divide it up and find the area of each shape separately. For example, to work out the area of this L-shaped room

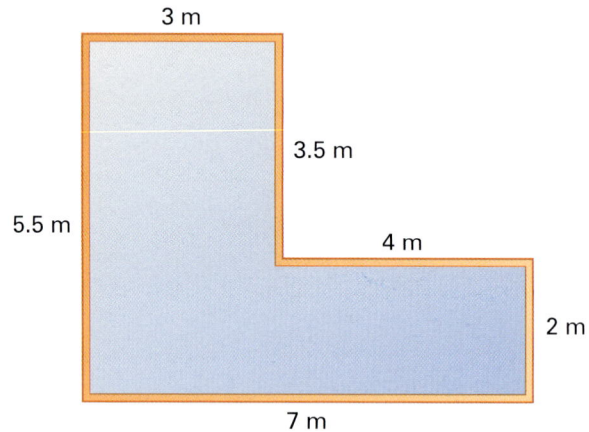

first divide it into two rectangles, A and B.

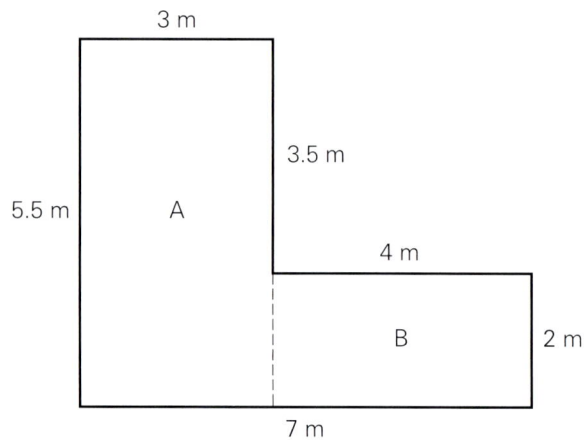

Area of rectangle A = $3 \times 5.5 = 16.5m^2$

Area of rectangle B = $4 \times 2 = 8m^2$

Total area of room = $16.5 + 8 = 24.5 \ m^2$

You could divide the rectangle in the example above into two different rectangles, C and D, like this:

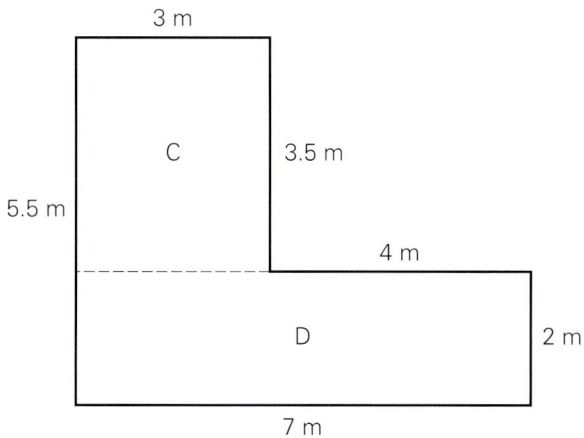

Check that you get the same total area.

Some shapes can be divided into rectangles and triangles. For example, to find the area of this wooden floor, divide the floor into a right-angled triangle, A, and a rectangle, B.

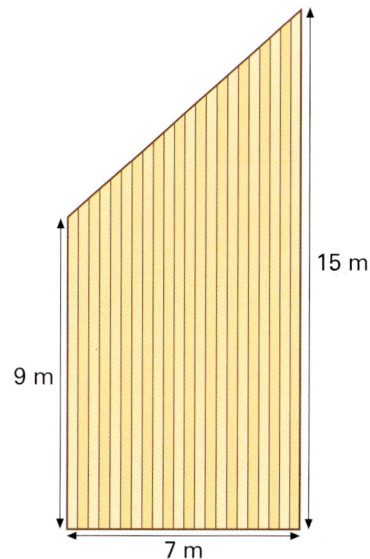

Triangle A has vertical height 6m and base 7m

Area $= \frac{1}{2} \times b \times h$

$= \frac{1}{2} \times 7 \times 6 = 21 \text{ m}^2$

Area of rectangle B $= 9 \times 7 = 63 \text{ m}^2$

Total area $= 21 + 63 = 84 \text{ m}^2$.

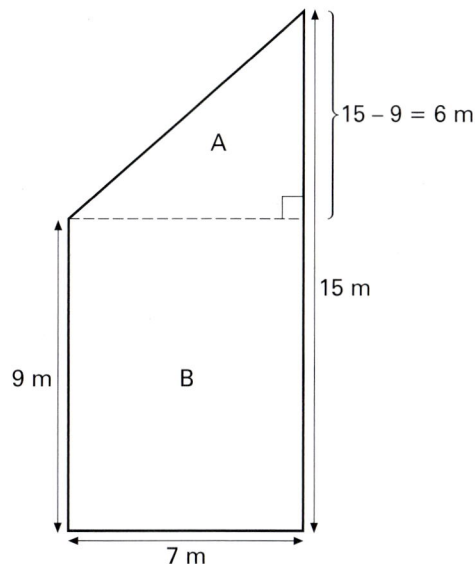

Units of volume

Volume is measured in cube units such as mm^3, cm^3, m^3. The volume of this cube is $1\ cm^3$ or $10 \times 10 \times 10 = 1000\ mm^3$.

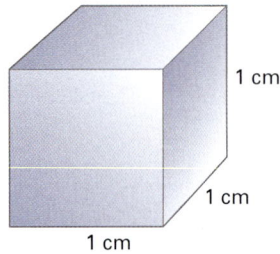

The volume of this cube is $1\ m^3$ or $100 \times 100 \times 100 = 1,000,000\ cm^3$.

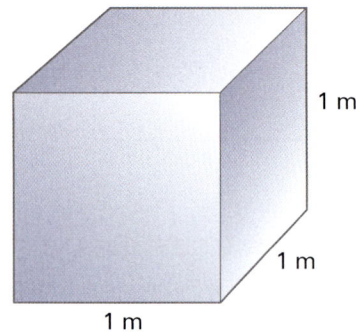

Remember

$1\ cm^3 = 1000\ mm^3$

$1\ m^3 = 1,000,000\ cm^3$

A cuboid is a 3-D shape with rectangular faces (like a box). The formula for the volume of a cuboid is $V = l \times w \times h$. For example, we can calculate the volume of the cuboid (right):

(a) in cm^3

(b) in m^3

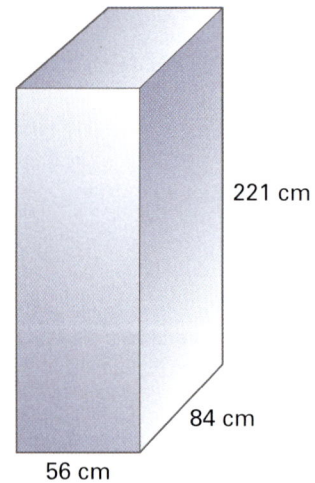

(a) $V = l \times w \times h = 56 \times 84 \times 221 = 1,039,584\ cm^3$

(b) $1,039,584 \div 1,000,000 = 1.039584\ m^3 \approx 1.04\ m^3$ (to two decimal places)

Calculations

Area and volume are used to carry out important calculations for many plastering jobs. You can calculate the method of payment for laying floor screeds by area and you can calculate the amount of material required (i.e. that you need to order) using the volume of the floor screed.

Area

Payment for floor screeding is by the area completed. For example, if you have been given a price of £11.50 per m², how much would you earn if you laid 30 m²?

Payment = £11.50 × 30 = £345.

Volume

The mix proportion for floor screed is 3:1 or 4:1. The amounts of sand and cement required for a given volume of floor screed are calculated as follows.

1. A room measures 10 m × 3 m = 30 m². This is then multiplied by the thickness of the floor – in this case 50 mm.

2. Metres cannot be multiplied by millimetres. So 50 mm becomes 0.050 m.

3. So volume = 30 m² × 0.050 m = 1.5 m³

4. The mix proportion is 1:3, one part cement and three parts sand. So one out of the four parts is cement, i.e. ¼ of the mix.

5. 1.5 m³ divided by 4 = 0.375 m³ of cement.

6. 0.375 m³ × 3 parts of sand = 1.125 m³ of sand.

7. (As a check) 0.375 m³ cement + 1.125 m³ sand = 1.5 m³ of material.

You cannot order exactly 1.125 m³ of sand so you would need to round it up to the nearest unit amount that can be ordered – this may be 1.5 m³ or 2 m³.

For cement, there is approximately 0.045 m³ of cement in a 25 kg bag. So, to calculate the number of bags required, take 0.375 m³ and divide by 0.045 m³ = 8.3 bags.

You now need to order 9 bags of cement (although this does not allow enough for wastage).

On the job: Rendering info

Mike was about to start a rendering job in the village but before he could start, he required certain information from the architect. This included drawings that showed elevations of the work which needed to be rendered, and specifications of the proposed render finish and the ratio of all mixes required.

1. Why did Mike need this particular information before he could start the job?

Knowledge check

1. Briefly explain why we use drawings in the construction industry.

2. What do the following abbreviations stand for: DPC; hwd; fnd; DPM?

3. Sketch the graphical symbols that represent the following: brickwork; prepared timber; sawn timber; hardcore.

4. When producing a drawing using third angle projection, where is the view from above placed?
   a. above the front view
   b. below the front view
   c. to the left of the front view
   d. to the right of the front view

5. Can you name the main types of projection that are used in building drawings?

6. What are dividers used for?

7. What type of information could be found in a drawing's title panel?

8. Name two ways in which you can find out the height of an OBM?

9. In isometric projection, at what angle are horizontal lines drawn?

10. What type of information can be found in specifications?

chapter 4

Tools and equipment

OVERVIEW

This chapter will give you a basic introduction to the tools and equipment that are used within the trade of plastering. Not every plasterer will use everything that is described in this chapter. As a plasterer, you will probably become attached to certain tools that other plasterers may not even use. You build up your own 'kit' over the years, and most plasterers have their favourite trowels and brushes, for example.

All tools and equipment should be treated with respect and handled properly to ensure that they last and help you to produce a quality job.

In this chapter we will look at:

- Health and safety
- Hand tools
- Power tools
- Other equipment
- Personal protective equipment

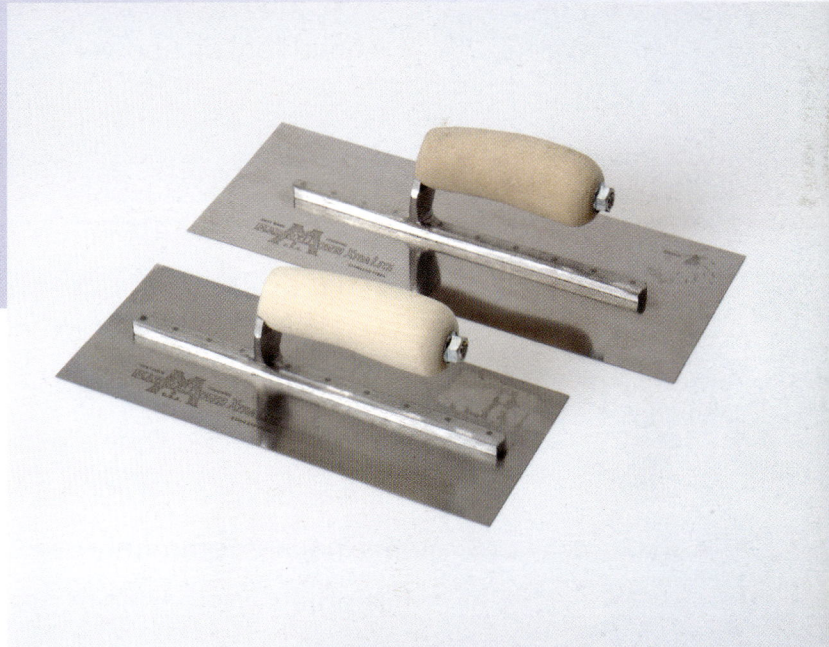

Health and safety

All tools are potentially dangerous, and the plasterer – as a user of tools – must make sure that all relevant health and safety requirements are always observed. This will help ensure that you do not cause injury to yourself or, equally importantly, to others who may be working around you, or the general public. Make sure you follow any instructions and demonstrations you are given on the use of tools, as well as any manufacturer's instructions provided on purchase of the tool.

Basic health and safety rules

1. Always make sure that you use the correct personal protective equipment for the tool and the job that you are carrying out.

2. Never 'make do' with tools. Using the wrong tool for the job can be dangerous, and usually breaks health and safety laws.

3. Never play or mess around with a tool, regardless of its type, whether it is a hand tool or a power tool.

4. Never use a tool that you have not been trained to use, especially a power tool.

Hand tools

The tools described in this section are integral to the plasterer's ability to carry out the work. They are usually kept in a toolbag, or in a bucket, which is carried from job to job. Some of the tools in this section are general-purpose items that are commonly used by construction workers in various trades, while others are specific to the plastering trade.

Transporting and applying material

Handboard or hawk

These allow you to transport an amount of plaster to the area being plastered. They are produced in various materials.

Hawks made from structural foamed urethane provide a surface that is stable, rigid and hard-wearing, yet also light in weight. The material can be warm to the touch, the one-piece moulded handle makes it comfortable to use, and it is easy to clean.

The plastic hawk is the cheapest of all, but it is still more than capable of doing the job required of it, and is ideal as a starting piece of equipment. The aluminium hawk is suitable for heavier-duty use. It has smooth, straight edges and rounded corners. It has a detachable handle, which is connected by a bolt through its length, and is padded to help prevent the development of calluses on the hand.

Handboards or hawks

Hand-made hawks can be constructed from a square piece of exterior plywood with a round piece of timber for the handle. A sponge can be used to prevent calluses.

Trowels

Trowels are used to apply plastering materials to a background. Manufactured from steel or stainless steel, these come in a variety of sizes and from different manufacturers. Common makes of trowel used by plasterers are Marshalltown, Ragni and Tyzack. Other, cheaper trowels can be obtained from DIY outlets, but they are not likely to produce as good a finish.

Gauging trowel

Gauging trowels are made of steel with a wooden handle. They are generally used for mixing small quantities of material and working with small amounts of plaster. When laying floor screeds, a gauging trowel is used for placing small amounts of materials into awkward areas of floors and for cleaning down equipment and tools during and after screeding.

Maintenance: Wash, dry and lightly oil steel.

Gauging trowel

Bucket trowel

This has a tapered blade, which makes it suitable for scraping out plaster from a bucket, or similar container, without damaging the base of the container.

Bucket trowel

Finishing trowel

This is used for skimming and finishing the top coat when plastering walls and ceilings. It is generally a trowel that has been **worn in**, and the front corners are slightly rounded to prevent lines in the plaster.

Floating trowel

This is used for applying the backing coat of plaster to walls. It is generally a cheaper, more rigid trowel, or a new trowel that is not yet ready to be used for skimming.

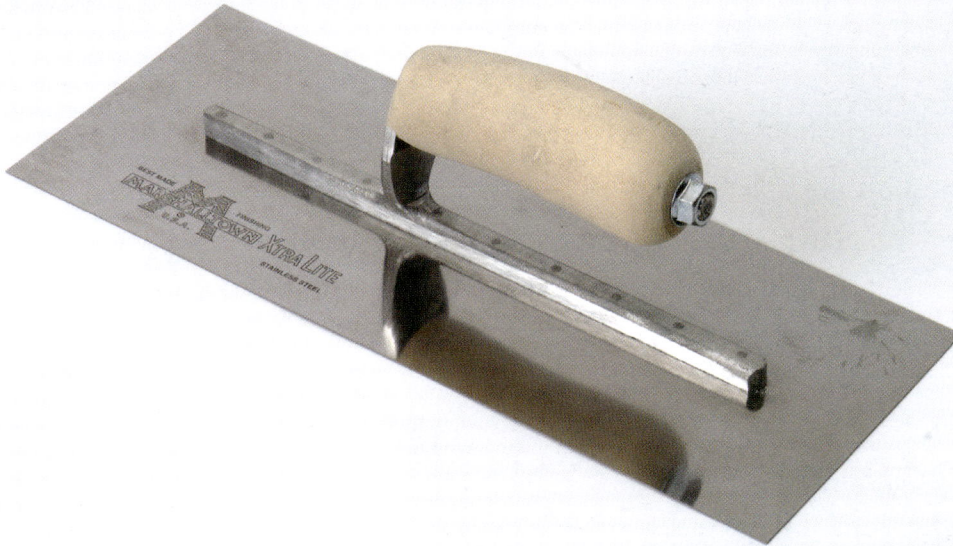

Floating trowel

> ### Definition
>
> **Worn in** – refers to a trowel that has been used mainly for floating, which makes it less rigid. A worn-in trowel reduces the lines left in the finishing coat of plaster, making it more suitable for skimming to produce a good finish

Floor laying trowel

This is used for placing sand and cement for flooring, and trowelling in the face of the screed to a smooth finish. It comes in two sizes: 400 mm and 455 mm long. Constructed from rigid steel or stainless steel metal, this trowel is tapered with a pointed end for getting into corners. It can have a **double shank** for strength, with a plastic or wood handle.

Maintenance: Straight after use, clean thoroughly and dry and, if the trowel is non-stainless steel, lightly oil it. Protect edges from damage.

Safety: Do not run your fingers down the edge of the trowel as it may be sharp enough to cut you.

Internal/external angle tool

This is used to finish internal and external corner joints. It helps in producing a good, clean and smooth finish. This tool is used in one long, sweeping motion to achieve a line that is true to the eye.

Internal/external angle tool

Taping knife

The taping knife is a metal blade with a wooden handle. It can be obtained in different widths – 100 mm is about the most useful. It is used for applying tapes or small areas of filler when dry lining.

Taping knife

A trained plasterer may be best suited to using a hawk and finishing trowel when hand taping and jointing because he or she will have full control of these tools.

Applicator

This is a 200 mm rigid blade with a plastic or wooden grip, which can be used as an alternative for applying jointing materials when dry lining.

Floats

There are three main floats that plasterers use. The plastic float is generally used on external rendering or floor screeding for filling in hollows in the floor after ruling in, but it can also be used when skimming, to assist in getting the surface flat. A devil float is used to help to close in the surface of the backing plaster and iron out any bumps. It has nails slightly protruding at one end in order to key the surface for the next coat of plaster; this is known as **rubbing up**. A sponge float may be used to assist with the finish of external sand and cement.

Maintenance: Wash directly after use. Be careful not to damage the face of the float as it will affect the finished face of the screed.

Definition

Rubbing up – the process of closing in the surface, rubbing out any small imperfections on the surface and providing a key for the finishing coat of plaster to adhere to

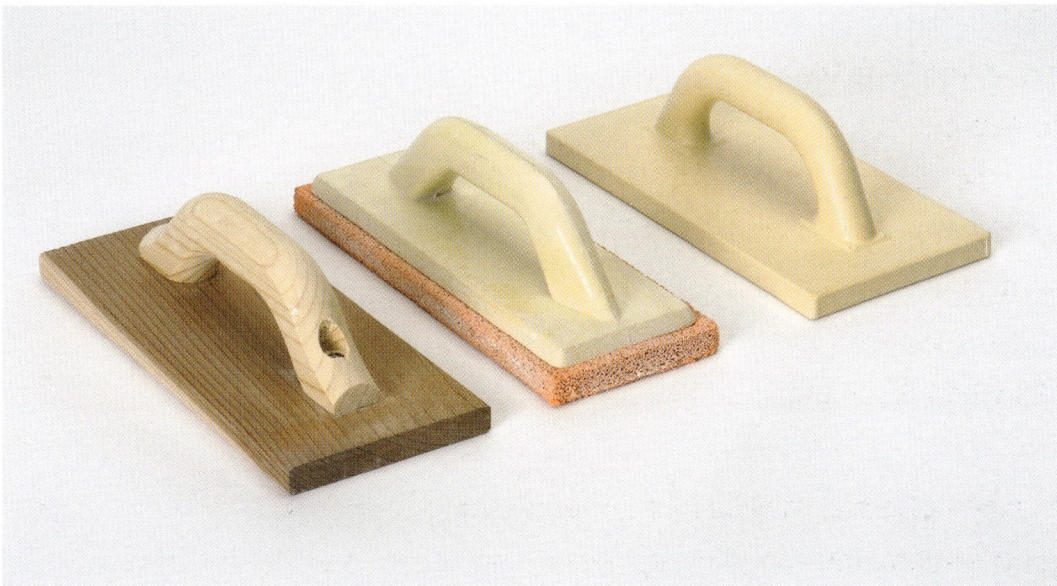

Floats

Darby

The darby is a type of rule used to smooth walls and ceilings. It is flat, with lipped edges and adjustable wooden handles. Darbies are available in two widths, and can be made of lightweight aluminium or polyurethane, with a rigid back support to prevent bending.

Did you know?

Both the darby and the metal feather edge rules (page 118) can be used for ruling in one-coat plasters

Darby

Jointing sponge

This is a circular plastic sponge fixed to a circular timber or plastic back with a handle. It is used for feathering out material used on taped joints in dry lining during the **jointing sequence**.

Definition

Jointing sequence – taping plasterboard joints and applying material to seal the tape and joints

Jointing sponge

Measuring and levelling

Tape measure

A tape measure is important to the plasterer for measuring up for the job, in order to gauge the precise amounts of material needed.

Tape measures come in many sizes, from 3 m up to 10 m for the pocket type, and from 10 m up to 30 m for larger setting-out tapes – some can go up to 100 m. They are usually made with plastic or steel cases, with a steel measure. Some come with both metric (centimetres and metres) and imperial (inches and feet) measurements, although most have only metric measures. Larger tapes can be made of steel or fibreglass.

Always ensure that tapes are wiped clean after use, as moisture will result in the tape rusting, making it hard to release or retract. It is important to keep your tape measure free from plaster, as this can clog the mechanism up, thus preventing further use.

Remember

When using a tape measure, take care not to confuse metric and imperial measurements, as this can cause all kinds of problem

Tape measure

Steel rule

A steel rule can be used for measuring the thickness of floor screed required to match the specification.

Maintenance: Keep tapes and rules free from sand and cement. Do not allow nicks or cuts in the edge of the tape, as it will affect the ability to retract the tape.

Safety tip

Control the tape speed when it retracts back into the holder as the sharp edges can cause deep cuts, especially if the tape has a cut or nick in it

Flooring rule

This is used for levelling in screeds and ruling out the floor surface, and can be either wood or metal, usually 100 mm × 35 mm with a maximum length of 3 m. Shorter rules may be required for smaller areas. Timber rules should be straight, and the two 35 mm faces true and flat. The edges of the rules should be parallel along the full length: if not, it will not give a true reading when levelling in the screeds with the spirit level.

Flooring rule

Maintenance: Timber rules should not be allowed to twist. Store them straight, especially when wet. Do not use sharp tools to clean rules as this may splinter the edges and face of the rule. Metal and timber rules should also be washed but careful storage is not as important with metal as it will not distort.

Safety: Be careful when handling long rules because of strain on your back. Wooden rules can leave splinters in unprotected hands. Long rules should be handled carefully so as not to damage finished walls and ceilings.

Spirit level

A spirit level is a familiar tool to DIY enthusiasts, and it is an important tool for the plasterer. Plasterers use them for making sure that angle beads and walls are plumb and floors are level when floor screeding. For levelling in floors, a good quality and strongly constructed level should be used, made of metal, because it is to be used in areas where it may suffer damage. A good spirit level should have both horizontal and vertical block **vials**.

Before you use a level, it is best to check it first for true (accuracy). You can do this simply by placing the level on a flat surface or on previously levelled screws, making a mark at both ends and reading the bubble position. You should then turn the level around, reversing the positions of the ends and make sure they touch your marks. The bubble can then be read again. If the bubble is in the same position both times you read it, the level is accurate. If the bubble gives different readings, the level is out of true and the bubble will need adjusting to make the level accurate.

Spirit level

> **Definition**
>
> **Vial** – the glass tube containing liquid plus an air bubble

> **Remember**
>
> Damage to a spirit level can cause incorrect readings and seriously affect your workmanship. Always handle spirit levels carefully to prevent damage and avoid the cost of replacement

Check screws with a plumb line. Once reading true, put level across screws, then turn 180°: if reading is different, the level is not true

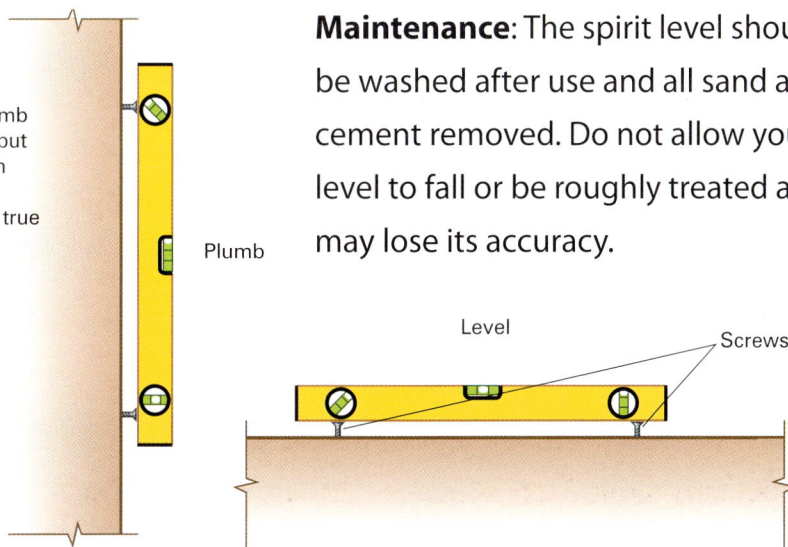

Plumb

Maintenance: The spirit level should be washed after use and all sand and cement removed. Do not allow your level to fall or be roughly treated as it may lose its accuracy.

Level

Screws

Figure 4.1 Checking levels for accuracy

Boat level

This is a smaller (hand-sized) level for checking small areas where you cannot get a larger level in. It is ideal for keeping in your tool pouch.

Boat level

Chalk line

This is used with powdered, coloured chalk for marking between two points to give a straight line. It is ideal for setting out and ensuring that you work to a correct line. In floor screeding, it is used for transference of the floor thickness datum points around the room. In dry lining, it is used for lining through on ceiling and/or floor, and establishing the position of each board.

Chalk line and chalk powder

Maintenance: Keep chalk line free from knots and keep sufficient chalk in the body of the chalk line.

Laser level

Lasers are a modern system for transferring levels to different areas of the work site. This is a small (but expensive) tool that allows setting out to be done accurately and speedily using a beam of laser light. Levels of this kind are often self-levelling and mounted on a stand. The laser will give you a straight horizontal line. Some laser levels will spin continuously through 360° allowing you to take your measurements from that line.

Laser level

Safety tip

Lasers, if not correctly used, can seriously damage eyesight, so only use them if you are trained and have the appropriate PPE

Remember

You will require supervision while using a laser

Square

This is a tool that provides an angle of 90°. It can be used to ensure that reveals are square when plastering.

Builder's square

This is used for positioning the screeds from the datum point. It can be self-made in timber or by using a metal builder's roofing square. Whatever type of square is used, it must be accurate.

Square

Maintenance: Clean all squares after use. If metal, lightly oil. Always check the accuracy of any square before use.

Water level

This simple tool consists of a length of clear plastic hose that is filled with water and is used to find levels. It is also used when floor screeding for transferring datum levels and setting out rises and falls to floors, as in a shower, for example. It is constructed from two glass tubes with measurements on the side and a length of rubber tubing attached to each end, containing water. One glass tube is held to a fixed datum point against a measurement on the tube. The second operative moves into the next room and raises and lowers the second glass tube until the water reaches the same mark as the fixed one. The wall is then marked.

Maintenance: Keep glass tubes clean and unmarked. Tubing should be free of kinks and cuts. Store carefully after use.

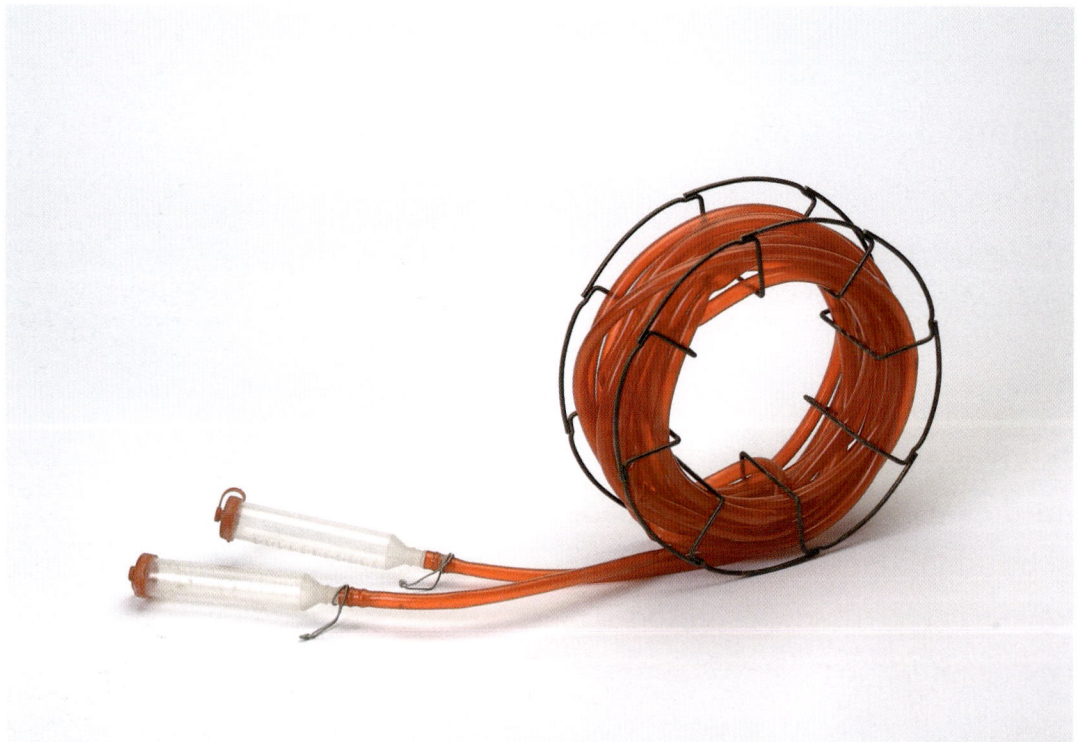

Water level

Sawing and cutting

Knife

A knife can be used to cut plasterboard and scrim to the necessary size, as well as for common tasks such as opening bags of plaster. It is important to keep your knife sharp in order to cut plasterboard and other items such as scrim cleanly, but this makes it a very dangerous tool. Some knives have retractable blades to make them safer.

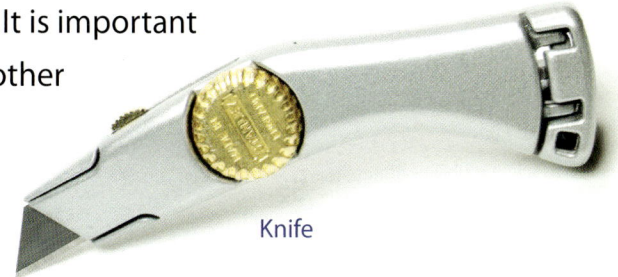
Knife

Saws

A saw is a common tool that you will find in most plasterers' toolbags. It can be used for a variety of tasks, including cutting plasterboard or making a quickly needed stand or handboard/hawk.

 **Safety tip**

Use knives with caution. Your hands are essential to your trade, and a cut to the hand can mean you being 'off the job' and thus losing money

Hacksaw

Hacksaws are useful for cutting small pieces of metal, such as angle beads. They are used mainly when cutting materials to be joined at particular angles (mitring).

Hacksaw

Board saw

A board saw is a special saw with a large tooth pitch (5 mm). It is shorter in length than the average saw and is used only for cutting plasterboards. Its larger teeth prevent the saw from becoming blunt and clogging with plaster dust.

Board saw

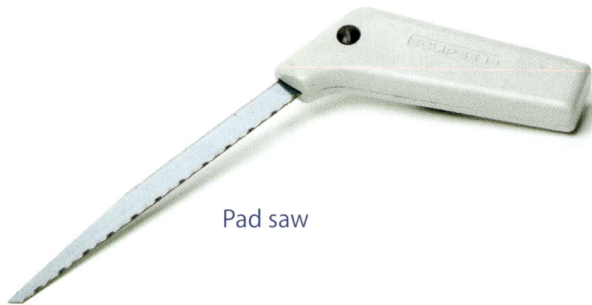
Pad saw

Pad saw

A pad saw tends to have a simple handle, no frame and a pointed end for easy penetration. This allows you to cut small apertures (holes or openings) in plasterboard. It is mainly used for making space for wires and pipes.

Mitre box

A compact mitre box can be made from either wood or plastic. It is used to guide the saw when cutting angles, particularly when cutting standard coving.

Mitre box

Coving mitre tool

Coving mitre tool

Often known by the trade name Wonder Mitre, this is used as an alternative to a mitre box for cutting coving. The shaped notches help to grip the coving firmly while cutting. The tool is suitable for both 100 mm and 127 mm coving.

Safety tip

When using tin snips to cut mesh, it is advisable to wear gloves to protect your hands, as the wire can cause serious cuts

Tin snips

These are used to cut metal such as angle beads, wire and sheets of expanded metal. Some are spring-loaded to make cutting easier. They are available in various sizes from different manufacturers.

Tin snips

Canvas knife or scissors

These are used for cutting canvas in a canvas bin. The knife and scissor blades must be kept sharp for easy cutting of the canvas.

Scraping and shaping

Joint rule

This is a stiff tool made from steel sheet with one end cut to an angle. The edge has a bevelled finish. The most common sizes of joint rule are 100 mm to 300 mm. It is most commonly used to form mitres, rebates, reveals and joints in fibrous plasterwork. It is also used for 'making good' and cleaning down benches.

Joint rule

Floor scraper

This is used to clean the floor area after plastering. It has a flat metal angled end and a long handle. The blades can be changed when they wear out.

Floor scraper

Did you know?

If you keep the knife on a chain secured to the canvas bin, you will not lose it

Safety tip

Be very careful when handling and using a canvas knife as it will be very sharp

Remember

The edges of joint rules should be protected and have no nicks in them. Also, all metal tools should be lightly oiled after use

Safety tip

Do not run your fingers down the edge of the joint rule because they are very sharp and can give you a deep cut

Rasp

Also known as a planer file, this is often referred to by the trade name Surform®, but is in fact a different tool. Rasps have a hard, rough surface of miniature teeth designed to smooth wood or metal by removing very small shavings. They are mainly flat, round or half round.

Rasp or planer file

Surform®

A Surform® is a flat tool with a serrated base like a cheese grater, and is used for planing the uneven edges of plasterboard before fixing or plastering. Surforms® differ from rasps because the teeth are punched right through the metal, enabling timber shavings to pass through. Hence, the tool is less inclined to clog up. They are also often used for taking down high points on plasterwork, and can be used for taking off high points on the **slipper** before the running mould is constructed.

Surform®

Definition

Slipper – part of the running mould that runs against the running rule. The running mould is used to form the shape of plasterwork, such as a dado. It is made using timber

Dressing – smoothing the surface of masonry or timber

Safety tip

When using a bolster, always wear goggles to avoid plaster debris or bits of aggregate getting in your eyes and possibly causing permanent damage

Bolster

This is a long-handled chisel made of hardened, tempered steel. Some bolsters have a plastic handle for better grip. It is used with a lump hammer for chopping off old plaster or **dressing** walls.

Bolster

Scratcher (scarifier)

This is used to provide a key on a base coat of plaster for the second coat to adhere to.

Scratcher

Hand sander and universal sander

These are flat-based hand tools used to **sand down** any edges or uneven surfaces. Both have sanding sheets which can be fixed to their faces by wing nuts and braces. They are often used when taping and jointing. The hand sander can be metal, plastic or wood and is gripped by a handle. The universal sander has a long handle or pole attached with a knuckle joint allowing the face of the sander to move in all directions – useful for reaching awkward areas.

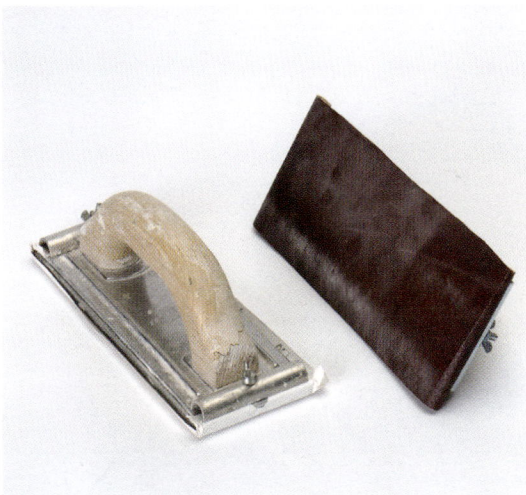

Hand sander and universal sander

Files

These are flat or half-round tools used to smooth the zinc profiles for a running mould. Needle files are used for shaping smaller, more intricate details in the zinc.

Files

French plane

This tool is often made by plasterers using hardwood and a hacksaw blade, but shop-bought versions are also available. It is used to remove imperfections in plasterwork by running it down the **arrises**.

Hammering

Lath hammer

A lath hammer has a head that is axe-shaped at one end and has a notch at the other end for pulling nails. It is typically used for trimming laths, but is also commonly used when preparing walls, to chop **snots** off the block wall before plastering.

Lath hammer

Claw hammer

This gets its name from its claw shape, and is used for pulling out nails. The claw hammer can also be used for levering. It is a common tool used by many trades, and most plasterers have one in their toolbag.

Claw hammer

Lump hammer

This is generally used with a bolster to give the force required to remove aggregate from the background.

Lump hammer

Panel or cross pein hammer

This is used for smaller tacks when fixing template to stock.

Panel or cross pein hammer

Water brush

Miscellaneous

Brushes

All plasterers have a varied selection of brushes to assist them while plastering. The larger ones are classed as water brushes; the smaller ones, such as the 13 mm and 25 mm, are used for tidying up and finishing mitres and the ceiling and wall lines for coving and cornices. You should also have an older, stiffer brush for washing your tools and cleaning out your buckets.

Splash brush

This can be made from horsehair bound onto a wooden handle by copper wire. It is used in casting, for applying the plaster into the moulds. Keep the splash brush wet when it is not in use, as this will stop the hairs from falling out: the wood swells and traps the hairs against the copper wire.

Splash brush

Busk

This is a small flat piece of pliable metal, commonly rectangular in shape but also available kidney-shaped for curved work. Busks are available in different gauges to allow flexibility, and are used to apply plaster onto joints to help smooth out any

Busk

> **Remember**
>
> Splash brushes must be kept clean after use and during casting as they will last longer and work themselves in, becoming easier to use

> **Remember**
>
> Take care of your tools: make them last and avoid costly replacements. Wash your tools each time you have finished using them. Check them for general wear and tear and for damage that could cause injury to you or others. Lightly oil metal tools after use

imperfections. They may also be used with a serrated edge for removing plaster where necessary. The tool is used in fibrous plasterwork to clean up the face of finished **casts**.

Small tool

This solid, one-piece steel tool is multi-purpose, and ideal for many jobs, such as raking out and filling, ornamental and complex plaster work, patching around pipes, and mitring coving.

Small tools come in four types:

- trowel end
- leaf end
- square end
- combination of all three.

Small tool

Picking tool

This is similar to the small tool, but triangular in shape. It can also be used for cleaning up casts, and when modelling plaster and doing **enriched work**.

Pouch

A pouch, with an adjustable waist strap, is used for carrying essential tools that are used frequently, and it provides easy access to them. You would generally keep in it items such as: tape measure, knife, pencil, snips, hammer and some nails or screwdriver and some screws.

Plasterer's pouch

Definition

Cast – piece of manufactured plasterwork that is ready to be fixed

Enriched work – any plasterwork that has a pattern or design

Power tools

Always treat power tools with respect: they have the potential to cause harm either to the person using them or to others around. All power tools used on site should be regularly tested (PAT tested) by a qualified person. There are several health and safety regulations that govern the use of power tools. Make sure that suitable PPE is worn at all times, and that power tools are operated safely. In some cases, you must be qualified to use them. The PUWER (Provision and Use of Work Equipment Regulations) 1998 can be referred to if needed (see Chapter 2 pages 42–43).

On site, transformers are used to reduce the mains voltage from 240 volts to 110 volts. All power tools used should be designed for this voltage.

Special care should be taken with electrical tools.

Always:

- check plugs and connections (make sure you have the correct fuse rating in the plug)
- inspect all leads to ensure no damage
- check that the power is off when connecting leads
- unwind extension leads completely from the reel to prevent the cable from overheating.

Never:

- use a tool in a way not recommended by the manufacturer
- use a tool with loose, damaged or makeshift parts
- lay a driver down while it is still switched on

Safety tip

When using power tools, always read the manufacturer's instructions and safety guidelines before use, to ensure that they are being operated correctly and for the correct purpose

- use a drill unless the chuck (the part in which the drill bit is held) is tight

- throw the tool onto the ground

- pass the tool down by its lead

- use a drill where it is difficult to see what you are doing or hold the tool tightly

- allow leads to trail in water.

Drills

Electric drill / screwdriver

Drills have two different settings and different speeds according to what you are using them for and what you are drilling into.

- **Drill**: this is a normal drilling action.

- **Hammer action**: this gives a striking action to the drill bit and is used to drill into solid backgrounds such as concrete.

- **Variable speeds**: these different speeds are good for fixing fibrous plasterwork because you can control the speed at which you drill: slow for drilling through the fibre cast (to prevent damage to the face) and then speeding up as you reach the background.

Electric screwdrivers make it easier to screw up casts, and they also have a depth gauge that stops the screw going too deep into the cast.

Electric drill / screwdriver

Whisk/drill

This is a power tool that has a long stem with a whisk on the bottom. It enables you to mix plaster easily and thoroughly and at a controlled speed.

Whisk/drill

Miscellaneous

Power leads

On site, power leads are generally yellow, and they should be regularly checked for any splits, cracks or broken wires.

Screw gun

This is a power tool that is used to drive screws into different backgrounds such as timber, metal or plasterboard. Always read and follow the manufacturer's safety guidelines.

Screw gun

Other equipment

This section refers to items that are too large for the plasterer's tool bag or bucket, but which are needed 'in the van' to carry out the job. Some are general-purpose and others are trade-specific, but all are vital pieces of equipment.

As with all tools and equipment, cleaning, maintenance and regular checks for wear and tear should be carried out. A split bucket can cost you time and money if, for example, you leak water in a customer's house!

Buckets

Buckets are an integral part of a plasterer's equipment. They are used for gauging out materials, mixing plaster, holding water, carrying small amounts of material, putting waste in and carrying tools. They come in a variety of sizes and colours.

Maintenance: Do not hit buckets with sharp tools to clean them out as the bucket may split. Always clean out after use.

Safety: Do not over-fill as this can put a strain on your arms and back.

Different buckets

Spot board

This is generally a flat piece of wood, which is placed on a stand at a comfortable height, and used as a place to keep the plaster before putting it on the handboard or hawk.

Stand

This is either a metal or a wooden folding stand which allows you to place a flat board on it and load it up with plaster.

Spot board on a stand

Stilts

Stilts give the plasterer extra height for reaching ceilings or for dry lining, and they eliminate the need for steps or ladders. However, these do need to be used correctly and require that you have a clear working area. Always follow the manufacturer's advice and safety guidelines; failure to do so could result in you toppling from the stilts and possibly injuring yourself.

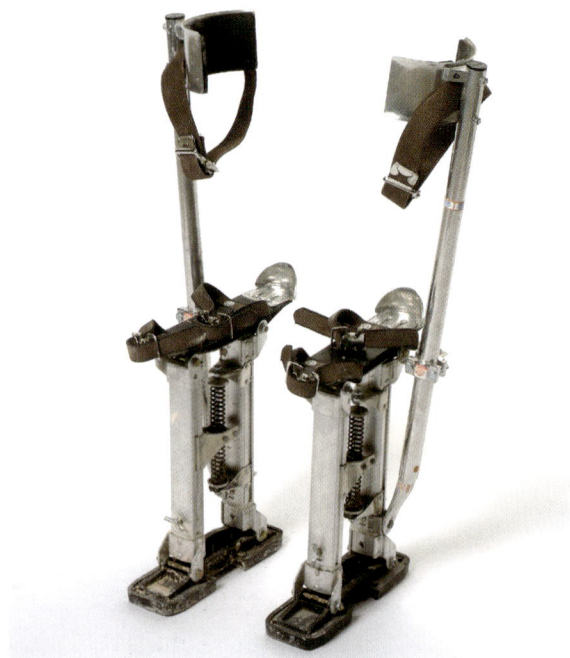

Stilts

Prop or dead man

This is an aid used for holding up a plasterboard single-handedly.

Prop or dead man

Safety tip

Do not struggle to raise boards on your own as you can injure your back through lifting too much weight, or lifting awkwardly

Foot lifter

This is a device that slides under the plasterboard and allows you to insert your foot and lever the board into place. It enables you to lift a wallboard up to 60 mm (2.5 inches) off the floor, leaving both hands free for securing the board in place.

Shovel

This is used for mixing materials such as sand and cement by hand, or for loading the cement mixer. It is also used in the cleaning up process. The best type of shovel is one with a metal shaft.

Maintenance: Wash and wipe after use. This allows for ease of mixing in the future – things naturally slide off a clean shovel face.

Shovel

Remember

Too heavy a load on the shovel will put a strain on your arms and back

Sweeping brush

Sweeping brush

This a common item on all building sites. It is generally used for sweeping up and keeping the area clean. However, plasterers also use them for sweeping dust off the walls they are about to plaster.

Wheelbarrow

Wheelbarrows are generally used for floor screeding where large amounts of material need to be transported over a distance. The best type of wheelbarrow for floor screeding is one specially designed to go through narrow door openings, and able to fit under the mixer being used. Always buy a good quality barrow.

Maintenance: Clean out after use. Do not hit the body of the wheelbarrow with a heavy object. Keep tyres inflated, as this will allow for ease of movement. Check that all metal stays are in place.

Safety: Do not overload the wheelbarrow as it will put strain on your back and arms. Approach the barrow between the lifting arms and hold the arms at the end, bend your knees and lift. The weight of the material should be over the wheel.

Bath

This is a trough for mixing plaster. Troughs are often made from heavy duty polyurethane but are also available in zinc from general hardware shops. They are quite robust so you can use shovels, whisks, etc. in them without causing damage to the bath. A bath lets you mix a large amount of backing plaster in one go.

Bath and drag

Drag or larry

This is a mixing tool with a fork-like device, bent at the ends. It is used for mixing backing plaster in a bath or trough.

Water dustbin

This is a dustbin used to store water for mixing. Using a water dustbin saves time as it allows buckets to be filled quickly by dipping rather than waiting for them to fill at a tap.

Straight edge

Generally made of aluminium, this can be used to check the true line of a finished wall or the ceiling line, for assistance in fixing angle beads plumb with a level, for ruling in floor screeds or to position boards when dry lining (and check that they are flat and true). This tool has traditionally been made of timber, and wooden versions are still available.

Straight edge

Feather edge

Feather edges come in various lengths and are used in the preparatory finishing of walls, sometimes when rendering and plastering, but mainly when floating to help eliminate slacks and hollows. These are again generally made from aluminium, with the leading edge tapered and the back edge thicker. The feather edge can also be used as a straight edge.

Feather edge

Larger items

Cement mixer

This is used for mixing sand, lime and cement, and can be either 110 V or 240 V electric, or petrol. It should be used with the correct PPE. The best type of mixer for floor screed is a paddle mixer. Larger mixers are generally mounted on wheels and smaller mixers on a stand.

Cement mixer

Maintenance: Mixers should be cleaned after use, both inside and outside the drum. Do not hit the drum with any heavy objects to dislodge set materials as this will damage the drum and prevent easy cleaning in the future. Do not leave water in the drum; allow it to drain out. Keep the electric lead clean, for ease of checking for damage. Use the correct fuel for petrol-driven mixers.

Safety: Do not overload the mixer. Do not use if damage is visible on the lead or plug. Do not repair the lead or plug yourself. Mind your back when tipping mixers on a stand. Do not clean out mixers while the drum is still turning. Do not allow water to get near the leads. When using petrol, keep away from naked flames, and handle with extreme care.

Cement pump

Used for moving floor screeds, which are usually pre-mixed, from the mixing area to a higher floor level. Cement pumps would usually be on hire and in some cases would be worked by the hire company.

Remember

If using a 240 V cement mixer, put an **RCD** into the socket outlet before plugging in

Definition

RCD (residual current device) – is used as a safety cut-out when using electrical equipment, to protect you from electric shock

Remember

The pump and hose must be kept clean at all times, and the floor screed will need to be wetter to be pumped through the hoses

Safety tip

Never play around with any hoses that are under pressure such as cement pump hoses, as the force contained in the hoses can cause considerable damage

Personal protective equipment

General personal protective equipment was looked at in Chapter 2 (pages 58–61), but there are some specialist pieces of PPE that plasterers use.

Gloves

Lightweight gloves are worn by many plasterers to stop the sand and cement drying out the natural oils from the hands. They can also help to protect your hands during the laying and mixing of the floor screed.

Safety boots

Always have good quality safety boots. When floor screeding, make sure you have safety boots which are waterproof because you will be walking on damp screed and wet floor areas.

Safety goggles

Safety goggles or glasses should always be worn when mixing with a whisk drill. They are now compulsory on some building sites.

High visibility vests

All building sites now require the wearing of high visibility (or High-Vis) vests.

Overalls

These will protect both your arms and your legs from possible burns from any cementitious material and will prevent the dust from getting into the pores of your skin.

Safety tip

Boots should be tied up because loose boots are dangerous and can cause fatigue

Remember

Keep your work clothes as clean and dry as you can to prevent health problems in the future

Knee pads

These are used mainly when floor screeding to protect your knees from strain and subsequent damage. They can be strap-on or incorporated within the overalls.

Knee pads

Remember

Damaged knees can affect your ability to work and earn money in the future

Barrier cream

Some plasterers use this to protect their hands from damage from the water and plaster dust when working.

Induction and PPE

When working on site, an induction will be carried out by the main contractor which will cover exactly which items of PPE are required. Each person working on site will receive the induction on their first visit.

On the job: Preparing backgrounds

James is a plasterer who works for a large plastering company. He has been sent to the site to float and skim a passage wall. He has organised his water supply and got his bags of material into the area ready for mixing when he notices that there are a lot of snots on the wall to be plastered.

- What tools might James use to chop the snots off the wall?

- What two items of PPE would James need to wear in order to protect himself?

On the job: Using power tools

Sean has been asked to use an electric mixer for a floor screed mix, but there are a few things that he is unsure about.

1. What safety checks should Sean complete before using the mixer?

2. What PPE should he be using during the mixing process?

3. For some unknown reason the mixer has stopped working. What should Sean do now?

FAQ

How do I know which tools I need, which ones are best, and where the best place is to buy them?

There are no 'best' tools: most plasterers have their own favourites and not all prefer the same. The tools that form the plasterer's 'basic tool kit' do not need to be elaborate or expensive; it is better to build up your kit as required by the job. A good idea is to take a look at another plasterer's tools and gauge which are the basics – a trowel, handboard/hawk, buckets and the contents of a pouch are a good start. It is not easy to know which tools suit you best; this comes with experience of using them, so it can be a little 'hit and miss' until you find tools that are comfortable and suited to you.

DIY shops provide basic tools fairly competitively and are ideal for many of the basics when starting out; whether the tools are 'branded' or not they will all do the job, although some cheaper tools may not result in the best finish. Builders' merchants usually stock more specialist tools with a wider range. Often old tools are handed down from other more experienced plasterers which can be useful for finding the best tool for you without the cost.

What should I do if the mixer falls off the stand it is on?

You should turn off the electric supply straightaway. Do not try to lift the mixer back onto the stand on your own, especially if it is full; always ask for help.

Why do I have to fully unwind a reel-up extension cable when I use one with a power tool? Surely the unwound cable could cause an accident?

An extension cable left wound around the reel can overheat and cause a fire. Unwind the cable fully but, to prevent an accident, make sure that the cable is not lying in the area where people will be walking.

Knowledge check

1. What tools might you use to get a wall flat when you are floating it with lightweight backing plaster?

2. What equipment would you use for mixing the backing plaster?

3. What is a 'snot'?

4. List four items of PPE a plasterer might use or wear.

5. What power supply voltage should be used for all power tools on site?

6. Explain the difference between a lath hammer and a lump hammer.

7. Sketch a lath hammer.

8. What is the piece of equipment called on which the plaster is placed ready to use?

9. When might a plasterer wear gloves?

10. What tools would a plasterer use when coving a house?

11. What would be the benefit to a plasterer of using barrier cream on his or her hands both before and during work?

12. What would a chalk line be used for?

13. Explain briefly the difference between a devil float and a sponge float.

14. What is the tool called that you use for holding the plaster before you apply it to the background?

chapter 5

Working at height

OVERVIEW

Most construction trades require frequent use of some type of working platform or access equipment. Working off the ground can be dangerous, and the greater the height, the more serious the risk of injury. This chapter will give you a summary of some of the most common types of access equipment, and provide information on how they should be used, maintained and checked to ensure that the risks to you and others are minimised.

This chapter will cover the following:

- General safety considerations
- Stepladders and ladders
- Trestle platforms
- Hop-ups
- Scaffolding

General safety considerations

You will need to be able to identify potential hazards associated with working at height, as well as hazards associated with equipment. It is essential that access equipment is well maintained, and checked regularly for any deterioration or faults that could compromise the safety of someone using the equipment and anyone else in the work area. Equipment is obviously not as important as people, but it can also be damaged by the use of faulty access equipment. When maintenance checks are carried out, they should be properly recorded. This provides very important information that helps to prevent accidents.

Risk assessment

Before any work is carried out at height, a thorough risk assessment needs to be completed. Your supervisor or someone else more experienced will do this while you are still training, but it is important that you understand what is involved so that you are able to carry out an assessment in the future.

For a risk assessment of working at height to be valid and effective, certain questions must be answered.

1. How is access to and **egress** from the work area to be achieved?

2. What type of work is to be carried out?

3. How long is the work likely to last?

4. How many people will be carrying out the task?

5. How often will this work be carried out?

6. What is the condition of the existing structure (if any) and the surroundings?

7. Is adverse weather likely to affect the work and workers?

8. How competent are the workforce and their supervisors?

9. Is there a risk to the public and work colleagues?

Definition

Egress – an exit or way out

Did you know?

Only a fully trained and competent person is allowed to erect any kind of working platform or access equipment. You should therefore not attempt to erect this type of equipment unless this describes you!

Duties

Your employer has a duty to provide and maintain safe plant and equipment, which includes scaffold access equipment and systems of work.

You have a duty:

- to comply with safety rules and procedures relating to access equipment

- to take positive steps to understand the hazards in the workplace and report things you consider likely to lead to danger, for example a missing handrail on a working platform

- not to tamper with or modify equipment.

Stepladders and ladders

Stepladders

A stepladder has a prop which, when folded out, allows the ladder to be used without having to lean it against something. Stepladders are one of the most frequently used pieces of access equipment in the construction industry and are often used every day. This means that they are not always treated with the respect they demand. Stepladders are often misused – they should be used only for work that will take a few minutes to complete. When work is likely to take longer than this, a sturdier alternative should be found.

When stepladders are used, certain safety points should be observed.

- Ensure that the ground on which the stepladder is to be placed is firm and level. If the ladder rocks or sinks into the ground, it should not be used for the work.

- Always open the steps fully.

- Never work off the top tread of the stepladder.

- Always keep your knees below the top tread.

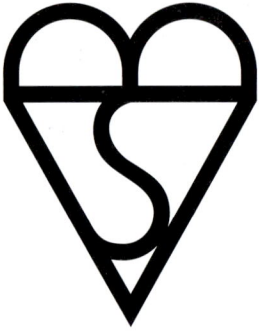

Figure 5.1 British Standards Institution kitemark

- Never use stepladders to gain additional height on another working platform.
- Always look for the kitemark (Figure 5.1), which shows that the ladder has been made to British Standards.

Several other safety points need to be observed, depending on the type of stepladder being used.

Wooden stepladder

Before using a wooden stepladder, check that:

- there are no loose screws, nuts, bolts or hinges
- the tie ropes between the two sets of **stiles** are in good condition and not frayed
- there are no splits or cracks in the stiles
- the treads are not loose or split.

Never paint any part of a wooden stepladder as this can hide defects that might cause the ladder to fail during use, causing injury.

Wooden stepladder

Aluminium stepladder

Before using an aluminium stepladder:

- check for damage to stiles and treads to see whether they are twisted, badly dented or loose

- avoid working close to live electricity supplies because aluminium conducts electricity.

Find out

What are the advantages and disadvantages of each type of stepladder?

Did you know?

Stepladders should be stored under cover to protect from damage such as rust or rotting

Aluminium stepladder

Fibreglass stepladder

Before using a fibreglass stepladder, check for damage to stiles and treads. Once damaged, fibreglass stepladders cannot be repaired and must be disposed of.

Ladders

A ladder, unlike a stepladder, does not have a prop, and so it has to be leant against something in order for it to be used. Together with stepladders, ladders are one of the most common pieces of equipment used to carry out work at height and gain access to the work area.

As with stepladders, ladders are also available in timber, aluminium and fibreglass, and require similar checks before use.

Pole ladder

Ladder types

Pole ladder

These are single ladders and are available in a range of lengths. They are most commonly used for access to scaffolding platforms. Pole ladders are made from timber and must be stored under cover and flat, supported evenly along their length, to prevent them sagging and twisting. They should be checked for damage or defects every time before being used.

Extension ladder

Extension ladders have two or more interlocking lengths, which can be slid together for convenient storage or slid apart to the desired length when in use.

Extension ladders are available in timber, aluminium and fibreglass. Aluminium types are the most favoured as they are lightweight yet strong, and available in double and triple extension types. Although also very strong, fibreglass versions are heavy, making them difficult to manoeuvre.

Aluminium extension ladder

Erecting and using a ladder

Certain points should be noted when considering the use of a ladder.

- As with stepladders, ladders are not designed for work of long duration. Alternative working platforms should be considered if the work will take longer than a few minutes.

- The work should not require the use of both hands. One hand should be free to hold the ladder.

- You should be able to do the work without stretching.
- You should make sure that the ladder can be adequately secured to prevent it slipping on the surface it is leaning against.

Pre-use checks

Before using a ladder, check its general condition. Make sure that:

- no rungs are damaged or missing
- the stiles are not damaged
- no **tie-rods** are missing
- no repairs have been made to the ladder.

In addition, for wooden ladders ensure that:

- they have not been painted, as this may hide defects or damage
- there is no decay or rot
- the ladder is not twisted or warped.

Erecting a ladder

Observe these guidelines when erecting a ladder.

- Ensure that you have a solid, level base.
- Do not pack anything under either (or both) of the stiles to level it.
- If the ladder is too heavy to put it in position on your own, get someone to help.
- Ensure that there is at least a four-rung overlap on each extension section.
- Never rest the ladder on plastic guttering as it may break, causing the ladder to slip and the user to fall.

Definition

Tie-rods – metal rods underneath the rungs of a wooden ladder that give extra support to the rungs

- Where the base of the ladder is in an exposed position, ensure it is adequately guarded so that no one knocks it or walks into it.

- The ladder should be secured at both the top and bottom. The bottom of the ladder can be secured by a second person; however, this person must not leave the base of the ladder while it is in use.

- The angle of the ladder should be at a ratio of 1:4 (or 75°). This means that the bottom of ladder is 1 m away from the wall for every 4 m in height (see Figure 5.2).

- The top of the ladder must extend at least 1 m, or five rungs, above its landing point.

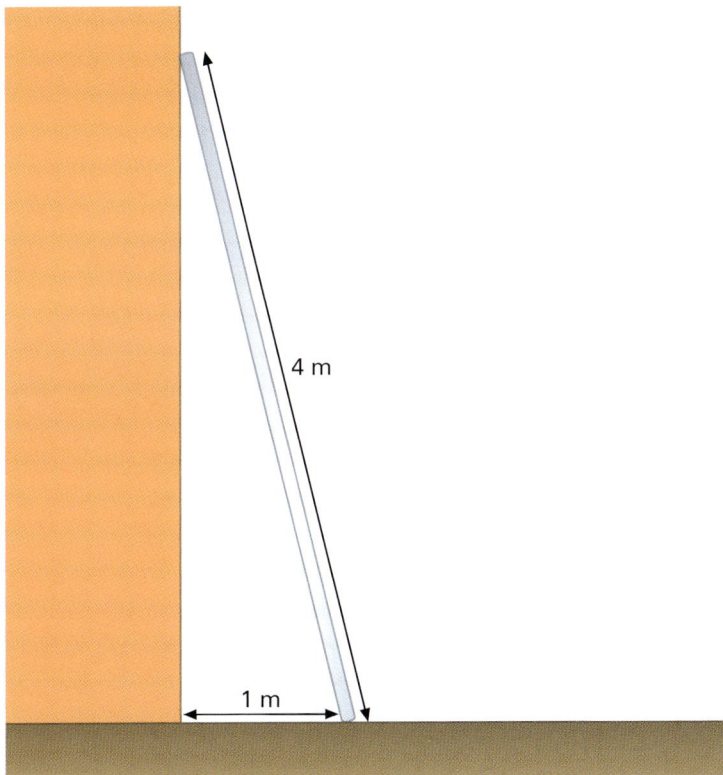

Remember

You must carry out a thorough risk assessment before working from a ladder. Ask yourself, 'Would I be safer using an alternative method?'

4 m

1 m

Figure 5.2 Correct angle for a ladder

Trestle platforms

A trestle is a frame upon which a platform can be placed. A trestle should be used rather than a ladder for work that will take longer than a few minutes to complete. Trestle platforms are composed of the frame and the platform (sometimes called a stage).

Frames

A-frames

These are most commonly used by carpenters and painters. As the name suggests, the frame is in the shape of a capital A and can be made from timber, aluminium or fibreglass. Two are used together to support a platform (a scaffold board or staging board) – see Figure 5.3.

Safety tip

A-frame trestles should never be used as stepladders as they are not designed for this purpose

Figure 5.3 A-frame trestles with scaffold board

When using A-frames:

- they should always be opened fully, and must, in the same way as stepladders, be placed on firm, level ground

- the platform should be no less than 450 mm wide

- the overhang of the board at each end of the platform should be not more than four times the thickness of the board.

Steel trestles

These are sturdier than A-frame trestles and are adjustable in height. They are also capable of providing a wider platform than timber trestles – see Figure 5.4. As with the A-frame type, they must be used only on firm and level ground.

Figure 5.4 Steel trestles with staging board

Platforms

Scaffold boards

To ensure that scaffold boards provide a safe working platform, before using them check that:

- they are not split
- they are not twisted or warped
- they have no large knots, which cause weakness.

Staging boards

These are designed to span a greater distance than scaffold boards and can offer a 600 mm wide working platform. They are ideal for use with trestles.

Hop-ups

Also known as step-ups, these are ideal for reaching low-level work that can be carried out in a relatively short period of time. A hop-up needs to be of sturdy construction and have a base of not less than 600 mm by 500 mm. Hop-ups have the disadvantage that they are heavy and awkward to move around.

Scaffolding

Tubular scaffold is the most commonly used type of scaffolding within the construction industry. There are two types of tubular scaffold.

1. Independent scaffold – this is a free-standing scaffold that does not rely on any part of the building to support it (although it must be tied to the building to provide additional stability).

2. Putlog scaffold – this scaffolding is attached to the building via the entry of some of the poles into holes left in the brickwork by the bricklayer. The poles stay in position until the construction is complete, and they give the scaffold extra support. This type of scaffolding should not be used for external rendering.

Did you know?

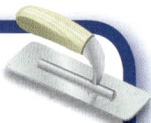

It took 14 years of experimentation to finally settle on 48 mm as the diameter of most tubular scaffolding poles

Special types of scaffold have been designed for use on staircases. The main site contractor may request that your plastering firm use them as they are designed to make plastering on walls above staircases safer.

No one other than a qualified **carded scaffolder** is allowed to erect or alter scaffolding. Although you are not allowed to erect or alter this type of scaffold, you must be sure that it is safe before you work on it. You should ask yourself a number of questions to assess the condition and suitability of the scaffold before you use it.

Definition

Carded scaffolder – someone who holds a recognised certificate showing competence in scaffold erection

- Are there any signs attached to the scaffold that state that it is incomplete or unsafe?

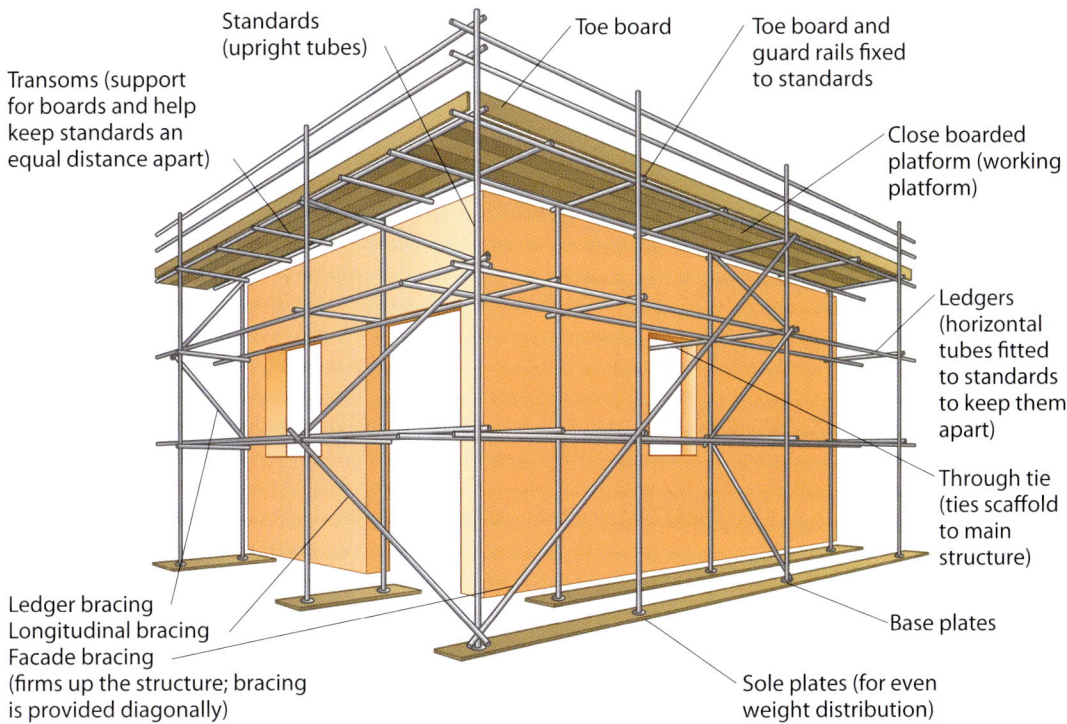

Standards (upright tubes)

Toe board

Toe board and guard rails fixed to standards

Transoms (support for boards and help keep standards an equal distance apart)

Close boarded platform (working platform)

Ledgers (horizontal tubes fitted to standards to keep them apart)

Through tie (ties scaffold to main structure)

Ledger bracing
Longitudinal bracing
Facade bracing
(firms up the structure; bracing is provided diagonally)

Base plates

Sole plates (for even weight distribution)

Figure 5.5 Components of a tubular scaffolding structure

Remember

If you have any doubts about the safety of scaffolding, report them. You could very well prevent serious injury or even someone's death

Right angle coupler – load bearing; used to join tubes at right angles

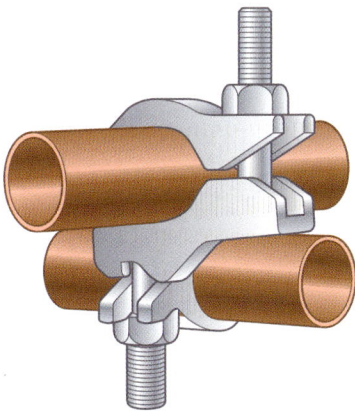

Universal coupler – load bearing; also used to join tubes at right angles

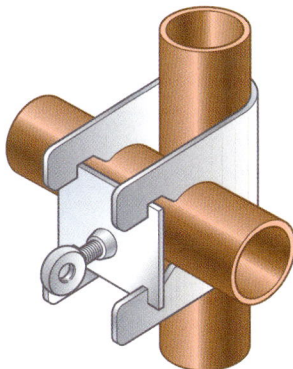

Swivel coupler – load bearing; used to join tubes at various angles e.g. diagonal braces

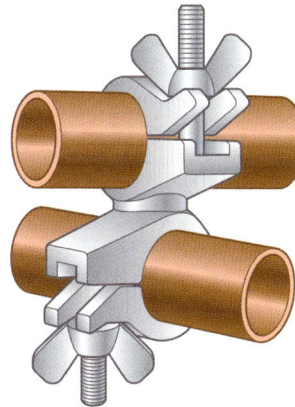

Adjustable base plate or base plate used at the base of standards to allow even weight distribution

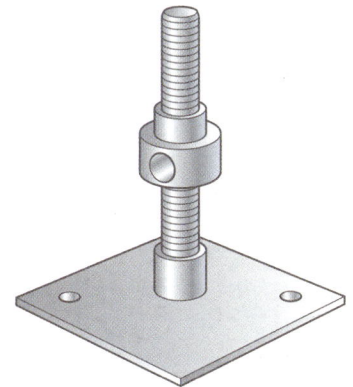

Figure 5.6 Types of scaffold fittings

- Is the scaffold overloaded with materials such as bricks?

- Are the platforms cluttered with waste materials?

- Are there adequate guardrails and scaffold boards in place?

- Does the scaffold actually *look* safe?

- Is there the correct access to and from the scaffold?

- Are the various scaffold components in the correct place (see Figure 5.5)?

- Have the correct types of fittings been used (see Figure 5.6)?

Mobile tower scaffolds

Mobile tower scaffolds are so called because they can be moved around without being dismantled, thanks to lockable wheels. They are used extensively throughout the construction industry by many different trades. A tower can be made either from traditional steel tubes and fittings or from aluminium, which is lightweight and easy to move. The aluminium type of tower is normally specially designed, and is referred to as a 'proprietary tower'.

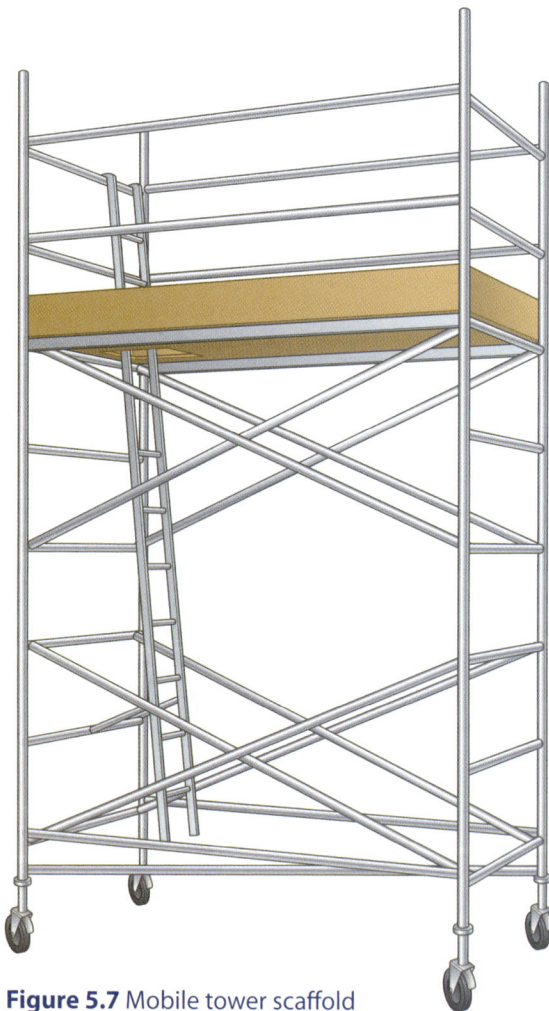

Figure 5.7 Mobile tower scaffold

Low towers

These are a smaller version of the standard mobile tower scaffold and are designed specifically for use by one person. They have a recommended working height of no more than 2.5 m and a safe working load of 150 kg. They are lightweight and easily transported and stored.

These towers require no assembly other than locking the platform and handrails into place. However, you still require training before you use one, and you must ensure that the manufacturer's instructions are followed when setting up and working from this type of platform.

Figure 5.8 Low tower scaffold

Erecting a tower scaffold

It is essential that tower scaffolds are situated on a firm and level base. The stability of any tower depends on the height in relation to the size of the base.

- For use inside a building, the height should be no more than three-and-a-half times the smallest base length.

- For outside use, the height should be no more than three times the smallest base length.

The height of a tower can be increased provided the area of the base is increased **proportionately**. The base area can be increased by fitting an outrigger to each corner of the tower.

For mobile towers, the wheels must be in the locked position while they are in use, and unlocked only when they are being re-positioned.

There are several important points you should observe when working from a scaffold tower.

- Any working platform above 2 m high must be fitted with guardrails and toe boards. Guardrails must be fitted at a minimum height of 950 mm.

- If guardrails and toe boards are needed, they must be positioned on all four sides of the platform.

- Any tower higher than 9 m must be secured to the structure.

- Towers must not exceed 12 m in height unless they have been specifically designed for that purpose.

- The working platform of any tower must be fully boarded and must be at least 600 mm wide.

- If the working platform is to be used for materials, the minimum width must be 800 mm.

- All towers must have their own access, and this should be by an internal ladder.

Definition

Proportionately
– when one thing increases in step with something else

Safety tip

Mobile towers must *only* be moved when they are free of people, tools and materials

Safety tip

Never climb a scaffold tower on the outside, as this can cause it to tip over

FAQ

Am I protected from electrocution if I am working on a wooden stepladder?

No. If you are working near a live cable on a wooden stepladder, if any metal parts of the ladder, such as the tie rods, come into contact with the cable, they will conduct electricity and you may be electrocuted. Take every precaution possible in order to avoid the risk of electrocution – the simplest precaution is turning off the electricity supply.

What determines the type of scaffolding used on a job?

As you will have read in this chapter, only a carded scaffolder is allowed to erect or alter scaffolding. They will select the scaffolding to be used according to the ground condition at the site, whether or not people will be working on the scaffolding, the types of materials and equipment that will be used on the scaffolding and the height to which access will be needed.

On the job: Attending to fascia boards

Pete has been asked by a client to take a look at all the fascia boards on a two-storey building. Depending on the condition of the fascia boards, they will need either repairing or replacing. The job will probably take Pete between two and six hours, depending on what he has to do.

What types of scaffolding do you think might be suitable for Pete's job? Can you think of anything Pete will have to consider while he prepares for and carries out this task? Think about things such as exit points, whether or not the area is closed off to the public and how long Pete will be working at height.

Knowledge check

1. Name four different methods of gaining height while working.

2. What must be done before any work at height is carried out?

3. What are your three health and safety duties when working at height?

4. As a rule, what is the maximum time you should work from a ladder or stepladder?

5. How should a wooden stepladder be checked before use?

6. When storing a wooden pole ladder, why does it need to be evenly supported along its length?

7. Explain the 1:4 ratio (or 75°) rule that should be observed when erecting a ladder.

8. When should a trestle platform be used?

9. What two types of board can be used as a platform with a trestle frame?

10. Why should you only use a specially designed hop-up?

11. There are two types of tubular scaffolding. What are they and how do they differ?

12. What are the eight questions you should ask yourself before using scaffolding?

13. In order to increase the height of a tower scaffold, what else has to be increased and by how much?

14. How high should scaffold guardrails be?

15. What is the only way you should access scaffolding?

chapter 6

Fix sheet materials

OVERVIEW

In the last years of the nineteenth century, a man called Augustine Sackett developed a new material: plasterboard. This material can be considered as a background and a backing coat combined in one.

Plasterboard consists of a sheet of prepared gypsum sandwiched between two layers of stout, specially processed paper. Plasterboard was first manufactured in the UK over 90 years ago. Since then, it has been developed into a range of modern high-performance lining products to meet the demands of buildings as diverse as houses and cinemas, hospitals and schools.

Today's plasterboards offer durable, high quality linings for walls and ceilings, lift shafts and stairwells, corridors and auditoriums. They offer a wide variety of solutions from simple space division through to demanding fire, sound, thermal, moisture and impact resistance.

Another type of sheet material that plasterers use is expanded metal lath (EML). The advantage of metal lathing over plasterboard is that it can be used for both internal and external work, and can also be used for curved work because of its flexibility.

This chapter will cover the following:

- About plasterboard
- Types of plasterboard
- Storage and handling
- Cutting and preparing
- Fixing to ceilings
- Plasterboard coving
- Lathing and trims
- Timber beams and wall plates

About plasterboard

Plasterboard is made from gypsum processed into a board and usually faced with a paper covering.

Gypsum

The gypsum used in the manufacture of plaster and plasterboard is derived from a number of sources. In the UK, it is mined at three main places: Sussex, Lincolnshire and Yorkshire.

Gypsum is a white rock, but impurities can colour it grey, brown or pink. Its scientific name is calcium sulphate dihydrate and it is composed of 70 per cent calcium sulphate and 21 per cent water by weight. The chemical formula is $CaSO_4\ 2H_2O$.

Gypsum is also produced synthetically as the by-product of a number of industrial processes. Flue-gas desulphurisation (FGD) of power station emissions is the largest production method for the gypsum used in plasterboard manufacture. The emission stacks of fossil fuel power stations incorporate 'scrubbers', which remove much of the sulphur from the waste gas, thereby reducing emissions of sulphur dioxide. The by-product of this process is gypsum. This gypsum is also sometimes referred to as desulphogypsum (DSG). Its use is increasing as FGD technology is installed in more power stations, and it is increasingly being used in plasterboard manufacture as it is a very pure form of gypsum.

How plasterboard is manufactured

To manufacture plasterboard, the raw material is first processed by grinding the rock to powder. The powder is heated at around 150°C, causing it to lose about three-quarters of its water, and is then called hemi-hydrate gypsum plaster ($CaSO_4\ \frac{1}{2}H_2O$) – commonly known as plaster of Paris. It is then remixed with water to form a paste, which is spread and sandwiched between the layers of facing paper. When the paste sets and hardens, it has effectively reverted back to being gypsum rock.

Many different types of plasterboard are made, such as:

- different thicknesses

- boards with specialist properties such as being particularly fire- or moisture-resistant, or for sound insulation (acoustic) uses

- composite boards formed from plasterboard with layers such as insulation bonded to it.

The finished plasterboard

Fibre-reinforced gypsum building boards are also made, which do not have paper facings and are therefore not described as plasterboard.

Types of plasterboard

Plasterboards are used in a number of ways, so different types of board with various edge and surface finishes have been developed.

Standard performance

Plasterboards are the modern way to provide high-quality linings for today's buildings. They are available in an unrivalled range of types and sizes, enabling you to select the right product for every application. Manufacturers British Gypsum, Knauf and Lafarge produce plasterboards of different types, colours, sizes, widths, lengths and thicknesses.

The standard plasterboard is suitable for most applications and is compatible with direct decoration or plaster finishes. It has ivory-coloured facing paper.

Some plasterboards have controlled suction characteristics; these boards have a specialised paper covering which controls the level of suction across the surface of the board, making the application of plaster or finishing material easier.

Plasterboards with either a negative edge or a bevelled edge profile are used to provide fine joints.

Typical applications

Residential:

- dry lining masonry and timber frame external walls
- ground-floor and upper-floor partitions in masonry and timber frame built homes
- dry lining masonry and timber frame separating walls
- in the construction of both mid-floor and top-floor ceilings.

Commercial:

- partitions in all institutional/commercial and leisure buildings
- separating walls in all institutional/commercial and leisure buildings
- ceilings in all institutional/commercial and leisure buildings.

Acoustic performance

Noise in buildings is not only a nuisance factor but can also significantly reduce comfort and efficiency. **Part E** of the 2007 **Building Regulations** stipulates minimum levels of **acoustic performance** for all residential buildings. There are a number of specific acoustic plasterboards available for different applications. Boards with a higher density core can be used in partition walls, separating walls and ceilings between flats and houses.

Definition

Building Regulations – a set of rules for various products relating to fire safety, sound insulation, drainage, ventilation and electrical safety, dictating how and where they should be installed. The regulations aim to ensure the health and safety of people in and around buildings

Part E – the regulations dealing with the transmission of sound

Acoustic performance – controlling and reducing the noise levels within buildings

Plasterboards with a layer of glass mineral wool backing are commonly used in existing buildings where an extra layer of sound insulation needs to be installed.

Acoustic performance plasterboards have pale blue facing paper.

Fire performance

A number of plasterboard types are available which provide effective fire protection under Part B of the Building Regulations. It is crucial that the fire protection requirements for a building are identified and incorporated to ensure that the occupants are able to escape safely from the building in the event of a fire. These plasterboards include glass fibre and other additives in the core material, giving increased fire protection qualities. Some types of board also include other innovations such as a vapour membrane which helps to prevent the spread of fire.

Fire performance boards have pink facing paper.

Typical applications

Residential:

- housing-integral garage ceiling linings
- protected fire-escape routes (stairwells in common areas of flats, etc.)
- separating floors in flats and apartment developments.

Commercial:

- ceilings below timber or concrete floors in institutional/commercial and leisure buildings
- high fire performance in institutional/commercial and leisure buildings
- enclosing stairwells in institutional/commercial and leisure buildings
- enclosing service ducts in institutional/commercial and leisure buildings.

Moisture performance

Certain buildings or areas of buildings require extra moisture protection, and today's modern plasterboards can have various moisture-controlling and water-resistant properties.

Moisture performance boards have green facing paper.

Typical applications

Residential:

- external soffits in sheltered positions
- dry lining wet-use areas such as kitchens and bathrooms
- as the base for ceramic tiling.

A sheltered external soffit

Commercial:

- as the base for ceramic tiling

- dry lining wet-use areas such as kitchens and bathrooms.

Another variant is available which includes vapour-checking qualities to provide condensation moisture control where there is a likelihood of higher moisture levels. Vapour check boards have ivory facing paper, with a metallised polyester film on the reverse. They are used where vapour control and plasterboard lining are required in one fixing operation.

Thermal performance

Part L of the Building Regulations concerns the thermal performance for external walls and roofs in almost all types of new and some existing buildings. Specific plasterboards are available which have an additional layer of expanded polystyrene attached during manufacture. Different thicknesses and densities of this layer provide varying levels of thermal performance.

Plasterboard used as an insulating layer

Typical applications

Residential:

- clear cavity construction in new homes

- on masonry external walls

- where a substantial upgrade in thermal insulation is required, such as solid walls in existing buildings.

Commercial:

- on external walls where high levels of thermal insulation are required.

Impact performance

Certain buildings or areas of buildings can be exposed to greater wear and tear, such as public or high traffic areas. Plasterboards can contribute to providing greater impact resistance. Certain plasterboards have higher density cores and are therefore able to withstand impact.

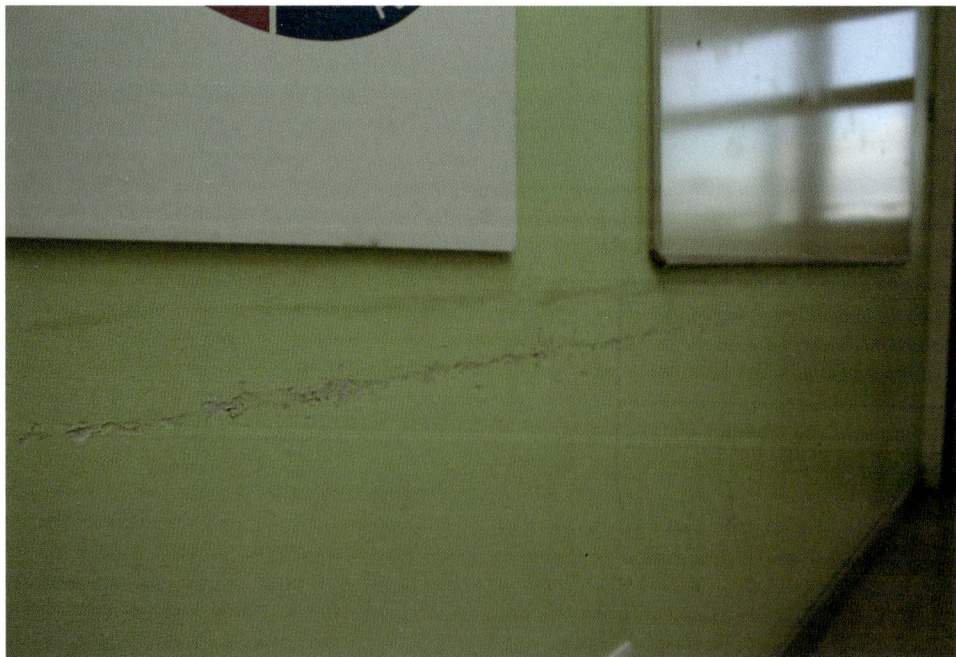

A wall in an impact-prone area

Typical applications

Residential:

- hallways, stairs and landing areas.

Commercial:

- high traffic areas such as corridors, reception areas, etc. in institutional/ commercial and leisure buildings

- in exposed areas of healthcare and educational buildings, such as central kitchens, hotels, etc.

Lath board

This is narrow plasterboard with two grey faces and produced with rounded edges. These are used where ceilings require floating and not just setting. Lath boards are designed to act like wooden lath ceilings, the idea being that you don't scrim the boards before setting with plaster. As you plaster the ceiling, the plaster is pushed through the gap and grips the board together as it did when working on old wooden lath ceilings.

Storage and handling

To protect the surface of plasterboards from damage they are bundled in pairs with the ivory surfaces innermost, and bound along their cut ends by means of an easily removable tape.

To prevent damaging the ivory surfaces, the boards should not be separated until they are required for use. Plasterboards should always be carried on edge in pairs with the ivory surfaces together. The boards should not be carried with surfaces horizontal as this imposes an undesirable strain on the core.

Did you know?

Plasterboard contains microscopic pores into which the wet plaster adheres

Remember

Plasterboard should always lie flat and not be stood up against a wall. Sheet materials on edge will bend owing to gravity and plasterboard can become bowed by moisture

When stacking boards, the edges of the boards should be placed down first and then the boards should be turned into the horizontal position. In no circumstances should the boards be slid one over the other as this is likely to scuff the surfaces.

Plasterboard must be stacked flat in a dry place, on a level surface, and must be properly protected from rising damp and inclement weather. Whenever possible, the boards should be stacked inside a building but, if stored outside, the stack must be out of contact with the ground, on a level platform, and completely covered with a securely anchored polythene sheet or tarpaulin.

A suitable platform can be constructed from 100–125 mm wide timber bearers of a length not less than the width of the boards, which should be placed not more than 400 mm apart.

Storage on **bearers** spaced wider than 400 mm may result in permanent deformation of the lower boards in the stack. The ends and edges of the boards should be neatly aligned so that there are no projections, and it is good practice to ensure that the height of each stack does not exceed 900 mm.

Cutting and preparing

Tools and PPE

- craft knife
- retractable tape measure
- straight edge
- pencil
- rasp
- gloves
- goggles
- safety boots
- face masks

Definition

Bearers – pieces of timber placed on the ground to stack material on to keep it away from the ground

Did you know?

On many sites, plasterboard waste is placed in separate bags or skips for recycling

Measure the length and width required.

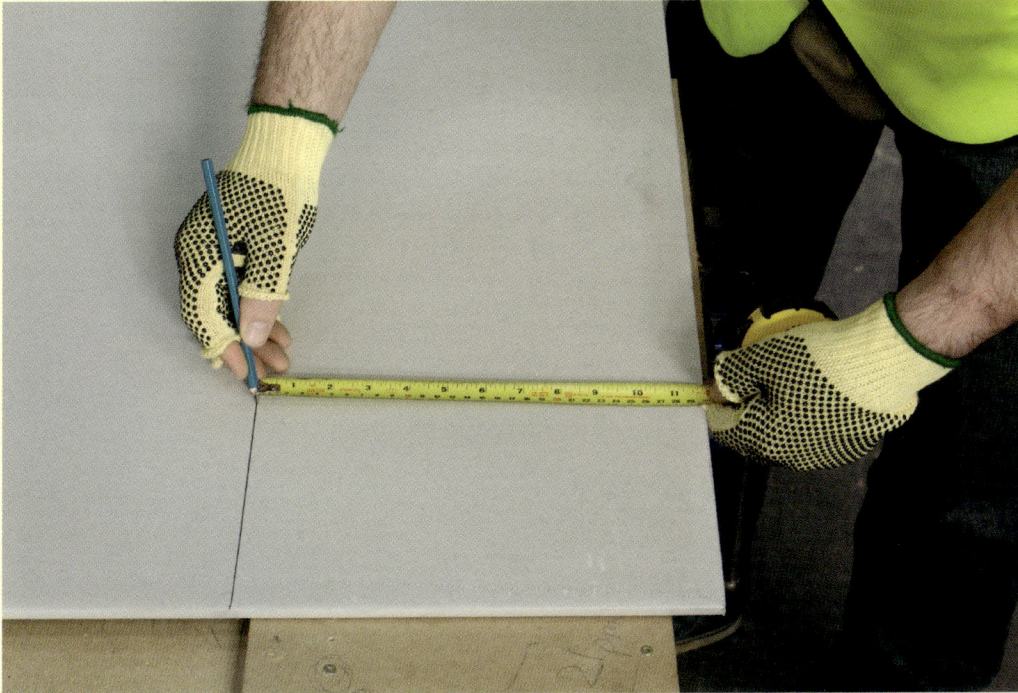

Using a pencil, mark the measurements onto the plasterboard ivory side. Using a level or straight edge, join the marks up with a pencil. You may wish to use a straight-edge to do this.

Using a craft knife score the board along a metal straight edge. Ensure hands, arms and legs are safely out of the way of the blade.

Lift the board on edge and lightly tap the scored line to snap the board.

Safety tip

Keep your fingers clear of the blade

When using a rasp on the cut plasterboard edges, it is advisable to wear a dust mask to prevent inhalation of dust

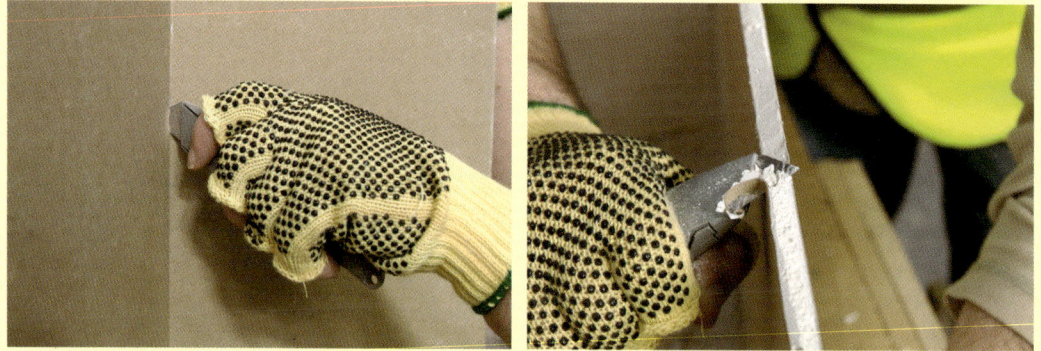

Remember

When cutting plasterboard, make sure that the area on which you are cutting the board has been swept clean as any loose debris will damage the board

Run the knife along the back of the cut to separate the two pieces of board.

Trim the edge with the knife or, using a rasp, rub down the edge to make it smooth and level.

Fixing to ceilings

The methods used in fixing should ensure that the boards are well supported by nails or screws, and that continuous joints across the ceiling are avoided if possible, to reduce the chance of cracks developing in the finished ceiling.

Each board should be nailed at 150 mm centres with 30 mm galvanised nails for 9.5 mm boards or 38 mm nails for 12.5 mm boards. Care should be taken to ensure that the head of each nail just grips the paper of the plasterboard without puncturing it.

If the nails are left with a space between the head and the plasterboard, later the ceiling will vibrate and push off small circles of plaster the size of the nail head. If the heads are allowed to puncture the paper, the plaster behind the nail head will have been crushed. Again looseness of the boards can occur and, in extreme cases, the plasterboad can even fall off. This is referred to as 'nail popping'.

Boards should be nailed no closer than 13 mm to the board edges.

When fixing plasterboards to a ceiling, the boards should be positioned so that the long bound edges are at right angles to the joists. It is important to fix the boards so that the uncut, unbound edge rests halfway on the furthest joist that the board will reach.

The exposed margin should be parallel to the joist edge. If succeeding boards are also fixed with uncut edges on the two adjacent exposed board edges, the boarding will be kept parallel and square. Succeeding rows are bonded to avoid an unbroken joint across the ceiling as this is likely to cause cracking.

Plasterboard fixed to ceiling joists

Key points

- Each board has two bound and two unbound edges. The bound edge must span the joists.

- The boards are fixed with 30 mm galvanised clout nails at 150 mm centres.

- A gap of 2–5 mm must be left between each board and the next.

- All boards must be bonded to avoid continuation of joints formed with unbound edges.

- Boards must be fixed with the printing facing up to the joists.

- The paper surfaces of the boards contain microscopic pores, and the plaster applied to the boards contains jagged, microscopic crystals which penetrate the pores, thus creating adhesion. Therefore it is important that fixed boards are plastered as soon as possible to avoid dust materials rising with warm air and filling the pores.

Fixings used for plasterboards

Plasterboards can be fixed by using either of the following:

- galvanised or zinc-plated clout nails

- galvanised screws.

Plasterboard thickness	Screws	Nails
9.5 mm	25 mm	30 mm
12.5 mm	38 mm	38 mm
15 mm	38 mm	40 mm
19 mm	42 mm	50 mm
12.5 mm double boarded	60 mm	65 mm

Points to remember when fixing boards.

- Screws provide a superior fixing to nails.

- Drive fixings home without damaging the board surface.

- Using screws minimises the risk of nail popping.

- Screws can be fixed at 300 mm centres.

- Nails need to be fixed at 150 mm centres.

Remember

The screws or nails should not puncture the paper on the plasterboard – this can cause the boards to become loose

Repairing damaged plasterboard – patching to a hollow plasterboard background

Where it is necessary to cut back damaged plasterboard to a ceiling or wall, as it would not be time- or cost-effective to re-board the whole area, the following procedure can be applied.

1. Cut back the damaged area, leaving a square cut.

2. Clean up the plasterboard edges and make sure that the back of the existing plasterboard is free from debris.

3. Cut a piece of new plasterboard, making sure that the width will fit through the cut hole in the ceiling but the length is long enough to cover the hole.

4. There are two methods of fixing the piece of plasterboard into place. One is by drilling two small holes into the new plasterboard and then threading string through the holes. The other option would be to pull the board into place by using the head of a nail; when the board is set in place, the nail can be pushed into the ceiling space.

5. Apply some plaster to the back of the new piece of plasterboard and place the board into position, pulling the board tight with the string or nail.

6. When the plaster has set, fill in the hollow either by using plaster or by dabbing a piece of plasterboard into position and re-plastering the damaged area.

This method can also be used on walls.

Damaged area cut back

New plasterboard placed in position

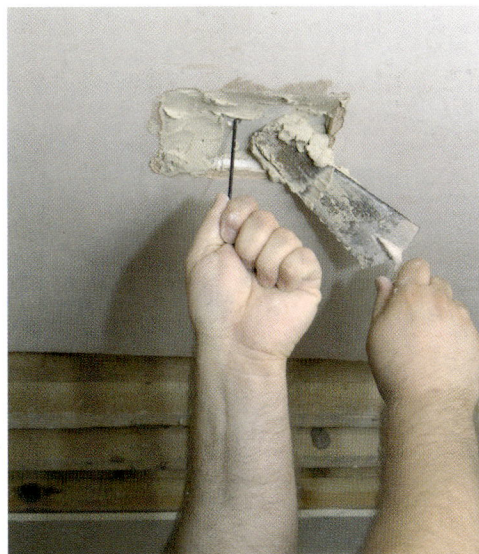

Hollow filled in

Plasterboard coving

Plaster coving is a strong flexible product composed of a fire-protective plaster core encased in an ivory-coloured paper. It can be used to enhance plastered walls and ceilings, and provides a true cove/cornice profile to decorate a room at the wall/ceiling line. Plasterboard coves are intended for direct decoration and are used to improve the appearance of, and to hide any cracks in, the wall and ceiling angle (this is more common in new build).

Types of coving are:

- cove
- cornice
- cornice strips.

They come in these sizes:

Type of coving	Length	Girth
Cove	300 mm/4200 mm	100 mm/127 mm
Cornice	3000 mm	135 mm
Cornice strips	1200 mm	25 mm

Tools and materials required

Tools

- hammer
- saw
- measuring tape
- tool brush
- small tool
- joint rule
- chalk line

- pencil
- mitre box
- template
- nail punch
- square
- basic hand tools

Materials

- cove adhesive
- plaster cove
- galvanised nails
- galvanised screws
- PVA
- steps
- mixing bowls
- sandpaper

Handling and storage

- Always carry the coving on edge.
- Stack coving in a dry place.
- Store coving on a flat surface.
- Keep coving off the ground.

Preparation of background surfaces

Before fixing the coving, the wall and ceiling area adjacent to the internal angles must be cleaned and any old or painted plaster surfaces keyed by scratching. Guidelines should be snapped using a chalk line around the room, 82 mm away, on the ceiling, from the wall/ceiling angle for 127 mm coving.

Cutting and mitring coving

The lengths of the cove should now be measured on the wall line and the mitres cut, in a mitre box if available. Alternatively, the first length may be butted into the angle and a scribed joint formed against this. Joints of 3 mm should be allowed between straight lengths, and it is an advantage to cut the joints at an angle instead of them being square butted: on internal and external joints, it is easier to hide the joint or seam than when they are butted together.

To avoid a great deal of making good, mitres should be cut accurately. You can use a number of methods and equipment to cut along the coving:

- a cove mitre box
- a paper template provided by the manufacturer
- a plastic mitre template
- a metal mitre template.

When the lengths have been cut, preferably with a fine-toothed saw, the sawn edges should have the burrs smoothed off with fine sandpaper. The cut lengths should be checked, in position, for accuracy before fixing. If the corner is not exactly square and will need finishing with additional material, PVA can be added to the exposed plaster of the cove to prevent the finishing material from setting too quickly.

Fixing coving

If the cove is to be nailed or screwed, the positions of the joists should be found and marked on the ceiling. Special bedding materials, some of which are recommended for mixture with hot water, are available from manufacturers.

The bedding mix should be made to a fairly stiff consistency and spread about 3 mm thick along each bedding edge, on the reverse side of the cove. This mix can be pressed into position with a sliding action until solid.

Galvanised nails or screws may be inserted at each end of the cove length and also in the middle if the adhesion or key is suspect. The nails or screws should be driven tightly enough to make a slight impression in the paper, but they should not to penetrate through the paper into the core.

Joints should be butted and made good as the work proceeds. Excess joint filler should be cleaned off while it is still soft, and nail/screw holes should be filled with this mix. When it is dry, any set material left on the cove surface can be rubbed down with sandpaper or wiped clean with a damp cloth.

Coving cut in a mitre box

Coving being fixed in position

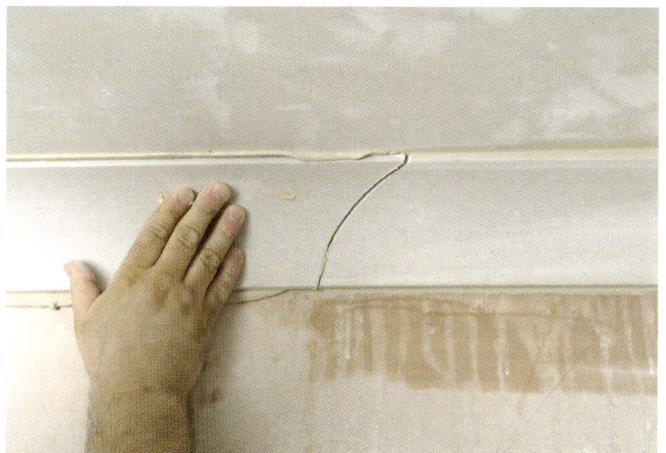

Mitre joints formed (above and right)

Lathing and trims

Lathing provides an excellent key for finishing materials on masonry, ceilings, suspended ceilings and timber frame buildings. Suitable for internal and external applications, lathing is easily formed, allowing designers to create free forms such as arches, domes and vaults in a trouble-free, effective manner. Lathing can also be used as a carrier for fire protection finishes to structural steelwork. There is also a wide range of metal trims that plasterers will use in their trade; they are simple to use and fix, and easy to work with. The range is designed to provide durable, effective solutions, whatever kind of plastering or rendering work your job entails.

Expanded metal lathing (EML)

This is made from good quality steel plate, cut and expanded to form diamond-shaped meshes. It is also available in stainless steel and with a galvanised coating for internal work. An advantage over plasterboard is that it can be used internally and externally where there is damp in the air. Because of its flexibility it can also be used for curved backgrounds. EML comes in different weights and mesh sizes to suit different situations.

Expanded metal lathing is normally supplied in sheets of 2700 mm × 700 mm. In the case of fireproof construction, it can be fixed to timber joists or metal runners.

When fixing EML to timber joists, the long direction of the diamond mesh should be nailed or screwed at right angles to the run of the joists. The sheets should be cut to the correct size, held in position and nailed to the centre joist first, using 30 mm galvanised nails or staples at 100 mm centres. The sheet should then be nailed outwards from the centre in each direction, nailing into each joist in turn to keep the EML as taut as possible. To help in pulling the EML taut, the nails should be **togged** in at an angle away from the centre joist, and bent over.

All joints should be lapped 25 mm over adjoining sheets, and wire ties should be placed every 150 mm along the loose ends using 18 gauge

Safety tip

Wear the correct PPE when cutting EML – gloves

Definition

Togged – nailed at an angle

EML being cut with tin snips

(1.2 mm) galvanised wire. At the joints with the wall, the EML should be bent down 75 mm flat to the brickwork. Joist spans recommended are 300 mm centres for 0.5 mm metal and 450 mm for 0.95 mm metal.

Rib lath

This is EML stiffened by steel ribs 10 mm deep and formed in the same sheet of metal. This type is available in sheets of 2500 mm × 700 mm.

When fixing rib lath, be sure that the ribs are in contact with and at right angles to the supports. The methods of fixing to timber or steel joists are similar to those for ordinary EML, except that the joist should be lapped 50 mm at the ends of the sheets on supports.

Rib lath

Laps between supports are not advised, but if these are unavoidable, the sheets must be overlapped by at least 100 mm and wired together with at least two ties to each pair of overlapping ribs. At the joints with the wall, a strip of ordinary EML, 150 mm wide and bent to form a right angle with two 75 mm flanges, can be fastened into the angle of the wall and ceiling by nailing or tying with wire.

Hy-rib

Hy-rib lath has strengthening ribs pressed into it during manufacture. Hy-rib, being stronger than rib lath, does not need to be fixed to bearers at centres so close together. Rib lath is fixed to beams at 600 mm, whereas Hy-rib lath can be fixed at 1200 mm or 1500 mm.

Plasterboard resilient bars

Resilient bar is a thin metal channel designed to substantially improve the sound insulation of plasterboard walls and ceilings. The channel isolates the plasterboard from the studwork, stopping direct contact and so dissipating sound which would normally be transferred through the frame.

This system is easy to install and produces excellent results, especially when used with ceilings. Resilient bars can easily be cut with tin snips or a hacksaw. They are fixed directly to the underside of an existing ceiling: 50 mm battens should be screwed to the ceiling at approximately 600 mm centres, at right angles to the joists. Care must be taken to ensure that the fixings used are secured to the joists and not to the plasterboard.

On walls, the bars should be mounted at right angles to the frame, at a maximum of 600 mm centres, with the narrow flange at the bottom and the wider flange at the top. This allows the plasterboard to draw itself away from the studwork.

A double layer of 12.5 mm plasterboard should be fitted to within 5 mm of the surrounding walls or ceiling. Joints should be staggered in all directions. All joints should be secured to the resilient strip with the appropriate length screw at 230 mm centres. Secure the first or thickest layer of plasterboard to the resilient bars with the correct length screws.

Double boarding

Fixing ceilings to timber joists is an established form of ceiling construction, which is widely used in both new housing and refurbishment. Ceilings are often specified as fire- and sound-resisting in residential units such as flats and apartments. Loft conversion and most new builds require double boarding to meet the requirements of national Building Regulations.

1. Mark the position of the joists and noggins at the perimeter prior to fixing the first layer of plasterboard.

2. After the first layer of boards has been fixed, transfer these dimensions to the lining, and mark lines to indicate the position of the timber supports.

3. Fix the second layer of boards with edges against the centre line of the supports, with all joints staggered in relation to the first layer. Finally, fix the boards in place with screws.

Timber beams and wall plates

During the fixing of plasterboard, the plasterer may come across timber beams and wall plates that need covering before plaster can be applied. Plasterboard can be fixed to the timber either by nailing or using screws. Alternatively, EML can be fixed taut with nails or screws; then a pricking up coat can be applied and keyed before the final application of plaster.

On the job: Taking delivery

Michael has been asked by his foreman to take charge of a delivery of plastering materials on a new-build site. As the materials are unloaded from the lorry, Michael is checking that the quantities and the amounts are correct according to the delivery note. Michael notices that the boxes with the angle beads have been damaged. He tells the driver, but the driver tells Michael to sign the delivery note anyway and says that, when he gets back to the depot, the driver will report it and send some new angle beads later on.

1. Do you think Michael should sign the delivery note or should he check first with his foreman?

FAQ

What does the term 'staggered joints' mean?

The idea behind staggering boards is so you do not get a continuous joint line. This is to prevent cracking in ceilings when they are plastered. When fixing the boards, you should leave a 5 mm gap between each board to allow movement. The joints are scrimmed before the application of plaster.

Knowledge check

1. How should plasterboard be stacked?

2. What might happen if you stack plasterboard incorrectly?

3. What preparation should you make before fixing coving?

4. What is the correct PPE to wear when cutting EML?

5. Suggest one method that you can use to repair damage to plasterboard on a ceiling area.

6. Name two different types of plasterboard.

7. How should plasterboard be correctly fixed to a ceiling?

8. What is the required gap between each board when fixed to a ceiling using staggered joints?

9. Why must EML be fixed taut?

chapter 7

Internal solid plastering

OVERVIEW

Internal plastering is the covering of walls and ceilings with any one or more of a variety of materials to provide a sound, flat, smooth surface for decoration. A good finished surface may well be the only decoration needed. As well as providing a base for decoration, plastering will also help with better sound and thermal insulation and fire resistance, as well as improving levels of hygiene (allowing for wiping down).

We shall cover the following topics in this chapter:

- History of plastering
- Preparation of backgrounds
- Materials used in plastering
- Proportioning and gauging plastering materials
- Mixing
- Plaster coats – method of work
- Bead (metal and plastic trim)
- Forming window openings, reveals and piers
- Floating and setting coat to a ceiling
- Floating a beam
- Patching a ceiling
- Making good to a wall

History of plastering

The British Museum has a sample of plaster that is at least 4000 years old, taken from one of the Egyptian pyramids. The Greeks also produced exquisite pieces of plasterwork 500 years before the birth of Christ. But it is when the Romans brought their own 'art and craft' of plastering to England that we were introduced to the skill of the plasterer.

In 1254, King Henry III visited Paris and admired the whiteness and fineness of the walls, and so he introduced the same material – gypsum plaster – to England. This is how the name 'plaster of Paris' became associated with this material.

Over the following years, the art and craft of plastering became more and more important; in London plasterers formed a separate guild company. In 1501, Henry VII granted this guild a charter, and they became the 'Worshipful Company of Plaisterers', one of the original 13 that set up the City and Guilds of London Institute.

Fine plasterwork

Plastering today

Internal plastering is a highly skilled craft: it is not enough just to be able to spread plaster to a wall or ceiling and bring it to a good finish. Any good craftsperson will need to have a sound knowledge not only of the materials used and what their characteristics are, but also of their suitability for any given situation. They will also need to be able to put right any problems that may happen with their own work and that of others.

Internal plastering will allow you to develop the hand and eye skills needed to produce good quality work. You will need to be able to forward-plan your work, have physical strength and show the ability to think on your feet.

Although over the years many new materials have been introduced, many of the methods and techniques used today are remarkably similar to those used hundreds of years ago.

Preparation of backgrounds

A background is the surface that the first or only coat of plaster is to be applied to. Some solid backgrounds produce a good or bad bond for plastering, and some preparation is needed to make sure of a good **adhesion**.

The preparation of any background before plastering is very important. In plastering, what you do first will affect the standard of the finished work. For example, if the background is not prepared well, the plaster that you are going to apply to it will not stick properly (this is known as loss of adhesion or bond failure). When plaster sticks well to a surface, it is said to have a good bond.

> **Definition**
>
> **Adhesion** – the ability of the plaster coat to stick to the surface

A typical background

Suction and adhesion

No two backgrounds are the same; they have different **absorption** (**suction**) depending on how solid they are.

There are two different ways that a background can cause problems for a plasterer. If it is a high suction background, the material may shrink, crack or not get to its full strength, and it may be difficult to rule in and get flat because of the loss of water. If it is a low suction background, the material may slip and slide, making it very difficult to rule in.

Types of background

A plasterer will think of backgrounds as just high or low suction, but in British Standard 5262 they are divided into:

- dense, strong and smooth materials
- moderately strong porous materials
- moderately weak porous materials

Definition

Suction or **absorption** – the ability of the material to soak up water. The more water soaked up, the greater the suction

- no-fines concrete

- expanded metal lathing

- brick containing soluble sulphates.

Dense, strong and smooth materials

Materials in this section include *in-situ* concrete, dense concrete blocks, concrete bricks and dense clay blocks.

- Do not apply rendering to these backgrounds until they have a good key, or the material may fall from the wall.

- Use a spatterdash coat to make a good key (see page 173).

- The material applied onto the spatterdash should be no more than 15 mm thick.

Moderately strong porous materials

Materials in this section include clay and sand, lime bricks and most lightweight aggregate concrete blocks.

This type of background has a good suction but, if you are going over different types of background, a spatterdash coat should be applied.

Moderately weak porous materials

Materials in this section include aerated blocks and some lightweight aggregate blocks and softer types of brick.

With these, it is not easy to get a good key. Some backgrounds will have a high suction, but you can get over that by wetting before plastering.

No-fines concrete

Materials in this section have large holes between the aggregate.

The material already has its own good key because of its open face, but water will not be absorbed into the background because of its open texture.

Expanded metal lathing

This type of background is discussed in Chapter 6, pages 162–164.

Brick containing soluble sulphates

Although mentioned in the British Standards, this type of background is very rarely seen and is not something the Level 2 student is likely to come across.

Composite backgrounds

Where a background contains a range of the materials listed above, it is called a composite background.

These types of background can give problems to the plasterer because the different types of materials that they contain have different levels of absorption and suction.

Key

All backgrounds should have a good key: this is what gives the background a grip (bond) for the plaster to stick to.

When the plaster sticks easily to a rough or open surface, it is said that the surface has a good key.

A key is formed in many ways.

Mechanical key

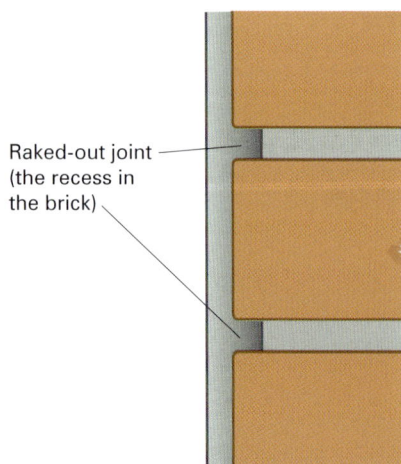

Raked-out joint (the recess in the brick)

A mechanical key is where the brick/block mortar joints are raked out to a depth of approximately 10 mm, or the surface is pre-keyed by the use of special keyed bricks or the keyed face of a lightweight block.

Figure 7.1 Section through a wall showing raked-out joints

Spatterdash coat

A spatterdash coat is a slurry (a wet mix) of cement and sand or cement, sand and **PVA** glue in a mix of one part cement and one part sand and PVA glue plus water. The spatterdash is applied by machine (Tyrolean gun) or small hand shovel or a dashing trowel. Used mainly with cement, limes and mixes.

Liquid PVA or EVA

You can use a liquid PVA (or EVA for external use) on smooth surfaces. If the surface is absorbent, a priming coat of 1:5 bonding agent to water can be applied according to manufacturer's instructions.

Some plastering manufacturers make an adhesive that is coloured, which makes it easier to see where you have applied the adhesive onto the background. It is applied the day before plastering, but you must check with the manufacturer to see what type of plaster can be applied to the adhesive.

One manufacturer has produced a new primer, B 100 (blue in colour), that can be sprayed onto the background and a tack coat, P 60 (pink in colour), that can be rolled on to the B 100. Any type of plaster can be applied to the adhesive up to a thickness of 13 mm. A heavy-duty adhesive (G 12) is produced for thicknesses up to 20 mm.

Hacking the surface

This process is as simple as it sounds and involves physically hacking the wall surface to create a key. This is usually done with a bricklayer's toothed hammer or a compressed-air-driven scabbler (this has teeth that spin at speed and roughen up the surface).

Definition

PVA – polyvinyl acetate, a chemically manufactured glue

Remember

PVA can act like a plastic skin over the surface but, if not applied correctly, it can be peeled off. PVA must be tacky when you work onto it

Preparation checklist

- Brush down the background to remove all loose materials and dust, etc. to make a good sound background.

- Remove all mortar **snots** from joints, internal and external angles.

- Make a key, if needed, to the background.

- Test the background for suction (this is done by splashing a little water onto the surface and seeing how quickly it gets sucked into the background). Treat the background if necessary.

- Drop boards (scaffold boards or old pieces of plasterboard) can be placed at the bottom of the wall to catch any material that is dropped. This allows the material to be reused, and keeps the floor cleaner.

- Fix EML to all timber wall and sole plates as necessary (this stops the plaster from cracking and falling off the wood).

- Fix angle beads.

- Set up the spot board and stand, and wet in the board.

Type of background	Surface key or suction	Preparation
Normal clay bricks or blocks	Good key: When joints are raked out Keyed blocks When keyed bricks are used Moderate key: Flush brickwork or blockwork	Brush and damp down according to suction Soft joints could be raked out in old brickwork
Dense clay brickwork, blockwork, calcium silicate blocks, concrete blocks	Good key: When joints are raked out Keyed blocks When keyed bricks are used Poor key: Flush brickwork or blockwork	Test suction if poor and apply a spatterdash coat
Dense concrete, engineering bricks	Poor key: Unless surface has been keyed in manufacture	Mechanical key, hand key or spatterdash coat
Painted brickwork, glazed tiles, glazed brickwork	Poor key	Treat with bonding agent (PVA). Painted surfaces should be tested before applying bonding agents, to ensure that the joint has a good bond within the brickwork. Brickwork could be hacked or covered with EML. Glazed surfaces should be degreased and a bonding agent applied. Lightweight plasters are best used

Table 7.1 Background preparation

Materials used in plastering

Make sure that the material you choose is compatible with the background.

One rule for choosing a material is that it should not be stronger than the background it is going on: if it is, the plaster will blow or become hollow and fall off the wall.

The plasterer has to identify the type of materials that they are going to use. This information comes from the **specification**.

Information in a specification includes:

- type of material

- number of coats

- thickness of plaster

- standard of work.

Plasterers need to check that the plastering material supplied will:

- spread easily

- build up to the given thickness (use backing coats)

- stay on the surface

- finish to a good surface.

The plasterer deals with a number of materials, and it is important to have an understanding of each of them. They include:

- sand

- lime

- various types of cement, including ordinary Portland cement (OPC)

- plaster.

Sand

Sand is a fine aggregate formed by the breakdown of rocks. For plastering, sand should conform to British Standard 1199.

There are two main sources of good sand: pit sand from inland quarries and river sand.

Sea sand is not good for building because it contains salt that has to be washed out completely before use, adding to the cost. If it is not washed properly, and the salt comes out from the surface at a later stage, it is called 'efflorescence'.

River sand does not make a good internal plastering sand because it has no sharp angles: these have been taken off by erosion caused by the moving water in the river. This type of sand does not have good wearing properties and tends to **work short**.

A good sand should be well graded – this means that it has a mixture of large, medium and small sizes of grains, to fill all the voids in the mix. If there are only large grains, the sand will need a lot of cement or lime to make a good strong, dense mix. This will make the mix expensive and cause extra shrinkage.

Sand should not contain loam (leaves, etc.) or iron as each will have an effect on the quality of the finish.

Sand can have a little bit of clay in it because this will help with the spreading of the material, but if it is above 4–5 per cent, it can cause the following faults.

- The setting of the cement will take longer.

- The retarders (used to slow down the set) in Class B plasters are attacked by the clay and so the set is speeded up.

> **Definition**
>
> **Work short** – where the water runs out of the mix because there are no **fines**
>
> **Fines** – the small bits of sand that help to hold in the water

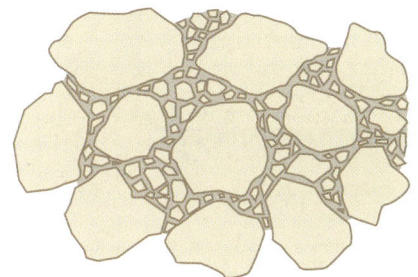

Figure 7.2 Well-graded sand has medium-sized grains to fill in the large voids, and small grains to fill in the smaller voids

- Cracking and blowing will happen because more water is needed to improve the spreadability of the mix and so, when the water evaporates, the material will shrink and crack.

- The shrinkage of the clay itself on drying out will also cause cracking and blowing if the clay is in balls.

The purpose of the sand in a mix is to:

- help the mix to shrink evenly during the setting and hardening (if the shrinkage is at a different rate it can cause cracking)

- lower the cost of the mixed material and provide the bulk of the mix (it is an inactive or inert filler)

- help with the workability of the mix, especially on thicker coats such as floating coats.

Bulking

When water is added to dry sand, it causes it to swell or 'bulk', and take up more space than dry sand. So, when preparing a mix, remember that a bucket full of dry sand contains *more* actual sand than a bucket full of wet sand. If the sand is dry, you don't need as many bucketfuls as you do when the sand is wet.

Silt

This is very fine grains of sand. A little, as for clay, is good because it helps with the spreading of the mix. It plasticises the mix – makes it flow more easily – but too much silt will cause faults such as those shown with clay.

Remember

Do not use soft sand – otherwise known as builder's sand – which is used for bricklaying. Use a medium sharp plasterer's sand

Symptom	Result	Possible causes
Delayed set or total failure	Weakness, shrinkage, cracking and delayed expansion	Sand containing excessive amounts of clay
Very slow set of gauged lime mortar	Delay in building programme	Sand having too much clay, animal matter or vegetable matter (humus) Note: especially common in cold weather when leaves fall
Low finished strength of mortar	Poor sticking of backing coats	Too much sand in mix Sand having too much clay
Efflorescence, dampness and rusting of metalwork	Unsightly appearance Damage to brickwork	Sand containing too much natural salt
Poor workability	Lots of droppings Poor stickability	Badly graded sand Sand having too much clay in it Note: too much water will need to be added and so will cause shrinkage cracks
Rust-coloured staining	Lots of expansion because of metal taking in oxygen Bond failure	Sand having too much iron impurity
Blowing of sanded plasters and external rendering	Damage to brickwork and rendering	Sand having clay balls or coal particles

Table 7.2 Failures caused by poor quality sand

Lime

Lime is manufactured by crushing limestone (which is mainly calcium carbonate) and heating it in a kiln to drive out the carbon dioxide content to produce calcium oxide. This results in the material known as burnt lime, lump lime, quicklime or just lime.

Two types of lime are used in rendering – hydrated lime and hydraulic lime.

Hydrated lime

Hydrated lime is produced by **slaking** calcium oxide (lime) with water to produce calcium hydroxide. It is used in sand and cement rendering mixes for application on all types of background.

The process of slaking lime

Hydrated lime offers a number of advantages.

- It prevents shrinkage cracks in the render mix.
- It improves the workability/spreading of the render mix on the background.

- It improves adhesion to the background.
- It prevents a dark sanding appearance being drawn to the surface when consolidating plain face render.
- It adds suction in the background to prevent sagging when applying decorative finishes to a plain face background.

Hydrated lime can also be made into lime putty by mixing it with water in a container and leaving it to mature over a few days (the longer the better). It is then added to sand and used as an 'undercoat' for internal plastering. This is known as 'coarse stuff', but when it is mixed in the correct proportions (two parts fine-washed sand and three parts lime putty), it can be used as a finishing material on top of the coarse stuff. The finishing material is known as 'setting stuff'.

Hydraulic lime

Hydraulic lime is produced by slaking lime made from limestone that contains clay and other impurities. Unlike hydrated lime, which has no set, hydraulic lime sets like cement once it is mixed with water, but far more slowly.

Hydraulic lime is preferred for use on older buildings that were built using lime mortar. It allows the building to 'breathe'; cement mixes are too dense and brittle for this type of background.

Lime is starved of carbon dioxide, which is removed during manufacture, and so it slowly absorbs carbon dioxide from the air. This will give the lime a thin hard skin, but just below the skin the lime is still soft. Over many years, the lime will continue to take in carbon dioxide. This soft layer beneath the surface will allow the lime to move with the building as the structure changes and the weather conditions change, allowing the building to 'breathe'.

Did you know?

Coarse stuff and setting stuff are normally used in restoration work to match the existing materials

Did you know?

Cracks will open in old lime-based ceilings and walls in the dry weather of summer and close up in the wet weather of winter

Lime used in old buildings and restoration work

Ordinary Portland cement (OPC)

Portland cement is artificial cement produced by a technique invented by Joseph Aspden in 1824. The raw material used in the manufacture of cement is limestone or chalk and clay or shale, roughly in the proportions of 75 per cent limestone (chalk) and 25 per cent clay (shale).

Portland cement is the basic active ingredient of render mixes. It is a closely controlled chemical combination of calcium, silicon, aluminium and iron, plus small amounts of other ingredients. Gypsum is added in the final grinding process to regulate or retard the setting of the cement.

Safety tip

Always wear gloves when handling cement or lime to protect against skin burns

Each step in the manufacture of Portland cement is checked by frequent chemical and physical tests in plant laboratories. The finished product is also analysed and tested to ensure that it complies with all specifications.

Several different manufacturers make cement, but the product must always be manufactured in accordance with British Standard EN 197–1 *Cement: Composition, specifications and conformity criteria for common cements*.

Different manufacturers will produce cement of different colours because they use material coming from different areas of the country. Try to use only one cement manufacturer when working with cement-based mortars, especially when using coloured mortars.

The manufacture of cement

Hardening and curing

Cement is used to bind and harden the mix for rendering. Therefore it is important to **gauge** the mix correctly. Mixes that are weak (not enough cement) will crumble. Mixes that are strong (too much cement) may create stresses that could cause the render to blow from the background. Also, any slight movement in the building will cause cracks to show on the face of the wall.

Definition

Gauge – measure the correct proportions of materials in a render mix to achieve full strength when set

Cement will have two sets. The first set should not be less than 45 minutes and the final set not more than 10 hours. Cement-based materials should not be re-knocked back after the 45 minutes, although many plasterers do this.

Hardening starts after the final set. There must be enough water available for continued hydration (chemical action between water and cement). This means that cement should be cured to stop the loss of water.

Curing can be completed by covering the plaster in plastic and allowing the cement work to sweat and the water to drop back onto it. Also, you can spray it with water or cover it with wet sacking.

Curing usually takes four to seven days.

Remember

Proper curing is very important, especially in hot weather, because the cement will not reach its full strength if it dries too quickly

Other types of cement

- **White Portland cement** This is manufactured from pure limestone and white china clay.

- **Coloured cements** Coloured pigments are mixed with white cement for light colours, and mixed with OPC for darker colours.

- **Rapid hardening cement** This is a finer material which is manufactured at a higher temperature. The setting time is no less, but hardening is faster. It must be used very carefully.

- **Masonry cement** This is OPC plus finely ground materials that improve the workability. It does not need the use of lime or manufactured plasticiser.

Plaster

Plaster is manufactured from raw gypsum (crystalline hydrated calcium sulphate, $CaSO_4$ $2H_2O$). Gypsum is mined, cleaned, crushed and calcined (heated) to drive off three-quarters of the combined water. This process produces a material with a chemical formula of $2CaSO_4$ H_2O. This material in its purest form is plaster of Paris. Under British Standard 1191 it is a Class A plaster. Because of the speed of the set (approximately 15 minutes) a retarder is added for site work, as this allows a longer working time.

Plaster produced in the Midlands area of the UK is pink in colour because the particular minerals present within that area of the country stain the gypsum. Plaster that is produced in the north of the country, in Cumbria, and in areas south of the river Thames, tends to be grey as a result of being stained by clay which is present in those areas of the country.

The different colours of plaster are not significant – it is produced in the same way and each type satisfies the requirements of British Standard 1191. However, a plasterer who is used to pink plaster may not like to use grey plaster and vice versa, because they may feel that the different coloured plaster works differently even though they are the same.

Pure white plaster (plaster of Paris) is found in a small area of the south coast at Hastings.

Setting of plasters

When plaster is mixed with water, this replaces the water that has been taken out during manufacture – the so-called 'water of crystallisation' – and new crystals start to grow. These crystals begin to interlock, forming a solid set material (this process of crystallisation is known as 'hydration'). To slow down the rapid set of plaster, retarders are added during manufacture to give the plasterer time to work with the material. The setting time for both undercoats and finishes is approximately 1½ to 2 hours.

When plasters set, they can get quite warm. This is because of the chemical reaction that takes place during setting, which releases some of the heat used in manufacture. This is referred to as 'heat of hydration'. When the heat has disappeared from the plaster, the plaster has completed its set.

Remember

If you try to stop the set of the plaster by **knocking it back**, you will break off the new crystals and so affect the strength of the set plaster

Definition

Knocking back – the dubious practice of adding extra water to plaster and working it with the trowel so that it can continue to be used even after it has begun to set

Remember

Always use bagged material before its use-by date. All bagged materials such as sand, cement and lime and pre-mixed modern renders should be rotated – this is where older stock is brought to the front to be used before any newly delivered stock

Storage of plaster

If left uncovered, plasters take in water from the air and this causes them to set in the bag (this is known as 'air set'). It can also happen if the plaster is badly stored in the open or in damp conditions. Always store plaster and any bagged material off the floor and away from damp walls. Do not stack any higher than five bags of material. Keep the material covered and rotate it. This means that when a new load of bagged material comes from the builders' merchant, you should put the new material at the bottom of the stacks.

Each bag of plaster has a date of manufacture printed on it so that you know when it has reached its use-by date – also known as its 'shelf life'. If the bags have been stored correctly, a bag of plaster should have a shelf life of three months.

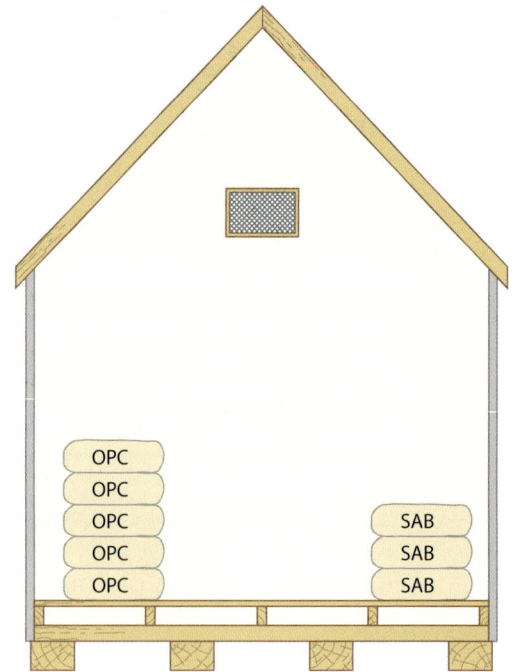

- Dry, ventilated shed

- Stock must be rotated so that old stock is used before new

- Not more than five bags high

- Clear of walls

- Off floor

Figure 7.3 Storage of cement and plaster bags in a shed

Additives

To give the range of plasters which are used on site, additives are used during their manufacture.

Expanded perlite This is used in lightweight aggregate mixes with gypsum plaster and Portland cement. It is a mineral, a glassy volcanic rock that contains a small amount of water.

Vermiculite This is mined as an ore that contains water. It is then heated and the water is driven off and the ore expands (exfoliation). The processed vermiculite contains millions of air layers, which make it a good heat insulator.

Both perlite and vermiculite improve the plaster's heat-insulation and fire-protection properties, and reduce the build-up of condensation because of its warmer surface.

Lightweight cement This is used as a backing coat and contains perlite as a lightweight aggregate. Also, a lightweight cement is produced for use on a damp background or where a chemically injected damp proof course has been installed. The finish for this material is unusual because it comes from Class C of British Standard 1191, but with lime added. This means that, when the plaster has been mixed, it will stiffen up after five minutes and will need **tampering back**, and then it will go creamy. This is a matt finished plaster, and not a lot of water should be applied when finishing as you will return it back to its creamy state.

Fibre-reinforced mortar This mortar comes with glass fibre added, in containers similar to those used for ready-mixed dry sand/lime/cement mortars. It helps to eliminate shrinkage cracks because of the glass fibre. As with ready-mixed sand/lime/cement, it avoids on-site mixing and ensures uniformity of mix.

Coloured pigments These are used in coloured mortars and should not have any lime in the mixes. They do not fade; nor do they weaken the strength of the cement.

Plasticisers These are added to the water to improve the workability of cement-based mortars. They also reduce the amount of water needed and so reduce shrinkage cracking.

Waterproofing This prevents water from penetrating into cement-based mortars and, in cement-based undercoats, also helps to reduce suction.

Definition

Tampering back – adding water to the mixed plaster on the spot board and re-mixing

Universal plasters These are plasters that can be applied by hand or machine (spray plastering) and contain both a backing plaster and a finishing plaster. They will go onto any type of background. The material still needs the skill of straightening and finishing.

When mixing plasters, *do not*:

- mix plasters and cement together

- mix different types of plaster together

- mix plasters with dirty water, because this will affect the speed of the set and the strength of the finished set

- mix plaster with hot or warm water as this will affect the speed of the set

- mix plaster that is still hot in the bag from its manufacture because this will affect the speed of the set.

Proportioning and gauging plastering materials

Definition

Proportioning – dividing into parts

When different plastering materials are to be mixed together, they have to be mixed to a ratio or proportion, usually by volume.

To achieve this, you measure out the materials in parts. This is known as **proportioning** by volume.

To gauge out, you can use a set container such as a bucket, wheelbarrow or gauge box for proportioning the materials.

A gauge box is a four-sided box with no bottom. The materials are put into the box and then levelled off at the top. The box is then lifted up and the process repeated.

Safety tip

Mixing plasters should be done in a well-ventilated area, and a face mask suitable for small dust particles should be worn

Note: if you use bagged materials such as cement and lime, the gauge is best designed to be based on one bag of material.

Different mixes and mix proportions should be used for different cement-based material. The mix proportion for cement:lime:sand most often used by plasterers is 1:1:6 but, because of the fines of the cement now produced, and the weaker backgrounds it has to go on, many plasterers now use a 1:2:9 mix. This is a weaker mix but it has the ability to move a little with the building and so limits cracking.

Mixing

Mixing in a trough

A trough is usually used for mixing lightweight plasters.

1. Pour in the correct amount of clean water (usually 2 to 2½ buckets of water per bag of plaster).

2. Add the plaster.

3. Mix by pushing the plaster and water together with a shovel, or by raking, and turn the plaster over from one end of the trough to the other until well mixed.

Instead of using a shovel, plasterers sometimes use a mixing drill.

Mixing in a trough

Mixing in a bucket or drum

Most finishing plasters or one-coat plasters are mixed up in a drum or bucket.

1. Add clean water to a bucket or drum until it is three-quarters full.

2. Pour in the plaster and allow it to settle.

3. Mix the plaster and water together with a whisk or plunger.

Mixing in a bucket or drum

Always clean out the mixing equipment when you have finished because dirty equipment and dirty water will affect the set of the material, and always follow the manufacturer's instructions. Check the bags for date of manufacture – it is best not to use bagged material if it is older than three months or if it shows any signs of dampness.

Mixing by cement mixer

Always start up the mixer before adding any material as this puts less strain on the mixer.

1. Add clean water to the turning mixer.

2. Add a small amount of sand.

3. Add the binder (cement or cement and lime).

4. Add the rest of the sand.

5. Add more water if necessary to get the right consistency of mix. Plasterers have the mortar according to their likes; the main thing is that it can be spread with some ease.

6. Allow the mix to turn for at least 2 minutes to get air into it for ease of spreading.

Once the mixer has been emptied, put a little water into the drum and let it turn for a while. If you have finished with the mixer, clean it out well by putting water into the drum with a few small bits of old brick. Allow it to turn for a while before turning the drum and letting the water run out into a container.

Mixing by hand

This is best done on a good, firm base such as concrete or a banker board (a large plywood sheet).

1. Turn the dry materials over with a shovel three times to make sure that all the materials are well mixed together.

2. Open up the centre of the heap to form a large ring (a well).

3. Pour in enough water to wet the mix.

4. Turn in the dry material from the edges of the ring. Do not allow the water to escape from the ring as it will take away the cement and lime contained in the mix.

5. Now add more water into a new well to get a suitable consistency.

6. Always turn over the mix three times, away from the centre of the heap, so that the material is well mixed.

7. Once it is finished, make sure that the base is cleaned well, ready for further mixes.

Plaster coats – method of work

Applying a coat of plaster

There are different types and numbers of coats of plaster, and different methods that are used for each coat, but the aim is to obtain good quality flat walls.

A layer of plaster is known as a coat. Internal plastering can be in one, two or three coats.

Plaster coats are generally known as (in order of application):

1. the render, pricking up or scratch coat

2. the floating or straightening coat (this is used to provide a true, even surface for the setting coat)

3. the setting or finishing coat, also known as a skimming coat (the setting coat, used internally, is the last to be applied and is brought to a smooth finish).

The number of coats that you apply will depend on the type of background you are to work on and the information from the specification. Opposite are the general rules used for the number of coats.

One-coat work

This is mostly in the form of a finish coat applied to a maximum of 5 mm, although one-coat plasters are available that are applied at approximately 13 mm thickness by hand. One-coat is applied as a setting coat only to sheet materials such as plasterboard.

Special one-coat plasters are now used to replace two-coat work and are applied to the same thicknesses as two-coat work. These are not setting coats.

Two-coat work

This is the most common form of wet solid internal plastering and is made up of an undercoat or floating coat and a finish coat (this is known as float and set). This is used on most solid backgrounds such as brickwork and blockwork.

Three-coat work

This is made up of two undercoats and a finishing coat.

The first undercoat is known as a render coat or scratch coat. The second undercoat is called a floating coat. The finishing coat can be called by any of three names: finishing coat, setting coat or skimming coat. This process of three-coat work is known as render, float and set. It is used on hollow or perforated surfaces such as expanded metal lathing; a render coat is applied to provide suction and to stiffen up the background.

Dubbing-out coat

If the background you are plastering on is in very poor shape (especially on refurbishment work), an extra coat of plaster will need to be applied. This layer is known as 'dubbing out', and is a coat of material used to fill in hollows to bring them into line with the rest of the background. The thickness should not be more than 10 mm.

Remember

The dubbing-out coat is not treated as part of the rendering coat or floating coat when pricing up the job

This is then keyed with a comb scratcher in horizontal lines. This is then left to harden up ready for a render coat on hollow backgrounds such as EML, or a floating coat on solid backgrounds.

Render coat

This is the first application of three-coat work. It is applied to the surface and ruled out to a basic shape, filling in any hollows and removing any bumps. The render coat brings out the background to a fair line and controls unequal suction.

Application

1. Lay on materials with a laying-on trowel.

2. Rule out to a fair line, filling in any hollows and removing bumps, to a thickness of 6–10 mm.

3. Key the surface with a comb scratcher in readiness for the floating coat.

Keying by the use of a comb scratcher should always be horizontal, never vertical, because, with vertical keying, the next coat will slide down the wall. Some plasterers key with a wavy line.

Broad screed systems

This is a method of applying a floating coat to a wall.

Walls should be floated using one of the two following systems.

Broad or box screed system

Using this system, which is normally used on smaller areas, does not give the highest standard of work, although it gives a far better quality than working freehand.

In Figure 7.4, the broad screed has been plastered into the corner of a wall using a floating rule. You can also see the up-and-down movement of the rule from top to bottom of the wall.

1. Apply the material to the surface.

2. The floating rule is passed across the material until it is at a thickness of approximately 11 mm.

3. The rule is passed over the material in an up-and-down movement.

4. Areas that have been missed are filled in and re-ruled.

5. Waste material is now removed from the angles, ceiling and wall lines, which are then cleaned with a wet brush.

6. Another vertical screed is then placed in the opposite corner and ruled in.

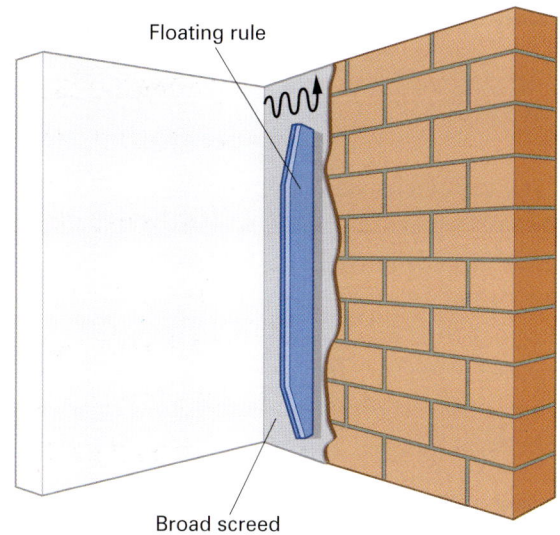

Figure 7.4 Broad screed system

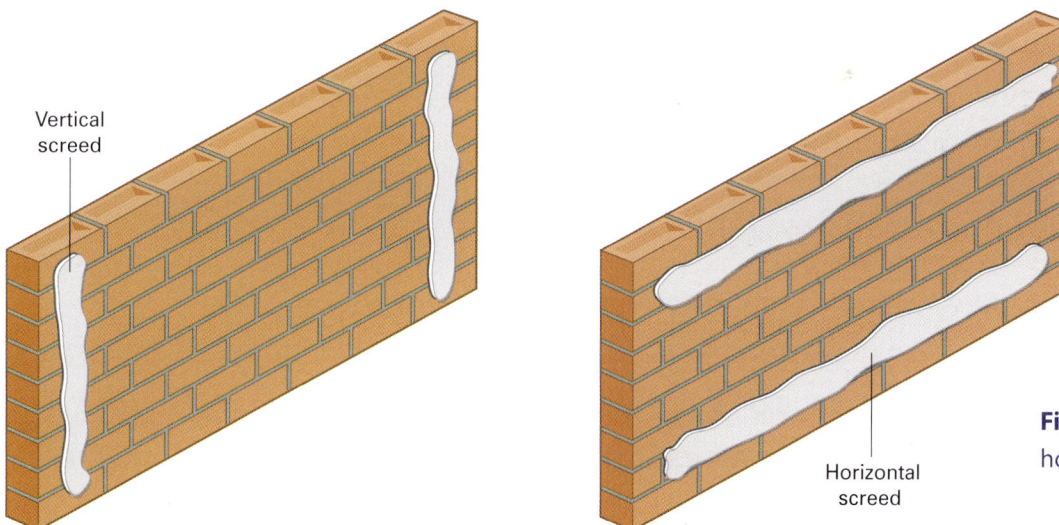

Figure 7.5 Vertical and horizontal screeds

Do not put any screeds in between the end screeds (screeds against internal wall angles) as this will give a bump on the wall where the screeds are.

7. Place a horizontal screed at the skirting line at the bottom of the wall about 25 mm off the floor, and another one the length of the rule further up.

8. Rule in the horizontal screeds off the vertical screeds.

9. Lay the rule flat onto the vertical screed and, without digging in, rule off carefully. Now go down to the other vertical screed and do the same. Then move to the middle of the screed and, watching both ends of the rule, rule off the material until the rule lies flat on the finished horizontal screed. It may be necessary to place another horizontal screed if the wall is high.

10. Fill in any hollows and re-rule in.

11. Starting at the top of the wall, fill in between the screeds then rule off. You can rule off the vertical screeds if it is a small rule, or off the horizontal ones. If you rule off the horizontal screeds, the material not needed will fall from the rule onto the floor or drop boards.

A simple method that can be used after you have achieved some experience is to use just horizontal screeds to rule off.

Dot and screed system

The dot and screed system is sometimes called plumb and dot (or the 'Rolls Royce' system of plastering a wall) and is rarely used for normal work. It can be used to advantage on long or high walls, or when the work has to be absolutely plumb (for example, when a staircase well is plastered and the staircase is to be added afterwards).

This system is not recommended for work below 19 mm in thickness, and is used in two- or three-coat work.

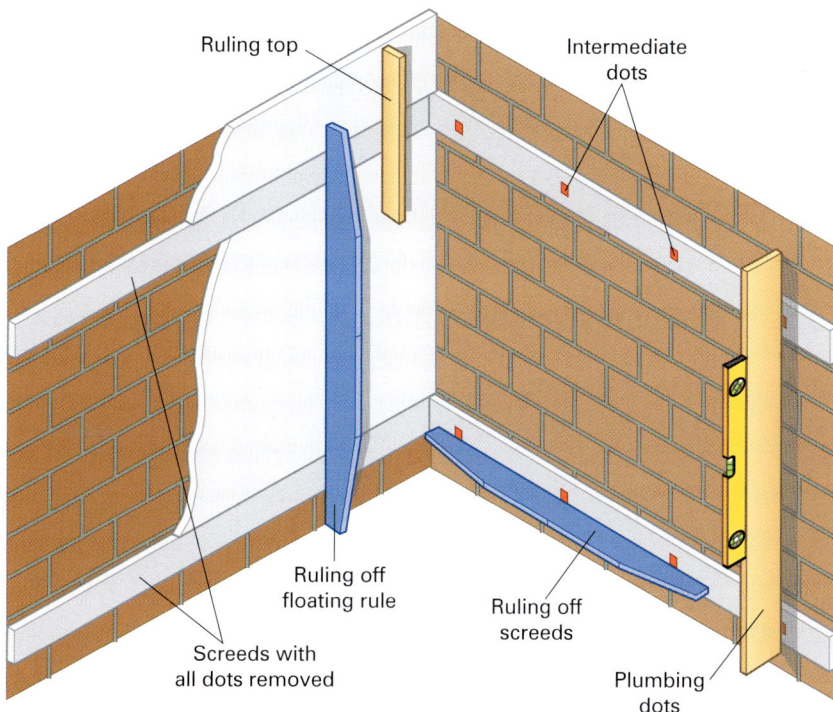

Figure 7.6 Plumbing, dotting, screeding and ruling

Figure 7.6 shows a way of plumbing in a wall of average height.

1. Start by placing a dot of mortar (Figure 7.7) onto the wall near to the internal angle at the height of the floating rule.

2. Place a second dot at the bottom of the wall.

3. Plumb in the two dots with the floating rule. Either tap in the wood or bring the wood out until the two dots are in line.

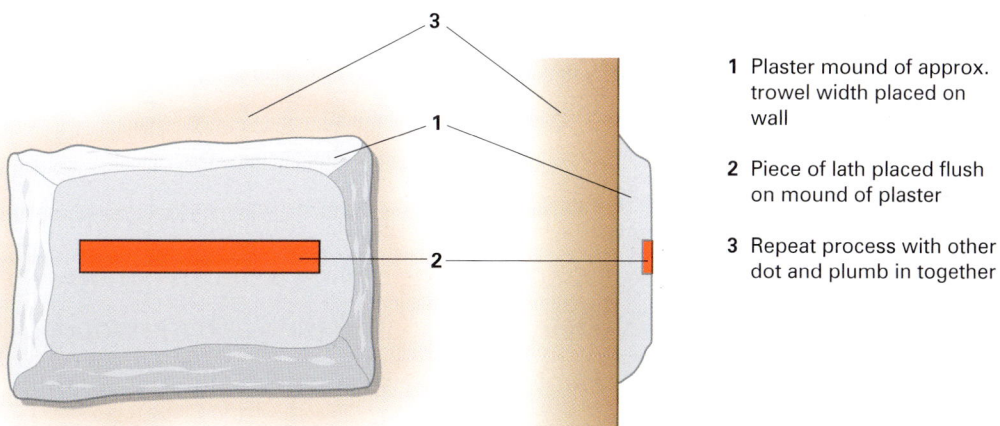

1 Plaster mound of approx. trowel width placed on wall

2 Piece of lath placed flush on mound of plaster

3 Repeat process with other dot and plumb in together

Figure 7.7 Structure of a dot

4. Repeat steps 1 to 3 at the other end of the wall.

5. Place intermediate dots between the two main ones, directly above each other.

6. Line through the intermediate dots off the four main dots horizontally by the use of the rule, and check them for plumb with their partners below. The wall should be now plumb to within 3 mm.

7. Join the dots together as per the broad screed system.

8. Once the screeds are completed, remove the timber from the dots and fill in.

9. Fill in between screeds and rule off.

For higher walls, a plumb bob is needed. This can be bought from a shop and is a weight on the end of a piece of string. (You can make your own by using a screwdriver or similar tied to a piece of string.) With the plumb bob, you will need two wooden gauges made by yourself. These gauges must be cut at the same time to make them accurate.

A dot is placed at the top of the wall and then directly below the dot another dot is placed – and it does not matter how high the wall is. It can be that one person is at the top of the scaffold and other plasterers are on each of the other scaffold lifts. The plasterer at the top wraps the string around the gauge so that it passes through the 'L' of the gauge, and drops the bob down to the plasterer at the bottom. This plasterer then moves the wooden dot in or out until the string passes through the 'L' of his or her gauge. The wall is now plumb. The plasterers on each lift now do the same to their dots using their own gauges. This is repeated at the other internal angle.

Dots are then placed horizontally between the dots already in position. A nail is then fixed to the background and a string line is drawn tightly over the top of the dots. A nail is then slid in between the string and the wooden dot at the ends, and left there. A nail of the same size is then slid in between the line and the intermediate dots.

Remember

For lightweight plasters you only need to cut back a small amount from the angle – about 2 mm – but for cement-based mortars you will need to cut back more – perhaps 3–4 mm. This stops the finishing coat from ending up in front of the angle

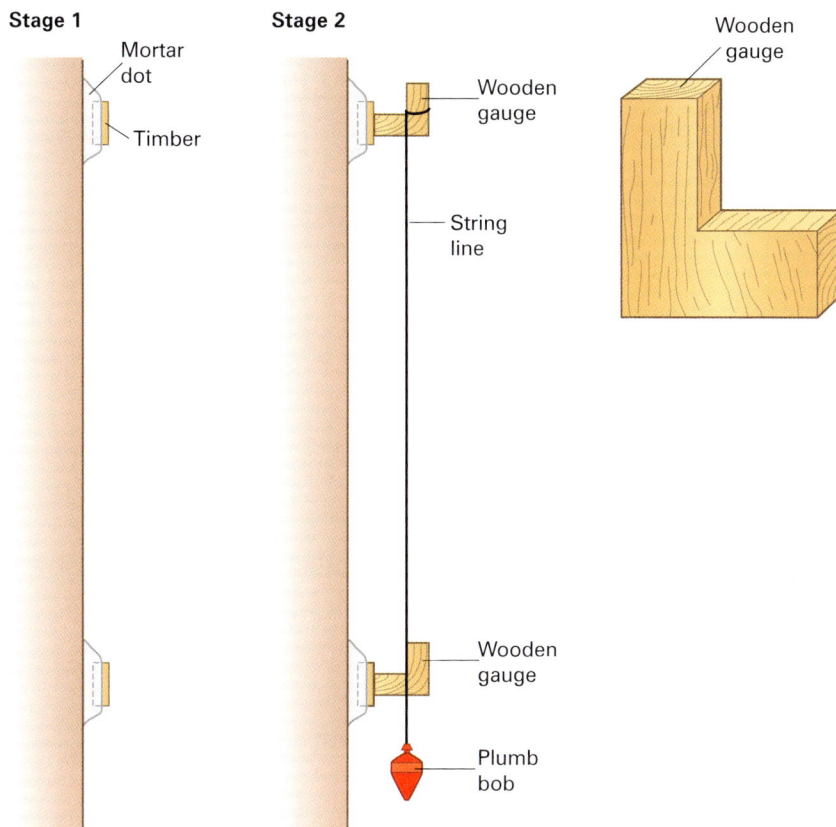

Figure 7.8 Using a plumb bob to line up dots on high walls

Note: the string must not move when the nail is passed between the string and the wood inside the dot.

The wood inside the intermediate dots may need to be pulled out or pushed back until the string is clear. Now follow stages 6 to 9 above.

Once the mortar on a floating coat has started to **pick up**, the screeds will need to be keyed. This is done by the use of a devil float. As you key the background, you should also, at the same time, fill in any hollows left from the ruling in. Keying can be done using figure-of-eight movements or a circular movement, but whichever you use, the background must be well keyed.

A floating coat or render coat that is not well keyed will allow the next coat applied to fall off, or become hollow. The use of the devil float will help to consolidate the background – to close in or tighten up the face by removing large hollows and misses.

Definition

Pick up – another term used to describe the process of a material setting or 'going off'

Remember

Before finishing your work for the day, always check the standards of your workmanship by running a rule around the walls, checking that there are no hollows or bumps. It is easier to improve the job while it is still soft than the next day, when it is hard

Once you have completed the process of keying, clean out all internal and external angles by using the back edge of the trowel, running it flat down the floating coat into the angle on both sides. For external angles, cut back from the angle with the edge of the trowel.

Always clean down the ceiling line with a wet brush and, when using lightweight plasters, keep the tools clean at all times by washing them in a bucket kept under the spot board stand.

Setting coats

The setting coat or finishing coat is also know as the skimming coat, and the method of applying the finish will depend on the type of floating coat that has been applied and the strength of the background.

Generally, the finishing coat should not be stronger than the floating coat, or there will be a danger of the setting coat shelling off from the face of the floating.

A setting coat is applied in order to provide a flat, smooth surface for decoration, and is applied directly to plasterboard in a one-coat system or as a finishing coat to a floated background.

Finishing coat to a floated background

Before starting the finishing coat, the floating coat should be checked for flatness. Any snots are removed by passing the trowel over the surface. All floated internal angles are cut out and cut back from angles.

All equipment must be clean, and good quality, clean drinking water should be used for mixing.

Clean water is poured into a clean bucket, then the finishing plaster is sprinkled into the water until all of the water has been soaked up. The plaster is then mixed by hand or drill. Plasterers will have their own preference as to the thickness of the finishing material.

The skimming mix is applied in an even coat with a finishing trowel starting from the left-hand side (if you are right handed).

Remember

If using a drill, do not over-mix the plaster as you will affect the setting time. Also, never re-temper the finishing plaster if it is stiffening up or setting – this will affect its strength

The mixed finishing plaster

Always start from the top left-hand side of the wall and from a hop-up if necessary.

Starting from the top helps you: you only have to do a small amount of work from the hop-up because the biggest part of the wall can be done from the floor. It will save you energy because you are not up and down the hop-up and you will not drop any plaster down a finished surface.

Applying a finishing coat

The setting system

Trowel, trowel

This is two applications, not two coats.

Each trowelful should overlap the previous one, with the toe of the trowel tight to avoid gathering on a double thickness at the overlap. Once this coat is completed and picked up (this is almost always immediately), a second coat is applied with a tight coat of the same material approximately 1 mm in thickness. If working from a hop-up for the top of the wall, when you work from the floor you should first run the trowel at the bottom of the finishing material to remove the excess material and flatten it in.

You may need to make a second mix; if so, keep the two mixes apart on the spot board. You can still use the rest of the first mix but, if they are mixed together, the first mix will send off the second far quicker.

When the setting material has picked up enough, it is ready for the trowelling up process. This involves going over each part of the wall methodically at least twice with a clean trowel lubricated with water. The trowel is held at an angle of about 45° or greater to the wall surface, with a fair amount of pressure. On the final trowelling, clean water is splashed onto the wall surface, with the water brush about 150 mm in front of each trowel stroke, until a matt finish is obtained.

- It sometimes pays to run a dry trowel over the wall surface at the end to remove any watermarks and fat marks. Also, if you are setting a wall with natural light shining down on it from a window, a series of last trowel runs horizontally approximately between the height of your knees and your shoulders will improve the appearance of the wall.

- When the wall is complete, the ceiling line should be cleaned, the power boxes cleaned out, and all excess material cleaned at the skirting lines. One way of doing this is to hold your floating rule on the setting, approximately 25 mm from the floor, and draw your trowel along it. Then remove all finishing plaster below this line.

Remember

Do not over-trowel the finish to produce a polished surface, because this stops the paint from sticking to the plastered surface. The following painter may charge you for rubbing down the plasterwork to form a key for the paint

Note: this system can be used for setting to lightweight floated surfaces; it may also be used on plasterboard. The finished thickness should be no less than 2 mm and no more than 5 mm.

If you do not hold the trowel firmly or the trowel does not pass smoothly over the plastered surface, it will leave what plasterers call 'fish scales'. These are lots of lines that are close together and form ridges in the plaster. They must be removed by hard trowelling or back trowelling (holding the fingers on the back of the trowel and scraping back over the fish scales).

A further problem that can occur is blisters. This usually occurs when the face of the floating coat has not been closed in enough during floating. Air gets trapped in the hollow and forms a blister on the finished surface. To remove this, do the same as for fish scales.

Trowel, float, trowel

Three applications of material.

On sand-and-cement-based backgrounds, you should complete the finishing coat in three applications. This is because you need to put on a thicker coat of material to cover the grains of sand. It also means that you have a better quality of finish than two-coat work.

The use of the float will also straighten out any irregularities there may be in the floating coat. The float is a good tool for this purpose because it is rigid and not flexible. This allows small amounts of material to be worked into any hollows.

Three applications may also be required on plasterboard. This will increase the thickness of material on the boards, cover the reinforcement and slightly straighten out any boarding which is not flat.

If a client needs a true flat surface to plasterboarded surfaces, you will need to complete the job in two-coat work (float and set).

If the floating is of a poor quality and the internal angles and skirting line are not straight, this can be improved by applying a thicker amount of finish

Remember

When you are trowelling off, a very light pinkish material will be found on the trowel. This is called fat and should never be reused to fill in any misses or hollows because fat has no strength in it and will shrink back from the finished face and still leave a hollow and misses on the face

with the first coat, and ruling out with a feather edge rule. This coat is then allowed to stiffen before continuing in the normal manner. This system will only take out hollows of about 5 mm.

The best time to put on a finishing coat is while the background is still green. This is while the floating still contains 'free' water: in other words, it comes down to how well you organise your work. The simple rule is: float in the morning up to dinnertime; clean up, cut back and set in the afternoon. The exception to this rule is cement-based materials, which should be left for 4–7 days for complete hardening and shrinkage to take place before setting.

Floating coats that have been allowed to become dry lead to difficulties such as loss of workability, peeling and blistering. As the plaster is applied to the surface, the background will suck the water out. This will lead to the next trowelstroke developing a double thickness at the joint unless extra pressure is applied. In the trowelling off process, the surface sometimes peels away in tiny flakes when the trowel is edged. This is because the plaster has dried before setting has taken place.

PVA can be used as a solution to high suction problems

Overcoming this problem

One way of controlling high suction of floating coats is to reduce the suction. (You always need a little suction to help with the setting of the material.) Soaking the background with water can do this. This can cause a problem if a wooden floor is in place, so a high-powered water spray can be used, which will soak a wall without mess.

A PVA glue watered down five parts water to one part glue is often used as a solution to suction problems. You should always wet the background so that the watered-down glue does not get completely sucked into the background, leaving a plastic film on the surface that can be easily peeled off. For best results, apply two coats and, when the second is tacky, plaster.

Setting coat to a plasterboard ceiling

A plaster recommended by the manufacturer should be used for the setting coat. You will also need a scrim (jute), usually 75 or 90 mm wide and sold in 100 m rolls, for reinforcing the joints between the boards.

Also, cotton or bandage scrim (53 mm wide) can be used, although this is a more traditional method. Increasingly over the last ten years, self-adhesive glass fibre mesh tape (50 mm wide) and dry lining paper tape (53 mm wide) have been used to reinforce the joints between boards.

For the setting coat to the board, use a low-level scaffold or use stilts.

The joints of the board and the angle between ceiling and walls are reinforced with the scrim or tape, etc. to reinforce them and help to eliminate some of the possible cracking at the joints.

Application of jute, cotton and tape

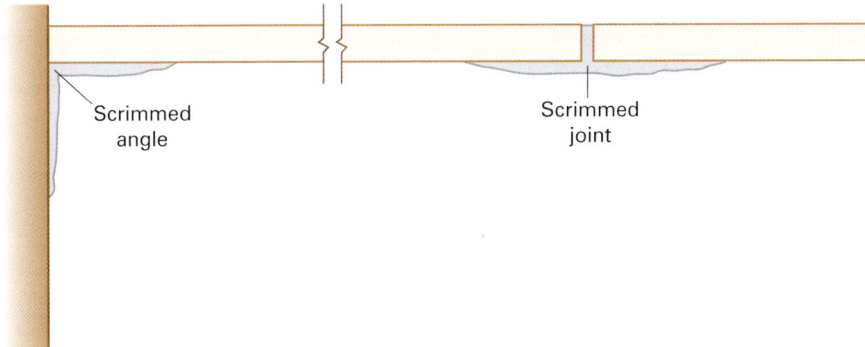

Scrimmed angle

Scrimmed joint

Figure 7.9 Scrimmed joints and angles

Did you know?

If plasterboard coving is to be fixed around the room, you do not need to reinforce the wall/ceiling angle

1. Cut scrims to length, making sure that they do not overlap and are not less than 25 mm apart.

2. Apply a strip of board finish over each joint, one joint at a time.

3. Lay the scrim over the trowel and, walking backwards, squeeze the jute into the plaster tight to the background.

4. Trowel back over the scrim with a little bit of plaster to make sure that the jute is all covered.

5. When applying scrim to angles, the same system is used but the scrim is pasted onto the wall and the board.

Self-adhesive tape

Make sure that the plasterboard is clean and free from dust, otherwise the self-adhesive tape will not stick.

1. Cut tape to length as for 1 above.

2. Stick the tape to the plasterboard joints as above.

3. Cover the tape by squeezing plaster over the surface.

Plastering a ceiling or wall on plasterboard one coat 3–4 mm thick

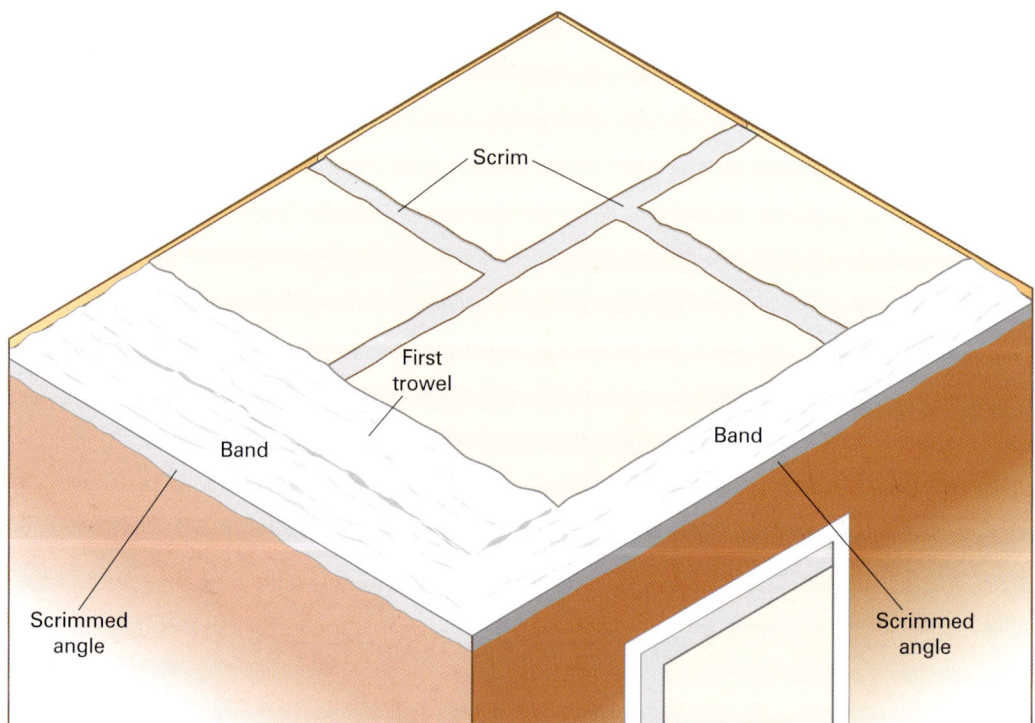

Figure 7.10 Applying a setting coat to a plasterboard ceiling: first coat with the trowel

Remember

The system shown is for applying a 3–4 mm coat to cover the jute scrim. For self-adhesive tape, paper tape or cotton, you do not need such a thick coat, so the floating application can be ignored. This is known as 'trowel, trowel'

Ceiling

1. The scrims having been cut and applied, spread a band the length of the trowel up to the ceiling/wall line in the left-hand corner (for right-handed plasterers) up against the scrim.

2. Spread the first application in between the scrims, starting from the left-hand side, covering the whole ceiling.

3. Straightaway, apply another application of plaster using the float over the whole of the ceiling, including the scrims. This application is used to straighten out the ceiling.

4. When this application has picked up, apply a final laying down coat. This should be left free from lines, gauls and marks.

5. Trowel up the final coat as for finishing to walls.

Walls

The same system is used as for the ceiling. The wall should be started at the top left-hand corner for right-handed plasterers.

Remember

Moisture-resistant plasterboard (as used in shower areas) must receive a PVA or similar preparation before applying a setting coat

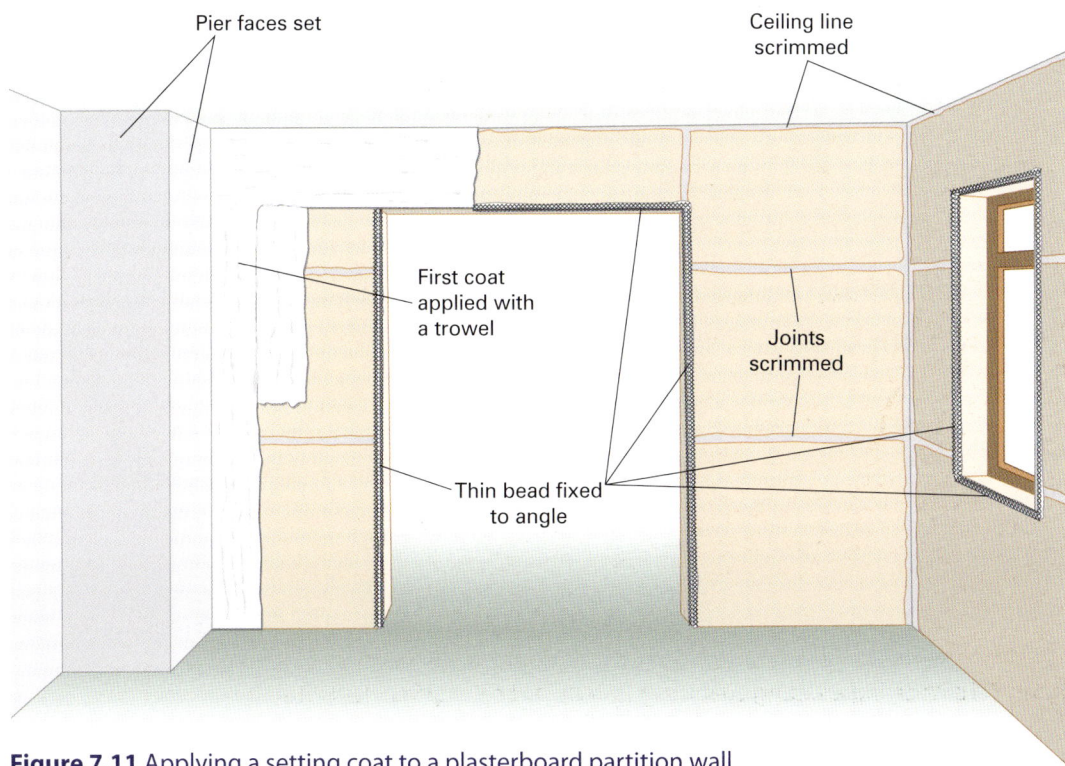

Pier faces set

Ceiling line scrimmed

First coat applied with a trowel

Joints scrimmed

Thin bead fixed to angle

Figure 7.11 Applying a setting coat to a plasterboard partition wall

Bead (metal and plastic trim)

A bead is an edging, manufactured from galvanised metal, stainless steel or plastic. Beads are also known as trims.

Beads help to save time for the plasterer in forming arrises (external angles), stops (a break between one material and another) and movement joints, plus other decorative features. The use of these beads helps to strengthen the edges where they are being used.

The nose of the angle bead is not sharp but a pencil round: a sharp angle is more liable to be damaged than a slightly round one. If beads are not available, the angles, edges and features must be formed by hand.

Types of bead

- **Angle bead** This is used for forming external angles.

- **Stop bead** This reinforces edges of plaster when no other material meets the plaster. It is also used when butting up to another material when no cover such as an architrave is being used.

- **Architrave and feature beads** These are special beads used against frames to form shadow lines.

- **Movement bead** This is fixed over building movement joints or where building movement is expected.

- **Thin coat bead** These beads are designed to be used with thinner plaster coats – both angle and stop beads are produced.

Remember

A movement joint in a building allows the building to move naturally. This means that any material over the joint will have a tendency to crack. To prevent this, the movement joint must continue through any plastering or tiling put onto that background

Fixing of angle bead

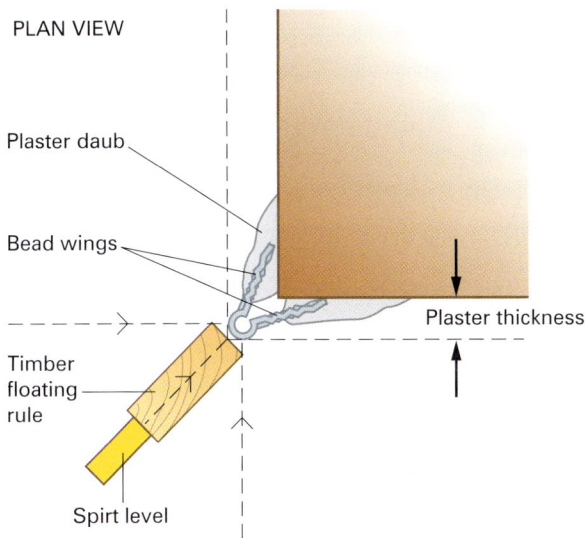

PLAN VIEW

Plaster daub

Bead wings

Plaster thickness

Timber floating rule

Spirt level

Figure 7.12 Checking an angle bead

1. Measure the length of the bead required.

2. Cut the bead to length using tin snips or a hacksaw.

3. Trim back the bead wings (the mesh part of the bead) from the top and bottom of the bead from the **nosing** of the angle bead.

4. With the trowel, and using stiffened finishing plaster or a bonding type plaster, place daubs of plaster at 600 mm intervals (four dabs per standard angle height) on both sides of the angle, and bed the bead (as shown in Figure 7.12) or fix with galvanised nails into soft blocks or hardened nails into bricks.

5. Using a floating rule and spirit level held in one hand, with the floating rule resting on your foot, move the bead in or out until it is plumb against the rule and the level. There should be no daylight between the rule and the bead. Plumb in the angle bead, checking on both sides of the bead and the nosing of the bead. The wings of the bead should be below the surface of the plaster when finished.

> **Definition**
>
> **Nosing** – the curved central strip of the bead to which the wings are attached

6. When the bead is in position, extra plaster may need to be spread over the daubs to make sure the bead is well secured. Sometimes it may be necessary to key the daubs of plaster.

Beads are supplied in various lengths (check manufacturers' catalogues for information). If necessary, lengths can be joined together by inserting a nail in the back of the nosing and squeezing the nosing slightly together to hold the nail in position. This will ensure true alignment and continuation of the nosing.

The standard of fixing of the bead will affect the quality of the finished wall surface. This is because you will be ruling off the beads when applying a floating coat. If the bead has a hollow, so will your wall, and so on.

When the floating has been completed, the bead should be cleaned down and cut back.

Beads for plasterboards

Perforated thin coat beads

Perforated thin coat beads are used for plasterboard external angles that need a finishing coat of no more than 3–6 mm. With this type of bead, the background will govern you; you cannot plumb or level these beads. The beads are nailed with rust-proof nails or screwed up.

For backgrounds that are in poor shape and need straightening out, this should be done in two-coat work and a standard angle bead used. Although the beads cannot be plumb, they can be straight within themselves.

Plasterboard stop beads

These are used to produce strong, neat finishes to openings and abutments.

Did you know?

Daubs are used rather than spreading plaster the full length of the bead so that the floating coat can have the mesh wings to key onto. Otherwise it would be liable to shell off the plaster that holds the bead

Thin coat stop beads

These are available in thicknesses of 3–6 mm. They are made up of two back-to-back stop beads with building paper placed underneath. This prevents plaster material from crossing the expansion joint and preventing the natural movement of the building. Jointing mastic can then be squeezed between the beads. This is a cheaper method of producing a movement bead.

Movement bead

This is specially manufactured for movement joints and is limited to about 10 mm maximum movement. This has a plastic strip over the bead so that, when the plastering is completed, the plastic should be visible and cover the joint.

Plasterboard edging bead

This bead provides protection for the edge of plasterboards. The edging beads are made in lengths of 35 mm, for use with 9.5 mm or 12.5 mm thick plasterboards.

Forming window openings, reveals and piers

The formation of window openings, reveals and attached and independent piers involves plastering to angles. Plastering to angles can be done in two ways:

- by the use of metal trims
- by the use of wooden rules.

The method of fixing beads is the same as for external angles.

Beading up around windows

When fixing beads to a window, the first point you need to know is the depth of the floating coat so that the beads are positioned at the right depth.

This is the sequence for fixing beads and rules.

1. Cut all beads, both uprights and for the head (top) of the window. It may not be necessary to use a bead on the sill because a window board will be fixed there.

2. Fix the head bead in position, checking for level. Hold a square up against the top of the window frame, and hold the bead at both ends and in the middle, to check that the coverage of plaster will just clip the window frame.

3. Lay a floating rule along the front face of the bead to check that 11–12 mm of floating can be put on the wall. Also check that the bead is running parallel to the face of the wall.

4. Fix the two uprights so that the nose of the beads line up with the head bead.

5. Check for plumb on the face and inside edge of the window reveal (the return back to the window). Also check that the bead is straight, with no gaps to the floating rule, and that there is enough thickness of floating above and below the window.

6. Again, check for how square the reveal is by holding the square onto the window and the bead; again, it should be approximately 11–12 mm. You can also hold a square in the corner between the head bead and the upright beads.

7. For the window sill, a piece of wood or plasterboard can be placed on the sill, lined up with the upright beads, and weighed down with bricks.

You can use a tape measure to check the reveal and soffit (head of the window) for equal measurement at top, middle and bottom of the reveal, and at each side and the middle of the head. The problem with this is that it depends on the window frame being put in plumb; if it is not, your window wall will be out of plumb itself. This can cause a problem if the window is plumbed in at a later date.

Use of rules to form window openings

Sometimes it may be necessary to use wooden rules instead of beads. For the use of rules, this is the system:

1. Cut the rules for the inside of the window opening. Cut the head of the window first, then the uprights and lastly the window sill (to sit in between the uprights).

2. The rules are best wedged into place rather than nailed: this allows for easy removal at the end of working.

3. The rules should be checked for plumb and straightness, and check that you have an average coverage of plaster over the whole of the wall.

4. When the wall has been floated, remove the rules gently by sliding them away from the angles so that you do not damage them.

5. Holding the rule taken off plumb from the reveal angle, form the reveal. (For this you will need an extra pair of hands.) Alternatively, you can nail the rules up into position on the face of the wall. The rules should be squared into the window frame as in step 6 on page 212.

> **Did you know?**
>
> If you gently tap the rules before removing them, it will loosen the material from the wood

Forming reveals

When forming reveals, the reveals are ruled in by the use of a reveal gauge (Figure 7.13).

A reveal gauge can be made from a piece of wood (there used to be purpose-made plastic reveal gauges – they may still be available). To make a gauge, first lay a piece of wood with a square edge against the rule or bead and the window frame. Then lay a square on top of the wood and against the bead/rule and window frame. Square up the wood and then, with a pencil, mark the edge of the window frame onto the piece of wood. Drive a headless nail into the end of the piece of wood so that part of the nail is showing. The wood can now run up and down the window frame and the bead/rule, forming the reveal square.

The problem with this system is that you may need to move the nail for the other side of the window and the head.

Another system is to do the same as above but, instead of using the nail, cut a square notch out of the wood so that it can run up and down the frame.

Some plasterers use the trowel to form the reveal. This system can lead to wavy reveals that are also out of square, and need a float and a good eye for straightness to straighten them out.

Remember

Whatever system you use, be careful of plastic window frames as they can easily be scratched and marked. Protect them by keeping the plastic protection strip on the framing

Figure 7.13 Reveal gauge

Returns and corners to attached piers

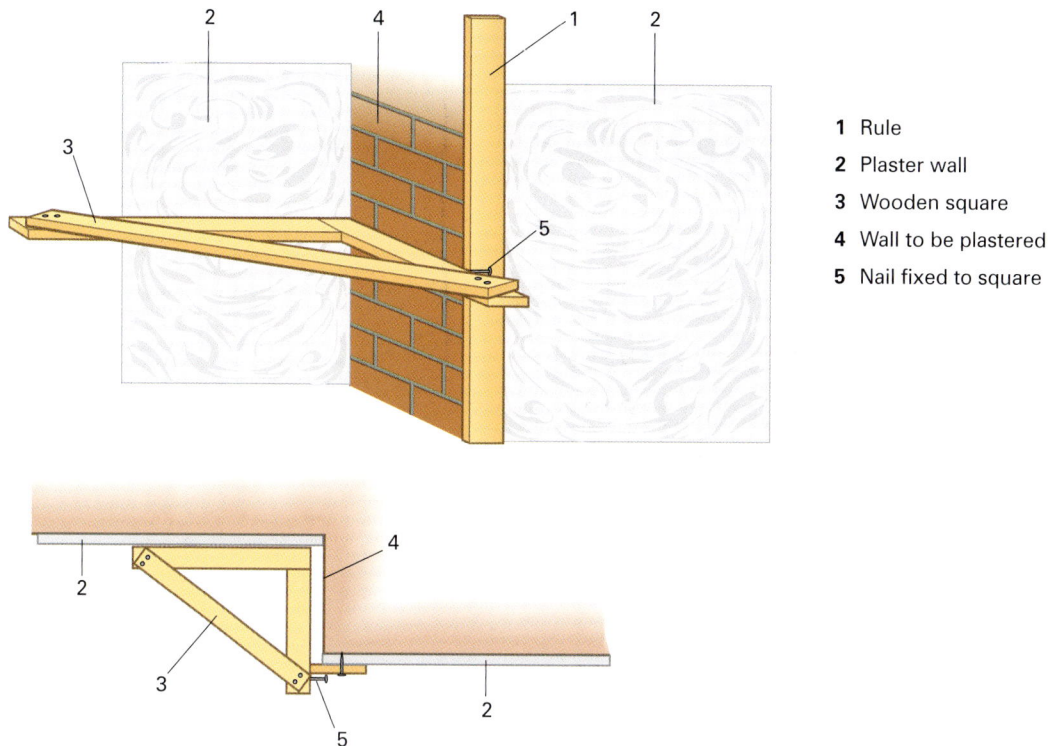

1 Rule
2 Plaster wall
3 Wooden square
4 Wall to be plastered
5 Nail fixed to square

Figure 7.14 Use of a builder's square

Use of wooden rules and beads is as follows (see Figure 7.14).

1. Make sure that a builder's square is held flat to the background and flush with the bead/rule.

2. Fix the bead/rule, as described in step 5 on page 213.

3. Float the wall.

4. Hold the square on the floated wall and insert a headless nail into the timber rule so that it slides up the bead/rule, so that the square remains in the same position.

An alternative method is to form a small screed at the bottom and top of the wall by the use of the timber square, and then rule in the return vertically off the screeds. This is easier than handling an awkward square for ruling in.

Remember

Always finish off any working to reveals and returns using the same method as for any form of internal floating

Attached and independent piers

When working to attached and independent piers, the beads/rules must be fixed accurately. If the beads/rules are not fixed accurately, this will make the rest of the returns and walls inaccurate.

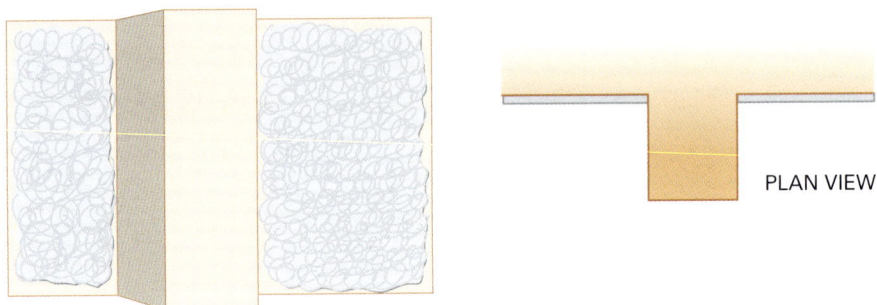

PLAN VIEW

Figure 7.15 The wall with the attached pier ready to start.

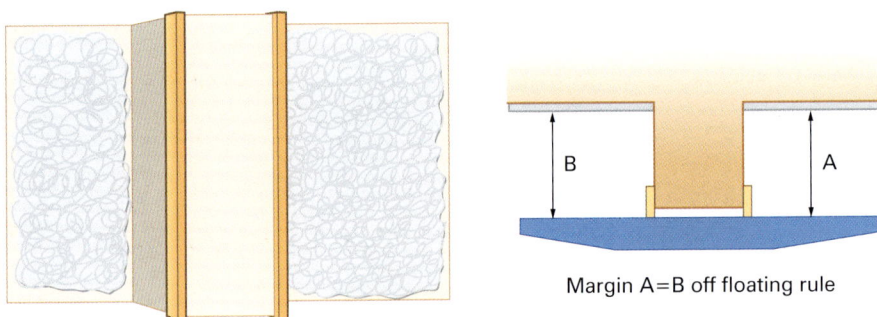

B   A

Margin A=B off floating rule

Figure 7.16 The beads/rules are fixed plumb and parallel to the back wall.

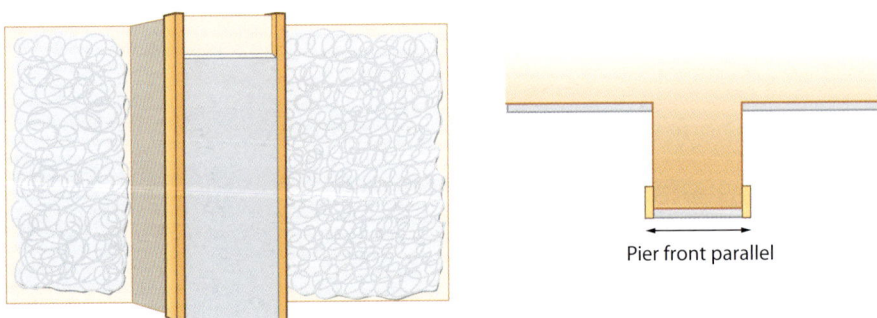

Pier front parallel

Figure 7.17 The face of the pier is ruled off first. This must be flat, true and plumb. Remove rules if used.

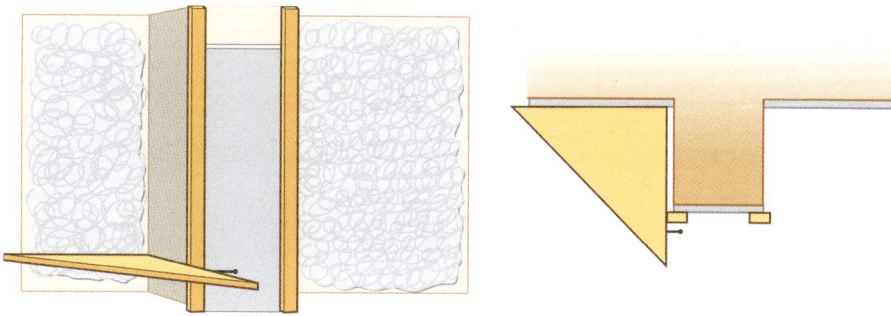

Figure 7.18 If the returns are 110 mm or less, they can be floated and ruled off the marked wall and the beads/rules with a square. If the returns are too wide for this method, then screeds are used.

Attached piers

Lining in attached piers and lining in independent piers are very similar. There are a few points, however, that need to be noted.

A string line is attached to the piers. This lines in the first two beads with the newly fixed beads. It is important to remember that at no point should the string line touch the beads, but there should be a piece of wood inserted between the string and the beads. When the new beads are fixed, you can easily check whether they are in line, rather than having the string line pushed out of place by the beads.

Figure 7.19 String line attached to the piers

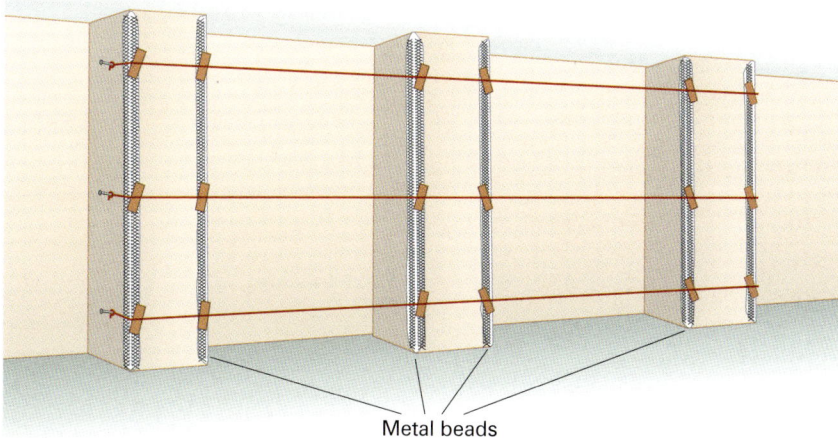

Metal beads

Independent piers

Plastering of a single or a series of independent piers is not very different from plastering a single or series of attached piers. When plastering to a single independent pier, the following points should be followed.

1. Check the pier for suction.

2. Check the pier for plumb.

3. Choose appropriate plaster.

4. Prepare the background.

5. Mark out, on the floor around the pier, the line of the finished work using a floating rule and a square (Figure 7.20).

6. Fix beads/rules to the marks on the floor (Figure 7.21).

7. Plaster to beads/rules as usual.

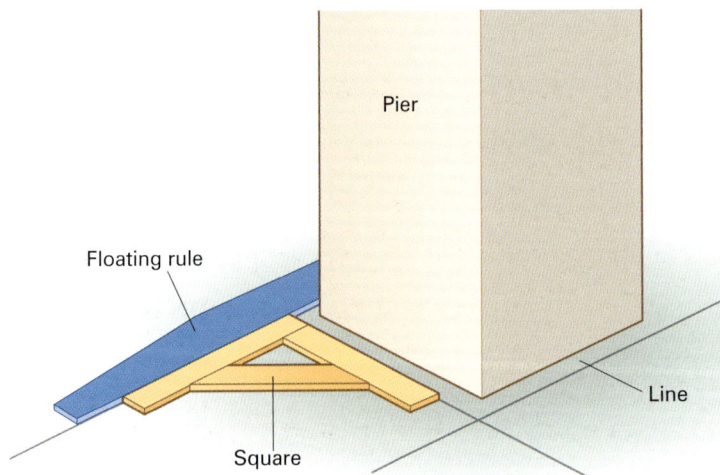

Figure 7.20 Setting out an independent pier

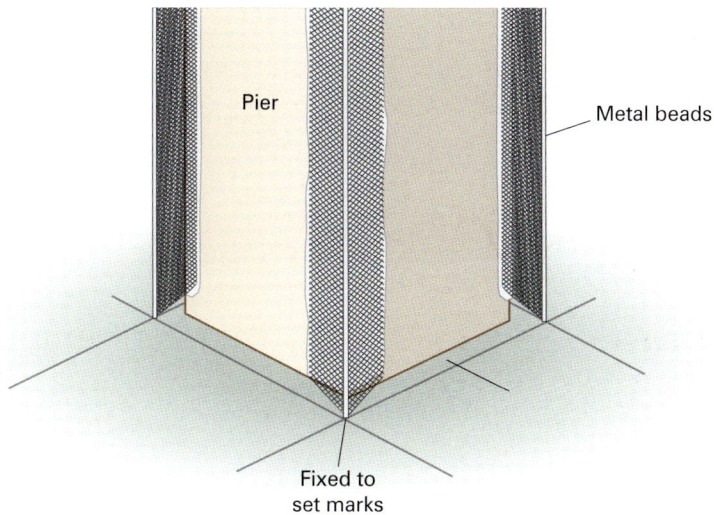

Figure 7.21 Metal beads fixed in position

Floating and setting coat to a ceiling

For this task, the assumption is that the walls have been previously floated plumb.

The reason for floating a ceiling is to provide a true, flat surface and to increase fire protection. Its use will mainly be on concrete ceilings or in a prestigious development that requires a high standard of workmanship. The thickness of floating material will depend on the type of material being used and the manufacturer's information. However, one rule of thumb is to keep the floating as tight as possible.

The floating of a ceiling is a difficult task and should not be tried until a degree of tool skills has been developed.

It is important that a good, stable low-level scaffold is set up, to allow the plasterer to move around with ease, because the plasterer will not be able to watch where they place their feet.

Remember

This task can be a very messy one because you are working above your head and ruling in the floating material. Safety goggles and overalls will be of great use during this task

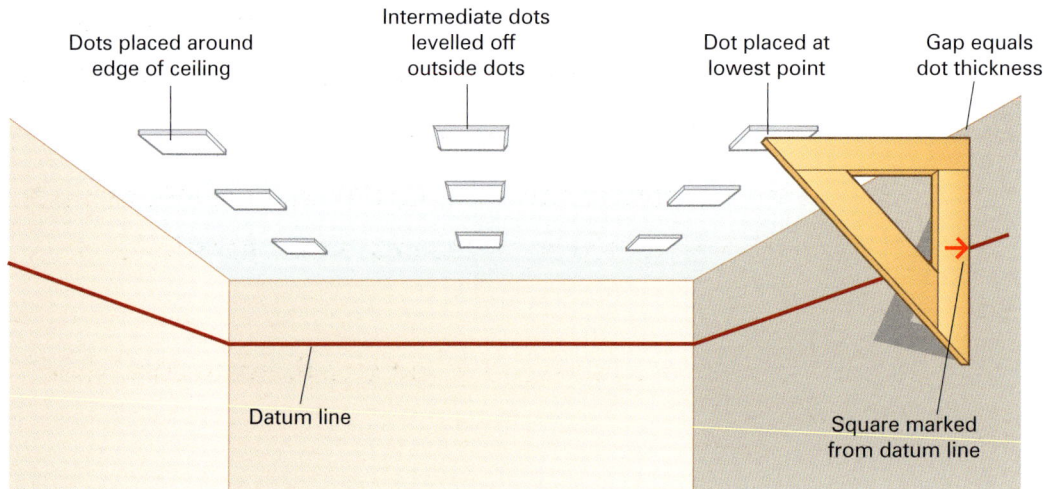

Figure 7.22 Setting out the dots on the ceiling

Snap a level datum line around the room about 225 mm from the ceiling. If the room contains a beam, snap the line below the soffit of the beam.

Select a point on the ceiling about 150 mm in from the wall that looks as if it is the lowest point of the ceiling. At this point, place a dot with a lath or piece of plasterboard bedded into it. Hold a square onto the floated wall and the dot. Tap the dot in or pull it out until the square sits squarely on the wall and the dot.

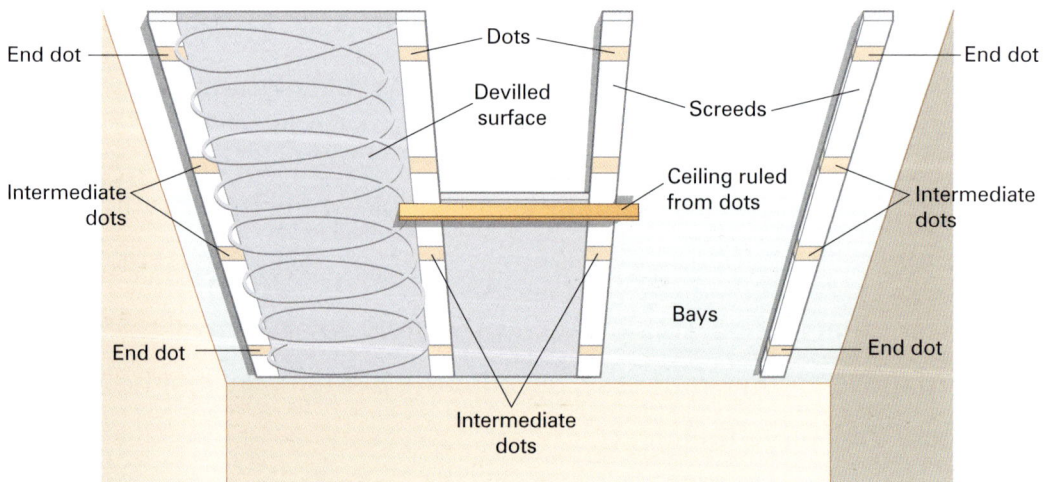

Figure 7.23 Ceiling floated and ruled in

Having positioned the first dot, a mark is made on the square in line with the datum point. Further dots can be positioned on the ceiling and lined up with the marks on the square and the wall (Figure 7.22).

Screeds can now be formed between the outside dots and the intermediate dots. The ceiling can then be floated and ruled in to a true, flat surface (Figure 7.23).

Devil and consolidate the floated surface and put on a finishing coat when the material has set.

Floating a beam

Concrete beams or plasterboard beams are floated to increase the fire rating (especially with plasterboard beams that are encasing a steel structure), and also to improve the straight lines of the beams themselves.

The floating of a beam is not too dissimilar to floating a ceiling.

Angle beads should be fixed along either edge of the beam (Figure 7.24).

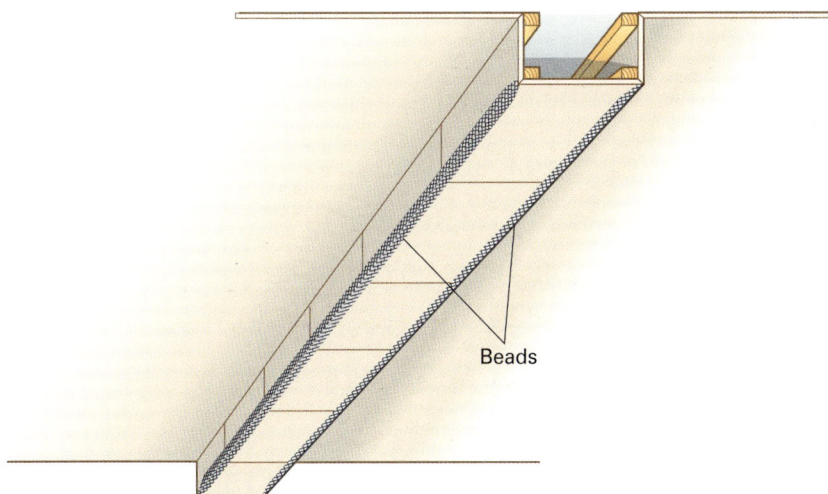

Did you know?

You can use a nail in the square instead of a pencil mark, to check the bead

Beads

Figure 7.24 Beads fixed to beam

The beads can be squared in from a floated ceiling (as described earlier) by holding the square flat onto the ceiling and marking the square, where it touches the bead, at one end of the beam. As long as the ceiling is true and flat, the square can be held along the length of the bead at regular spacings, so that there is equal distance between the angle bead and the ceiling.

Repeat the process on the other side (or cheek) of the beam. This will give an equal measurement on both sides of the beam.

Using a piece of wood, plasterboard or tape measure, check the measurement between the two angle beads on the soffit of the beam. The measurement between the two beads should differ by no more than 3 mm along its length.

Check the straightness of the angle beads by holding a straight edge rule on the face and underside of the bead. If the ceiling is true and flat, there should be no gap showing between the bead and the rule.

When this is complete, again using the square resting on the ceiling and touching the bead, put in a small screed on both cheeks of the beam. Do this at distances that match the floating rule. Now float in the beam cheeks and the soffit of the beam.

When the material has set, skim in the normal manner.

If the ceiling has only had a finishing coat applied, you are limited to how much you can straighten out the beam. First, temporarily fix a skim bead at both ends of the plasterboard beam. Then, holding a straight edge on the soffit with a level, fix a temporary nail in the centre of the bead. Now measure the distance between the skim bead and the ceiling, at both ends and at the middle. Check the measurement: if there is more than 3 mm difference, there is very little you can do to make the beam run parallel with the ceiling. If this is the case, just make sure that the skim bead is straight.

Remember

It is very difficult to get a ceiling dead flat, so some allowance is given – usually 3 mm in a 1.8 m floating rule

Patching a ceiling

Wood lath ceiling

Plaster patching on wood lath ceiling can be carried out by different methods. If the patch is about one metre square, the repair can be made good by nailing or screwing a piece of plasterboard, cut to size and as near to the shape as can be made. The edges of the plasterboard may need some undercoat to fill in the gaps between the new plasterboard and the old ceiling. When the floating plaster has set, slightly cut it below the existing ceiling and coat the edges of the old ceiling with a coat of PVA adhesive. This is in case you overlap the finishing plaster from the patch onto the existing ceiling. Then skim the surface of the plasterboard to bring it in line with the original ceiling.

Where there is sufficient thickness of material to be put onto the patch, the edges of the boards can be reinforced by the use of scrim to avoid the possibility of cracking at the joint.

If the thickness between the laths and the existing ceiling does not allow for a piece of plasterboard to be nailed up, the wood laths must be carefully removed back to the centre of a joist nearest the patch. The plasterboard can then be nailed/screwed onto the joists. The plaster method is as above.

Remember

It is better to screw the plasterboard up in a wood lath ceiling. This means that you do not disturb, by hammering, the key between the plaster and the wood laths on the back

Remember

An irregular shape is easier to lose (i.e. not be noticed when decorated) than a regular shape

Making good to a wall

The ultimate test for any good **making good hand** is that their work should never be seen. If, even after decoration, the repair can still be seen, then the making good hand has not done a good job. It is very difficult to get experienced making good hands; most are older plasterers with a good level of skill.

The damaged area should first be removed, carefully, so as not to damage the surrounding area. In a number of cases, the repair may well be completed in a room that is in use, so extra care must be taken to protect the surrounding areas, furniture, etc.

1. Brush down the damaged area to remove any dust.

2. Rake out mortar joints if possible, to form a key.

3. With a gauging trowel, pointing trowel or similar, carefully remove any plaster to form an undercut under the existing plaster (Figure 7.25). This will help to secure the loose plaster around the repair.

4. Wet in the background area to be repaired, and the undercut, or coat with PVA adhesive.

5. When the PVA is tacky, or while the area is still damp, apply the chosen plastering material to the repair.

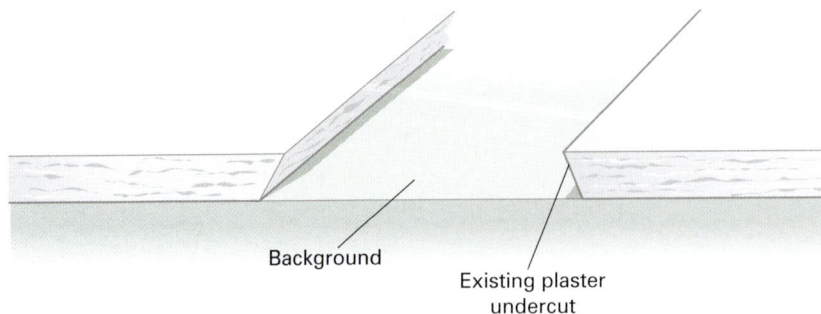

Background

Existing plaster undercut

Figure 7.25 Forming an undercut in the existing plaster

6. Rule in the floating coat level with the existing finish (Figure 7.26), and key the floating ready to receive the finishing coat.

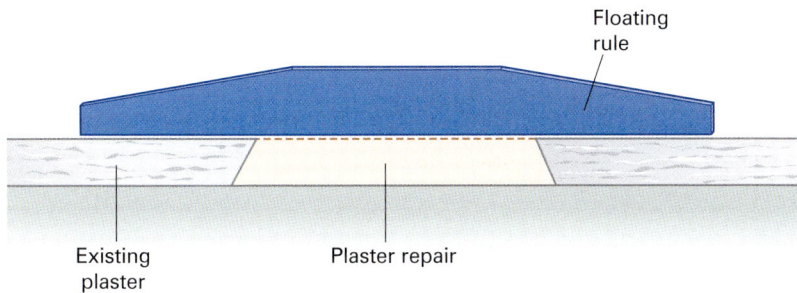

Figure 7.26 Floating coat ruled in

7. When the plaster has set, cut back the floating by about 2 or 3 mm, by scraping back with the back edge of a trowel. Cut back especially around the edges of the repair to give an extra thickness of finish (Figure 7.27), which will allow for a better blending in of the old and the new plaster.

8. Wet in the surrounding area of the repair and apply the finishing coat.

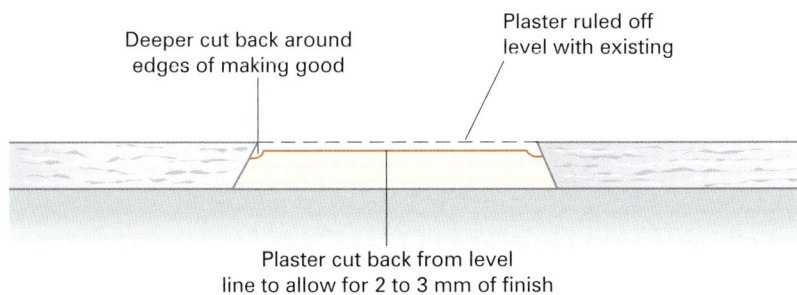

Figure 7.27 Plaster cut back and finishing coat applied

Did you know?

It is OK to use plaster that is near the end of its shelf life when making good small damaged areas. This is because it will set more quickly, so a larger number of repairs can be completed in a day

Remember

If you are liable to go over the existing plaster with your finish because of the poor finished standard of the existing plaster, you must coat the existing plaster with PVA adhesive

On the job: Internal plastering

1. Lewis has been asked to float and set a wall that has three windows in line, all of the same size. What method should he use to make sure that, when the wall is finished, all of the external angles are in line?

2. Clare has been asked to skim a ceiling. What inspection should she make on the low-level scaffold that has been erected for her and what should she do if she finds a fault?

3. Michael has been asked to float and set a wall in cement/lime/sand. When he gets to site he sees that the wall is painted. What should he do now? Should he make his own mind up and, if he does, what treatment should he give the wall before starting to float it?

FAQ

Can I put a finishing coat on top of cement-based mortars and lightweight plasters straight after I have finished floating the wall?

This is not recommended, especially on cement-based mortars. On these floated backgrounds, the cement needs to attain its full strength and be allowed to shrink before setting. On lightweight plasters, it can be drawn into the floating but it will be more difficult to obtain a good quality finish. It can also lead to blistering of the finishing coat.

Can I mix two different types of lightweight plaster?

This is not recommended by the manufacturers if you are putting two different lightweight materials one on top of the other. However, if you are mixing them together in the mixing trough it will work.

Can you add water to materials that are setting off on the spot board?

Again, this is not recommended because it will weaken the material and affect the set and so you will end up with a poor quality job.

Can I bed plasterboard into the face of a metal lintel to bring it out to the wall line?

Yes you can, as long as it is the correct material used for plasterboard. In fact, it helps to save on material and time.

Knowledge check

1. Name two cement/lime/sand mixes.

2. What does three-coat work mean?

3. When setting a ceiling that has canvas on the joints, from where should the first coat be started?

4. If you are left handed where should the setting coat for a wall begin?

5. How do you check an angle bead for plumb?

6. What part of the window is the head?

7. What is the purpose of a reveal gauge?

8. Name the system used to make a large hall wall true and flat.

9. Besides an angle bead, name three other types of trim.

10. If an internal angle shows up as not straight during the setting coat, how could you straighten it out?

11. What is the purpose of the box screed system of floating?

12. On lightweight plaster, what system is used for applying the finishing coat?

13. How do you prepare a lightweight block background before plastering?

14. Before applying a setting coat, what must you do to the angles?

15. What type of key is formed on a floated background to make it ready for the finish?

16. Name four pieces of equipment required for floating a wall.

17. Name four tools used for applying the finishing coat.

18. Name four reinforcing materials for plasterboard joints.

19. In plastering, what are fish scales and what causes them?

chapter 8

External solid plastering

OVERVIEW

Render provides a weatherproof surface that prevents the penetration of moisture into the outside of the building, and forms a decorative finish.

In the mid-eighteenth century, rendering was carried out using a mortar of hydraulic lime and sharp sand. This provided a breathable render, but it took a long time to set. It was replaced by mortars of cement and hydrated lime, which had a quicker setting time – essential in the housebuilding boom after the Second World War. New renders are being developed to meet today's needs. These new renders are pre-mixed so that they are uniform in colour and have a consistent strength. Traditional lime renders are still used however, especially for restoration work.

Key issues when choosing render are: planning regulations and conservation requirements; fire and insulation properties; the background; climatic exposure; the client's requirements; and, of course, cost.

This chapter will cover the following:

- Materials used for external rendering
- Additives
- Preparing backgrounds
- Bonding adhesives
- Mixing and applying render
- Plain float finish
- Metal trims

Materials used for external rendering

It is important to choose the correct materials to produce render. This will produce high quality render mixes that will not develop faults such as cracking and blowing of the surface, which affect the appearance and allow moisture to penetrate.

Sand

Sand makes up the bulk of the render mix. For traditional external rendering mixes, the following types of sand are used:

- pit sand – quarried inland, usually red in colour

- dredged sand from the river or sea bed, usually a dark yellow colour

- artificially created sand, available in different colours.

Modern render mixes are made with artificially created sand. This is formed by crushing stone or gravel to the required grade. It is available in different colours, such as white, red or black.

When mixed with cement and lime, the sand will form the bulk of the mix; the sand is known as the aggregate.

As with internal plastering, poor quality sand will cause the external render to crack and become loose and hollow, or it may eventually crumble. In good quality sand, the particles are irregular in shape (not rounded), and well graded. The largest grains should not be more than 5 mm. This is assessed using a sieve test to ensure no grains over 5 mm are present in the sand.

The sand should have been washed to remove impurities. Clay and silt particles in the mix prevent the cement from bonding to the aggregate, so each load delivered to the site should be checked for 'cleanliness'. The amount of silt must not be more than 10 per cent of the volume of aggregate. The silt test is used to check this.

Silt test

Materials and equipment

- sample of sand
- water
- salt
- glass jar or measuring cylinder
- tape measure.

Method

Step 1 Place 25 mm of water into the jar, add 1 teaspoon of salt and gradually add the sand until the level of the top of the sand reaches 50 mm.

Ingredients being added to water

Step 2 Shake the jar for 1 minute.

Step 3 Leave to settle for 3 hours. Measure the height of the aggregate and the thickness of the silt layer.

To work out the percentage of silt in the aggregate, calculate the following sum:

$$\frac{\text{Thickness of silt}}{\text{Total height of aggregate and silt}} \times \frac{100}{1}$$

Jar after shaking

For example, if we measure the sand to be 45 mm and the silt thickness is 5 mm:

Jar after 3 hours

$$\frac{5}{45 + 5} \times \frac{100}{1}$$

$$\frac{5}{50} \times \frac{100}{1}$$

$$0.1 \times 100$$

$$= 10\%$$

Conclusion – this sample would be suitable, but only just.

Storage of sand

Sand should be stored in a clean bay, and covered with a tarpaulin to reduce contamination from animals, leaves and other aggregates.

Stored sand

Cement

Cement has been covered in detail in Chapter 7, pages 182–184, and the information included here is relevant to its use in external solid plastering.

Two types of cement are commonly used with external renders. Ordinary Portland cement (OPC) consists essentially of 75 per cent limestone and 25 per cent clay. It is grey in colour. White Portland cement contains 75 per cent limestone and 25 per cent white china clay. It is white in colour, and is used when a whiter, lighter appearance is desirable in the render finish.

On an external rendering job, cement should be stacked off the ground in a container or shed to keep dry.

Setting time for cement

The setting of cement is a chemical reaction, and so it is affected by temperature. In warmer climates, cement will set more quickly than in colder areas. The initial set of cement is 45 minutes, but the final set is not more than 10 hours.

Special-purpose cements

Sulphate-resisting Portland cement (SRPC) is used in situations where sulphates are present in concentrations that would damage normal Portland cement mortar. This type of damage results in white salt stains appearing on the face of backgrounds that could penetrate through the render.

Rapid-hardening Portland cement (RHPC) is finer than OPC, and is used in concrete to ensure a higher rate of early-age strength development.

Lime

Lime has been discussed in detail in Chapter 7, pages 180–182. It is commonly used in external solid plastering on older buildings or on restoration projects.

Safety tip

When cement is mixed with water an alkaline solution is produced. Take precautions to avoid skin contact with wet cement, fresh concrete or mortar, and prevent dry cement from entering the eyes, mouth or nose. Wear suitable protective clothing, gloves and eye/face protection

FAQ

What types of lime would you use when rendering, and when?

Hydraulic lime is used mainly for listed building work, whereas hydrated lime is used on modern buildings.

Additives

Additives are commonly used in cement-based render mixes, whether for the dubbing-out coat, scratch coat or top coat. Additives are liquid or powder ingredients, and should be carefully measured in accordance with the manufacturer's instructions before adding them to the mix.

There are several types of additive that can be added to cement-based render for external applications:

- **plasticiser** – improves the workability of the mix and its ease of application

- **waterproofer** – improves workability, forms a waterproof barrier in the render and equalises suction

- **retarder** – this can be added to the mix in warm conditions to slow down the setting process

- **accelerator** – this can be added in cold conditions to speed up the setting process.

Some modern pre-mixed renders have additives included during manufacture. This will eliminate problems caused by adding too little or too much when mixing by hand.

On the job: Using additives

Peter the labourer mixed my render, but used too much plasticiser. This resulted in the mix not achieving its correct strength, and later it crumbled. What should Peter do to prevent this happening in future?

Preparing backgrounds

Most modern houses and other buildings are built from blocks, which require little preparation. Older buildings will require some type of preparation before rendering. This is essential to ensure a good bond between the render and the background.

New blockwork only requires damping down of the surface before rendering, whereas all other backgrounds require preparation.

Table 8.1 identifies the procedure for preparing backgrounds prior to rendering.

Remember

Some backgrounds may still have old render. This will need to be prepared by hacking off

Table 8.1 Preparation of backgrounds

Type of	Hack off old work	Rake out joints	Brush and dampen	Apply slurry adhesive
New brickwork			✓	✓
Old brickwork	✓	✓	✓	✓
New blockwork			✓	
Old stonework	✓	✓	✓	✓
Concrete surface			✓	✓

Bonding adhesives

Applying a slurry coat

Some backgrounds have poor adhesion properties. The plasterer must be able to identify the background correctly, to determine what type of surface treatment or bonding adhesive may be required to create a key or bond when applying the render to the background.

The traditional slurry coat was called a spatterdash coat: a mixture of wet sand and cement spattered on to the wall surface to form a key.

There are various modern versions of the slurry coat available from manufacturers. These include:

- **Cementitious polymer-modified material**. This is usually supplied in powder form, and includes a bonding agent. It is added to water on site to make a slurry, which is then brushed onto the background, forming a stipple to provide a key for rendering.

- **Heavy-duty slurry**. This is supplied ready mixed. It is applied by roller or trowel to a previously sealed and primed background to form a stipple effect.

Bonding adhesives are designed for use on poorly keyed dense surfaces; they improve adhesion between the background and the first render/scratch coat. They come in either powder or liquid form. Some require mixing, while others are pre-mixed.

There are many bonding products on the market. One example is SBR. This is latex-based. It is used in areas subject to humidity, dampness or continuous water contact to improve the water resistance of cement mixtures. SBR comes in liquid form. It is either mixed with cement to make a slurry and applied to the background with a brush, or added to the render mix in the proportions 30 per cent SBR to 70 per cent water.

Insulation board and EML are commonly used on houses with poor insulation properties. This type of board or cladding is fixed by drilling and plugging to the background surface. Specialist lightweight renders are required for this background; sand and cement mixes are too heavy.

Mixing and applying render

Safety tip

Always wear the correct PPE when mixing render: dust mask, boots, hard hat and gloves

Render is normally mixed mechanically in a petrol or diesel mixer.

When mixing any type of render, it is essential to gauge all mix materials correctly with a bucket measure. This will ensure that all mixes will be of the correct strength and colour throughout the work.

Remember

Good housekeeping and storage of materials are always important, but particularly if space is limited in the mixing area

Gauging render

Modern renders are pre-mixed to the required strength.

It is essential to use clean water when mixing renders. Dirty water may weaken the mix or stain the face of the finished surface.

External rendering to the background surface can be applied as either two-coat or three-coat work.

Two-coat work

Two-coat work comprises the scratch coat and the top coat.

Scratch coat

This provides the backing coat for the render finish. It is normally applied to straighten out uneven backgrounds such as block or brick surfaces. It usually includes a waterproofing additive. The scratch coat must be between 9 and 12 mm thick to prevent the brick or block background showing through. Once an area is covered, a wire comb scratcher is used to form a key on the surface: this will enable the final coat to bond when applied.

At this stage, it is necessary to form any angles and **reveals** in the work area.

Method

1. Hold a timber rule plumb on one side of the wall to a thickness of 10–12 mm.

2. Apply render up to the timber rule.

> **Definition**
>
> **Reveal** – the side of a window opening or doorway which is at right angles to the face of the work

Applying a render

Remember

Always protect windows and doors when carrying out render work. They could be costly to replace if damaged

Definition

Bellcast – a curve built into the bottom edge of a roof or wall surface designed to throw off water. It looks like the edge of a bell, hence bellcast

Safety tip

Always keep working areas and platforms free of any obstacles that could cause a tripping hazard when carrying out render work

Slide rule away

Working render to the angle

3. Slide the timber rule upwards and away from the angle.

4. Hold the timber rule on previously laid render to a thickness of approximately 10–12 mm.

5. Apply render up to the timber rule.

6. Slide the timber rule upwards and away from the angle.

Bellcasts need to be formed at this stage. This is done by fixing metal trims above window and door openings, and also at DPC level to form the bellcast in the render finish. A bellcast is also known as a drip or weathering. Bellcasts can also be formed by fixing timber battens which are removed when the material is set.

Top coat

This is the final coat or layer applied to the scratch coat to form the finished render. However, first the reveals must be completed, as follows.

1. Remove any hard sand and cement left after the keying process by running a trowel over the scratched surface.

2. Fix or hold a timber rule on the main face of the wall, plumbing or lining it to the window or door frame to a thickness of 10–12 mm.

3. Apply top coat to the reveals.

4. Once the top coat starts to pull in (set), consolidate or rub up the surface with a plastic or wooden float.

5. Use a sponge to scour over the surface to close the face, if necessary.

Three-coat work

Three-coat work comprises a scratch coat, top coat and a final decorative finish such as pebble dashing.

In addition to these coats, a dubbing-out coat is used when the background surface is uneven and requires filling (for example hollows and crevices in a stone background).

Applying a dubbing-out coat will reduce the thickness of application, which could otherwise cause the work to sag and slide off the wall. Sometimes more than one dubbing-out coat will be needed to bring the surface flush with the face of the background.

Most cement-based renders are left for a minimum of 24 hours before the next layer is applied. This allows the render to cure and the mix to achieve its maximum strength. However, it is worth noting that the longer the scratch coat is left for, the more shrinkage and cracking may take place. Hydraulic lime mixes take longer to set and so should be left longer between each application than cement-based mixes. Lime-based renders are sometimes left for weeks to cure.

Find out

Buildings that require a dubbing-out coat are generally stone, slate or uneven brickwork. Can you think of any more?

Did you know?

Direct sunlight can cause the render to dry too soon, and this makes it weak because the cement has not set fully. Tarpaulin or timber sheets can be used to protect against direct sunlight

However, the principle of applying a weaker mix for each successive application or coat is the same for any render. Applying strong renders on weak backgrounds causes stress which will result in the render becoming loose.

Ratios of the render mix

Ratios are designed to help the plasterer know the right quantity of each material when mixing. Mixing the render too strong for a weak background may cause subsequent stress, resulting in cracking and blowing. Mixing the render too weak may cause no initial set and subsequent crumble.

The ratios for dubbing-out mixes for sand, cement and lime render commonly used on uneven backgrounds such as old brick, stone or slate are:

Sand	Cement	Lime	Additive
5	1	1	Plasticiser

or

Sand	Cement	Lime	Additive
4	1	½	Plasticiser

The ratio for mixes commonly used as a scratch coat applied to block or brick backgrounds is:

Sand	Cement	Additive
4	1	Waterproofer

The ratio for top coats commonly used for external render finishes applied to the scratch coat is:

Sand	Cement	Hydrated lime	Additive
5 or 6	1	1	Plasticiser

The ratios for hydraulic lime renders are:

Coat	Hydraulic lime	Sharp sand
Dubbing-out	1	1½
Scratch coat	1	2
Top coat	1	2 ½

The above ratios should be used as a guide only; they may vary from site to site. Architects may specify different types of mix for different parts of the country, depending on the climatic conditions.

Remember

No additives are used in hydraulic lime renders

Plain float finish

The picture shows a plain float finish, produced by consolidating the render surface with a wooden or plastic float, which leaves a sandstone effect. It is usually finished with masonry paint for added weather protection. It is time-consuming, in the cold winter weather, having to wait for the render to set before consolidating and achieving the finish, but this finish is commonly used in sheltered areas.

Other surfaces that are finished in the same way will include window reveals and heads, **plinths** below the DPC, special features such as **quoin** stones and smooth bands that divide large areas, or decorative bands around window or door openings.

Consolidation of plain float finish

Definition

Plinth – render applied below the damp proof course to ground level

Quoin – brick or large stone, set in an external corner of a wall

When applying plain float render finish:

- Check the background for excessive suction and treat accordingly. This will allow enough time to apply and rule the surface of the finish before it dries.

- Apply the rendering material working from the top to the bottom of the wall surface, to a thickness of 10–12 mm: applying the render too thinly will cause a dark sanding effect on the surface when consolidating.

- After applying the finish coat, rule the surface with a straight edge or darby to a flat, smooth finish.

- Allow the ruled surface to pull-in (set), then consolidate (scour) with a plastic or wooden float.

- Lightly apply a sponge to close the face of the finish, leaving a plain pattern.

A common fault with this finish is crazing: cracks appear on the face, caused either by suction in the background or by over-scouring of the surface.

Traditional sand, cement and lime renders had to be mixed by hand, and poor gauging could cause problems: renders blowing from the background, cracks appearing in the surface finish, and irregularities in the colour of the finished render. Modern renders are pre-mixed and bagged with all the necessary materials and additives, and just need the addition of water when mixing. This gives consistent results, with the correct strength and colour.

Modern renders can be applied by a machine that mixes the render, and pumps and sprays the material onto the background surface. Traditional plastering techniques are still needed to form the finish.

Renders based on hydraulic lime are still used today, mainly on old buildings that were built using lime mortar. This type of mix has better workability properties, and so does not need the addition of plasticiser or other additives.

External renders will need to be cured because of the cement content. This can be done by hanging wet canvas or plastic sheeting down the face of the render. A light hosing with water 24 hours after application will help the render to achieve full strength, especially in hot weather.

Metal trims

Metal trims were manufactured as an alternative to the use of traditional timber methods for forming angles, stops and bellcasts in the render finish. They are fixed to the background before the scratch coat is applied. For external work you should use stainless steel or plastic trims: galvanised trims can rust and weep through the render. Cut metal trims with tin snips.

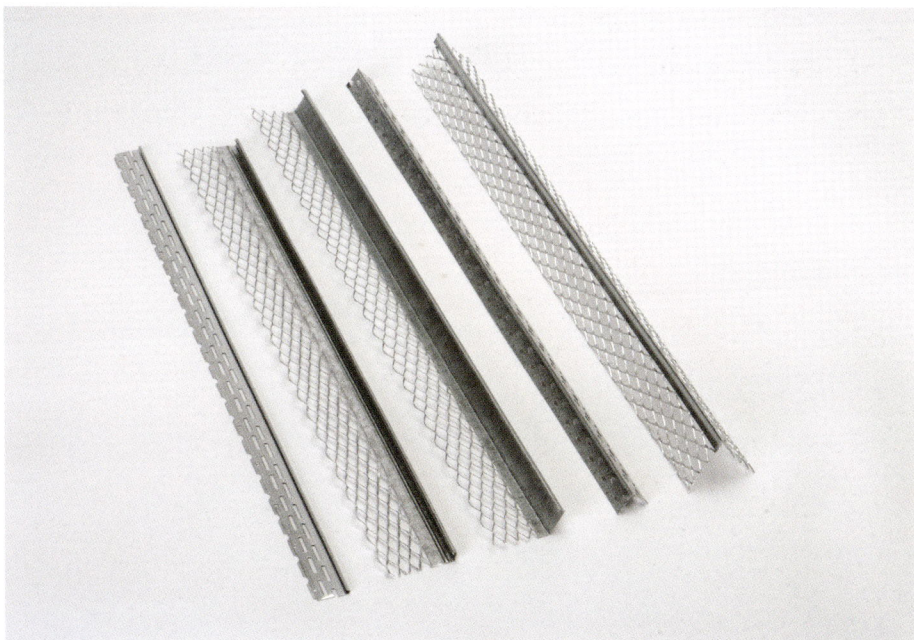

Types of metal trim

The types of trim used in external rendering work are:

- **bell bead** – forms a drip above windows and doors, and prevents bridging to DPC level

- **stop bead** – can be fixed up to facing brick or timber frames to form panels

- **angle bead** – used on external corners for straightness and strength

- **expansion bead** – used to allow movement when two walls meet each other as a straight joint.

All these trims are available in both plastic and stainless steel.

These can all be fixed in the same way, either by using nails or clouts (which must be rustproof), or by bedding them in position with the render material. Always position the trim to the correct line, with no bows or kinks, as this can show in the finished render.

Knowledge check

1. What is the purpose of a bell bead when rendering?

2. Name the type of slurry that is applied to a background that has a poor mechanical key.

3. State the two main reasons for plastering the outside of a house.

4. When preparing sand and cement mixes for rendering, what is meant by binder and aggregate?

5. Why is plasticiser added to a sand and cement render mix required for external render?

6. What type of render is used to restore and plaster old buildings such as churches?

7. What are the two raw materials for producing cement?

8. Why are stainless steel and plastic trims, rather than galvanised trims, used on the outside of buildings when rendering?

9. What is meant by well-graded sand?

chapter 9

Floor screeding

OVERVIEW

The purpose of floor screeding is to produce a true, flat, level, hard-wearing surface, which has the ability to be a base for additional coverings such as carpets, tiles, etc. It is important that the floor is level because kitchen equipment, furniture or expensive industrial equipment may be resting on the finished surface. Floor screeding can be a specialist skill performed by floor screeders, or may be part of a plasterer's range of abilities, which makes him or her an all-round plasterer. On larger jobs, floor screeding could be the last operation performed by a plasterer before leaving the building, so it is important that you work cleanly and without damaging already completed work.

We shall cover the following topics in this chapter:

- Hand tools and mechanical equipment

- Materials and storage for floor screeding

- Proportioning and mixing

- Types of floor screed

- Methods of laying floor screeds

- Curing

- Flooring faults

- Laying floors to falls

Hand tools and mechanical equipment

The selection of hand tools and the type of equipment selected help to determine, along with hand and eye coordination, the standards and quality of the floor screed that you will produce. It is important to maintain your tools properly and to be aware of any safety precautions that may apply to a particular tool.

Hand tools

For laying floor screeds, all tools are hand-held. There are no tried-and-tested mechanical levelling tools, although there is one mechanical levelling tool now on the market.

It is essential to have all the required tools, which should be of the best quality that you can afford.

The following hand tools are used in floor screeding:

- floor laying trowel
- plastic float
- spirit level
- water level
- gauging trowel
- chalk line
- measuring tools.

Equipment

You will also need to have the following equipment available for floor screeding jobs. These will be either 'in the van' or, for some of the larger items, hired specially for the job.

- Cement mixer – paddle mixer
- Wheelbarrow – narrow

- Shovel

- Builder's square

- Flooring rule

- Buckets

- Lasers

- Cement pump

Personal safety equipment

Appropriate PPE should be used at all times. The following items are particularly important for safety and protection when floor screeding:

- face mask

- industrial gloves

- safety boots

- knee pads

- overalls.

For more information and a full description of the tools, equipment and PPE required for floor screeding see Chapter 4, pages 87-124.

Materials and storage for floor screeding

The two basic component materials required for floor screeding are sand and cement. It is important to check the quality of the sand used and to store your materials correctly.

Sand for floor screeding

This should be a 'sharp' and 'gritty' sand. This means that it contains larger angular grains of sand for harder wearing qualities.

The sand should be clean and free from impurities such as dirt and leaves, etc.

Definition

Silt – very fine particles of sand which help with the ability to work the sand with the trowel. Too much silt is not good as it does not have a lot of strength and this can lead to cracking

Safety tip

Wear gloves, overalls and a face mask when handling cement. If it gets onto your body and you sweat, the cement mixes with the sweat and can cause very painful skin burns

Definition

FIFO – first in first out: a system of using stock whereby the oldest material is used first so that it doesn't perish

See Chapter 8, pages 231–232, for details of a simple site test to test the **silt** content of sand. This should show a uniform grading of sand and that it is clean enough to be used.

Cement

This should be ordinary Portland cement (OPC).

Storage

Bagged materials, such as cement, plaster and sand, should be stored in a ventilated, waterproof shed, with a sound (good condition) dry floor. They should be clear of the walls, and piles should be no more than eight to ten bags high.

On smaller jobs there may not be a shed available, so you will have to discuss with the client whether a suitable storage area can be found.

Bags should be used in the same order as they were delivered, known as 'first in first out' (FIFO).

Proportioning and mixing

In order to produce the required strength of floor screeding material, you must measure out the correct proportions of sand and cement. You must also use the correct method of mixing the floor screeding material in order to produce the best results for laying.

Proportioning

There are two recognised mixes for floor screed:

- 3:1 = 3 of sand to 1 of cement
- 4:1 = 4 of sand to 1 of cement.

The preferred mix when mixing by hand or with a cement mixer is 3:1. The material should be gauged out by the bucketful, and levelled off at the top and then tipped out onto the ground. It is then mixed together thoroughly on the floor, if mixing by hand, or tipped into the drum of the mixer.

Gauged materials ready for mixing

Keep count of the number of buckets measured as a mistake will affect the strength of the mix. It should be 3 buckets of sand and 1 bucket of cement. It may be that you or your mixer are not strong enough to mix more than 4 buckets, but it could be that you have 6 buckets of sand and 2 buckets of cement, or 4½ buckets of sand and 1½ buckets of cement. This still works out as a 3:1 ratio.

Definition

Bulking – the increase in volume of sand caused by it being wet

Well – in the mixing process, the sand and cement is spread out and a hole is made in the middle for putting in the water; this is called the well

Safety tip

In addition to the normal PPE, wear a face mask because of the cement content.

Definition

Balling – when the sand and cement mix does not have enough water, it will bind together in small balls, which will make it extremely difficult to lay the floor

When buying a pre-mixed floor screed you can specify 4:1 because they take out any human error, as it is mixed by computer and machine.

When doing your own mixing, be aware that sand that is wet '**bulks**': it expands when wet and so takes up more space than dry sand. This will affect the proportions and strength of the finished mix.

Mixing

When mixing by hand, the dry material should be thoroughly mixed together. A '**well**' is opened up in the middle and good clean drinking quality water is added. Sufficient water should be added so that when the material is mixed it is damp, but not wet.

A simple site test for correct water content is to press a ball of material in your hand and squeeze. Open your hand and the material should be in a tight ball without falling to pieces. If sand and cement is wet, it will stain the palm of your hand; if it is semi-dry, it will leave more of a dusting to the palm of your hand that can be easily brushed off on your trousers. If you need to wash your hand, the mix is too wet.

When mixing by cement mixer, first add a little water into the drum and then alternately add sand and cement. Do not put all the cement in first as it may stick to the drum. Adding too much water will affect the laying and strength of the screed.

Too much water will bring cement to the floor surface during laying and this will weaken the floor screed. Too little water will lead to the mix '**balling**' and being extremely difficult to lay. The mixing of floor screeding material is very important because it affects the ability to lay and the finished quality of the floor screed.

Types of floor screed

There are three types of floor screed: bonded, unbonded and floating.

Bonded floor screed

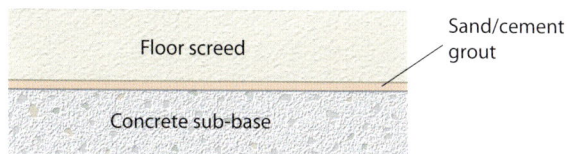

| Floor screed | Sand/cement grout |
| Concrete sub-base |

Unbonded floor screed

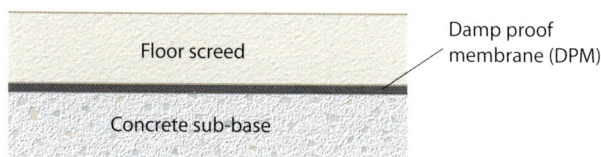

| Floor screed | Damp proof membrane (DPM) |
| Concrete sub-base |

Floating floor screed

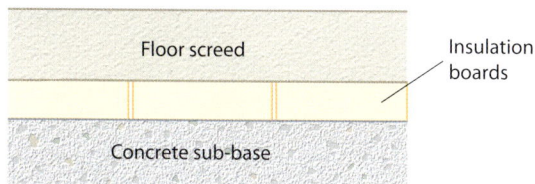

| Floor screed | Insulation boards |
| Concrete sub-base |

Figure 9.1 Types of floor screed

Bonded screed

This is the laying of a screed directly onto a pre-laid concrete tamped surface. The face of the concrete will be tamped down with a rule and left in this rough state with aggregate showing, which helps with the bonding process.

Preparation

Remove all old droppings of plaster and any other debris. All dirt and dust should be removed. The concrete base should be given a good soaking overnight before levelling screed is laid. Brush off any excess water before 'grouting'. Grout is 1:1 sand/cement mixed with water in a bucket. This is applied to the wet concrete and brushed in. A PVA bonding agent can be applied to help bond the sand and cement to the base.

Remember

Always stir the grout before application so that sand and cement are well mixed

Thickness

This should be a minimum of 25 mm, but no more than 40 mm; above this thickness there will be a loss of adhesion.

Unbonded screed

This system is laid onto a new or an old renovated concrete sub-base. As the name suggests, the screed is not bonded to the concrete base.

Preparation

The sub-base should be clean and smooth, ready for any damp proof membrane (**DPM**), so that the DPM is not damaged. This will prevent any damp rising up through the floor. Any hollows and cracks in the sub-base should first be repaired. No other preparation is required. Unbonded floor screeds can be used in underfloor heating for schools, commercial buildings (offices, shops, etc.) and conservatories.

Thickness

An unbonded screed should have a minimum thickness of 50 mm and be no more than 70 mm.

Definition

DPM – a layer of waterproof material placed under the screed to stop moisture coming up from the ground into the building

Floating screed

This form of screeding is used on top of rigid or semi-rigid insulation boards.

Preparation

The concrete base should be smooth and level. Any gaps between the boards and sub-base should be filled by grout or floor screed.

Thickness

When laid on a compressible layer, in a commercial unit, the thickness should not be less than 75 mm at any one point, and not more than 100 mm. For domestic units, the thickness should not be less than 65 mm, at any one point, and no more than 90 mm. (Commercial units refer to offices, shops, factories etc., whereas domestic refers to houses and flats, etc. where people live.)

Methods of laying floor screeds

When laying floors, first levels have to be formed from given datum points, then narrow screeds laid, within which the main floor screed can be laid.

Forming of levels

A datum point is used so that all levels are transferred from a fixed point. It is usual site practice for the general foreman or site agent to go around the site putting in the levels for the tradesperson to work to. A datum mark is a mark that will be placed on the wall or from a given point, such as the threshold of the front door, that the tradesperson will then transfer around the building to take their levels from.

A second method of forming the floor level, mainly in domestic housing, is to take the level from the bottom of the door frames or staircases.

The floor is prepared as in the previous section, and grout is applied by brush to the area on which the first narrow screed is to be laid.

The grout must still be wet when applying the screed material. The width of the first screeds should be approximately 300 mm, or slightly wider than your trowel. Lay approximately half of the required thickness of screed and **consolidate** it well. Place a second amount of material onto the compacted screed and rule it in with a flooring rule.

Flooring rules can be 3 m in length, which means that, with practice, you can rule in a screed of 4–5 m in length.

Now check the accuracy of the screed by checking against the chalked line around the room by the use of a builder's square. The square has a pencil mark on it, which lines up with the chalk line on the wall, as shown in Figure 9.4.

The second way of levelling in your screed is by working from the bottom of the door frame (Figure 9.5). Lay the screed as previously described, but this time use a level on top of the flooring rule to check the screed accurately.

> **Definition**
>
> **Consolidate** – compact or pack down hard

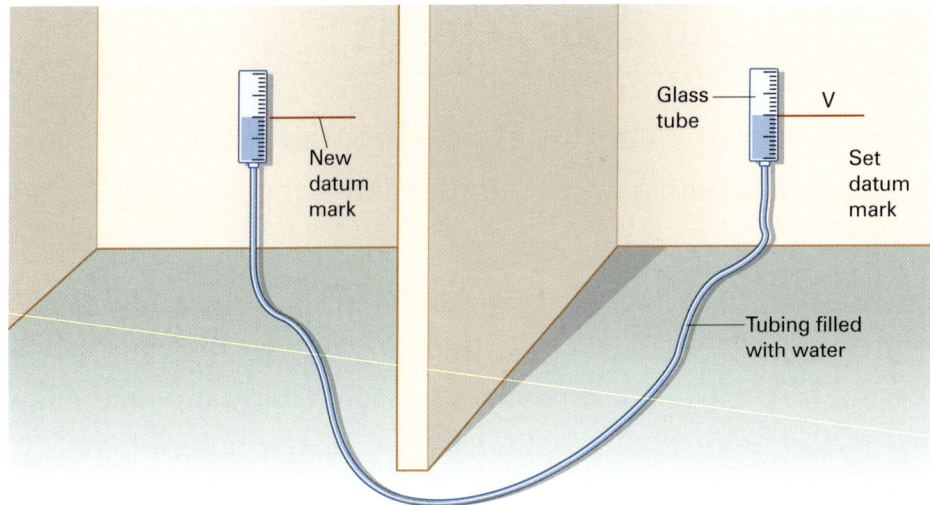

Figure 9.2 Use of a water level to transfer fixed datum points from one room to another

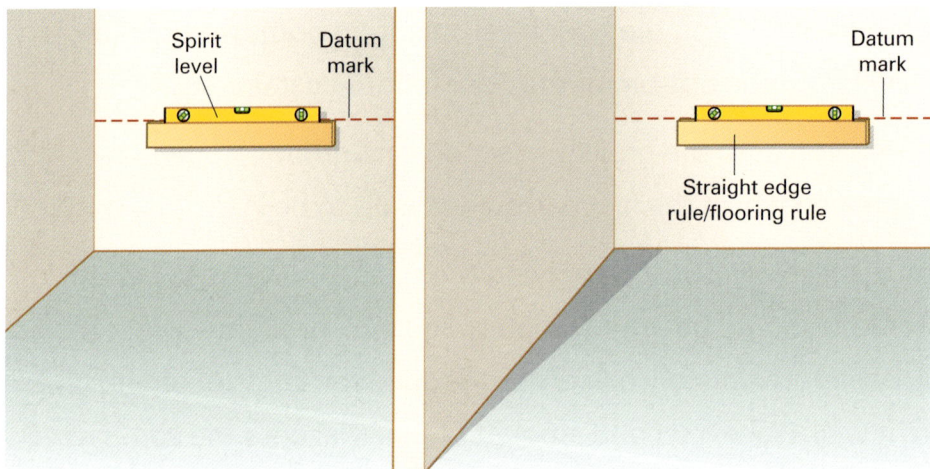

Figure 9.3 The datum mark can be taken round the room by reversing the level and rule. Alternatively, simple level marks are made on the wall and joined together by snapping a chalk line

You should reverse the level as you work around the room. This eliminates any slight inaccuracy in your level.

Take the screeds around the room and return back to were you started. It should now meet up to the other side of the door frame to within 3 mm.

The surface of the screeds should be finished off to the specified surface finish.

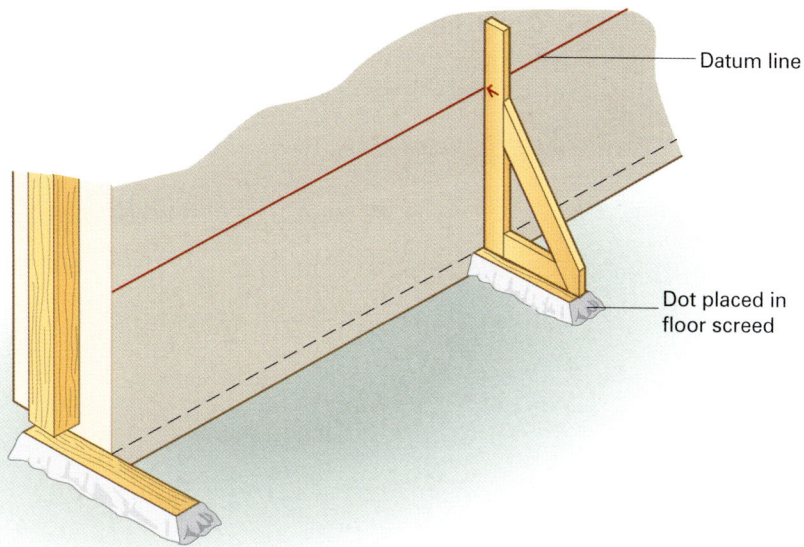

Datum line

Dot placed in
floor screed

Figure 9.4 Placing dots with a square on a datum line

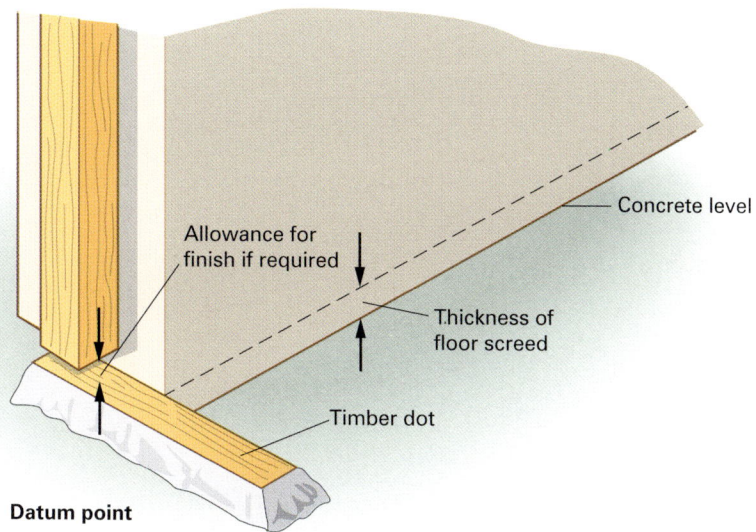

Concrete level

Allowance for
finish if required

Thickness of
floor screed

Timber dot

Datum point

Figure 9.5 Using the bottom of a door frame as a datum point

Filling in between the screeds

Grout up between the screeds and then spread out a layer of floor screeding material between the screeds. Consolidate the material.

Now bring the screed mix a couple of millimetres above the screeds and rule in using the finished screeds as your rule. The rule needs to be worked backwards and forwards filling in larger hollows as you go.

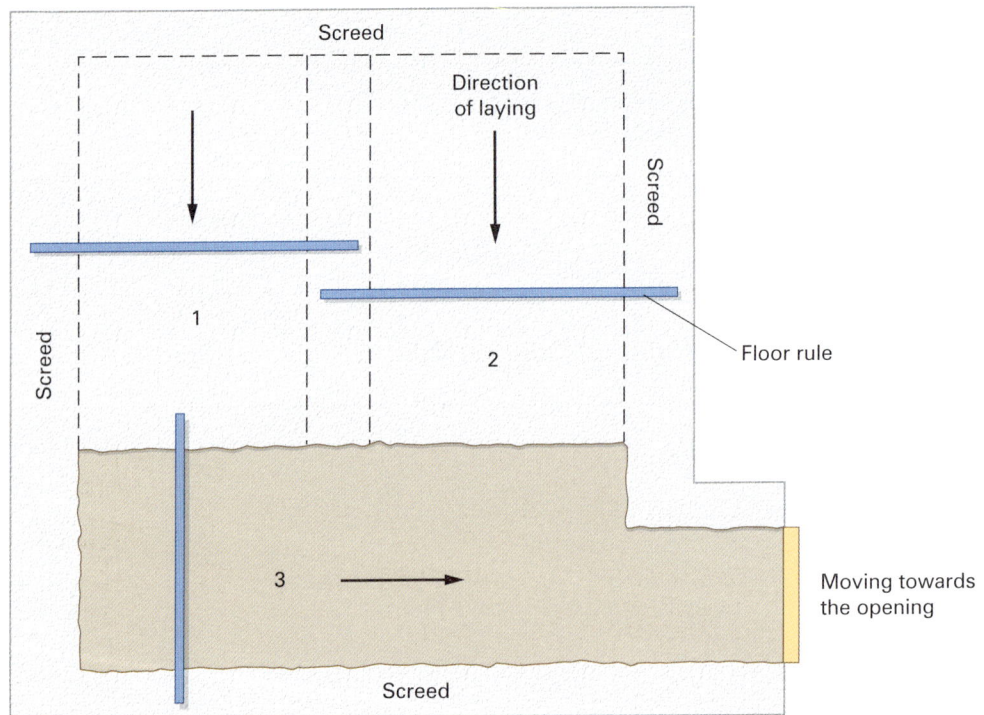

Figure 9.6 System of laying to screeds

Fill in any smaller hollows by the use of a large plastic float.

When the surface has been ruled in, check for level by laying the rule diagonally across the face of the floor and placing your level on top. Now bring the floor to the required finish as stated in the specification, either a float finish or trowel finish.

Now work your way backwards towards the door opening.

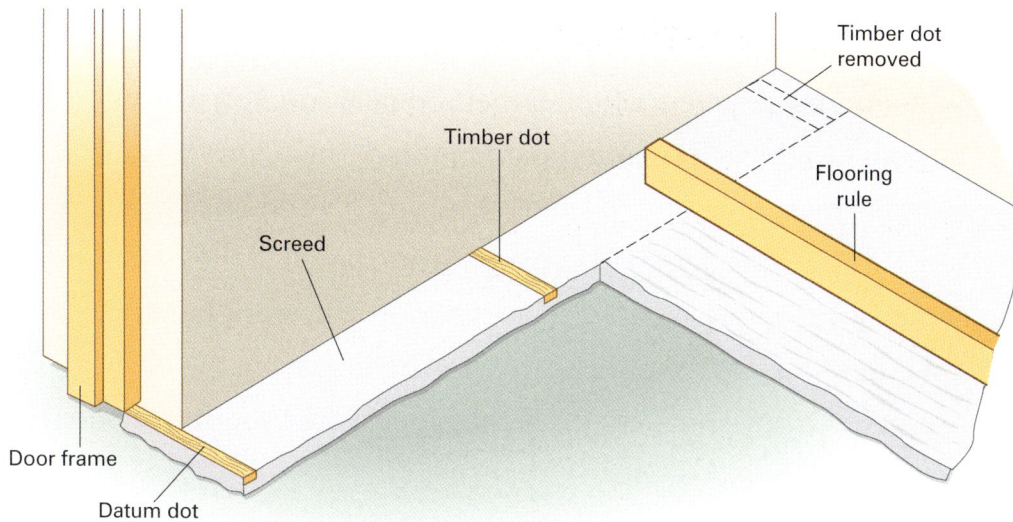

Figure 9.7 Using screeds for ruling in

> **Remember**
>
> British Standard 8204, *Screeds, bases and in-situ floorings*, recommends raking the compacted surface before applying a second coat

A third method of setting out your screeds is to use 'dots'. These consist of sand/cement dots to support timber pieces (Figure 9.8). They are used to help form levels. Because they are of a harder material, you can work the rule across them harder to get your levels.

These are lined in from the datum line as shown, and the first screeds are then laid between the dots.

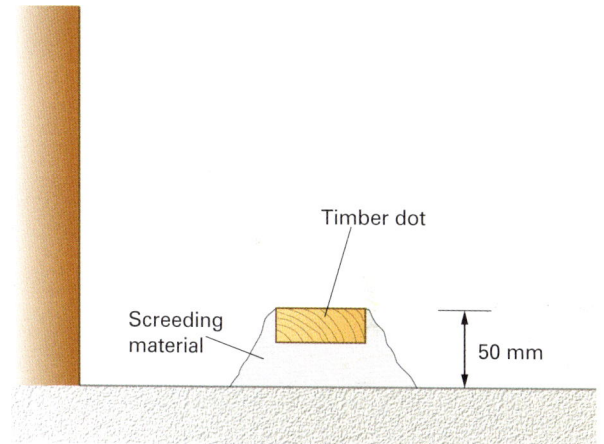

Figure 9.8 Dots used for setting out

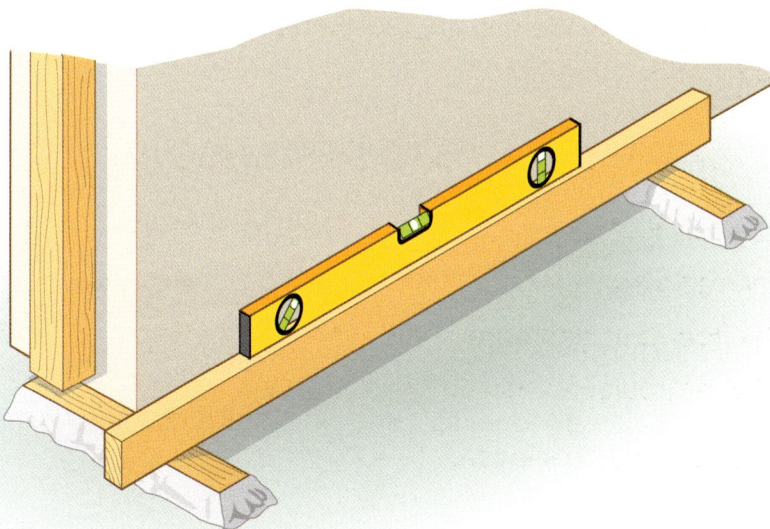

Figure 9.9 Placing dots with a rule and level

Laying larger floors

Larger floors may require a different method of laying. You may need to lay the floor in 'bays' in a chequerboard method. This allows you to walk between the bays. Referring to Figure 9.10, you may lay all of the bays marked '1' on one day and then come back and lay all of the bays marked '2' the next day. The joints in between are know as '**daywork joints**' and are just vertical butt joints. They should be grouted before laying the next day's bays. To prevent too many joints, try to lay the biggest area you can in one day.

1	2	1	2
2	1	2	1
1	2	1	2
2	1	2	1

Figure 9.10 Laying floor screeds in bays

Standards

There are set standards of flatness, as listed below; these are taken from BS8204-1: 2002. The one you are required to work to should be listed in the specification.

Class	Hollow size showing under a 3 m rule
SR 1	3 mm
SR 2	5 mm
SR 3	10 mm

For a floor to be classed as level, it should be plus or minus 3 mm over a 3 m distance.

Types of floor finish

There are three types of finish to the face of the floor screed.

Trowel finish

This finish should be created by using a flooring trowel, which will give a reasonably smooth finish to the face. This finish is best used if only a thin type of floor covering is to be placed on the floor later.

Float finish

This finish is completed with the large float, which tends to bring the grains of sand up to the surface. This finish is used if there is to be a covering of wooden blocks or thicker coverings, etc.

Latex finish

This is sometimes called a 'smoothing compound', but most people would know it as 'self-levelling compound' or 'latex finish'. It is a trowelled finish of cement and silver sand with glue additives, which is trowelled thinly onto the finished surface. It takes out all the small hollows and leaves a smooth finish.

Curing

There are two methods of controlling the curing.

The first method is to cover the floor with a plastic sheet and allow it to sweat under the cover. The water will drop from the plastic back onto the floor. A little water can be sprayed under the plastic over the next seven days to help the floor to cure fully. After seven days, the floor surface will be very hard.

The second method is to use a chemical curing agent which is sprayed directly onto the floor surface. After a number of days, this will break down and leave the face free of any curing agent.

> **Remember**
>
> Try to keep people and construction traffic off your floor for about seven days. Always put down scaffolding boards or wooden sheeting on top of the plastic if people have to walk on the floor

Drying-out periods

All floors should be allowed to dry naturally. A rule of thumb calculation is to allow one day for each millimetre of thickness. Under normal conditions, you need to allow about a month for 25 mm floors, two months for 50 mm floors and a 100 mm floor might need as much as four months to dry out.

Flooring faults

Poor workmanship can cause faults to happen. Some of the more common ones are listed in the following table.

Cause	Possible effects
Poor preparation of sub-base	Cracking and lack of bond
Mix too dry	Hard to lay and finish – gives a weak finished floor
Too much cement	Shrinkage cracks (not enough sand to bind onto the cement)
Too little cement	Shrinkage cracks and will break down when a load is put on the floor
Too much water	Hard to form a flat level surface, floor will shrink more as it dries out and surface will be weak
Poor mixing of material	Could leave pockets of sand with no cement, or vice versa
Over-trowelling / trowelling too soon	Brings water to the surface with cement, reducing strength and possibly causing cracking; when the floor dries, it leaves cement dust on the surface
Poor curing	Weakens the surface, causing curling at the edges and joints and possible cracking

Table 9.1 Flooring faults

Testing for lack of bond

This is a simple check to be used either side of any cracks in the screed, at the edges and corners of the bays.

Test by tapping with a hammer or rod and listen for a hollow ringing sound. This will show that the screed has not bonded with the base. You should do this test four weeks after laying.

Repairing hollows

Either drill holes into the screed at the area of the hollow and pour in a liquid synthetic resin, or cut out the hollow area, prepare the sub-base properly and re-lay a new screed.

Remember

Unbonded and floating floors will always sound hollow

On the job: Laying a floor screed

Phil has been asked by his employer to prepare the levels in house number 4 ready for him to come in and lay the floors. When Phil goes into the house, he notices that the radiators for the house are stored in the living room and that there are no datum points visible. He also sees that the door linings have been taken right down to the floor. What should Phil do now?

Laying floors to falls

The process of laying floors to falls is very similar to that of laying flat floors: the tools, materials and preparation of the subfloor are the same as for flat floors. The method of setting out and working from the initial screeds is the same as for flat floors. The mix proportions and the finish are the same. The difference is that this type of flooring allows for drainage to a given point, such as a drainage outlet. This type of floor is used in an area that may require washing down after use, such as a food preparation area.

This type of floor is very difficult for a trainee to lay, as it requires quite advanced skills with the flooring rules. It is best to practise on flat floors before attempting a floor to falls.

Setting out falls

If you are asked to lay to a fall of 1 in 100 or 1:100, this means that, for every 100 mm of length, the drop or fall of the floor will be 1 mm. Again, an example would be that a floor that is 10 m long to an outlet will have to fall by 10 cm.

Establishing the level

The equipment you use is the same as for flat floors, but you work to a given distance and a given measurement out of level. It could be that you use a flooring rule for setting out the screeds that is tapered to the required fall.

Other methods for use over longer distances are the cowley, water or dumpy level. These would be used with a calculated distance to give correct falls.

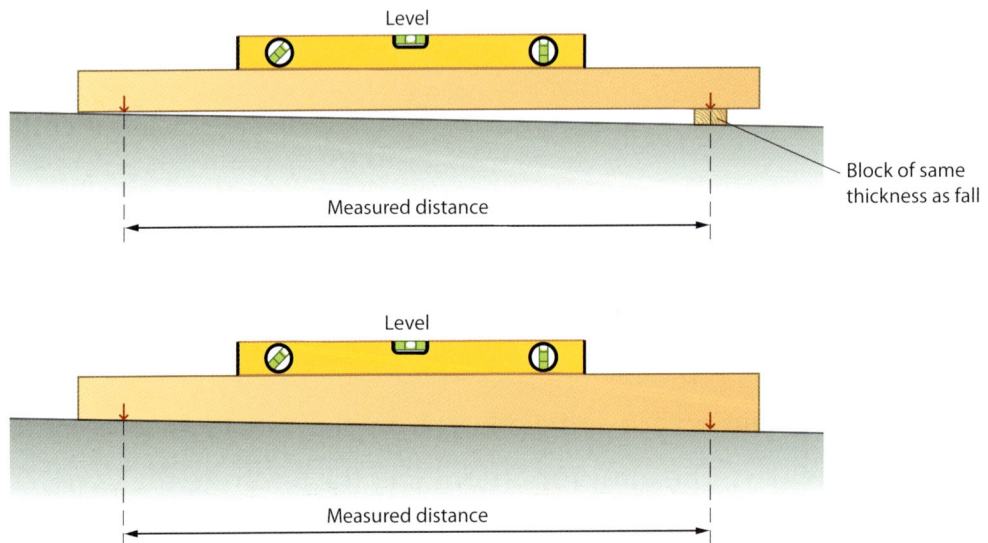

Figure 9.11 Using a flooring rule to set out the required fall

Laying the falls

First the gully that is to take the water away should be fixed in position before you start to set out the screeds. The preparation is completed in the same way as for flat floors. The screeds are taken from the corner of the gully back to the finished point of the floor, where it should pick up with the datum point set up for the thickness of the floor to achieve the required fall.

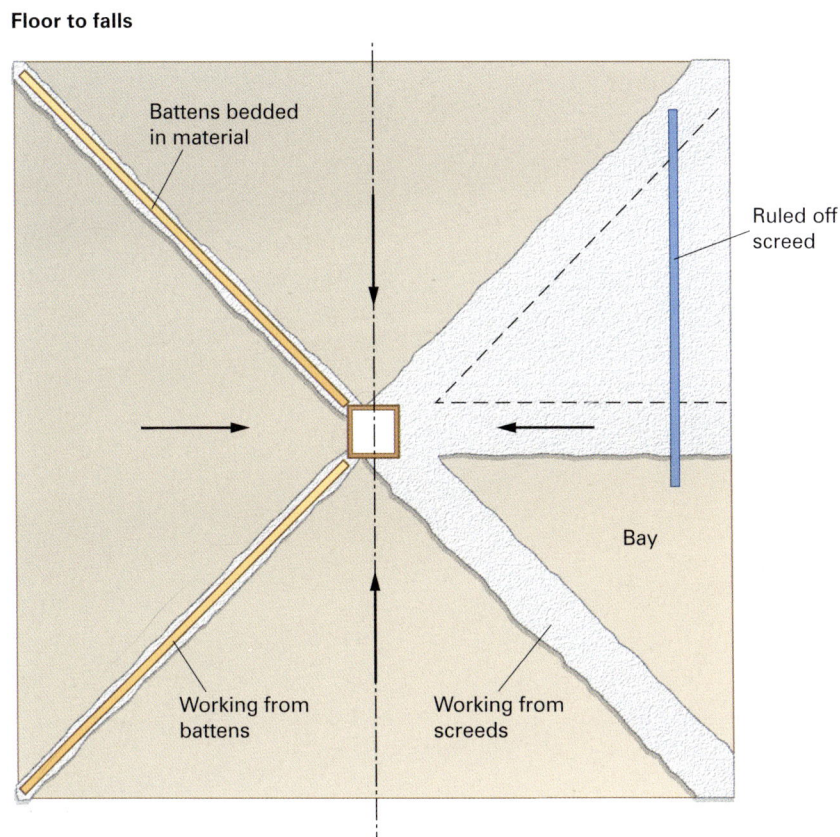

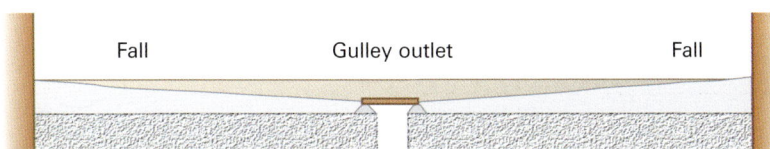

Floor to falls

Figure 9.12 Laying floor to a fall: top, plan view (alternative methods shown each side of centre line); bottom, section

The screeds can be either sand and cement or timber battens bedded into the screed.

The ruling in for the floor from the screeds is more difficult than for flat floors because it may well narrow down towards the gully, as you can see in Figure 9.12. This means that you will need to angle the rule as you work, otherwise you will dig into the sand and cement on your right and left.

The finish could be either float or trowel finished according to the specification.

FAQ

Can an ordinary plastering trowel be used for floor screeding?

Yes it can, but it should not be your finishing trowel: a small trowel can leave more trowel marks.

What should I do if my employer tells me to just lay the floor and don't waste time packing it down?

This is a problem because you may feel that your employer is not doing the job properly, and you want to tell him or her. It is important for you to be happy with the work that you do, as this could reflect on you personally and affect future work opportunities.

I am laying the floor and find that I cannot get the recommended thickness all over the floor. In one place it is very thin because of the unevenness of the subfloor. What should I do?

If you are a trainee, you should go straight to your employer and explain the problem. Your employer should go to a site supervisor and explain the situation because it could cost money if it is necessary to dig up the floor, lower the level of the sub-base and re-lay. If your employer explains the problem straightaway the problem can be sorted early in the floor-laying process.

What should I do if I cannot get a good finish on the floor surface?

Sometimes the screed will be too dry to form a good finish because of poor mixing, the screed hanging around too long before laying, or the mixed screed drying out, in the sun or near to the heating, etc. To get a good finish, you may have to wet down the mix a little, either by spraying with water, or by splashing water onto the face of the screed by hand or brush before trowelling off or floating up.

Knowledge check

1. What tool is used to transfer a datum point from one room to another?

2. Which type of cement mixer is preferred for mixing floor screed?

3. What is the purpose of using a float?

4. Name two types of power used for mixers.

5. What is the voltage rating for mixers?

6. What type of material is best for a level and why?

7. What is the recommended size of a floor screeding rule?

8. Why should kneepads be worn during the laying process?

9. Name three tools required for laying a floor.

10. What can dry out the natural oils from the hands?

11. Should builder's sand be used for floor screeding?

12. Name two places where your floor screed levels can be taken from.

13. Explain the reason for using grout.

14. Why are bays used in the laying of floor screeds?

15. When mixing by hand, what is the recommended mix proportion?

16. When using a 3 m long flooring rule, how far out of level can you be?

17. When laying a floor between the screeds, do you work away from the door or towards the door?

18. What thickness of floor screed should be used for a bonded screed?

19. What is the purpose of a dot?

20. Name two methods of finishing off the surface of a floor.

chapter 10

Dry lining by direct bond

OVERVIEW

Dry lining has developed more than any other form of plastering in the past number of years. It is now very hard to find any new building that does not have some form of dry lining in it, especially in the housing market.

Direct bond is a system that is classed as a dry method of producing a flat wall surface and is used mainly in the new housing market. It involves securing sheets of plasterboard directly to the background surface, leaving an air space between the plasterboard and the background. This system will produce a much warmer house than a traditional plastered surface because plasterboard is a better insulator than solid plaster, and the air gap forms an extra insulating layer. Its speed of construction makes it ideal for quick house building, and the drying-out time of the wall covering is a lot less than for solid plaster. This allows decoration to take place sooner and allows the new house owner to move in sooner, which means a quicker financial return for the house builder.

This chapter will cover the following topics:

- Tools and equipment
- Materials
- Background
- Setting out
- Fixing
- Taping and jointing
- Sealing

Tools and equipment

Tools

These tools would be used for the installing of the direct bond system (see Chapter 4 for more details, including photographs).

- Hawk and trowel for applying adhesive dabs
- Tape measure
- Pad saw
- Chalk line
- Spirit level
- Square for fixing returns
- Straight edge
- Foot lifter
- Board saw
- Internal corner trowel
- Taping
- Applicator
- Hand sander and universal sander
- Jointing sponge

Equipment

- Hand-held electric mixer (110 volt) – for mixing adhesives
- Whisk or paddle – for use with the electric mixer
- Plastic mixing drum – for large quantities of adhesives
- Hand plunger – for mixing smaller quantities of adhesives

- Different sizes of buckets or containers for different quantities of adhesive

- Spot board and stand

- Cement pan for keeping jointing material in – used with the taping knife

- Access equipment if required

Materials

Types of board

See Chapter 6 for a discussion of the various types of wallboard that are available. For dry lining by direct bond, the following types of board are ideal:

- tapered edged wallboards

- 9.5 or 12.5 mm thickness

- 900 or 1200 mm width

Tapered edge plasterboard is a board which is thinner at the edges.

Jointing materials

There are different jointing materials available on the market, some of which are pre-mixed and come in sealed tubes, and some of which come in powdered form and need site mixing. These are gypsum-based for a fast set with hand taping and jointing, and lime-based for a material that will set in the air and so take longer to harden. Each jointing material will have its own trade name according to the manufacturer. Jointing materials fall into several categories.

Setting material is used for filling in the joints between the boards. It does not need atmospheric or humid conditions as it will set on its own. It is usually used for hand application.

Safety tip

When using powdered fillers, wear a face mask when mixing them, and work in a well-ventilated area; thin protective gloves will also protect the hands during taping and jointing

Remember

If the setting material is applied too thinly, it may dry out before it hardens. If this happens, it may not allow the paper reinforcing tape to bind into the jointing compound

Air-drying material is usually applied thinly and needs air-drying conditions. It can be used for machine jointing or hand application, and can be used as a filler, but it will require a number of thin coats because a greater time needs to be allowed for joints with greater depth.

Part setting + part air-drying combines the two materials mentioned above. It can be used for two-stage application.

Mixing of jointing materials

The three types of material come in powder form but the air-drying material also comes in pre-mixed form. If the material requires mixing, make sure that it is well mixed as per the manufacturer's instructions. The jointing materials should be mixed to form a smooth paste with no lumps or small particles of hard materials. It is very important that all mixing tools and equipment are perfectly clean because small, hard particles will rip out the jointing area and prevent a fair face finish.

Joint reinforcement

To help prevent the joints between the boards from moving and cracking, reinforcement is needed. This comes in many forms and different operatives will have their own preferences.

Paper joint tape is a thick grade of paper that has minute holes or perforations in it to allow the jointing compound to bind into it. It has a crease running down the middle of it for internal angles, and is very strong.

Self-adhesive glass fibre mesh is a form of fibreglass tape that has its own glue attached during manufacture. It has an open mesh. It is also very strong, but it can be easily cut with a sharp steel tool.

Reinforced paper corner tape is a strong paper tape that has two strips of thin metal imbedded into one side of the paper, with a fold separating the two strips. It is used for external angles.

Drywall metal beads are the same as the metal beads used in internal plastering for reinforcing external angles when applying a finishing coat. Some manufacturers have the mesh of the wings smaller than for a finishing coat. These beads are easier to use on external angles than reinforced paper tape, but are more expensive.

Drywall plastic beads are similar to metal beads.

Glass fibre mesh is not recommended by manufacturers because of the greater ease in cutting the tape during application with sharp tools.

Background

Most backgrounds are suitable for direct bond except painted surfaces. Also, any background that has a damp problem should be cured first. The surface should be free from dust, foreign matter, oil and any large mortar snots. The masonry work should be of good quality and the line of blocks, bricks or concrete should be as level as possible. For a secure fixing, the **dabs** need to be no less than 10 mm and no more than 25 mm thick. A wall that is poorly built and is not level would need dabs that are outside of this range and the lining would therefore be less secure.

The ceiling should be boarded prior to the beginning of setting out the direct bond. This may have been done by a specialist known as a 'tacker' or 'boarder'.

The amount of moisture content in a background will change its suction characteristics. If the background is wet, you must allow it to dry out first, otherwise the adhesive will not bind into the background and will slip down the face of the wall.

In dry, hot conditions, try to prevent the adhesive drying out too quickly before the adhesive sets properly:

- Avoid through draughts of wind.

Definition

Dab – a trowel length of adhesive that is applied to the wall. It should be raised up and then tapered down to smear into the wall. This raised part of the dab is what holds the plasterboard to the wall, and the smeared part is what holds the dab to the wall

Remember

The background must be of a good standard – poor backgrounds may need a different system of dry lining to straighten them out

- Try to work so that you follow the progress of the sun as it works its way around the building.

- On very hot days, you may need to kill the high levels of suction by damping down the walls with a little water.

Try not to install dry lining before the building is adequately dry because it can have a bad effect on both the building and the lining itself. If you do not allow the background to dry out, it will retain that moisture. This water may well get into the plasterboard and affect its strength by making the boards wet. It can also lead to mould growth in the form of black mildew, and this can get into timbers such as the skirting boards.

Services

All electrical services should be passed behind the boards in the air void. Any wires or pipes that are thicker than the air void should be chased into the background if possible. If not, the air gap behind the board should be increased.

Lighting and electrical boxes should be cut out of the plasterboard as the work proceeds. All frames and door linings should be designed for the board thickness being used.

Setting out

Setting out for a plain wall

1. Find the high spot of the wall. This will be a brick, a block or a piece of concrete that stands out from the rest of the wall. The reason for finding this point is that, if you ignore the high spot and start at a low or hollow point then, when you reach a high spot, the board will stand proud of the rest of the wall and so cause a bump which will prevent the wall from being flat and true.

2. Transfer the high spot by plumbing it up to the ceiling as shown in Figure 10.1 and also down to the floor.

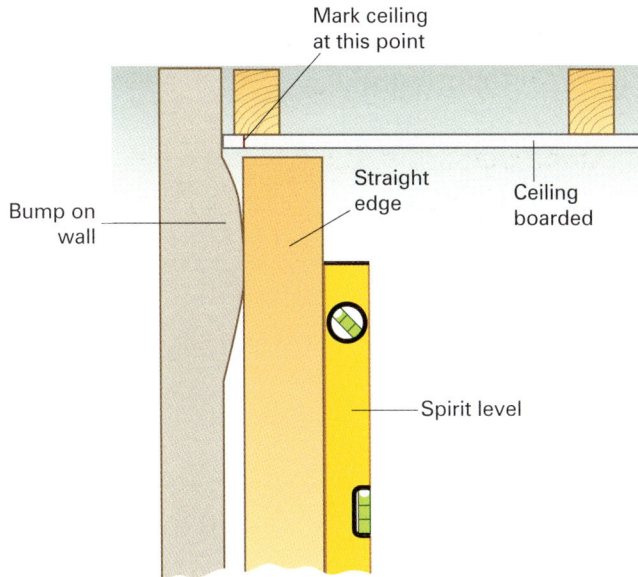

Mark ceiling
at this point

Bump on
wall

Straight
edge

Ceiling
boarded

Spirit level

Figure 10.1 Transferring the high spot of the wall

3. The ceiling will now have a pencil mark showing the high spot of the wall. So, from this mark on the ceiling, add 10 mm for the thickness of the dab of adhesive plus the plasterboard thickness onto this mark (Figure 10.2).

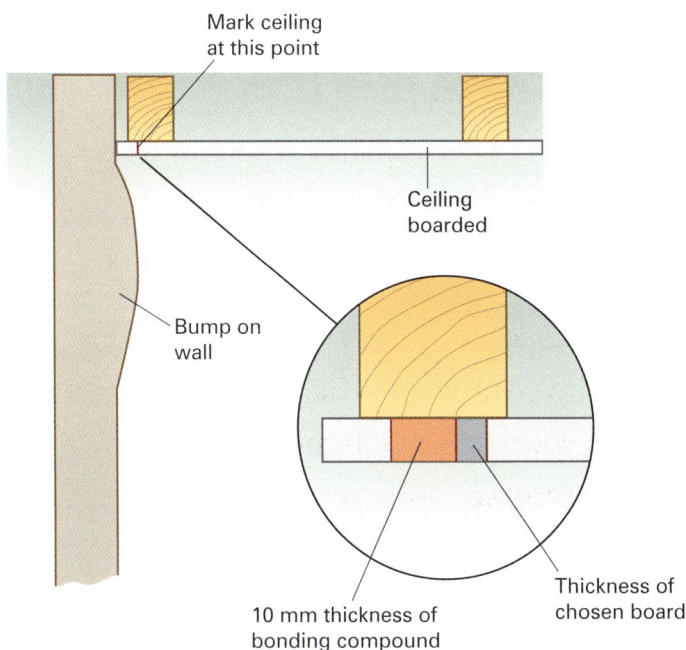

Mark ceiling
at this point

Ceiling
boarded

Bump on
wall

10 mm thickness of
bonding compound

Thickness of
chosen board

Figure 10.2 Additional marking out onto ceiling

Chalk line snapped along ceiling at a distance of high spot plus thickness of adhesive and thickness of board

Figure 10.3 Setting out with the chalk line

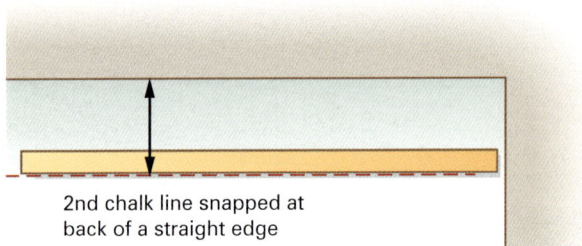

2nd chalk line snapped at back of a straight edge

Figure 10.4 Second line set out

4. Take the new measurement and transfer it to each end of the ceiling and re-mark it. Take the chalk line, shake well, and run out to the full length of the wall. With some help, take the line through the marks at each end of the wall and snap. There should now be a chalk mark on the ceiling, as shown in Figure 10.3. Alternatively, just have the one pencil mark and, using your eye, make sure that the chalk line is through the mark and running parallel to the face of the wall, and then snap the line.

Or, for ease of lining in the boards, when fixing, a second chalk line can be added. First, place the straight edge face onto the chalk line on the ceiling and mark the back of the rule. Complete this at both ends of the chalk line. When complete, snap a second line through these two points (Figure 10.4). The use of this second chalk line will make it easier when taping back the boards when fixing. When the back edge of the straight edge touches the line, the board is in the correct position.

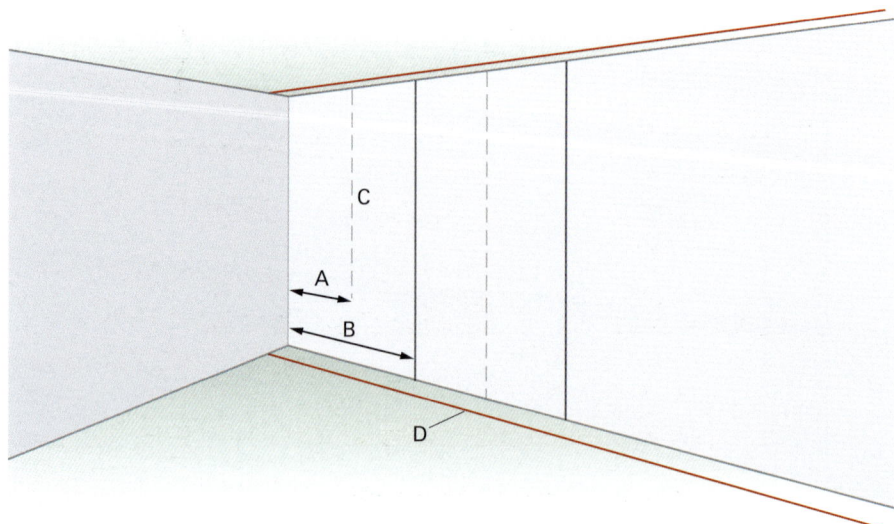

Figure 10.5 Marking out the width of the boards

5. Transfer these lines on the ceiling down to the floor by the use of a straight edge and level or plumb line. This will help you to keep the plasterboards plumb (vertical).

6. Working from the internal angle, mark out the width of the boards, either 900 or 1200 mm.

Then mark the centre of each board, 450 or 600 mm (A and C in Figure 10.5). The marking of the wall should be plumb and can be completed with a piece of old plasterboard. This acts like a piece of chalk.

Attached piers

If an attached pier is built into, say, the middle of a wall as shown in Figure 10.6, you should get the face of the pier running parallel to the back wall. To do this, lay a rule on the floor and then measure the distance from

> **Remember**
>
> Setting out is very important as it will affect the finished quality of your work

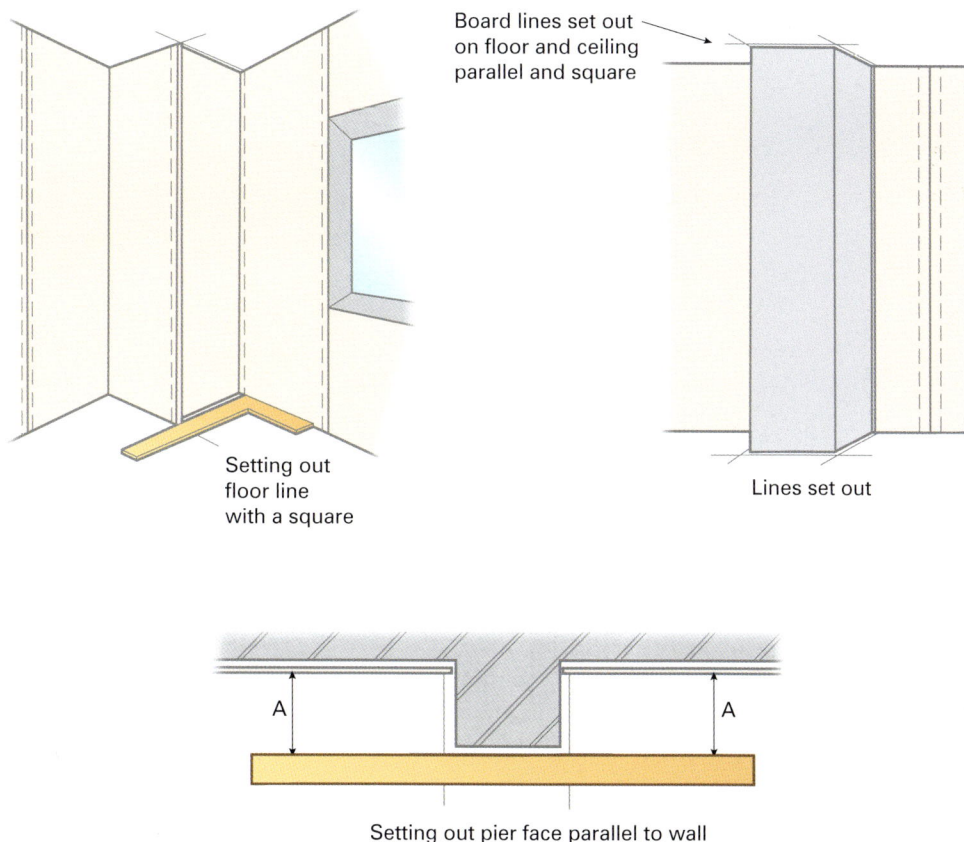

Board lines set out on floor and ceiling parallel and square

Setting out floor line with a square

Lines set out

A   A

Setting out pier face parallel to wall

Figure 10.6 Setting out for attached piers

the face of the pier at 'A' each side of the pier. Adjust the rule until the measurement is the same either side of the pier and then draw a line on the floor. Next, add on the thickness of the adhesive dab and the plasterboard and redraw the line to this thickness. Repeat this on the ceiling.

The plasterboard can then be fixed to these guidelines.

Window openings

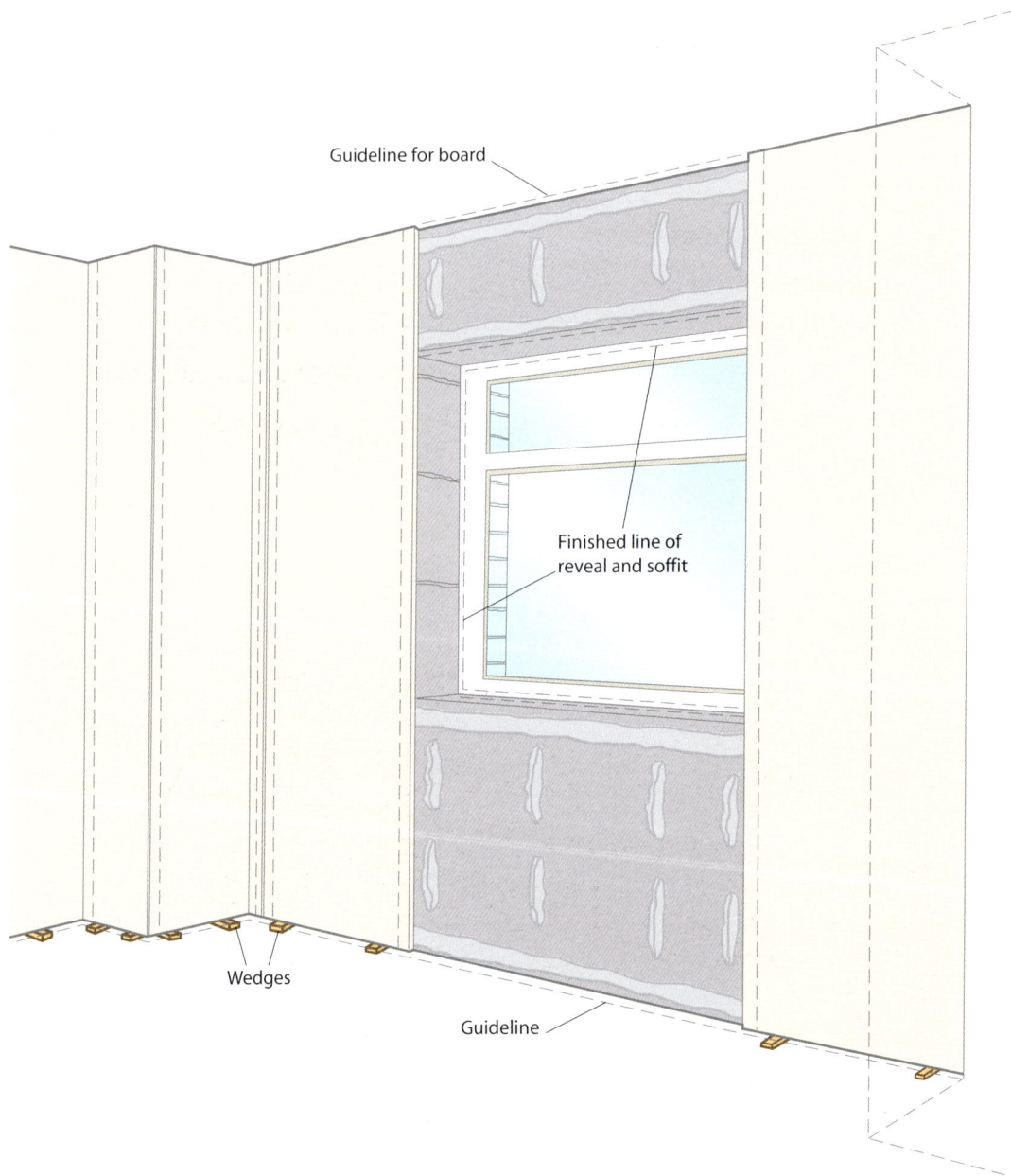

Guideline for board

Finished line of reveal and soffit

Wedges

Guideline

Figure 10.7 Guidelines marked out for boards around a window opening

To set out a wall in which there is a window opening, you should first follow steps 1–5 for setting out for a plain wall. You will now have the guidelines on the ceiling and floor which will help keep the wallboards plumb.

To mark out the width of the boards, start from the vertical external angles of the window opening, and mark out the full widths of boards from the window opening towards the internal angles at either end of the wall.

When planning the wall, always ensure that any cut edges of plasterboard are at internal angles or the sides of any windows or doors.

Make sure that the tapered edge of the first board overhangs the vertical external angle very slightly to allow for a neat external angle joint when bedding the plasterboard onto the window reveal/return.

The window opening may not be exactly the same width as a complete board (or multiple complete boards). If this is the case, a wallboard will need to be cut to fit. Mark out any full board widths (if the window opening is wide enough) and measure any gaps that will need to be filled by a cut piece of board.

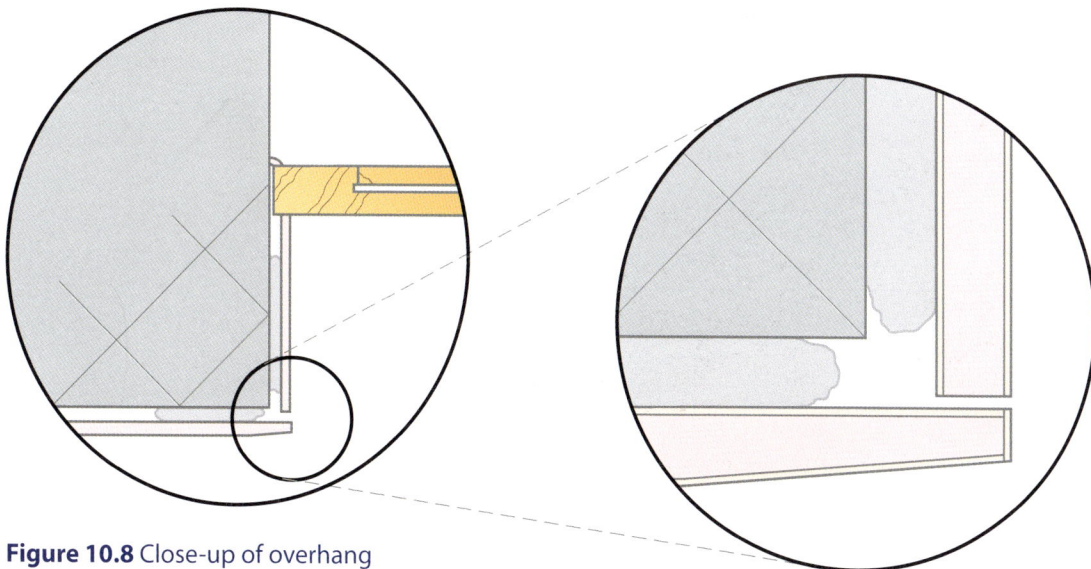

Figure 10.8 Close-up of overhang

Enlarged detail at the angle of the reveal

Wallboards will also have to be cut for the section of wall above the window opening, the same as for the board below the window.

Over the head of the window, a continuous strip of adhesive should be positioned to allow for fixing of curtain rails. Once the setting out is complete, the window wall should be completed as for a plain wall.

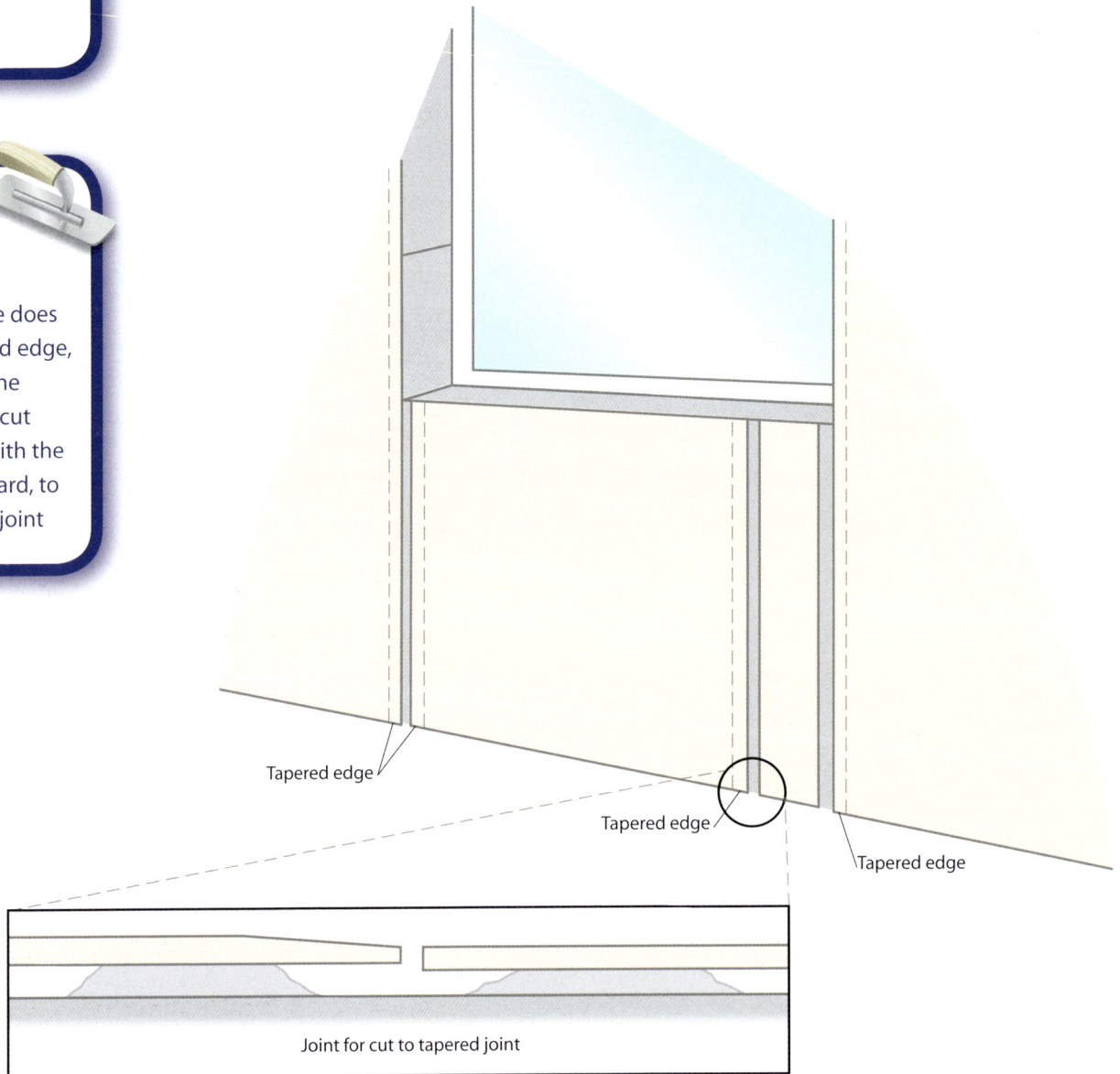

Tapered edge

Tapered edge

Tapered edge

Joint for cut to tapered joint

Figure 10.9 Wallboards cut to size under the window opening

Fixing

Fixing to a plain wall

1. Fix one board at a time (A in Figure 10.10) after cutting to the height of the room less 15 mm.

2. By using a trowel, apply a continuous fillet of adhesive around the perimeter of the wall (F and G), services and openings where required (Figure 10.10).

Figure 10.10 Fixing boards to a plain wall

3. Start the dry lining from a position so that any cut edges are at internal angles or the side of any doors or windows.

4. Apply adhesive dabs (C and D) approximately the length of a trowel (250 mm long) and about 50–75 mm wide. The dabs should be placed no nearer than 25 mm to the board edge lines. The dabs can be placed directly on the centre line and you should put a continuous strip of adhesive at the skirting line. There should now be three lines of adhesive.

5. Position the cut plasterboard, grey face inwards, against the dabs, with the bottom edge of the board resting on some old plasterboard strips (E).

6. Tap the board back with a straight edge until the board lines up with the chalk lines on the ceiling and floor (B). If an outside line has also been included, the board should be tapped back until the outside edge of the straight edge lines up with this second outside line, when the straight edge is resting against the board face.

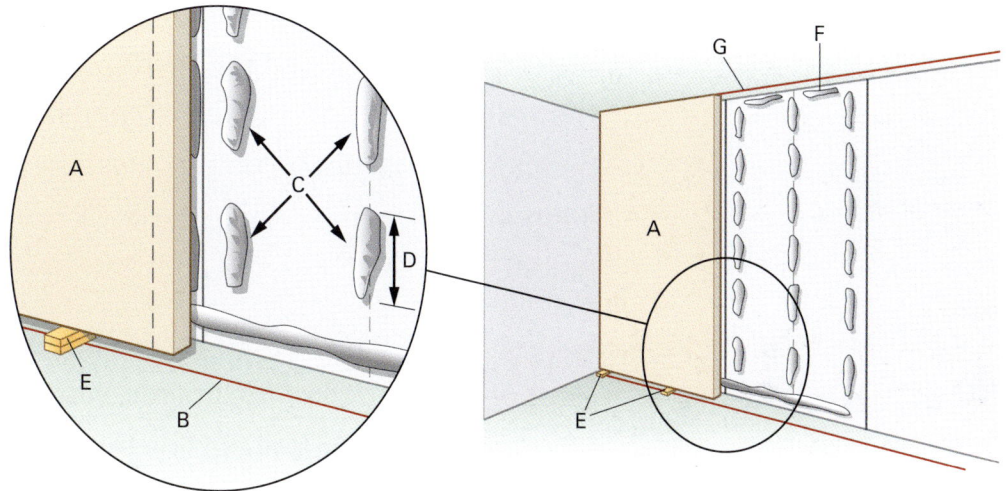

Did you know?

The adhesive at the bottom of the wall is for the skirting to be fixed to if nailing or screwing it. Extra dabs of adhesive are placed around power sockets and light switches, plus any specified points as required, to provide a solid base for any fixings

7. Slide in the foot lifter and lift the board tight up against the ceiling. Wedge the board in place with further strips of board and remove the foot lifter. The board should not slip down the wall. Place a level on the edge of the board to check for plumb. This prevents trimming of further boards. If the boards are not plumb by the time you get to the end of the wall you may have to trim a tapered board to fit. Also, if a board is not plumb it will not be tight against the ceiling line. If the board next to it is tight against the ceiling line it will open the joint between the two boards.

8. For the next sheet, prepare the wall as for step 4 and proceed as for steps 5–7. The edge of the boards should be lightly butted together. Check that the boards are in line by sliding the straight edge along the face and check diagonally.

A continuous band of adhesive (called a 'perimeter seal') is placed around the walls to prevent air movement. Also, any mortar gaps between the background of bricks and blocks must be filled to maintain the thermal insulation.

Separating walls

On walls that are built between houses, to fulfil Part E of the Building Regulations, to stop sound going from one house to another, companies have produced a 'parge coat', which is applied directly to the wall before direct bond is started. It is 6 mm thick, must not be scratched and must be left with a trowel finish. Sand and cement can also be used, but it must be 8 mm thick (check first with the specification).

When using 'insulation boards' in the direct bond system – for example, in a hall wall against an 'integral garage' (a garage built within a house) – a special type of nail called a 'nailable plug' must be used to fix through the dab into the wall after the adhesive dabs have set. This is in case of fire: if a fire starts within the garage, the boards will not fail by falling off the wall but will remain because they are nailed and so will maintain their fire-protection function.

Remember

Check with the specification what type of board is needed when using a parge coat

Attached piers

The boards should be cut according to the width of the pier plus an extra bit on the width of the plasterboard (for the adhesive dabs that will be needed for sticking the plasterboard to the pier returns).

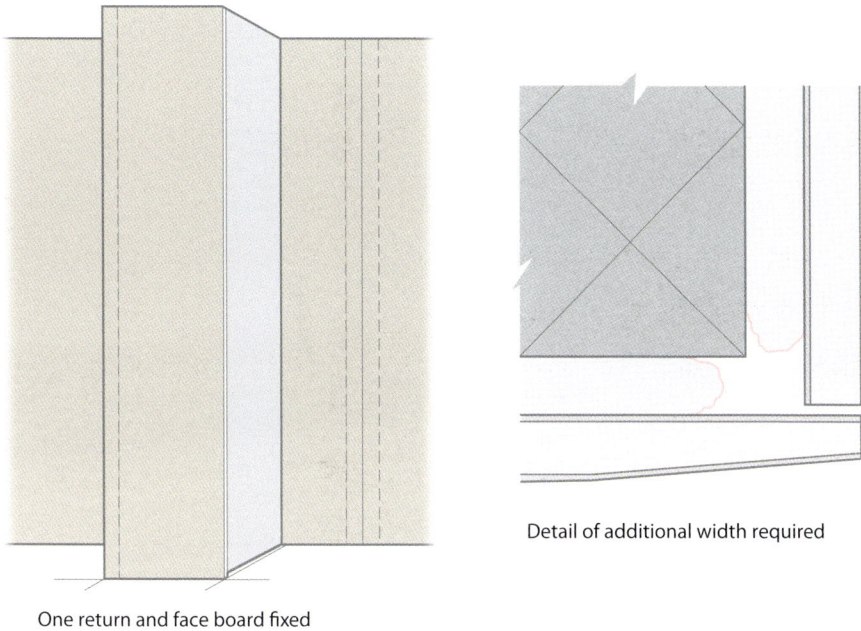

Detail of additional width required

One return and face board fixed

Figure 10.11 Fixing boards to an attached pier

All pier return plasterboard should be squared in from the plasterboard wall that the pier is attached to.

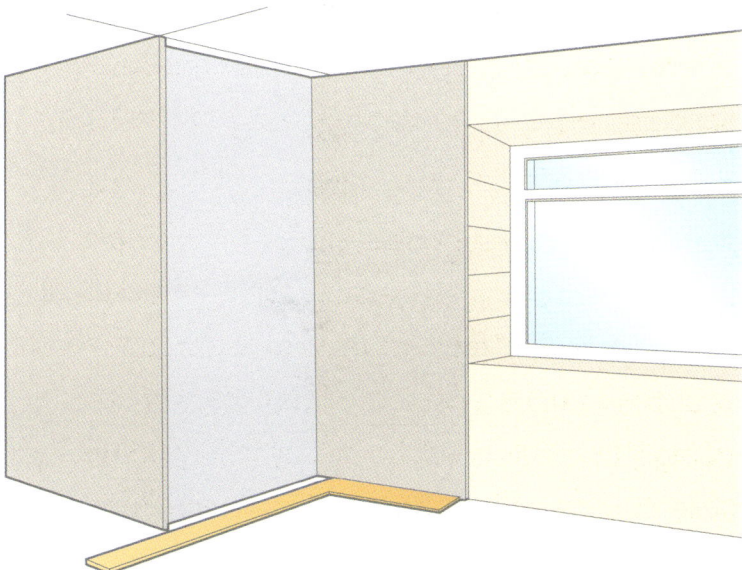

Figure 10.12 Returns squared in

Window openings

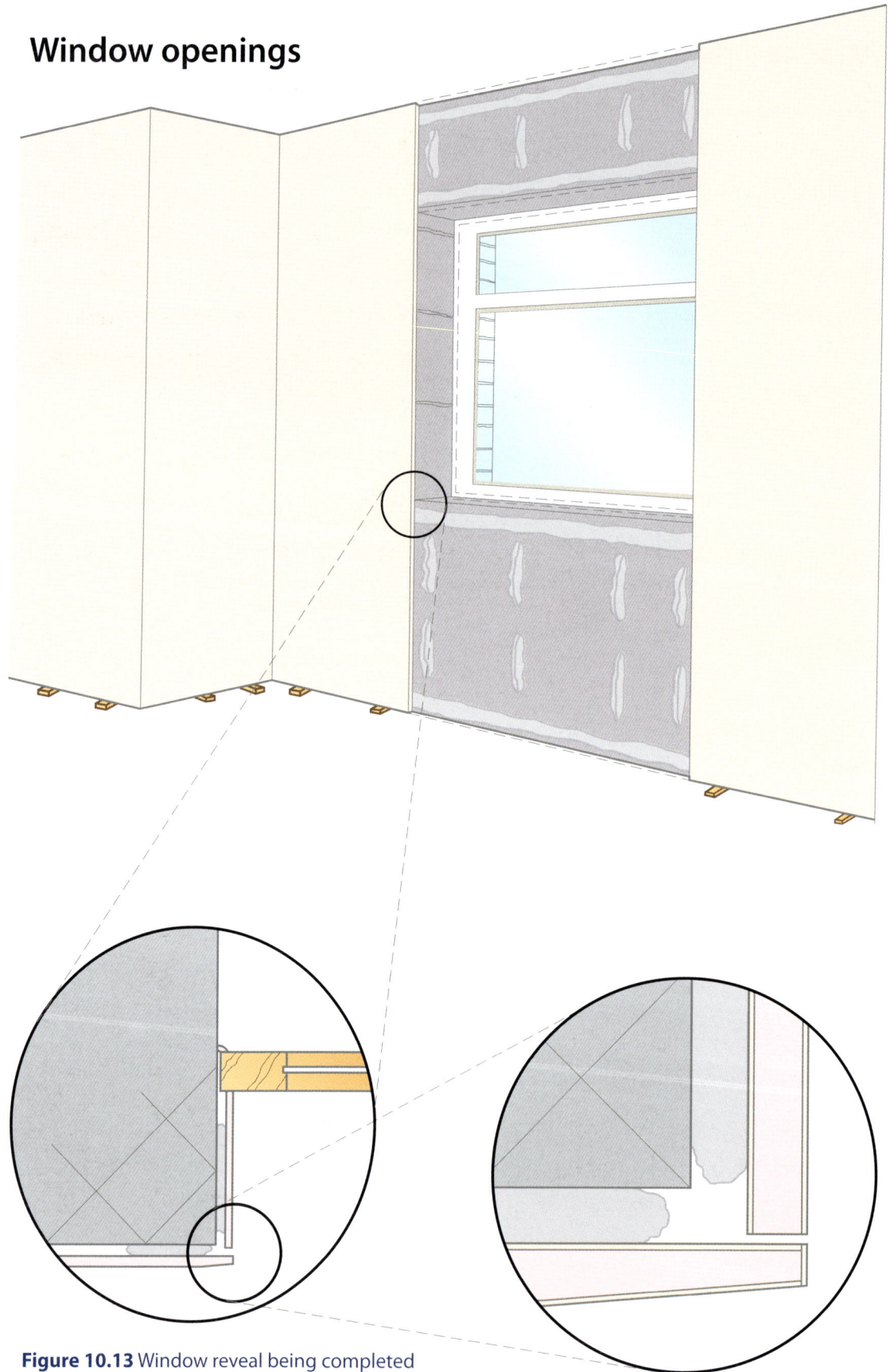

Figure 10.13 Window reveal being completed

1. Follow steps 1–7 described in 'Fixing to a plain wall' to fix the full boards to the wall in which the window opening sits. Remember to start the fixing so that any cut edges of board appear at the sides of windows and doors or internal angles.

2. Fix any full boards to the wall underneath the window opening following the same process. If necessary, cut wallboards to fit. If a cut wallboard is used, a cut square edge will butt up to an uncut tapered edge. Where this happens, taper back the cut edge so that it lines up with the tapered edge – this will make it easier to joint.

3. Over the head of the window, a continuous strip of adhesive should be positioned to allow for the fixing of curtain rails.

4. Fix cut boards to the wall above the window opening.

5. The window reveals are completed by cutting strips of board to the correct size. The board is then tapped back until it is in line with the edge of the face board (this should overhang to allow for this) and square with the window frame. Position the cut edge of the board to the window frame side of the reveal.

The plasterboard used on the soffit or head of the window opening will need to be held in position by wedging it in place with strips of plasterboard or lengths of timber (Figure 10.14).

Remember

Try not to have the cut end of the plasterboard showing on angles because it makes it harder to complete the jointing

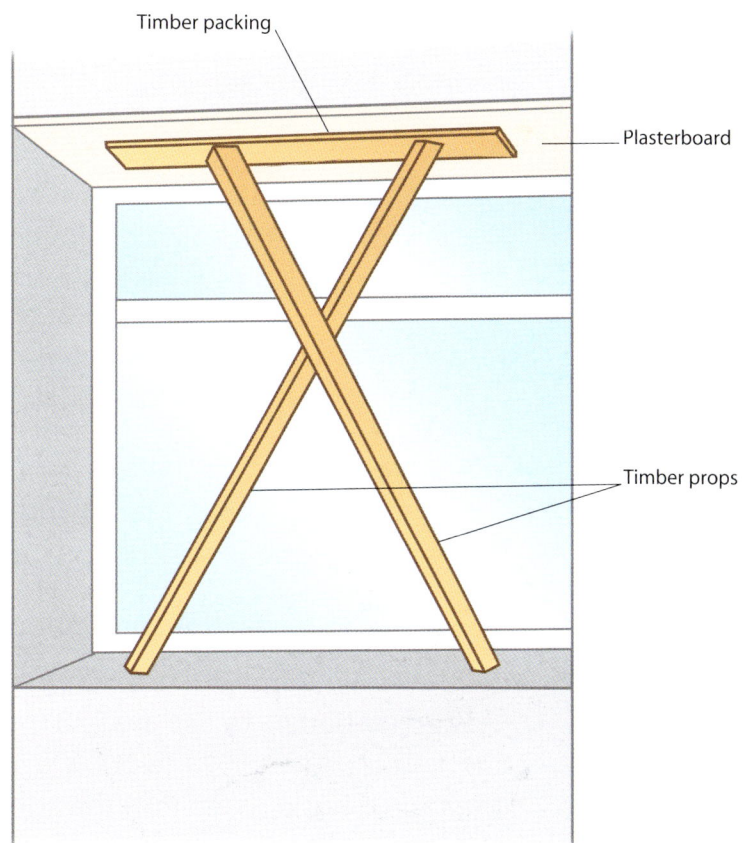

Figure 10.14 Plasterboard propped in position

Taping and jointing

Method of jointing

Here is a suggested order of applying joints:

1. internal angles

2. tapered edged joints

3. cut board edge joints

4. external angles

Method of forming straight joints

1. Cut tape to the required length allowing for the tape at ceiling line. Note that the ceiling/wall line will need to be taped unless coving is to be fixed later.

2. Apply a band of jointing material to the depression of the tapered edge board. This can be done with a trowel or a filling knife.

3. Press the tape into the filler with the toe of the trowel or filling knife. Press it in firmly. There should be no more than 1mm of filler under the tape. Ensure that all the air has been forced out so that no air bubbles are left.

4. Cover the tape with joint filler flush with the board. Use a damp jointing sponge to feather out excess filler on the face of the board.

5. Apply a further two coats of joint filler once each coat has dried, feathering each coat out beyond the previous application. Use a damp jointing sponge for feathering out.

6. Sand down each joint application to achieve a smooth finish. Be careful not to over-sand, otherwise it will roughen up the face of the paper tape.

   Sanding papers to use are 120 grit or 150 grit.

If the tape is not pressed into the adhesive as in step 3, it will blister. If blistering is found, it must be cut out and a new tape applied.

Any nail/screw holes should be 'spotted' (filled in) with the same number of jointing applications.

Method of forming internal angles

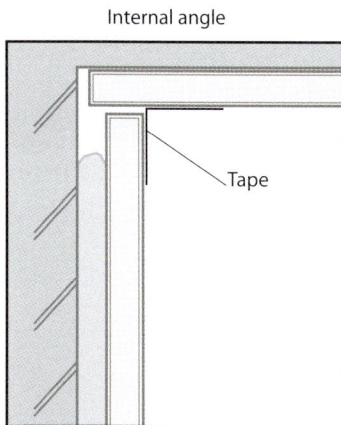

Internal angle

Tape

Figure 10.15 Taping internal angles

At internal angles the tape should be folded along the centre line. Jointing material should then be applied either side of the angle and the tape pressed firmly into it. The procedures and standards for straight joints should be followed.

Method of forming external angles

For exposed angles, use an external angle dry lining bead. For unexposed angles, use reinforced paper tape (this is a paper tape with two metal strips).

1. Spread jointing material 50 mm wide down each side of the angle. Ensure the area is well covered with material – a lack of material will create a bubble which will affect the quality of the angle. Bend tape at 90° and place into the material.

2. Using thumb and forefinger, press the tape into the jointing material. A slight pinching action will raise the nosing of the tape slightly, ensuring that further applications of jointing material do not overlap the paper tape.

3. Complete the jointing as shown from step 4 in the straight joint procedure described above.

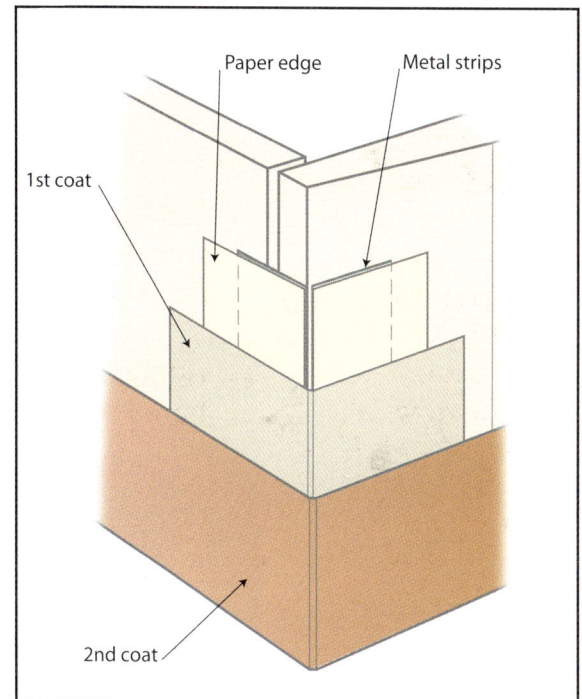

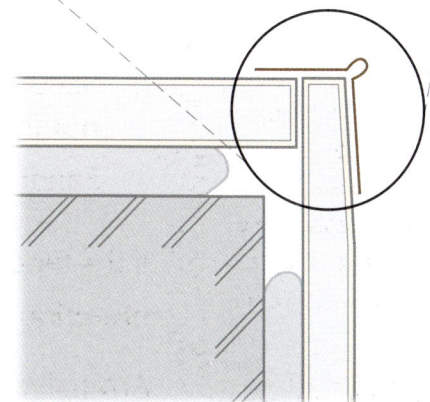

Paper edge   Metal strips

1st coat

2nd coat

Figure 10.16 Taping external angles

External angle paper tape

Sealing

When the jointing and sanding down have been completed, the boards should be brushed down to remove the dust. An application of proprietary board sealer should be applied by brush or roller over the boards and joints as per the manufacturer's instructions – this is called a 'sealing coat'. The faces of the board and the joint have different suctions, and the sealing coat seals both surfaces so that they are ready for decoration. Many problems and mistakes that people make with dry lining relate to this sealing process: if sealing is not completed before decoration takes place, the joints will be seen through the finished decoration. This gives the impression that the work is of a poor standard even though the joints may be true and flat.

On the job: Dry lining

Ben has been given the job of dry lining a wall that runs up one side of a staircase. Three-quarters of the way up the stairs is a small window. Describe the method of setting out and fixing the plasterboards that Ben must use for this wall.

FAQ

Why are dry lining plasterboards finished by applying a sealing coat over the surface rather than just taping and jointing the joints and sealing the board face?

This is because many DIY people use steamers to take off wallpaper and some of them were even removing the paper surface from the plasterboard thus exposing the plaster core within the board.

Why are many of the general public suspicious of dry lining?

The general public is more suspicious of dry lining because, unlike traditional plastered walls, when you tap them, they sound hollow. They also dislike fixing to dry lining because of the need for special fixings – this may be beyond the skills of a less than capable DIY person.

Also, repairing damage to dry lining is more difficult, especially if there is a hole in the plasterboard.

Fixing to the plasterboard was difficult, although better fixing methods have helped. Even so, fixing heavier objects such as radiators is still a major task, especially for the DIY person.

Knowledge check

1. Name two types of reinforcing used for dry lining joints.

2. What spacing is used between adhesive dabs?

3. What is the first and most important thing to do when setting out the wall for boarding?

4. What is a tapered-edged plasterboard and why is it used in dry lining?

5. What are the thicknesses of tapered-edged plasterboards?

6. What tool is used for positioning the plasterboard tight to the ceiling boards and how is the board then kept in that position?

7. Give two reasons why the joints in plasterboard may still be visible after decoration.

8. What can be done to the joints to help in the jointing process when the jointer is inexperienced?

9. What should be the consistency of the adhesive used for fixing the plasterboard?

10. Where should a continuous band of adhesive be positioned?

chapter 11

Fibrous plasterwork

OVERVIEW

Fibrous plasterwork is the ornamental, decorative side of plastering. It is completely different from any of the work covered in previous chapters. The tools to be used are different from other areas of plastering you may have read about or worked on to date. The plaster you will work with is pure gypsum.

Fibrous plasterwork is almost a trade within a trade. It has been said by many people that you cannot call yourself a plasterer unless you can work in all aspects of the trade, and produce good quality work.

We shall cover the following topics in this chapter:

- Operations of fibrous plastering
- Tools, materials and equipment
- Construction of running moulds
- Methods of running out mouldings
- Casting techniques
- Moulding techniques

Operations of fibrous plastering

Fibrous plasterwork is made in workshops away from site, and then transported to the site area, where it is then fixed in position.

You will need the ability to think in many cases in reverse, to have a knowledge of geometry, to be able to measure accurately and to work, in many cases, with a delicate hand. You will need a great deal of patience, and must be able to work at the bench and not walk around. Fibrous plasterwork is a bench trade, unlike solid plastering, which allows you to move around site. The only time you will visit site is to fix what has been made or to take measurements.

The basic operations involved in fibrous plastering are:

- **Mould cutting** – a process of producing a running mould, which is used to form shapes in plaster. It includes a timber framework and a supporting template.

- **Running** – the use of a running mould to form shapes using plaster of Paris. When the plaster is set the shape is called a 'run moulding'.

- **Moulding process** – the forming of the reverse shape of an item in solid or flexible materials. From the 'mould' will be produced the finished product known as the 'cast'.

- **Casting** – the method used to produce the finished product from a mould.

Tools, materials and equipment

The operations involved in fibrous plasterwork and described above require a range of different tools, materials and equipment, most of which were described in Chapter 4.

Tools for making running moulds

Metal and woodworking tools are used for making the running moulds, and sometimes you may need drawing equipment, such as compasses, squares, etc. if you are not given a drawing to work from.

It is important to have a good range of hand files and needle files. Be sure that, among your hand files, you have some square edge files with a **safety edge** on one side, and some half round files used for curved shapes. All the files should be of a fine cut, not too coarse.

Take care when using needle files that you don't dig into part of the template that you do not want to file.

Snips are also much used and, as well as the normal plasterer's tin snips used for cutting the metal, sometimes smaller-sized snips or even **jeweller's snips** would help with smaller cuts.

The following tools are also required for making running moulds:

- hand saw
- rasp or Surform®
- claw hammer
- panel or cross pein hammer
- square
- small tools.

See Chapter 4, pages 99–109 for full descriptions of these tools.

Materials for making running moulds

The following materials are required to make a running mould.

Definition

Safety edge – some square edge files have one edge that is smooth, so that you do not cut into the side against which you are working

Definition

Jeweller's snips – small delicate snips, which have straight or curved blades

Timber

Timber is used to construct the stock or horse (see Figure 11.3 on page 305) of the running mould. It is important that you have wood that has two straight edges and is not too twisted. You can use second-hand wood as long as it is in good condition.

Exterior plywood can also be used, especially for larger running moulds.

Metal

This is usually zinc, although steel can sometimes be used. Steel is more difficult to cut and file but it does last longer when running out, and does not bend when put under heavy pressure. The required profile is cut into the zinc plate. When attached to the stock of the running mould, it becomes the template. When cutting and filing zinc, be careful because it is very soft and mistakes can be easily made.

Nails

You will need different sizes of nails for different thicknesses of wood. Do not use too long a nail as it will come through the timber and cause cuts to your hands when handling the running mould. You will need panel pins for fixing the template to the stock.

Equipment for running out mouldings

Fibrous plasterwork needs a range of different items of equipment.

Buckets

These should be made of heavy duty plastic because they will take a lot of wear. Used for mixing larger amounts of plaster, carrying water and rubbish.

Bowls

These are usually made from plastic or rubber, for easy cleaning after use. They are used for mixing up small quantities of plaster and for holding water.

Benches

These should be made to last, with a strong timber frame, usually about 3m long and 1m wide, but sizes will be different depending on the area you have to work in. The benches are made up as shown in Figure 11.1, and will have a topping of plaster, which makes it easier to repair holes and damage to the face of the bench, and thus easy to maintain. Some benches are covered with hard-wearing laminate (like a kitchen worktop) for making plain face slabs and they can be used for running out small amounts on site. The bench must have a true, straight running rule of timber or metal on each side for running out mouldings.

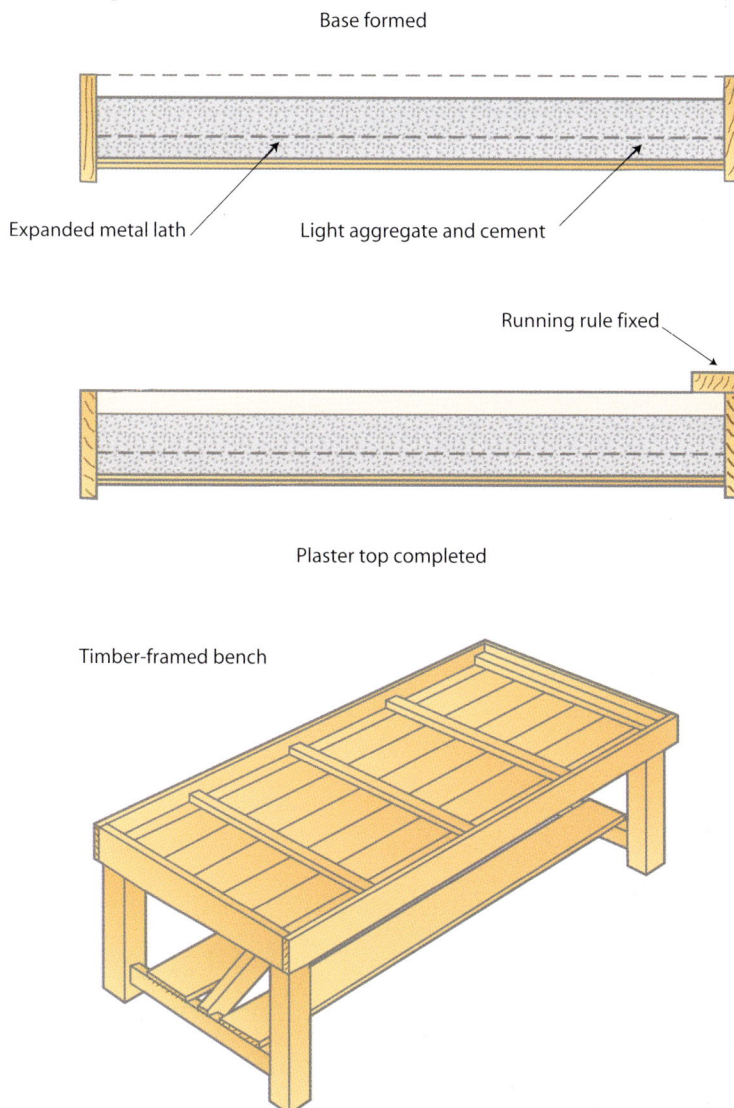

Base formed

Expanded metal lath   Light aggregate and cement

Running rule fixed

Plaster top completed

Timber-framed bench

Figure 11.1 Typical plaster bench

Remember

Old plaster slosh should be poured into a rubbish skip and not down the drain because it could cause a blockage

Plaster bin

This is used for the storage of plaster. It will keep it dry and out of the way, making the workshop cleaner and tidier.

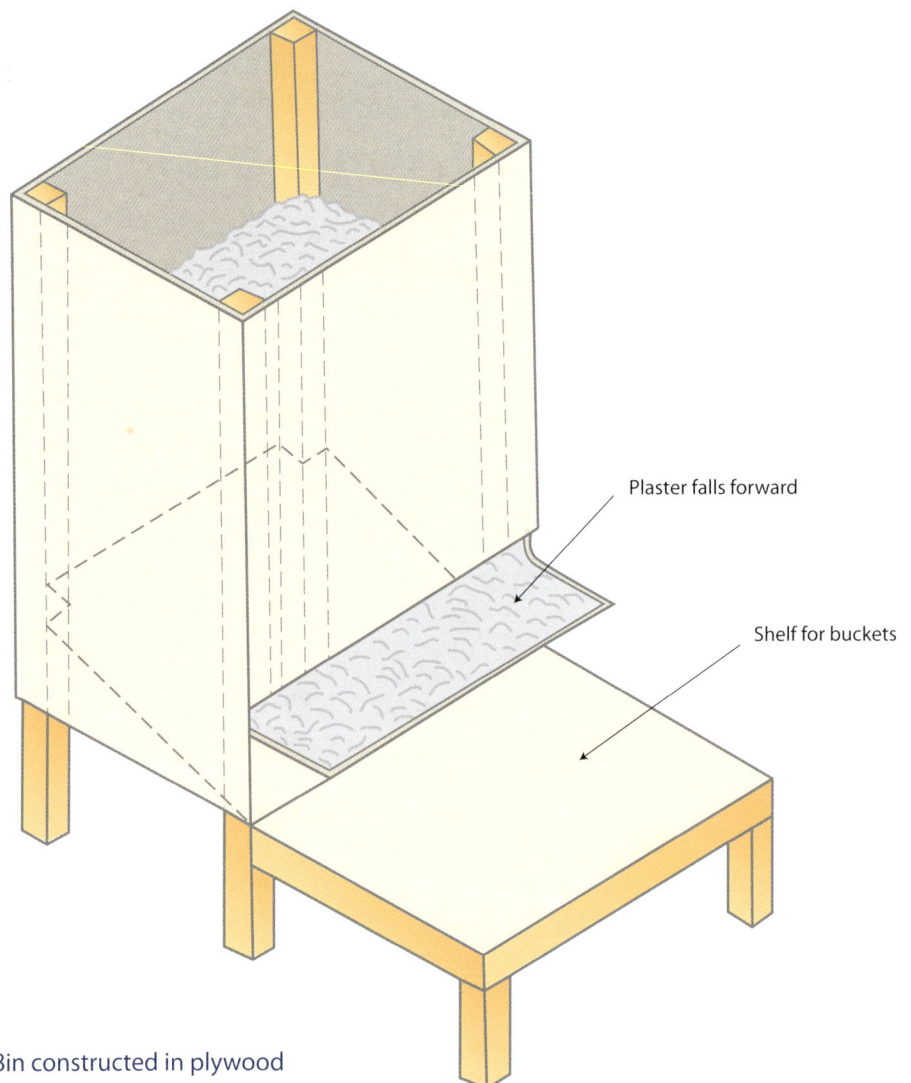

Plaster falls forward

Shelf for buckets

Figure 11.2 Bin constructed in plywood

Water tanks

Usually two water tanks are required. One is used for good clean drinking quality water for mixing of plaster; it may be connected to the water system by a valve that will keep the water topped up. A second tank would be used for cleaning out equipment and running moulds, etc. This tank is called a slosh tank, and will have to be cleaned out on a regular basis because the old plaster (or slosh) will build up. If left too long, it will begin to smell.

Materials for running out mouldings

Plaster

This is usually called casting plaster and is what you would know as plaster of Paris. The proper name is a hemi-hydrate plaster (Class A as specified in BS 1191). This means that, during manufacture, three-quarters of the water is driven off using heat. Your job is to replace that water to take the material back to a natural rock 'gypsum', but in the particular shape that you want. As the plaster sets it gets warm – this is caused by a chemical reaction which releases the heat put into it during manufacture, so when the plaster becomes cool, you know that it has set.

Casting plaster comes in different grades: fine, super fine and coarse.

Fine casting plaster is used for most casting needs, running mouldings and producing plaster casts. It is also the plaster that is used in fixing and mitring. It is the most used of all fibrous plasters.

Super fine plaster is a much finer material and is used for detail work, i.e. mouldings, etc. that have delicate shapes and lines. It is also used with fine plaster when casting. For example, the face of the cast would be in super fine ('firstings'), and then the fine would be used to back up the casts ('seconds').

Coarse plaster has its place (if it is available) for use in coring out moulds, because it is a lot cheaper. You will not get the same detail of reproduction as for fine or super fine.

Fibrous plasters also come in degrees of strength. Different manufacturers will have different ranges of plasters with different characteristics. They will also name them in different ways. It is best to read the manufacturers' information sheets to see what material is best for the job you want to do. For example, if you are producing mouldings that are liable to get damaged, you want a good hard plaster. Similarly, if you have a cast that may need a bit of work to get it out of the mould, then a slightly harder plaster is needed. A reverse mould that will have a lot of casts taken from it may need a hard face, so again it is sensible to choose a harder grade of plaster.

Hessian/canvas

Used as reinforcement for running out larger mouldings.

Grease/release agent

Used to prevent the plaster from sticking to the bench, and also helps with the running of the mould along the bench.

Shellac

Shellac is a painter's knotting or button polish that can be thinned down with methylated spirits. It is brushed onto plaster surfaces in three thin coats or until it has a polished surface: this will seal the plaster surface and prevent the water from any other coats of plaster that are applied being sucked out. This can be used on bench surfaces etc.

Tools for casting

A number of tools are required for the casting process which have been discussed and explained in Chapter 4.

- Splash brush
- Canvas knife or scissors
- Busks
- Joint rules
- Small tools
- Saws
- Hammers

Remember

Shellac brushes should be kept in neat methylated spirits when not in use or in the shellac itself; if not they will become hard

Materials for casting

Plaster

As discussed in 'Materials for running out mouldings' (page 297).

Size

Because casting plaster has a setting time of about 15 minutes, for most casting jobs it would be too quick, so to slow it down we use **size**. Traditionally plasterers use painter's glue size that is put into water to dissolve with a handful of lime. The lime is to stop the glue size becoming too stiff, because size needs to be in a liquid form.

The liquid material is boiled in a bucket, allowed to cool and then tested for strength to see how long it will stop the plaster from setting.

To test the strength of any new batches of size, mix up a full bowl of plaster and, before adding the plaster, add one capful of size (or one measure of whatever you are using to measure out your size) to the water and time the set of the plaster. Do the same with two, and three measures, and time all three bowls. Record the setting times on a piece of paper next to the size bucket.

> **Definition**
>
> **Size** – a gelatine-based material (gelatine, as used in jellies, which is made from animal bones)

Grease or release agent

Traditionally, this is made up from tallow (a form of animal fat) mixed with cheap engine oil or paraffin 50/50 in a metal bucket and melted down. It is then left to cool, after which it can be used to grease up your moulds using a brush or a piece of old canvas. The amount of oil will need to be reduced when the weather is hot because the grease will become too runny to use. Each fibrous plaster shop will have its own recipe for the amount of tallow to oil/paraffin.

Neat tallow can be used for greasing, especially when casts are removed from difficult reverse moulds. Just hold it in your hand to slightly soften the tallow.

Hessian or canvas

Plaster on its own has very little strength, so hessian or canvas is used as reinforcement. It is a jute material with a mesh of about 6 mm – the holes in the material are 6 mm apart. It comes in rolls of about 100 m long and widths of 75 mm, 150 mm, 100 mm and 300 mm, and can be kept in a canvas bin. Cut with canvas knife or scissors.

Laths

These are thin strips of sawn, rough timber that are usually about 3 m long and as straight as possible. They are 3 mm thick and 25 mm wide, and are used for reinforcement and for fixing the casts. Because they are likely to be very dry, they are best kept soaked in a long water trough to stop the water from the plaster being sucked out and also to stop the laths from twisting when they become wet. This movement could twist the cast and lead to possible cracking of the face.

Shellac

As discussed previously (page 298).

Equipment for casting

The equipment is the same as used for running out mouldings with the addition, if space allows, of a long water trough for the soaking of laths.

Tools for moulding techniques

Most tools used in moulding techniques are the same as previously covered.

Material for moulding techniques
Polyvinyl chloride (PVC)

This is a material made from vinyl resins known to fibrous plasterers as 'rubber', and also called hot melt compound or HMC. It comes in different types of flexible grades, and each grade is a different colour to make it easier to see the difference. It is melted down in a machine at temperatures ranging from 120 to 170°C. The main problem with PVC is its high temperature, as this can affect some **models**: air may be released from a model which has not been fully sealed, and these air bubbles will form holes in the rubber that will produce bumps on the casts from the mould.

There are several advantages of PVC.

- The mould does not lose its flexibility (unless it is continually melted down for reuse).

- The mould does not easily tear, although softer grades are more liable to, and if it has been re-melted many times it loses its oils and is more easily torn.

- When a mould is no longer needed, it can be cut up and the material reused, which makes it cheaper to use.

- No mixing together of materials is needed, thus cutting out mistakes.

- It is very convenient for one-off casts.

There are some disadvantages to PVC too.

- It needs expensive melting equipment with extraction facilities.

- You have to handle material at very high temperatures.

- The fumes can be very dangerous.

- You are not guaranteed a good standard of finished pour every time.

Cold pour moulding compound

This material is a flexible silicone rubber. It is kept in sealed containers that must be stored in a metal container called a blast storage bin, and it has a **shelf life** of about six months when stored to the manufacturer's instructions.

> **Definition**
>
> **Model** – the original moulding that is to be reproduced

> **Definition**
>
> **Shelf life** – the length of time that materials can be stored before they deteriorate

The cold pour consists of two chemical materials that are mixed together in the amount stated in the manufacturer's instructions. One of the chemicals is weighed out using a set of weighing scales, and the other is a type of catalyst that comes in a bottle with measurements on the side. The two materials must be well mixed together so that a proper setting or hardening process takes place. There are different types of cold pour, some of which, referred to as being 'thixotropic', allow you to work in the vertical plane – an upright mould. This allows you to take a mould of an ornament or section from an existing piece on the wall and ceiling.

The advantages of cold pour are:

- the mould does not lose its flexibility

- the mould will not easily tear

- no expensive equipment is needed and can be used on site

- almost a perfect pour every time if the preparation is done correctly

- will reproduce far better details from originals than PVC

- many more casts can be made from cold pour than PVC before it deteriorates beyond its practical use.

The disadvantages of cold pour are:

- expensive to use because it cannot be cut up and reused

- you must be able to weigh the materials accurately and measure out carefully to get the right mix

- requires special storage because they are potentially dangerous chemicals.

Clay

This is used in case moulding to:

- help form a case over a model (boards of clay)

- seal leaks

- provide support around models.

A board of clay being produced

Boards of clay are used to form the case over the model.

A board of clay is beaten out on a wooden board about 600 × 300 mm, with two lengths of wood of the required thickness nailed along each edge of the board. The board is brushed with French chalk to stop the clay from sticking to the board, and the clay – which must not be too wet or too dry – is then beaten into the board. Another piece of wood is then used to rule in the clay, nice and smooth, to the thickness of the rules. This is then loosely rolled to form the board of clay.

Equipment for moulding techniques

Holt melt machine

This is a very expensive piece of equipment – even a small one can cost over £1500. It must have an extractor fan above the machine that switches on as soon as the melting machine is turned on. The melting machine will have a thermostatic control to stop the rubber from burning and it will have an outlet in the bottom of the tank for letting out the rubber – this must be checked to see that it is shut.

The smaller melting pots hold only about ¾ of a metal bucket of rubber.

Safety tip

Melting PVC

Always wear a face mask designed for protection against breathing in fumes, wear heat-resistant gloves and apron, and make sure that your arms are covered. Also, the area around the machine must be kept clean and tidy because you are dealing here with a potentially very dangerous material.

Note: If the rubber does catch fire, immediately evacuate the building and call the emergency services because the fumes from the rubber can cause cancer

Metal buckets

Used for carrying the hot rubber from the melting machine to the model to be poured.

Metal funnels

Used for pouring the rubber into the mould.

Scales

Used for weighing out the cold pour.

Construction of running moulds

There are a variety of different ways of constructing running moulds, but we will look here at the method of constructing a simple panel mould for running straight and circular mouldings, and at the running mould required for forming a cornice reverse running mould. This method can be used for constructing most running moulds: only very small additions are required for other running moulds.

Template

The template of the profile is made from the zinc or steel sheet and follows the traditional shapes, as shown in Figure 11.4. The profile shape can be drawn on paper and glued onto the zinc. Cut around the zinc by using a pair of snips.

Place the template into a vice and, using files, file down to the profile line. Always check your lines and do not go beyond them. When you have filed up, a good check is to lay the profile onto an original drawing and make sure it matches.

When you have finished filing the shape, file off the burr at the back of the template and, using a piece of wet and dry paper, remove all the file marks left on the metal. If these file lines are not removed they will show on your finished moulding run.

Remember

Do not cut right up to the profile lines with the snips because one mis-cut and you will need to start again

Hand brace

Alternative fixing for stock using a housing joint

Stock

Horse/slipper

Template/profile

Minimum 40 mm

This end is called the nib of the mould

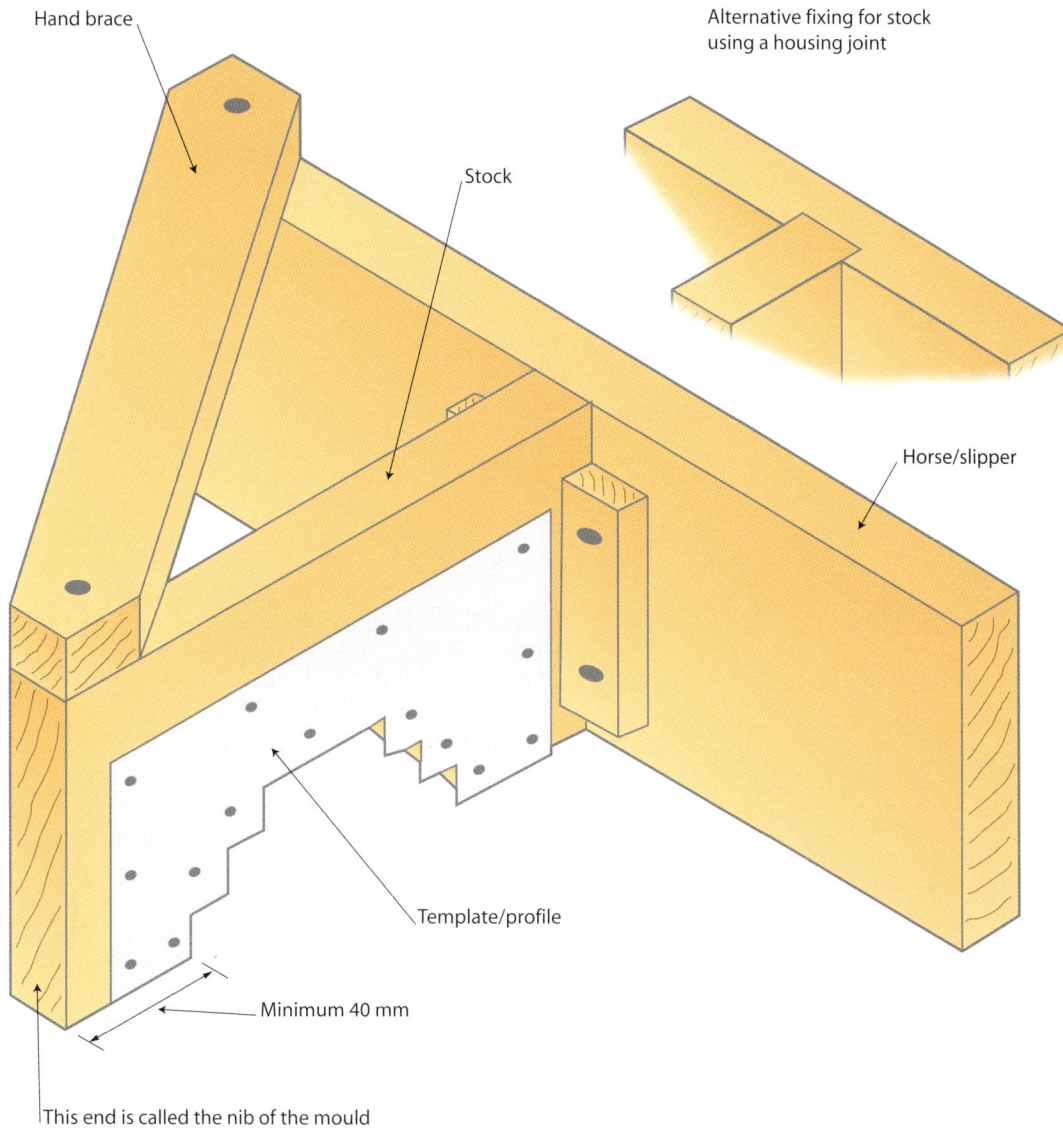

Ratio: The horse is 1$\frac{1}{2}$x the length of the stock

Figure 11.3 Running mould terms

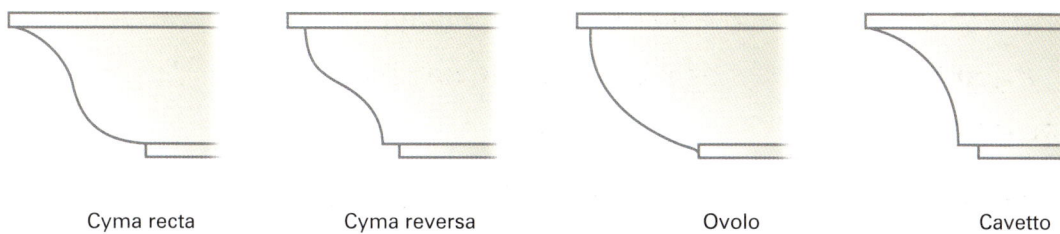

Cyma recta

Cyma reversa

Ovolo

Cavetto

Figure 11.4 Moulding sections or outlines

Stock

This is made from timber, and supports the soft zinc and stops it from bending during the running. Lay the profile onto the stock and draw around it with a pencil. Then redraw a pencil line following the template outline back about 5 mm. Then, using a saw and a coping saw, cut the wood out to this second line. The back edge of the stock should be splayed away; this can be done with a rasp. The splaying away stops the wood collecting the plaster or getting in front of the template.

Horse or slipper

This is the same height as the stock but 1½ times the length. It supports the stock, which is fixed to it at right angles with nails or a housing joint. This slipper will run along the running rule that is fixed to the bench.

Hand brace

This is fixed to the horse and slipper and helps to keep it firm. Some larger running moulds need two hand braces. The furthest point away from the slipper is called the 'nib', and if this moves too much it will cause **chattering**.

The mould will need to be braced against this movement because, the larger the moulding, the more swell there will be in the plaster upon setting.

Circular running moulds

A circular running mould is used for forming circular mouldings. The construction of this mould is very similar to straight moulds. In fact, you only slightly change your straight running mould to produce one. All you need to do is take a piece of wood called a gig stick, slightly longer than the radius of the circle required, and nail it on top of the stock and hand brace. Another way of forming this type of mould is to use an extended stock. The gig stick or extended stock should reach from the slipper to beyond the turning point, as shown in Figure 11.5. On the underside of the gig stick or extended stock, a piece of metal (called the turning eye) should be fixed with a hole in it about the size of a 50 mm nail at the radius distance. This will allow the running mould to rotate. The gig stick should be in line with the template face.

A turning block is fixed to the bench, as shown in Figure 11.5, by nailing into the bench and packing it with a **wad**.

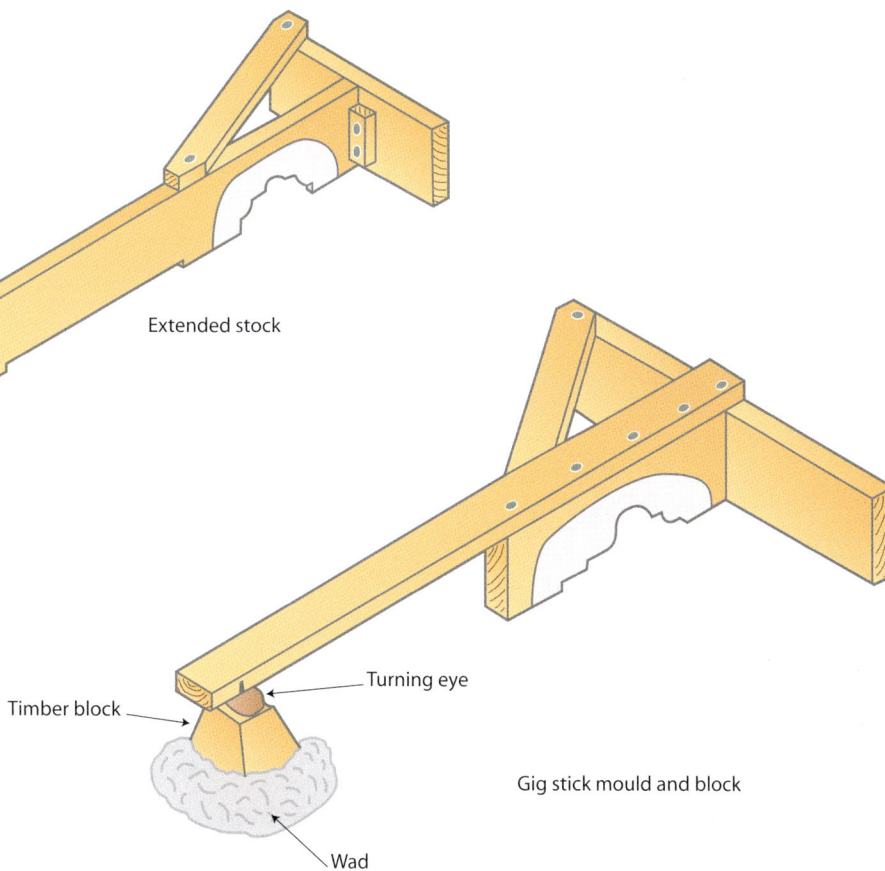

Definition

Wad – a piece of canvas soaked in plaster which forms an extremely strong fixing

Extended stock

Turning eye

Timber block

Gig stick mould and block

Wad

Figure 11.5 Circular running mould

Reverse cornice running mould

The construction of this running mould is the same as described and is shown in Figures 11.6 and 11.7. Note the difference in the template and the use of an additional brace for the cornice running mould.

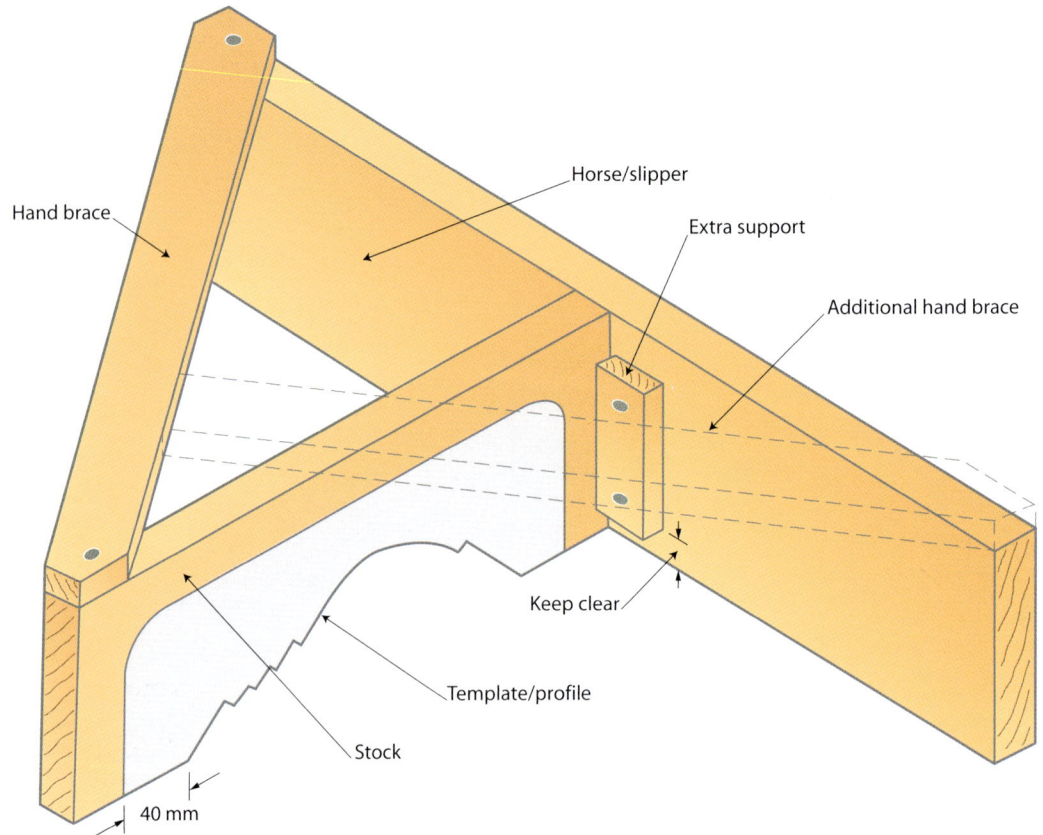

Hand brace

Horse/slipper

Extra support

Additional hand brace

Keep clear

Template/profile

Stock

40 mm

Figure 11.6 Running mould for a reverse cornice mould

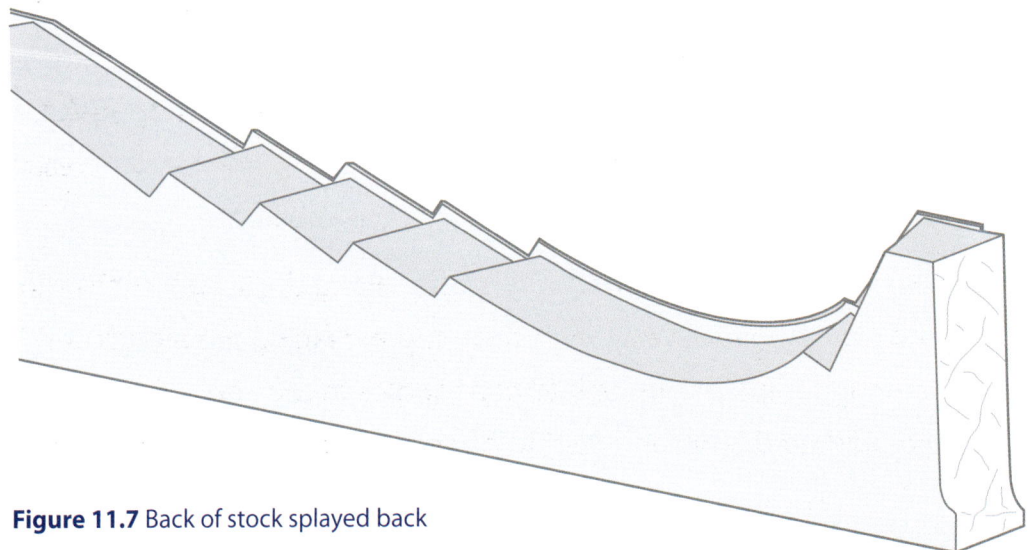

Figure 11.7 Back of stock splayed back

Methods of running out mouldings

Running out a simple panel mould

The running out of this type of moulding is the same method as for the running out of any moulding. It is only the size that changes.

1. First repair any damage and hollows in the bench by using casting plaster and a joint rule. The bench should be slightly wetted before making good. When the plaster has set and dried out, give the bench three coats of shellac. (You can speed up the drying process by brushing dry plaster dust onto the bench, and then taking it off by using a joint rule.)

2. Grease the bench well, including the running rule and running mould.

3. Mark with a pencil the length of moulding you need to run out on the running rule.

4. Beyond the run length, put a nail at the highest point of the template, in the bench. This is to stop the moulding slipping off as it begins to swell. Do not put one at either end, because when the plaster swells it has nowhere to go and so will snap. Use either a headless nail or one with a small head, over which should be a piece of clay in the shape of a pyramid to help with easy release of the plaster from the nail at the finish of the run.

5. Now you will need to mix up your plaster. The amount of plaster you need depends on the size of the moulding. (You may need help with this at the beginning.) Put clean water into a bowl and sprinkle plaster into the bowl until it is just below the surface of the water. Allow it to soak for a couple of minutes. Grease up your arms and hands using barrier cream and mix up the plaster making sure that there are no lumps.

6. At the bench, pour a small amount of plaster along the length of the run. Take your running mould and, with the template facing the direction you are going, stand in front of it at right angles to the bench. With your left hand holding the nib and resting on the bench and your right hand

Remember

The minute you start mixing up the plaster it begins to start its set, so do not delay – speed is a must. You do not need glue size in a running mix, unless the moulding is very large

holding the hand brace, walk backwards pulling the running mould. Your left hand will feed the plaster back into the running and will push it into the running rule. Your right hand does the pulling. Hold a bowl at the end of the run for catching the unused plaster. This can now be used again and cuts down on waste.

7. Repeat the process, adding more plaster each time, building up to match the profile. It will be necessary to clean the running mould in between runs by using a small tool or an old piece of lath.

8. When the plaster becomes too old, re-mix another mix for finishing off. This mix needs to be a bit wetter.

9. Once you have reached a good quality of finish, clean down the bench with a joint rule and saw the plaster to the required length. If the bench is well greased, the moulding can be slid across the bench, or use a gauging trowel to slide along the length of the moulding to release it from the bench. The moulding can now be lifted on edge to the storage area.

For circular running the system is the same, the only difference being the position of the hands and the removal of the running mould.

Your hands will need to be positioned with one hand on the turning point (if not too far away) and the other on the hand brace. Unless you are double jointed, you will need to reverse your hands at some stage.

When removing and replacing the running mould from the moulding, ensure that it is taken off and put back in the same place each time.

At the finish of the run leave the running mould in position for a short while, then slightly move it forwards. This will clean off any plaster wastage in front of the template.

Remember

Wet plaster must always be stored flat, because it will bend to the shape of whatever it is lying on

Running of a reverse cornice mould

The system for running out a reverse cornice mould is the same as for the panel moulding. The only difference is the setting up and the fact we are using a larger template section.

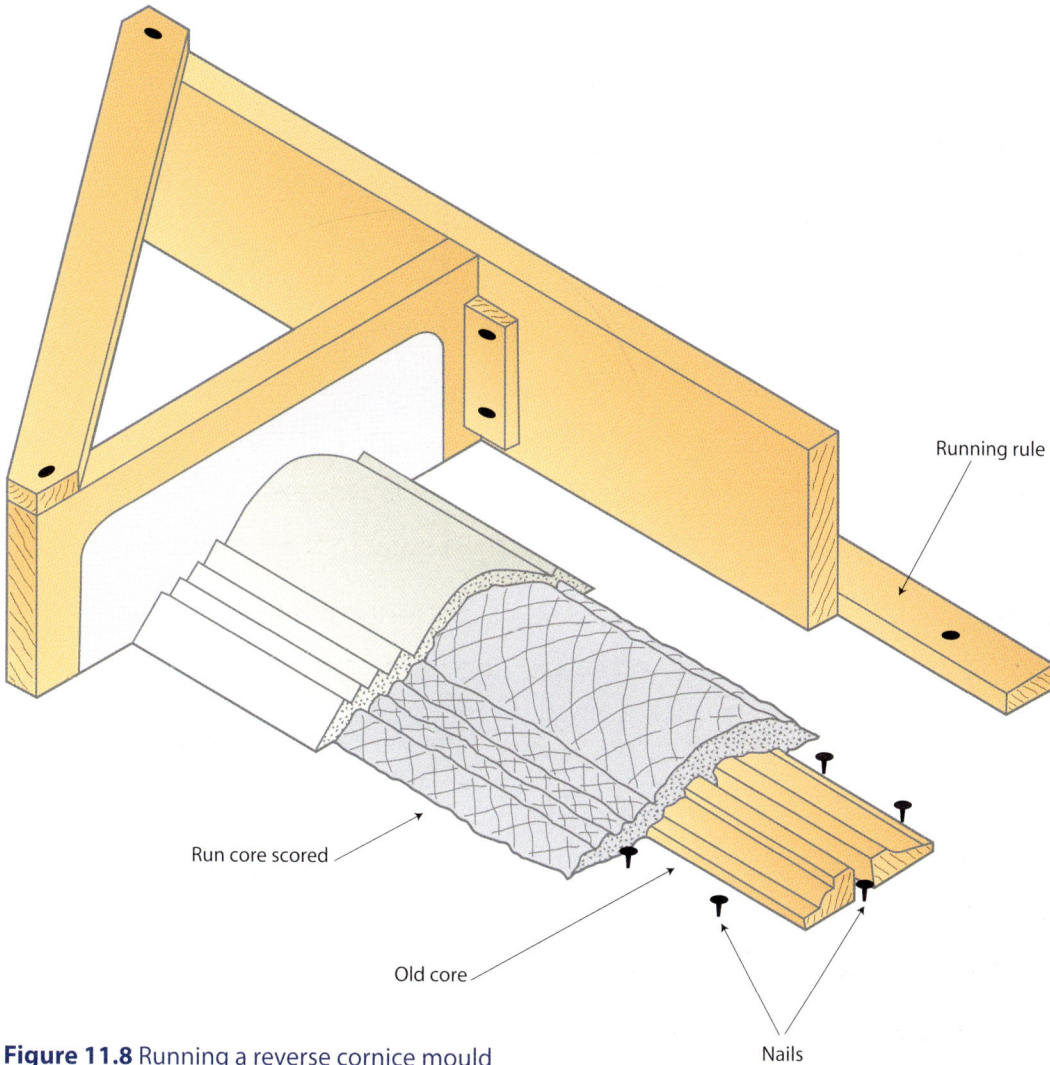

Running rule

Run core scored

Old core

Nails

Figure 11.8 Running a reverse cornice mould

1. Because of the size of the moulding it may need a **muffle**, as a large swell in the plaster can happen.

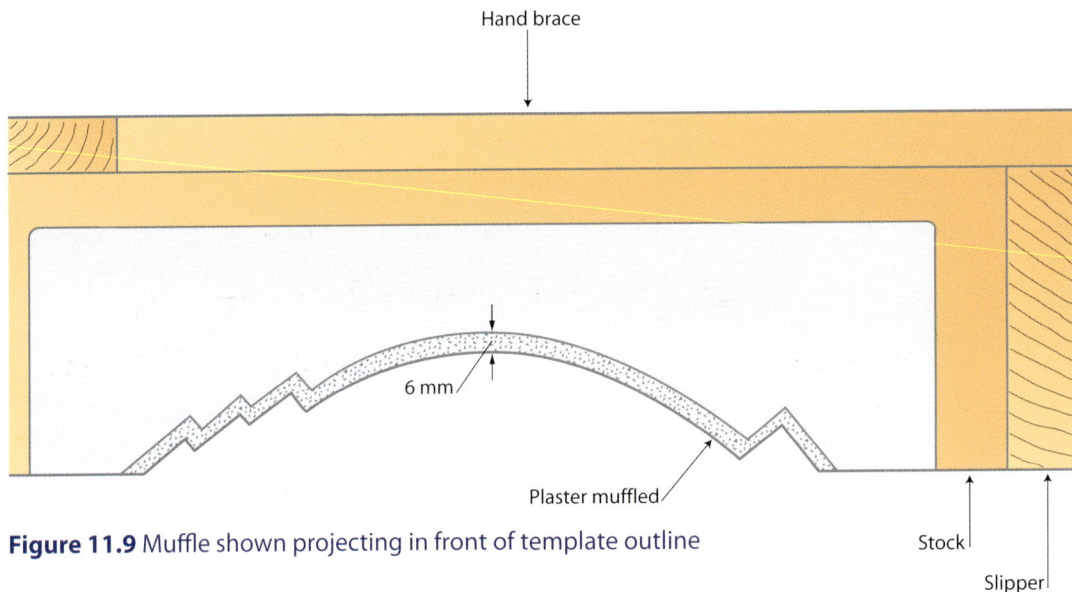

Hand brace

6 mm

Plaster muffled

Stock

Slipper

Figure 11.9 Muffle shown projecting in front of template outline

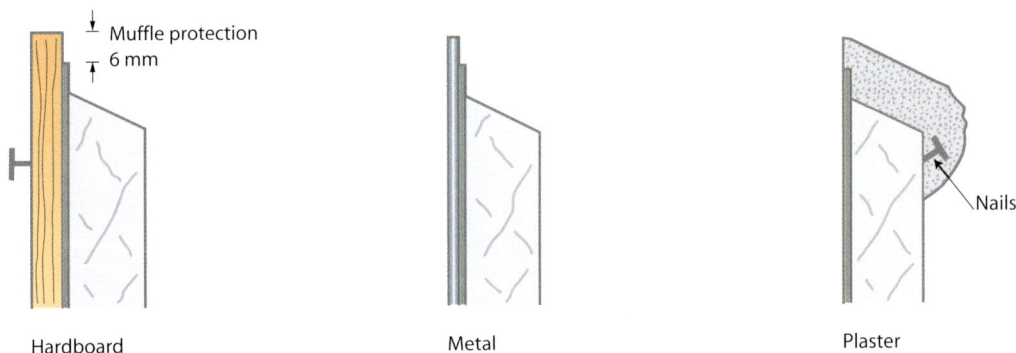

Muffle protection 6 mm

Hardboard

Metal

Plaster

Nails

Figure 11.10 Forming a false profile

2. Again, because of the size of the running, to save on plaster, a core of old plaster mouldings or plasterboard can be fixed down to the bench as shown in Figure 11.8. (Remember to grease the bench before laying down the core.) Lay canvas or hessian soaked in plaster over the core to hold it in position.

3. Because we may need the reverse mould to stay on the bench, the core can be nailed down to the bench.

4. Because this is a bigger moulding, you will need to mix up in a bucket.

5. Pour plaster as described above.

6. Run the mould over the core forming the shape of the muffle.

7. When you have completed this run, take off the old muffle, check the template for any damage and clean the running mould.

8. Use a craft knife to apply a deep criss-cross key to the core.

9. Re-grease the bench, running rule and running mould and continue to run out to the required finish.

10. When the plaster has set, square off the ends of the moulding to the required length, clean down the bench and, when the moulding has dried out, coat it in three coats of shellac.

So what type of running have you done? Well, the small panel mould is a *positive* moulding. This means that it is the finished product. The reverse mould is a *negative* moulding, which means that it is in *reverse* and casts are taken from it to produce the finished product.

Another type of run is the run cast. This is used when the amount of moulding is not enough to make a mould, but is too big just to run out on the bench.

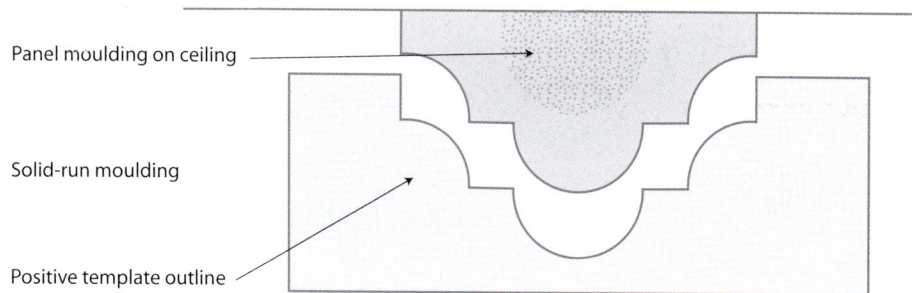

Panel moulding on ceiling

Solid-run moulding

Positive template outline

Figure 11.11 Setting out for templates positive and reverse moulds

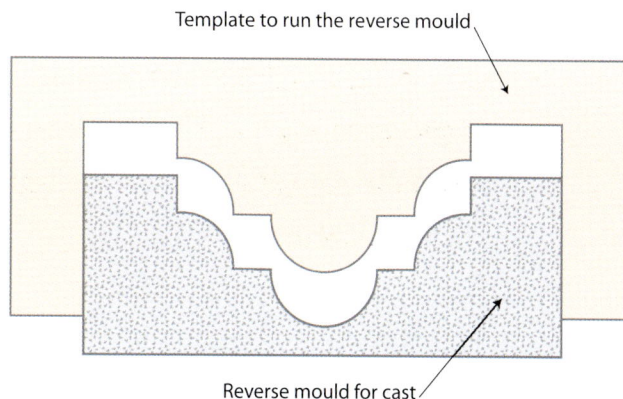

Template to run the reverse mould

Reverse mould for cast

Figure 11.12 Template to run a reverse running mould

So what do you do?

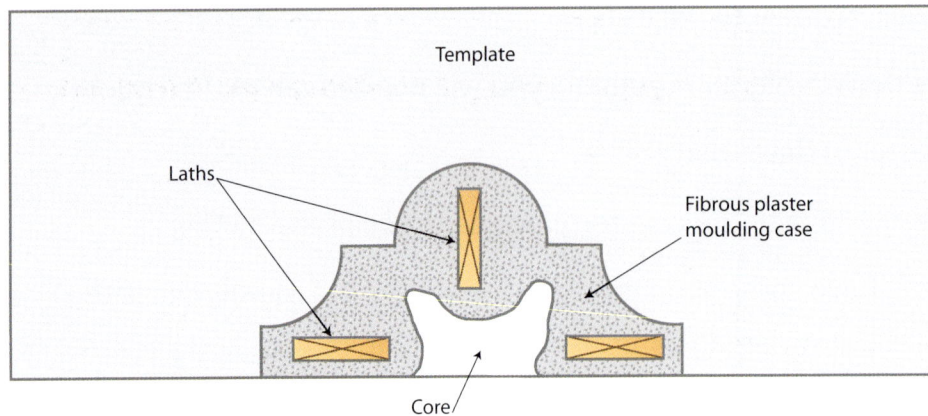

Figure 11.13 The template would run the shape required

1. Construct a running mould, but this time put on a false profile that will run out a plaster core. This core is then shellacked and well greased.

2. Cut canvas that is the length of the moulding and wide enough to lap over into the middle.

3. Cut timber laths slightly shorter than the length of the moulding run.

4. Gauge up the plaster and, using a splash brush, brush in a coat of plaster over the core.

5. Soak or lay the canvas onto the core.

6. Brush the laths with plaster and lay them flat on the bench either side of the core.

7. Turn in the canvas over the laths to meet in the middle. (You may be able to have further laths as shown in the diagram.) Brush in the canvas.

8. Run out the moulding as shown until the finish.

9. When the plaster has set, clean down and lift off the moulding from the core, and repeat.

Casting techniques

As an example, we will go through the system of casting a **plain face** slab.

Definition

Plain face – a flat plaster cast used for forming suspended ceilings or walls, or for use as a temporary bench to which to fix a model

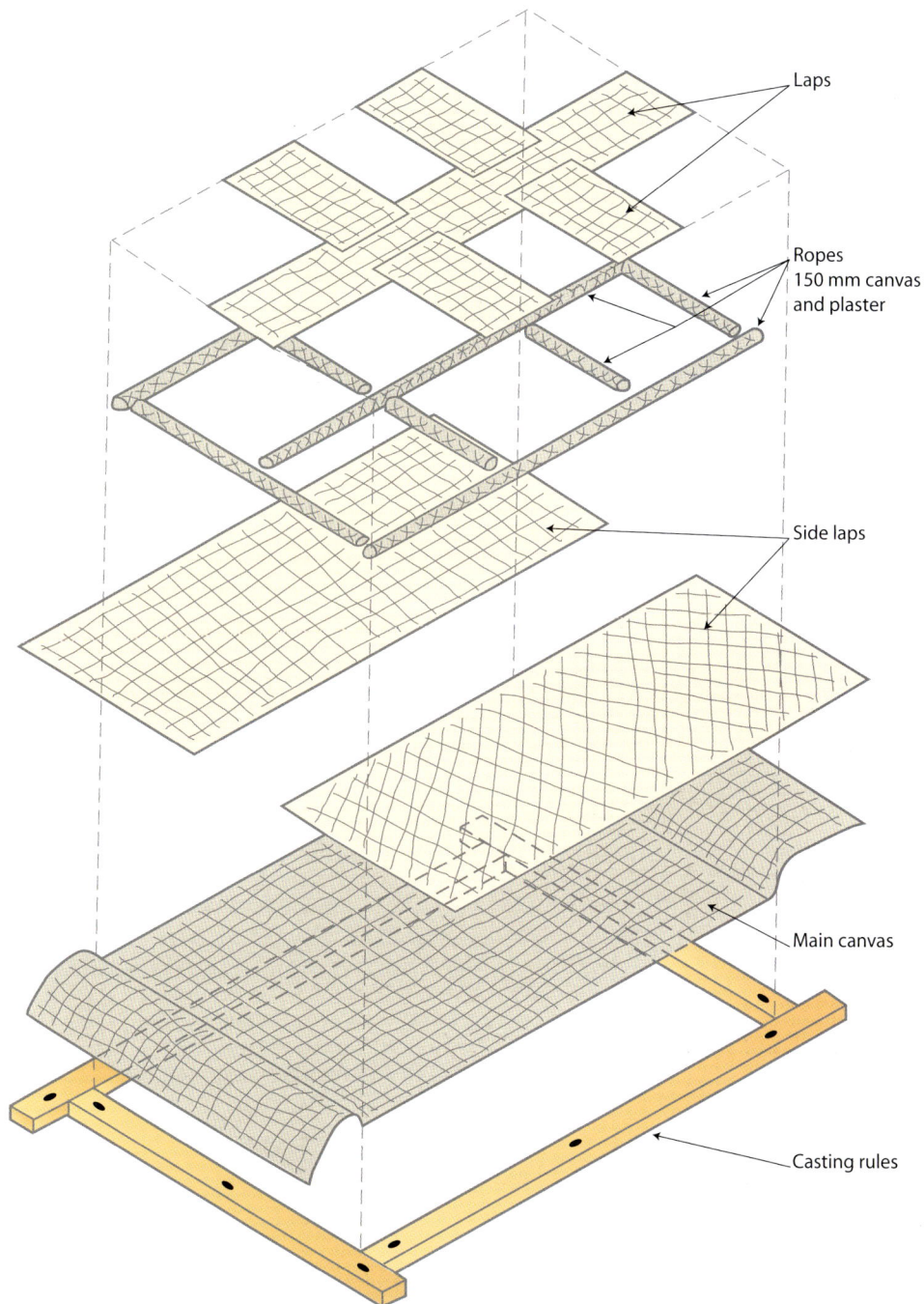

Laps

Ropes
150 mm canvas
and plaster

Side laps

Main canvas

Casting rules

Plain face 600 x 900 x 40 mm

Figure 11.14 Exploded view of plain face canvas

Preparation

1. Make good and shellac the bench.

2. Make up a framework from timber to the sizes required. Cut the timber slightly bigger than the required size. The timber is usually 25–35 mm in thickness. This will make the mould.

3. Fix the timber rules down to the bench, checking that they are square. Leave the heads of the nails slightly above the rules for easy dismantling.

4. Cut the canvas:

    *   Cut the main canvas sheet that is the width of the mould. Leave an overlap at both ends as shown in Figure 11.14.

    *   Cut two side laps which, when turned in, meet in the middle of the mould. This gives two layers of canvas.

    *   Cut a **rope** to go around the edge of the mould. It is used to go under the laths to help with fixing and preventing twisting of the laths.

    *   Cut smaller ropes to go under the cross laths.

    *   Cut laps to go over the laths for the back of the cast, as shown in Figure 11.14.

5. Cut the laths to go around the edge of the mould, but make them about 5–10 mm short, and laths for under the cross laps. Now soak the laths.

6. Lightly **French chalk** inside the mould. This will help when greasing because you can see where you have greased, and where you have not.

7. Grease up the mould, the timber rules and around the surrounding bench.

Mixing

We are going to use the two-gauge system of casting, which uses two different mixes of plaster: firstings and seconds. The firstings are mixed and used first and the seconds have size added, in order to slow down the set, and are used second.

Definition

Rope – in casting, a strip of canvas about 150 mm wide soaked in plaster, rolled and lightly passed through the hand

French chalk – a very fine powder

Why use two mixes? The face of casts must be free from canvas. If the canvas were pasted into soft plaster, it would show through on the face. To avoid this, an initial mix of firstings is used so that the face is formed and set (within 15 minutes) before the canvas and seconds are applied.

1. Put good clean water into a bowl and into a bucket.

2. Add size to the bucket (for the seconds). Ask someone who has used the size how strong it is. This will tell you how much you need to get the job finished before the plaster sets.

3. Mix up the firstings, and take it to the bench.

4. With the splash brush, brush a coat of firstings into the mould and up the sides of the timber. Make sure there are no misses. Run a finger around the mould between the timber and the bench to remove any trapped air and re-brush in the plaster.

5. Splash on a coat of firstings to give an even coat of about 6 mm.

6. Strike off using a piece of old lath along the top of the timbers (strike-offs) and remove any of the surplus plaster.

7. Wash out your bowl and splash brush in the slosh tank, and mix up seconds.

8. Test the firmness of the firstings in the mould and, when it stiffens up, brush in a coat of seconds.

9. Lay in the main sheet of canvas and the side laps.

10. Brush in the canvas with the seconds.

11. Soak the long rope and lay it around the edge of the mould, and soak the shorter ropes for under the cross laths.

12. Get the laths and lay them in the mould and brush both sides with plaster.

13. Lay them on top of the ropes, and turn in the canvas that is left, then paste the canvas in with seconds.

14. Soak the laps and lay them on top of the cross laths and brush in.

15. Again, strike off any spare plaster on top of the timbers.

16. Give a splash coat to the back of the cast for extra strength and to tidy up the back.

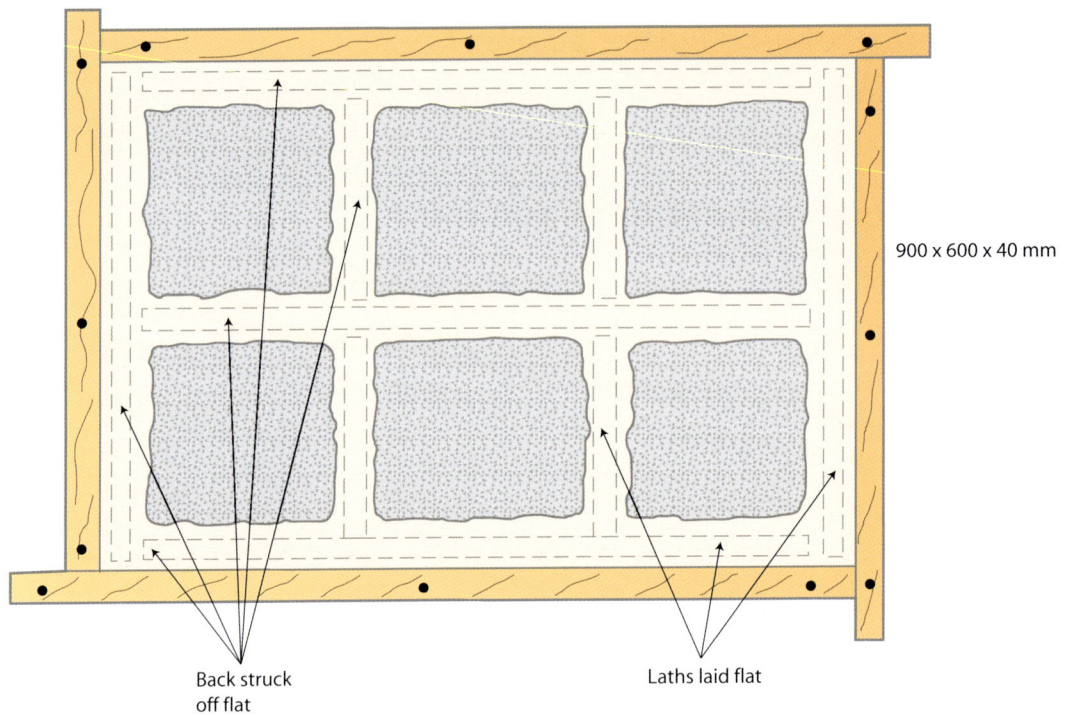

900 x 600 x 40 mm

Back struck
off flat

Laths laid flat

Figure 11.15 Casting a square edge plain face slab

17. Strike off and build up any points not yet in contact with the strike-off edges. This now finishes the cast.

18. When the cast has set, clean up around it and remove it from the mould.

19. The face of the cast will need to have the grease removed – this is done with a piece of canvas. A busk is used to clean up the face of the cast, removing any lines or imperfections.

Did you know?

Laths are used on edge for added strength, and for suspension by wire and wad. Laths are used flat to allow the cast to be screwed or nailed to the background

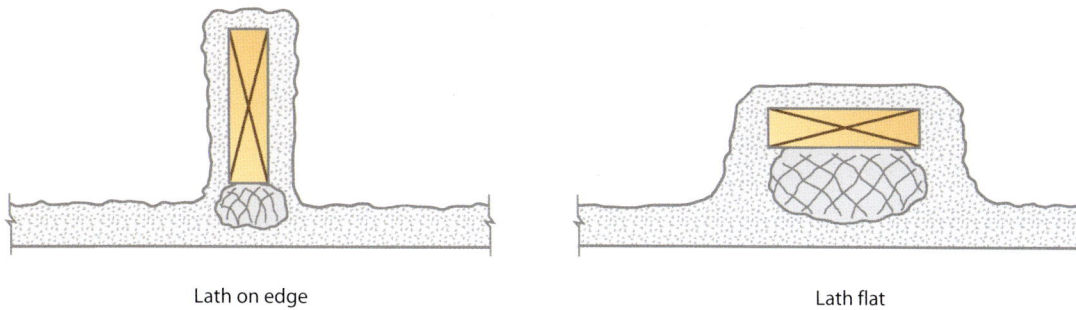

Lath on edge

Lath flat

Figure 11.16 Lath on edge, and flat

One-gauge casting system

Another system is the one-gauge system of casting.

1. Mix one gauge of plaster with size to control the set.

2. Brush on a coat of plaster, making sure all the mould is covered.

3. Splash on a coat of plaster.

4. Strike off.

5. Form a canvas bag filled with dry plaster and dust the back of the plaster in the mould to stiffen it up.

6. Strike off again.

7. Very carefully lay in the canvas as described in the two-gauge system, and continue casting in the same order.

Advantages

*   By using only one gauge, there should be no problems with different rates of swelling between firstings and seconds, which can cause **cockling**.

*   The cast, with the use of size throughout, is stronger at the face.

Disadvantages

*   Great care has to be taken throughout the casting that the canvas is not pressed through to the face – no pressure must be applied with the hands during casting.

Definition

Cockling – where the first coat expands and breaks up into the second coat

Method of forming different joints in plain face slabs

Plain faces have to be jointed to form a long flat surface. If you use butted joints, they can tend to crack out, but there are other edge designs that can be used:

- square
- rebated
- lapped
- lapped and rebated.

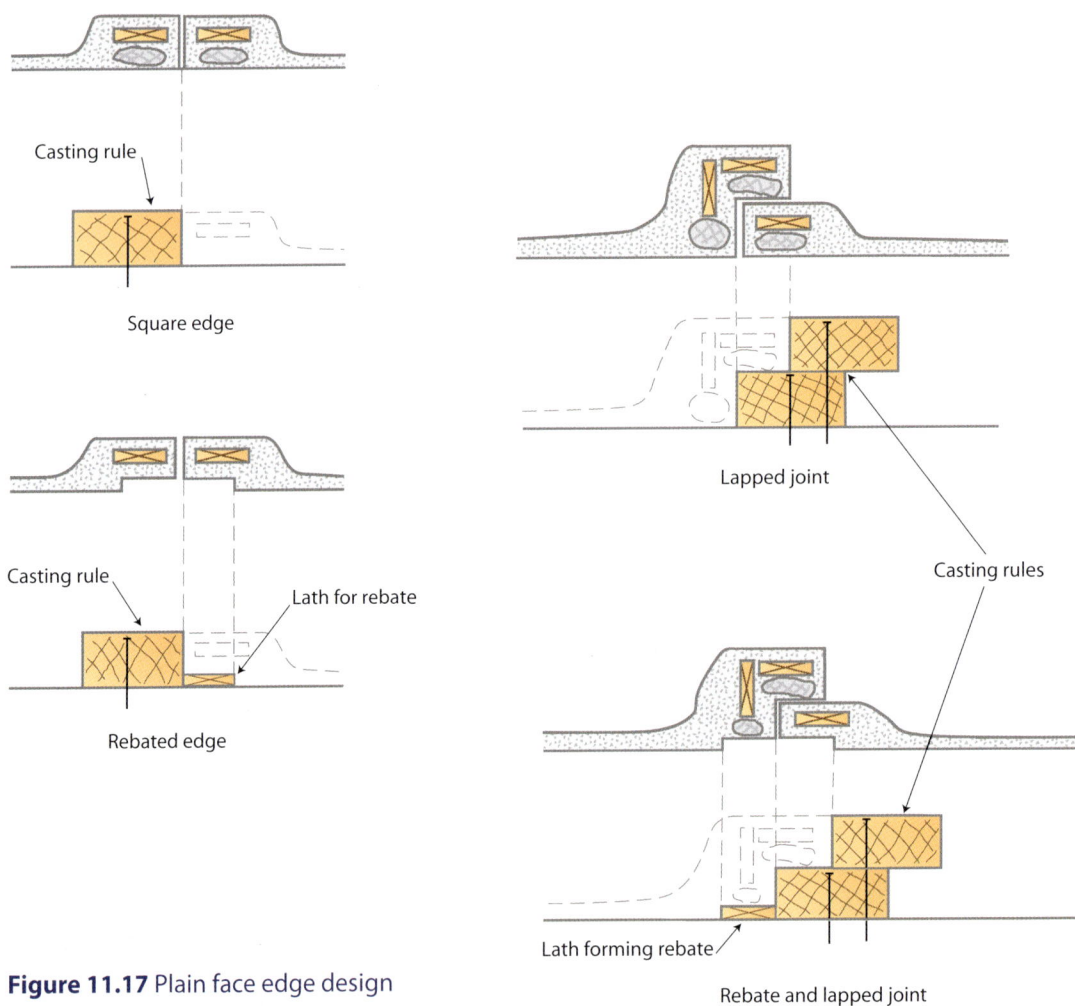

Casting rule

Square edge

Casting rule

Lath for rebate

Rebated edge

Lapped joint

Casting rules

Lath forming rebate

Rebate and lapped joint

Figure 11.17 Plain face edge design

Casting rules

Laths for rebates fixed to the bench

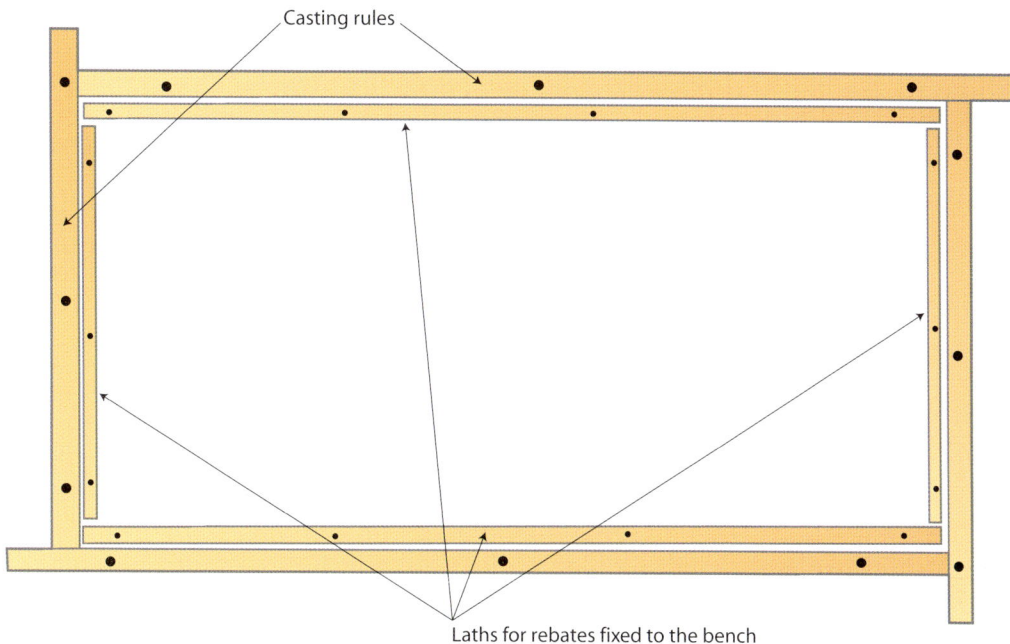

Figure 11.18 Reverse mould of a plain face slab

The rebated, lapped, and lapped and rebated edges have a recess cast into them. This allows for, after fixing, a length of canvas soaked in plaster to be laid into the recess. The faces of the two slabs are then levelled out together to hide the joint by the use of a busk or joint rule and a small tool.

Casting from a reverse cornice mould

The system of casting is the same whatever you are doing; it is only the shape that changes. You may change the amount and shape of the canvas you cut, and also the number and size of the laths. In some casts, you may have to put in larger pieces of wood or even use metal, but it does not change the system.

The preparation of the mould is as we have already described. The canvas is cut to the length of the mould plus about 100 mm of overlap at each end, which will be turned over during the casting for added strength at the end of the cast. This is important when joining lengths of cornice together.

The laths are cut 25 mm short at each end.

According to the size of the cornice, you will either need canvas laps that will go over the back of the cast or laths that are 'bruised'. To do this, take a piece of old lath and place it on the floor and then take a longer piece of lath and, with the axe head of a lath hammer, hit it lightly to bruise it into a shallow curve to fit the curve of the back of the mould.

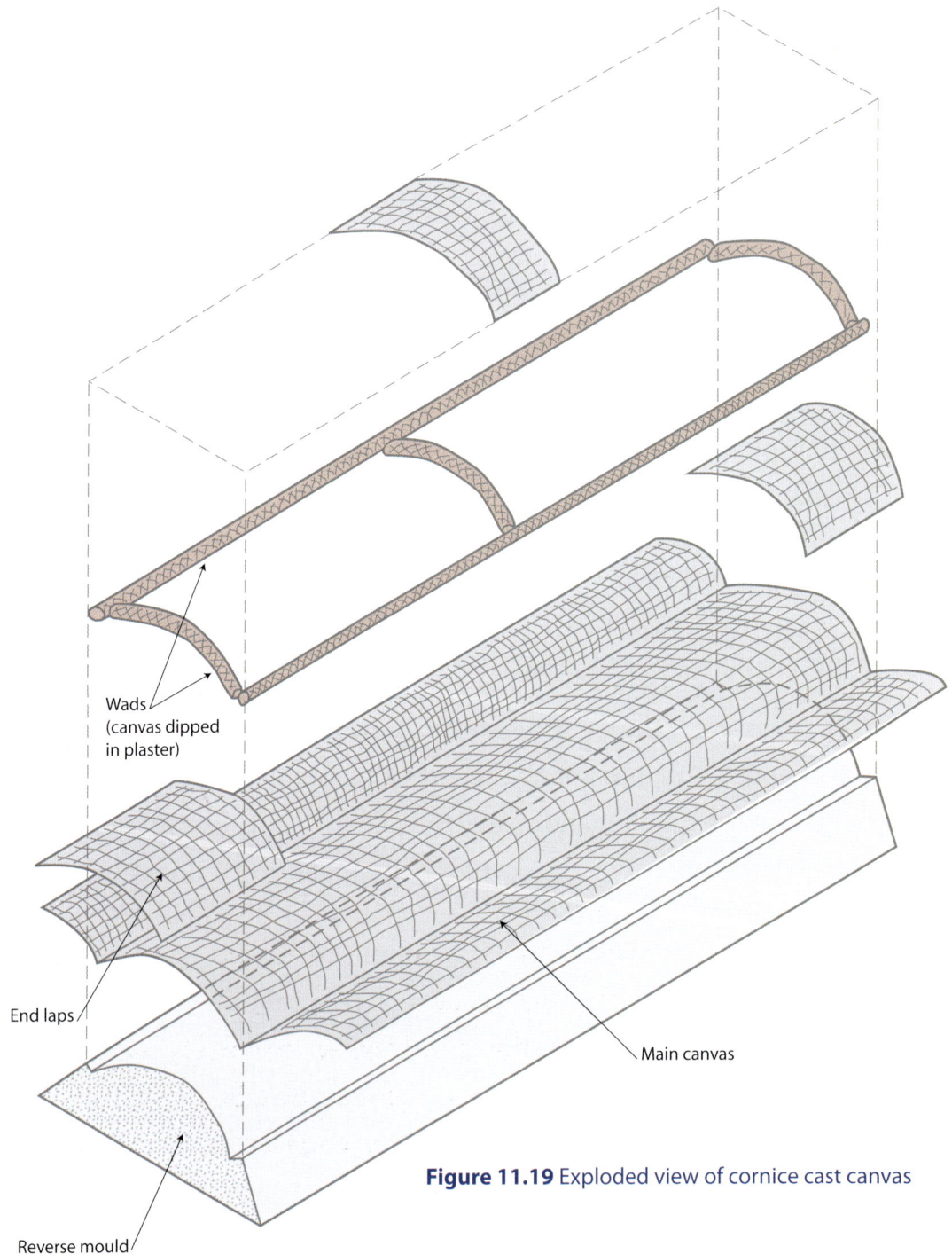

Remember

The laths for a cornice cast must be placed at the ceiling and wall line strike-offs. These are needed for fixing the cornice by nail, screw or adhesive to the ceiling and wall. If these two areas are not flat and have a build-up of plaster, the cornice cannot be fixed flat back to the wall or ceiling

Wads (canvas dipped in plaster)

End laps

Main canvas

Reverse mould

Figure 11.19 Exploded view of cornice cast canvas

For very large cornices, a 'knuckle joint' is formed. This is two pieces of wood placed on edge and crossed over at the high point of the curve in the mould. For even bigger cornices you can use metal brackets.

All of the reinforcements need laps placed over the back of them.

The laths, etc. at the back of the cast must be struck off flat again to make fixing easier.

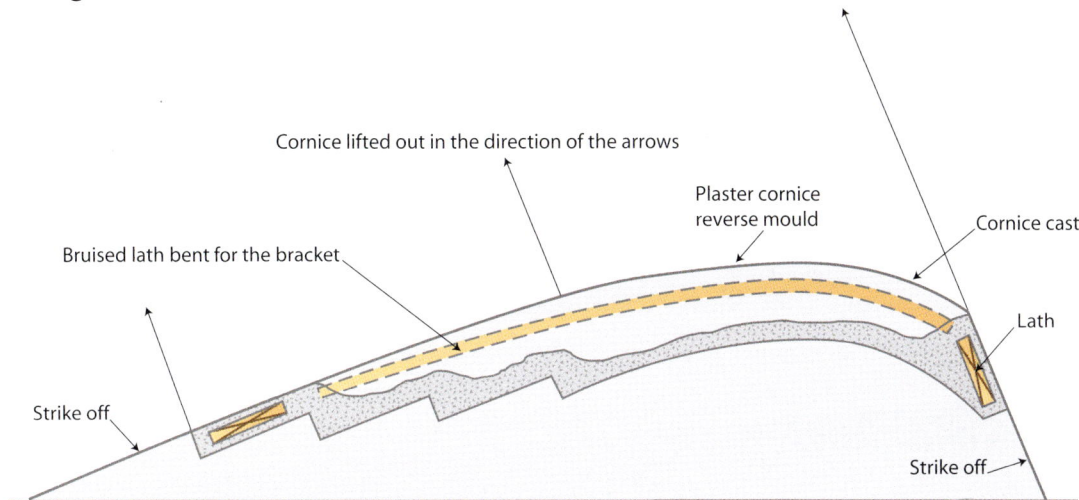

Figure 11.20 Section through a plain straight cornice cast filled in the mould

Storage and handling of casts

Fibrous plaster casts should be both strong and light to handle.

All casts should be well stored and protected at all times. What is the point of making good quality casts if you spoil them by poor handling and storage?

When you have removed casts, they should be handled very carefully and on edge. For heavy casts, ask for help in lifting them.

When storing, always keep casts as flat as possible, and be aware that wet casts will take the shape of whatever they are laid on. Cornices can be laid against a scaffold board resting against a wall face to face. This stops the faces getting damaged. The casts should be covered to protect them from any damage in the workshop. Tie the casts to the scaffold board so that they do not fall. Plain faces should be stored flat or on edge face to face. Always handle plaster casts or run mouldings on edge.

Faults that may happen in casting

Cockling

As already explained, this fault can happen in two-gauge casting. The face of the cast can look like a broken eggshell. The fault happens mainly on curved surfaces owing to the length of the curves and the greater expansion. One way of stopping this problem is to draw a line through the firstings at intervals as a form of expansion joint; this gives room for the expansion to take place.

Cast sticking to the mould

This mainly happens with plaster reverse moulds. It is caused by poor greasing (missed areas), and can also be the result of poor sealing of the plaster mould face that allows the grease to soak into the plaster face. It can also happen if the plaster is very wet when the shellac is brushed on.

Holes and misses

Poor brushing in of the firstings causes this fault. This happens mostly in flexible rubber moulds. If you run your fingers through the angles (arrises), it will get rid of the air trapped in these sharp members.

Grease on the face of the casts

This is caused by having too much grease on or in the mould. Excess grease should be removed, before casting, with a dry piece of canvas.

Cracks on the face of the cast

Cracks along the lath line are caused by twisting of the laths, mainly caused by poor soaking of the laths or not putting ropes under the laths during casting. This can also happen if a moulding compound material is moved or roughly handled during the casting system.

Loose laths during fixing

This is caused by not enough brushing in of the laths in plaster and in tucking in the laps around the laths during casting.

Strike-offs not correct

This is a common fault when learning – do not put too much plaster on the canvas around the laths at the strike-offs. The cast at the strike-offs should also not be left hollow; it should be built up with plaster – otherwise, during fixing, the cast is likely to crack or bow.

Moulding techniques

There are various different methods of forming moulds from a model:

- flood mould (sometimes called open mould or solid mould)

- case mould (sometimes called clay case mould or closed mould)

- skin mould.

With each method, the exact details will depend on a number of factors:

- the amount of moulding material available

- the amount of material needed to form the mould (this will be affected by how much money you have to make the mould)

- the time available to make the mould

- the equipment available for producing the type of mould.

Flood mould

This type of method of moulding can be used on either cold pour or PVC.

Advantages

Very little preparation is required: only a simple wood or clay framework. This makes this system very quick and simple.

Disadvantages

This method will use up a large amount of moulding compound, as it has to be higher than any point of the model. There should be at least 13 mm of thickness above the model.

Thick sections of any of the moulding compounds are difficult to handle. This can make the removal of casts more difficult and can lead to breakage.

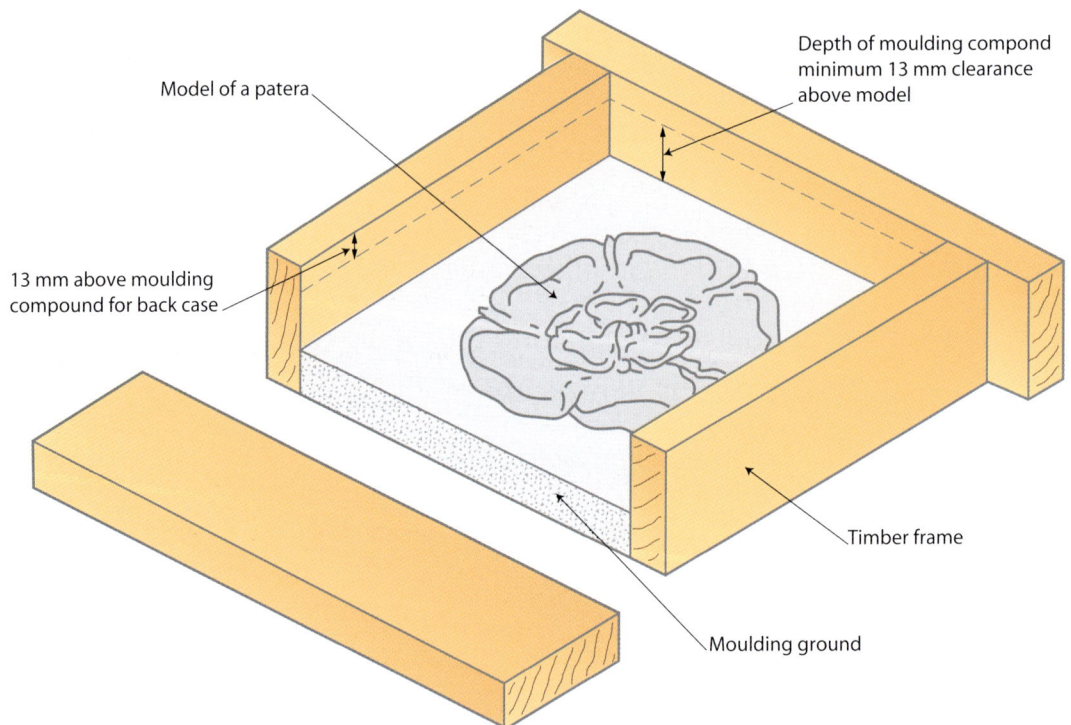

Depth of moulding compond minimum 13 mm clearance above model

Model of a patera

13 mm above moulding compound for back case

Timber frame

Moulding ground

Figure 11.21 Open, flood or solid mould (exploded view)

The model you use may be an object kept in the workshop as a stock item. It may have come from another job, or it may have been made by a specialist clay modeller or carved from wood. It may even have been taken down from a house, etc., but it is something that needs to be reproduced.

Method of forming an open mould

1. Mount the model on a moulding ground (this can be an old plain face – anything that is flat and can be sealed) and make good.

2. If an old stock piece is being used, clean it down and make it good, i.e. repair any damaged or missing parts of the model.

3. Make a frame or fence to go around the model with a minimum of 25 mm gap between the model and the frame.

4. If the model is an awkward shape, a clay fence can be used, with a minimum of 25 mm gap between the model and the fence.

5. Seal the frame or fence using shellac, and fix it to the moulding ground.

6. Seal all the junctions with plaster. This can also be used on the wood and clay to hold it to the moulding ground. The frame or fence must be well sealed because the liquid can find any small pinhole to leak through.

7. Now pour the moulding compound directly onto the moulding ground, making sure that its final depth is 13 mm or more than the highest point of the model.

It is important not to pour the moulding compound directly onto the model as it will cool very quickly and can leave some ugly seams that will have to be cleaned off afterwards.

Back case

When the moulding compound has hardened, plaster reinforcement with canvas can be cast over the back of the compound. The plaster should be 'struck off' level with the top of the frame. This case will give support to the compound and allow it stand level on the bench.

Case mould of a centrepiece

A case mould is a method that uses a fibrous plaster case to hold the moulding compound to form a reverse mould.

The purpose of a case moulding is:

- to reduce the amount of moulding compound that would be required for a flood or solid pour

- to allow for an even thickness of moulding compound that covers the complete model (the even thickness of moulding compound makes sure that it can be easily peeled off the model when the cast has been made).

The sequence of operations is as follows:

1. Mount the model onto a moulding ground and make good.

2. Beat out (hit with your fists) boards of clay (see page 303) to the required thickness – 13 mm for PVC and 8–10 mm for cold pour.

3. Cover the model with damp old newspapers.

4. Lay clay boards over the model, sealing any joints.

5. Form a lip or continuous **joggle** around the outside of the model. This is best formed using 25 mm clay strips on edge. These strips should be slightly narrower at the top. A wood template or gauge can be used to shape the lip into the clay. When the plaster case has been formed, this lip will hold the moulding compound in place.

Definition

Joggle – a location point used to prevent movement between the moulding compound and the plaster case

Figure 11.22 Case mould of a centrepiece

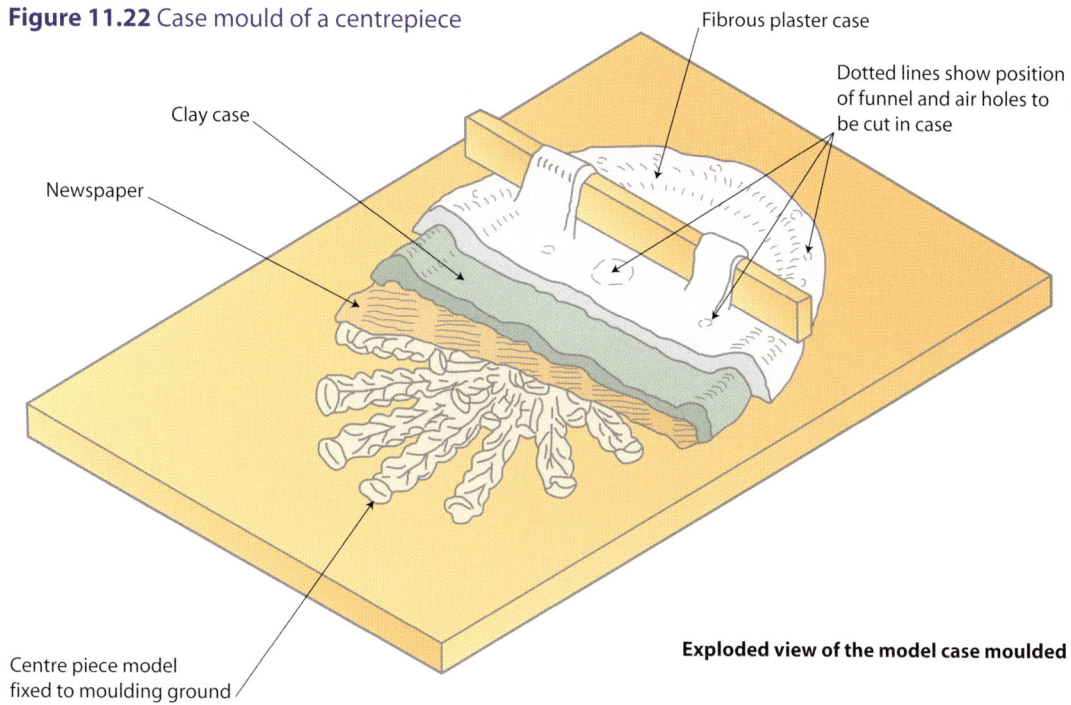

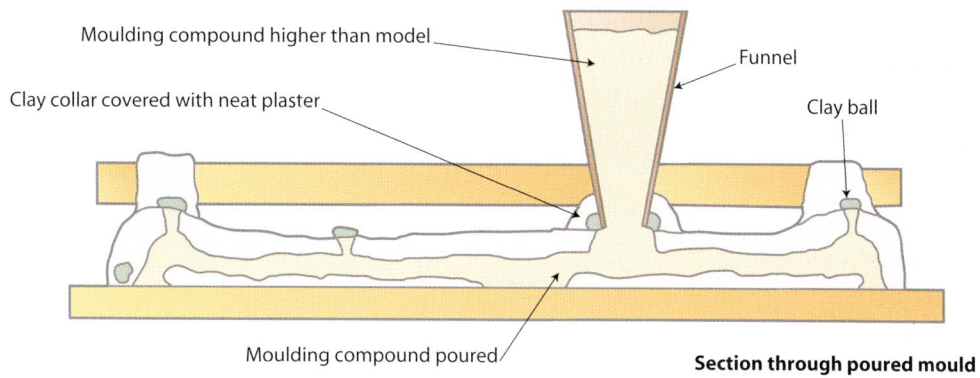

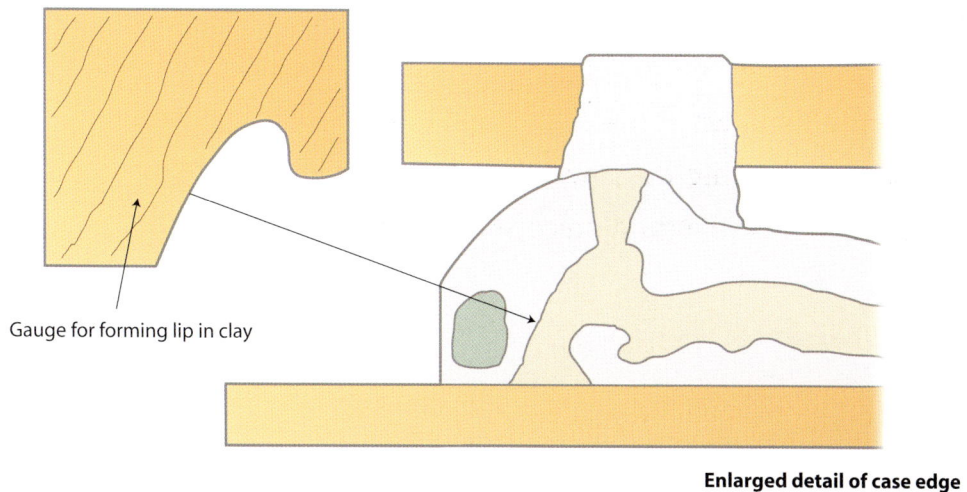

Fibrous plaster case

Dotted lines show position of funnel and air holes to be cut in case

Clay case

Newspaper

Centre piece model fixed to moulding ground

Exploded view of the model case moulded

Moulding compound higher than model

Funnel

Clay collar covered with neat plaster

Clay ball

Moulding compound poured

Section through poured mould

Gauge for forming lip in clay

Enlarged detail of case edge

6. Smooth all of the clay.

7. Cut strips or laps of canvas, enough to give two layers of canvas over the whole of the clay plus a 150 mm overlap around the outside.

8. Cut a rope long enough to go around the outside of the clay, and small pieces of timber to sit on top of the rope.

9. Cut two cross-timbers to act as reinforcement and bearers. (These bearers will allow the mould to sit level on the bench during casting from the mould.)

10. Cut laps to cover the cross-timbers.

11. Cast a case over the clay using 'firstings' and 'seconds' as previously described.

12. When the plaster has set, mark around the case with a pencil and put pencil marks around the case that line up with the same marks on the moulding ground. This will help when you have to put the case back. Remove the plaster case and set to one side.

13. Remove all the paper and then the clay, and clean the clay of any plaster. Put the clay back into a clay bin and lightly it wet down and cover it with wet sacking to stop it drying out.

Preparing the case for pouring

1. Clean off all the old clay slip by using a piece of old canvas.

2. Cut **air** and **pour holes** into the case. (Use 10–13 mm diameter holes for PVC and 4–6 mm for cold pour.) Air holes should be placed at the low spots especially. The more air holes the better – if air becomes trapped, it will prevent the compound from flowing and so will leave a missed area

Definition

Air hole – a hole cut into a case mould to allow air to escape as the compound is poured in

Pour hole – a hole cut into a case mould through which the moulding compound is poured

which spoils the pour. There is no need for a large number of pour holes; a lot will depend on the size of the model to be poured. The more pour holes you use, the more compound will be needed.

3. Clean out all loose debris and place the case back onto the marks you have made.

4. Wad down the case back in position by using clip wads onto the case and the moulding ground. (To make it easy for removing the wads later, small pieces of paper can be laid onto the back of the case and wads placed beyond the paper onto the case and the moulding ground.)

5. Fix pouring funnels into position by using clay and backing up with plaster. Keep the bottom of the funnel off the back of the case.

6. Roll up some clay balls ready for blocking off the air holes as soon as the moulding compound comes through.

7. Check that all joints are sealed.

8. Now you are ready for pouring – pour the compound carefully.

9. When the compound has set, remove all funnels by using a sharp knife, and remove wads and clay balls.

10. Remove the case from the model and turn it over.

11. Clean down the model and put it back into the stock cupboard.

12. Take out the compound from the case and cut the compound off flush from the air holes and the pour holes.

13. Shellac and grease the plaster case and replace the moulding compound.

You are now ready to make castings from your reverse mould.

> **Safety tip**
>
> It is important that the funnels do not fall over, especially with PVC because of the hot rubber inside

Skin mould

This is a method when you do not have a lot of moulding compound and you have to produce a mould quickly. The biggest problem with this method is that it must be treated with great care when using PVC.

The process is exactly the same as for the flood mould, but the difference is that a smaller amount of compound is poured onto the moulding ground. The compound is then carefully lifted from here with a piece of wood or small tool and poured over the model. This is repeated until a thin skin has covered the model. Then, again cover the compound with a plaster case.

On the job: Casting bonus

Emma has been given a new job by the shop foreman, to produce 84 casts of a cornice section in seven working days. Because she is experienced in the method of casting, she has been put onto a bonus. The bonus is that she will receive £5 for every cast that she produces over eight per day. For Emma to get the best bonus she can, and produce the number of casts required in the time given, what methods should she employ?

FAQ

Will I have to spend all of my time in the fibrous plaster workshop?

No. You should, as an apprentice, spend time with a mentor in the workshop casting, laying down models, etc. But you should also spend time out on site in the fixing team.

Once you have completed your training, you can then make a choice between being a shop hand or a fixing hand.

Do I need drawing skills?

Yes, having drawing skills is very important for being a fibrous plasterer. That is, you need not artistic skills but technical drawing skills: you may need to draw out the template sections required for a job. The ability to do a good sketch will also be useful for describing what you suggest for sections and layout of the fibre work.

What are the main requirements for a fibre hand?

You must have patience, and the ability to work much of the time in reverse. You must be able to look at an architectural drawing and plan the job from that: what type of casts are needed, what size they must be, and where the reinforcements need to be placed for future fixing.

Is there work available for me in the fibre industry?

Yes, there is, but it is limited to certain areas of the country. There is also the film industry that requires fibre hands for building film sets. Also, after training, there would be the possibility of starting your own fibre company in an area that is lacking one.

Knowledge check

1. Why is cold pour more costly than PVC?

2. When casting, into which mix do you put size?

3. When running out a small panel mould, is size needed in the mix?

4. Name two forms of reinforcing used in casts.

5. What are the two types of metal that can be used to form a template?

6. What is the ratio of slipper to stock?

7. What is the name used for the system of making a running mould?

8. What is the 'nib' of a running mould?

9. What is a hand brace is used for?

10. Name two parts of a running mould needed to form a circle.

11. What type of mould is required to form a number of cornice casts?

12. What is the difference between a flood mould and a case mould?

13. What should be added to the firstings to speed up the set?

14. When greasing, so that you do not miss any areas, what should you do to the mould?

15. What is the difference between a model and a mould?

16. What is a lap?

17. What is the purpose of a strike-off?

18. Name three tools required for forming a template.

19. What is size made from?

20. What is the purpose of a wad?

chapter 12

Fixing and repairing fibrous plasterwork

OVERVIEW

In this chapter we will look at simple methods of fixing and repairing fibrous plasterwork. The methods of fixing will depend on the background that the fibre is to be fixed to and also the size and weight of the fibrous casts and mouldings. Both modern and traditional fixing methods are covered in this chapter.

The repair of fibrous plasterwork is generally the same as working on new work. The biggest difference is in the way that you get your moulding outlines to match up with existing fibrous and, in some cases, solid-run mouldings.

The tools, equipment and materials for repairs and fixing will not be listed – they will be the same as in the previous chapters – although any new materials will be introduced and explained as they are covered.

We shall cover the following topics in this chapter:

- Basic fixing of fibrous plasterwork
- Fixing cornices to plastered walls and ceilings
- Fixing panel mouldings
- Fixing plain face slabs to timber ceilings
- Repairs to fibrous plasterwork

Basic fixing of fibrous plasterwork

Once the fibre has been made in the workshop, it is taken to site and fixed in position to produce the finished job. Usually, a site fixing team, who do not work in the workshop, completes the fixing. The method of fixing used will depend on the background as well as the weight of the cast, its size and shape, and also its position in the building.

The method of fixing will also depend on how the reinforcement has been positioned in the cast from the workshop.

Before starting any fixing, you should check against the architect's drawing that you have the correct mouldings as shown or listed on the drawing. The drawing should also show you in which room each moulding should be fixed and where.

The various types of internal moulding (see Figure 12.1) are:

cornice – a moulding between the wall and the ceiling

picture rail – a moulding on the wall below the cornice forming the frieze

panel – a square or rectangular area on a wall

Did you know?

'Cornices' are sometimes wrongly called 'coving', but coving is usually only used with plasterboard

Figure 12.1 View of internal mouldings

dado rail – a moulding at chair rail height (sometimes called a chair rail)

skirting – a moulding at the base of the wall

architrave – a moulding around a door or window

Fixing types

Different types of fixing are used, depending on the conditions.

Screws

For normal wood backgrounds such as timber joists, you should use sheradised, zinc-plated or brass screws. However, brass screws are very soft and so care should be taken as they can easily break. The size of the screw will depend on the size and weight of the cast and the depth the screw must go through to reach the fixing points.

Metal self-tapping screws are zinc-plated, self-drilling and tapping (they make their own hole) and are used for fixing fibre to metal sections.

> **Remember**
>
> All fixings should be of a type that does not rust

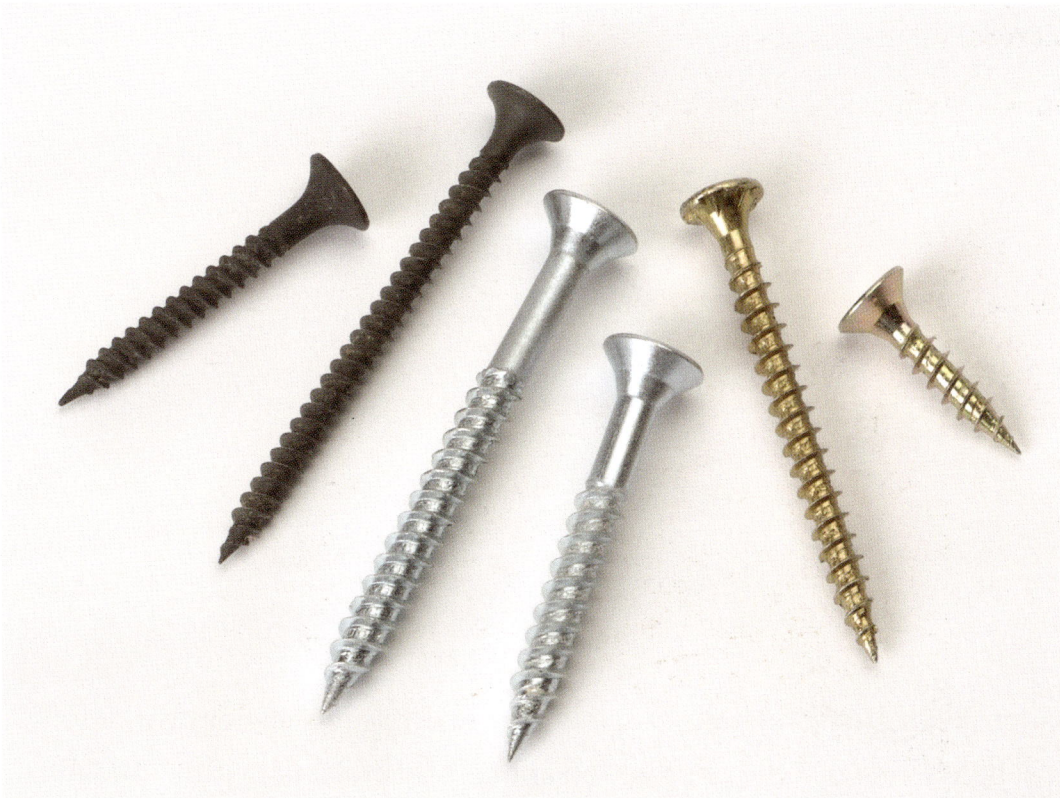

Nails

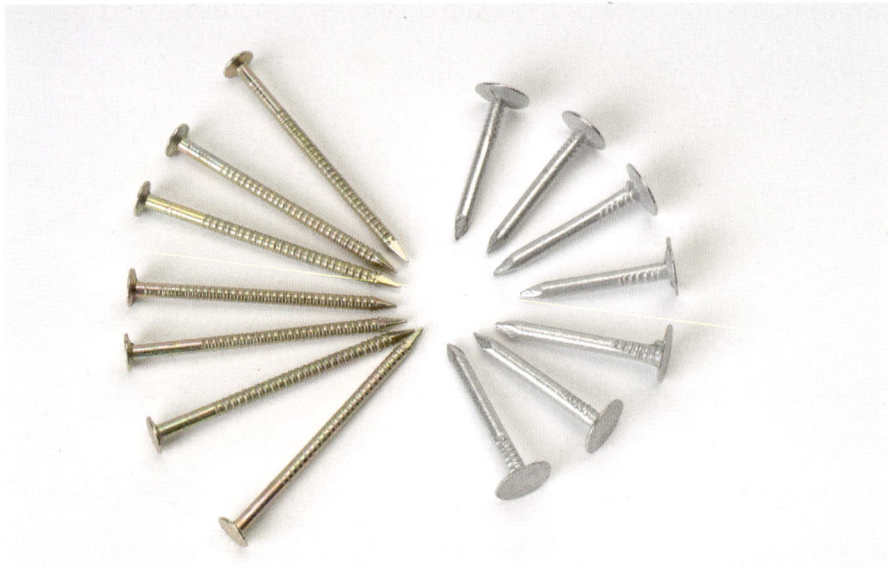

Plain galvanised nails or non-rusting nails have a ringed shank which increases their holding power. Again, the size of the nail will depend on the fixing to be carried out.

Bolts

Various different fixing bolts or screws are available for different conditions. Wall bolts (shown in the photograph above) and drill anchors are used into solid backgrounds, and toggle bolts for hollow backgrounds.

Plugs

Sometimes it is necessary to drill and plug a background to help with the strength of fixing for either nailing or screwing.

Wall plugs are produced by a number of manufacturers and they are commonly referred to by their brand name: Rawlplugs, Plasplugs, Fischer plugs. They are usually plastic (though sometimes you can make your own from wood), and different colours are used for different screw and nail sizes. Do not drill a hole bigger than the size of the plug because it will just pull out from the background.

A masonry drill bit is needed for drilling into brick, block or concrete. For timber, use a wood drill bit.

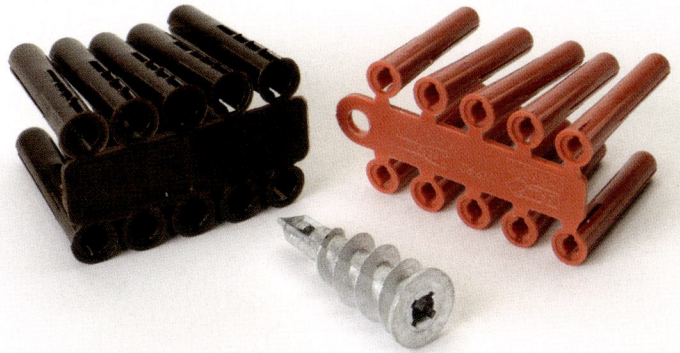

Tools for fixing and mitring

The following tools are required for fixing and mitring. See Chapter 4, pages 88–112, for a fuller description of these tools:

- multi-purpose saw
- Surform®
- bowls (large and small)
- tool brushes and fitches
- busks (square and kidney)
- small tools
- joint rules
- gauging trowel
- chalk line
- level

- hammer

- screwdrivers

- electric drill / screwdriver.

Other tools, such as normal woodworking tools, may be found in a fixer's toolkit along with setting-out tools such as tapes, measuring rules and squares.

Backgrounds for fixing

The backgrounds that fibrous work is fixed to should be:

- strong enough to carry the weight

- rigid, to prevent movement

- dry and free from dampness.

To check whether a background is sound, tap it lightly with a hammer. This will show any loose plaster; a hollow-sounding ring shows that the plaster is not bonded and could be pulled off by the fixings. Any loose plaster should be removed and made good.

A background with high suction can cause problems as it prevents the plaster from reaching its full strength and stops the plasterer from producing a high standard of finish. The suction can be 'killed' by applying PVA glue.

The flatness of the surface to fix to is important. The finished fibrous plaster surface can only have a good standard and straight line if the background is in reasonable shape. The background should have less than 3 mm deviation (bump or hollow) in a 1.8 m rule.

Setting out for fixing

All setting out should be carried out from datum points and centre lines.

In Chapter 9, on floor screeding, we explained the use of datum lines and how they are set out and worked from (pages 255–257). The system for fixing fibre is the same.

The use of centre lines is the best way of setting out mouldings that are positioned on walls or on ceilings. The centre line is positioned by measurement and all further measurements are taking from that line. Sometimes **grid lines** will be set out for fixing.

Fixing cornices to plastered walls and ceilings

When preparing cornices for fixing, it is important to make sure that the cornice is always the right way round. You need to be aware of two important elements:

wall line – the strike-off which is fixed to the wall

ceiling line – the strike-off which is fixed to the ceiling.

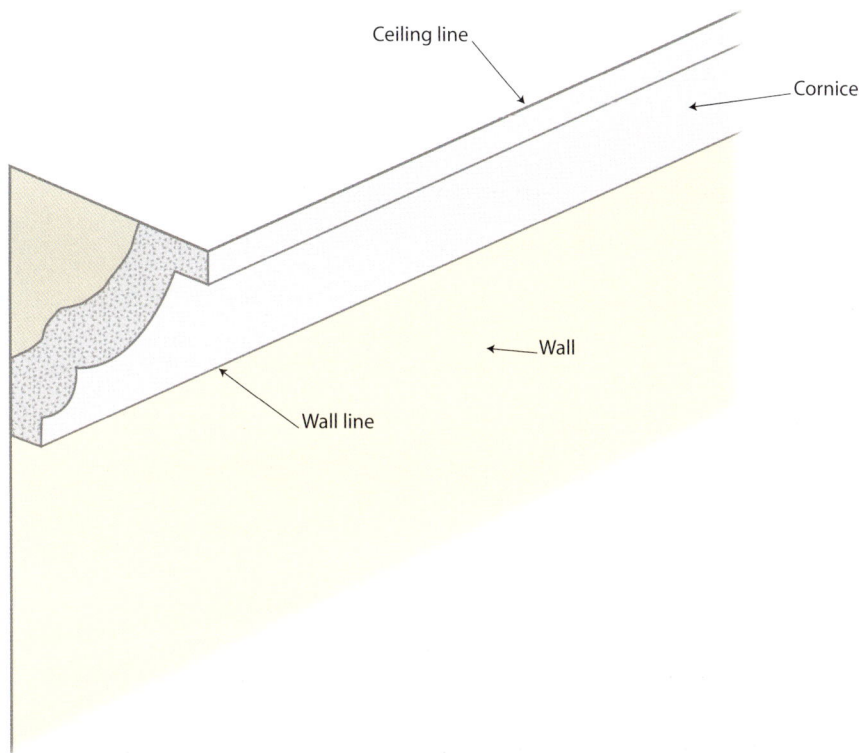

Figure 12.2 Cornice in position

> ### Definition
>
> **Grid lines** – equally spaced parallel horizontal or vertical lines drawn on the wall or ceiling, from which the setting out can be completed

Setting out

First find the **projection** of the cornice by laying the ceiling line on the bench and the wall line against a square. The projection is then measured as the distance between the square and the outer edge of the ceiling line.

Definition

Projection – how far something sticks out

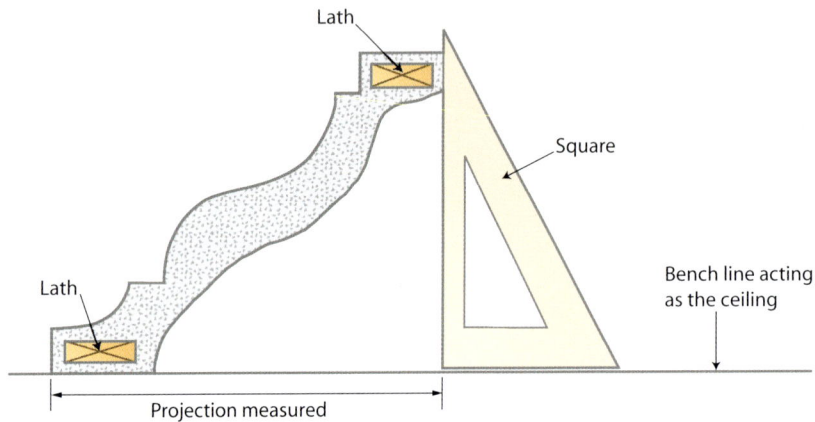

Figure 12.3 Cornice laid down on the ceiling line

Now make a mark on the ceiling at each end of the **run** of cornice.

Definition

Run – how much cornice needs to be fixed – the continuous length of cornice running along one wall

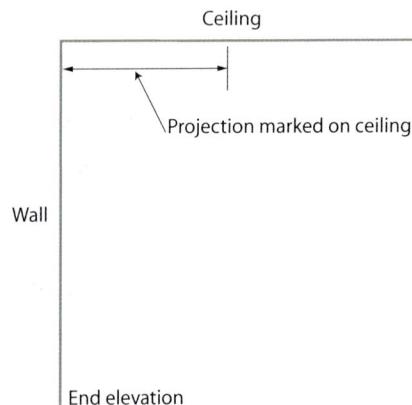

Figure 12.4 Marking a projection

Snap a chalk line through these points.

Repeat this for each length of wall.

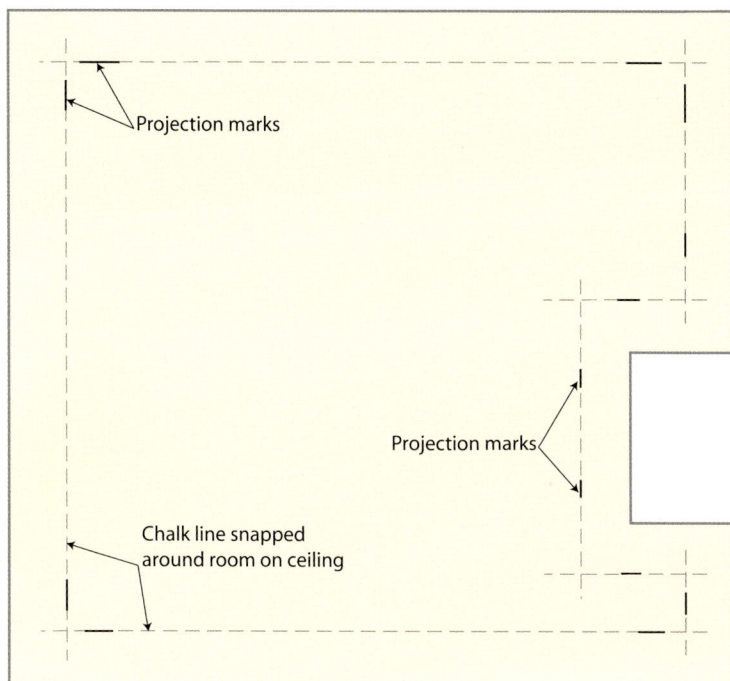

Figure 12.5 Reflected view of ceiling

Cutting cornice

Cornices should be cut to a mitre. Unlike carpenters, you do not need to have very tight mitres because you will need to reinforce the mitres so that they do not crack out at a future date. You can also make good the mitres to form a nice sharp angle.

Figure 12.6 shows a reflected view (worm's eye view) of a room with internal, external and splayed mitres. Most internal and external mitres are joints of 90° with the mitre cut at 45°.

Did you know?

A mitre joint between mouldings can be any angle but it should not be a straight joint

Internal mitre

a   b   c   d

f   g

External mitre

h

Projection

e

j

Splayed mitre

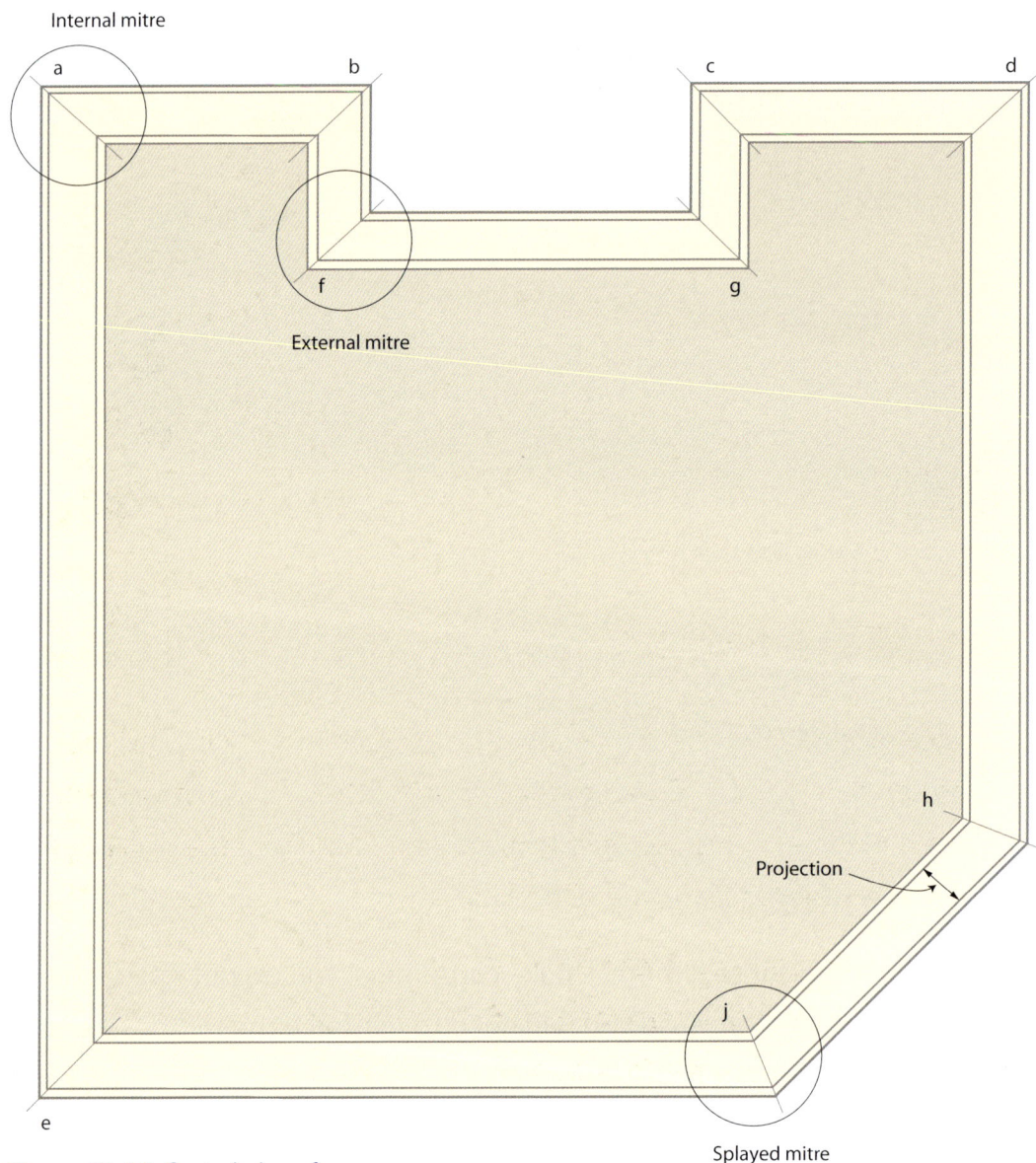

Figure 12.6 Reflected plan of a room

Measuring and marking mitres onto the cornice

Once the projection lines have been snapped onto the ceiling, the mitre lines can be worked out by drawing a line between the wall angle and the point at which the projection lines intersect. Figure 12.7 shows a reflected view of a ceiling above a bay window with the projection lines and mitre lines marked.

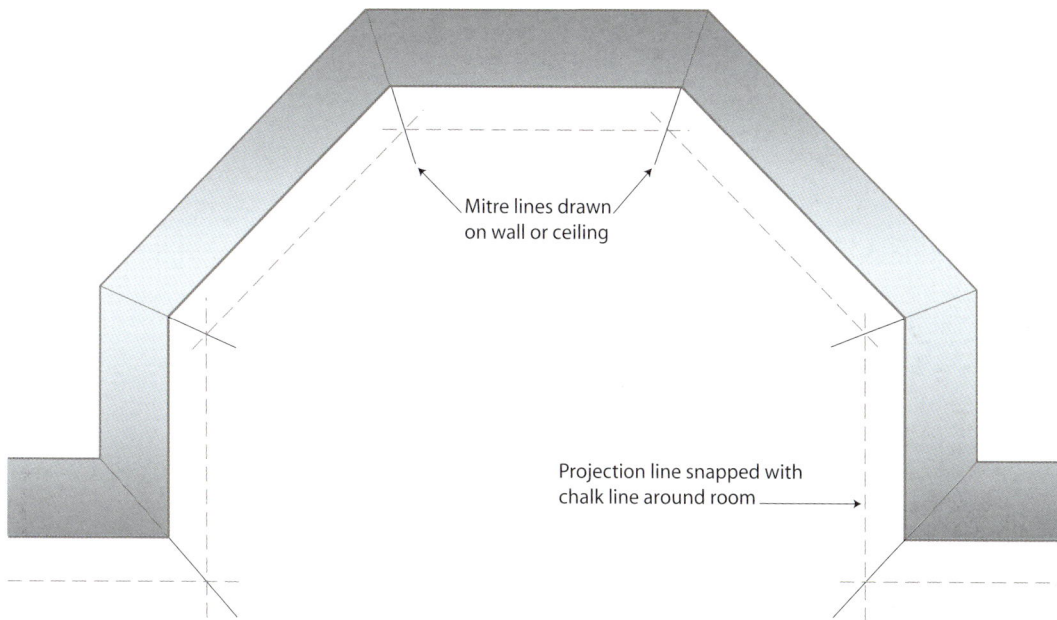

Figure 12.7 Reflected plan of a bay window

The cornice or moulding can be offered up to the projection line and the mitre line can then be transferred to the cornice with two markings: mark where the mitre line meets the ceiling line, then mark where the wall angle/ mitre line meets the wall line.

The method described above can be used for all types of mitre. A different method for marking splayed mitres is to place a small square on the point where the projection lines intersect down to the wall and mark the wall.

Now measure along the wall from the mark into the wall angle. The cornice wall line will be longer than the cornice ceiling line by this amount. Mark the cornice accordingly, using this measurement.

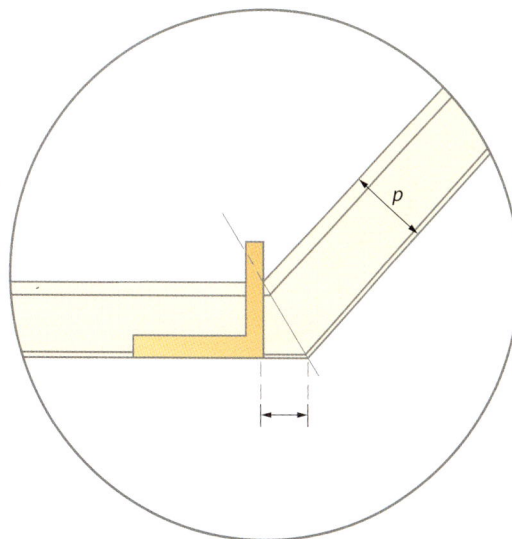

Figure 12.8 Splayed mitre: measuring the extra wall line length

Cutting the mitre

Wooden squares are fixed to the cutting bench so that the cornice can rest against them. A block of wood is then fixed in front to stop it moving (Figure 12.9).

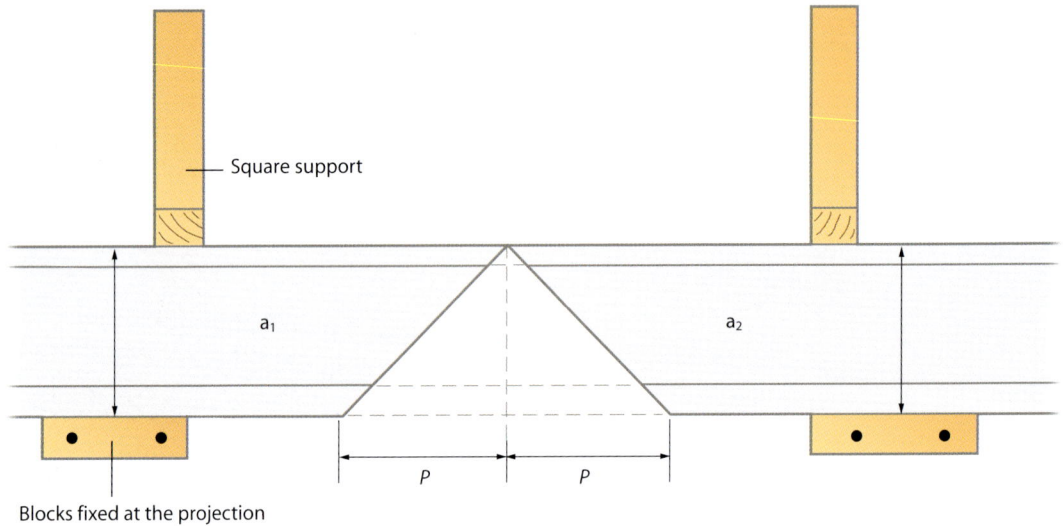

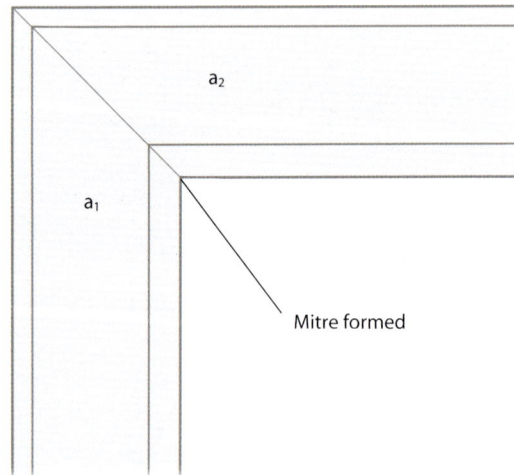

Square support

a_1

a_2

P

P

Blocks fixed at the projection

a_2

a_1

Mitre formed

Figure 12.9 The cornice on the cutting bench

With the cornice set up against the square supports, and the type of mitre that you wish to cut marked, you must now line up the saw by lining up, with your eye, the top of the saw with the marks you have put on the cornice. Always keep the saw upright and saw through to the marks. If you do not trust your eye, you can put a pencil guideline for cutting through.

It is important never to cut a cornice (or coving) with it lying down flat, as if it were a piece of wood, because you will end up with a very wide mitre. Also, never cut with the wall line on the bench because this will give you an incorrect angle for the mitre.

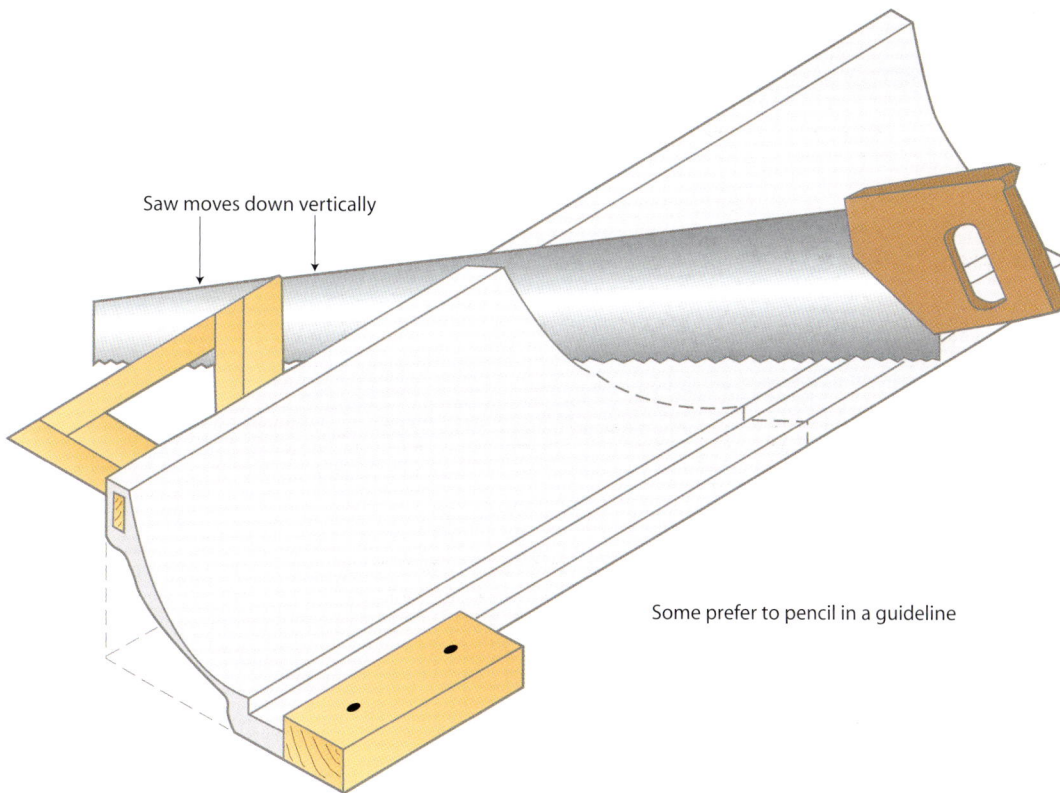

Saw moves down vertically

Some prefer to pencil in a guideline

Figure 12.10 Cutting the mitre

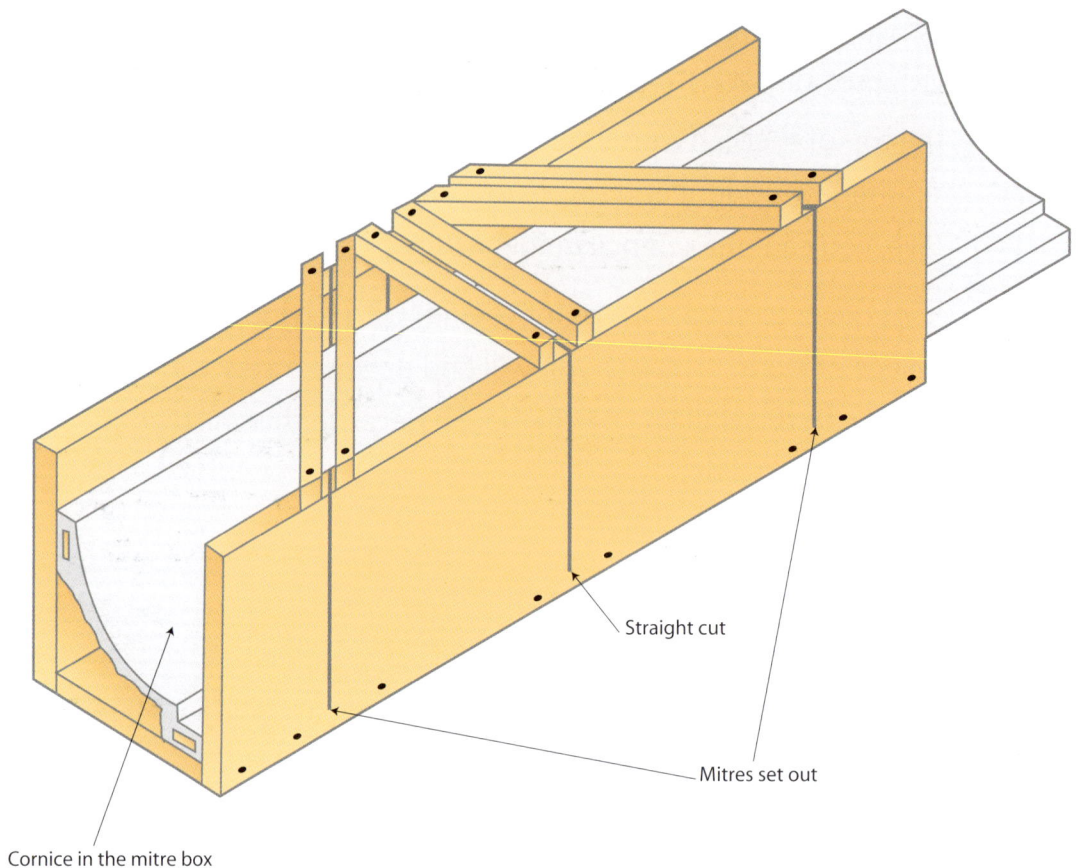

Straight cut

Mitres set out

Cornice in the mitre box

Figure 12.11 A mitre box

Use of a mitre box

An alternative method of cutting 90° and straight cuts is a box, which is best made for individual cornices, although fixers do carry around a large box big enough to cut most cornices (Figure 12.11). If the box is too big, the cornice will not be held firm and will move during cutting. A timber batten can be nailed into the box so that the cornice is held firm. The use of a mitre box also means that you must place the cornice ceiling line on the bottom of the mitre box, i.e. treat the bottom of the box as the ceiling.

Self-return or stopped end mitres

This is a method of stopping a cornice when required on a straight run. This is most commonly seen in the hall when the staircase pokes through the ceiling.

The mitre is just an external mitre with the run of the cornice cut off (i.e. it doesn't continue around a corner).

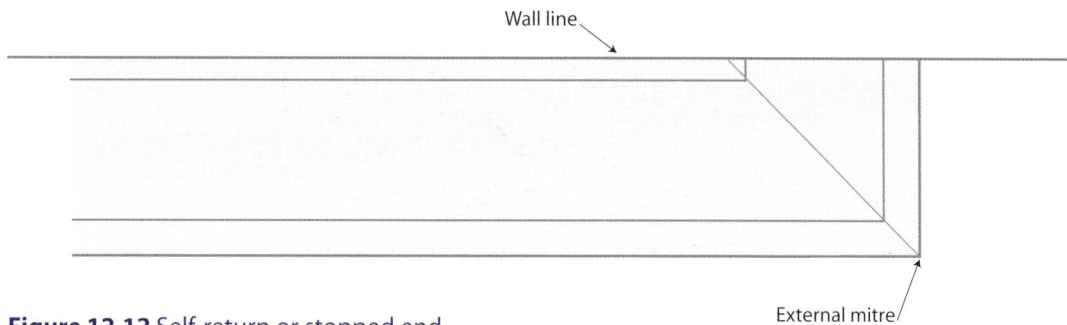

Figure 12.12 Self-return or stopped end

In practice it is often better to wad a short return with the external mitre cut and laid on the ceiling line. The self-return is wadded to the back of the main run of cornice. When the wad is set hard, the self-return can then be cut flush with the back of the cast so that it will lie flat against the wall and ceiling.

Fixing cornice

On some jobs, you may be required to use traditional methods, although there are easier, modern methods available.

Traditional fixing method

With the setting out is completed and the mitres are cut, the cornice can now be fixed in position. Fixing points can be marked on the wall and ceiling.

If you are working in a team of two, one person can hold the cornice cast in position and the second operative can drill a small **leader hole** through the laths at the strike-offs, marking fixing points on the wall and ceiling. With the cornice cast removed, a masonry bit can be used to drill the hole, and a wall plug inserted to receive the fixing. Now reposition the cornice and line up the leader holes with the drilled and plugged fixing points. The screws should be taken below the surface of the cast and screwed tight, pulling the cornice back, with the strike-offs flush with the wall and ceiling.

If you are working on your own, it is a more difficult job because you will need to drill and plug the wall and then mark the cornice in the same position that lines up with the holes drilled in the wall. The cornice is then propped up in position by the use of **fixing blocks** or, for smaller, lighter casts, nails could be used to provide temporary support for the cast during fixing. The cornice can then be screwed up into position.

All cornice lengths are cut and fixed in position and fixing blocks removed.

If the wall or ceiling lines are not flat back to the surface, packing pieces (wedges) can be placed in position against the fixing points to keep the cornice straight.

Sometimes it is not easy to get a fixing point, especially at the ceiling line or when fixing fibrous plain face slabs. To get over this problem, you may need to cut holes into the ceiling boards big enough to get your hands into. A wad is then soaked in plaster and fed through the hole onto the back of the cast and onto the back of the clean plasterboard (the cast will need to be supported until the wads are set). Once the wads are set, the holes in the plasterboard can be made good.

Modern fixing methods

An alternative method of fixing cornices, dado mouldings and lightweight moulding sections is to use one of a number of proprietary manufactured fixing adhesives. Always check with the manufacturer to see if they will hold the fibre you wish to fix.

One other adhesive used is tile adhesive, but it will need supporting until the adhesive hardens (note that it will shrink back from any wall or ceiling line).

The backs of smaller mouldings such as dado mouldings and the areas that the mouldings are to be fixed to must be keyed to form a good bond between the moulding and the background. This is usually a deep cross key with a slight undercut (a sharp craft knife can be used). The moulding should be soaked well in water until the bubbles disappear and the background can have a couple of coats of PVA applied.

Casting plaster can also be used to stick smaller mouldings. Mix the material and allow it to stand until it becomes like cream, and then apply it to the back of the moulding and squeeze it home tight (support it with nails or blocks of wood until the plaster has set). Clean away all plaster wastage that has squeezed out using a busk or joint rule, and use a tool brush to clean any plaster off the face of the moulding.

Fixing panel mouldings

Many panel mouldings are fixed to the wall in a design that has a quarter-circle in each of the corners. This makes mitring a little more difficult because you are mitring from straight to curve, and joint rules will not be curved to the same curve as the mouldings. To get over this problem the panel moulding should be drawn on the wall, including the inside and outside of the moulding.

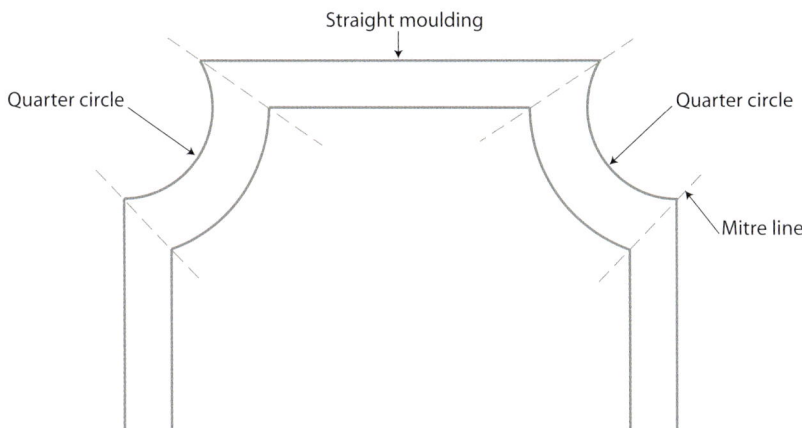

Straight moulding

Quarter circle

Quarter circle

Mitre line

Figure 12.13 Mitring straight to curved panel moulding joints

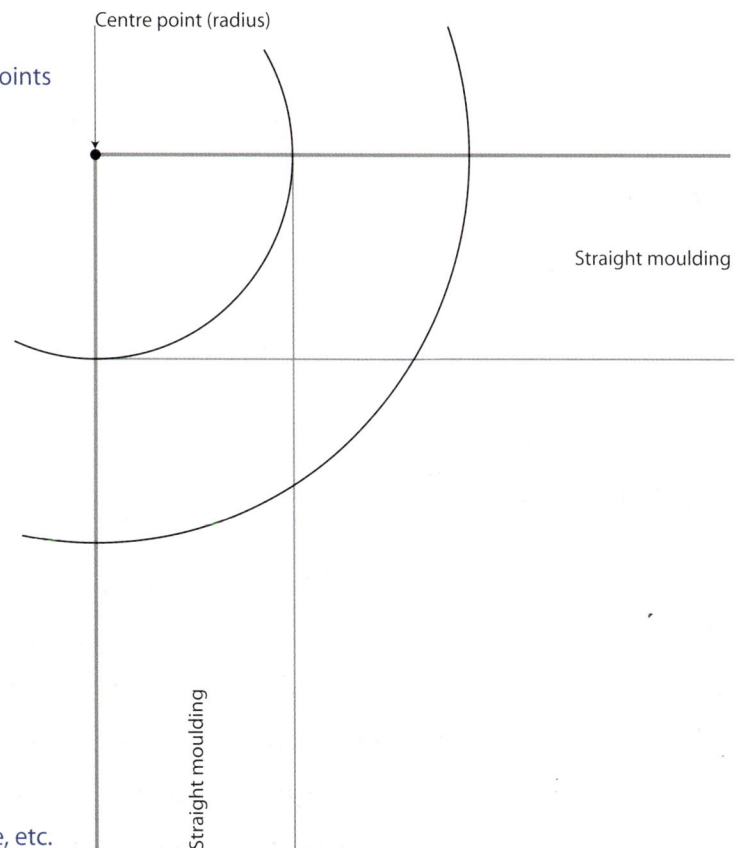

Centre point (radius)

Straight moulding

Straight moulding

Figure 12.14 Moulding drawn onto wall or plain face, etc.

Mitre line drawn approx. 5 mm from original mitre line

Original mitre lines

Mitre line drawn approx. 5 mm from original mitre line

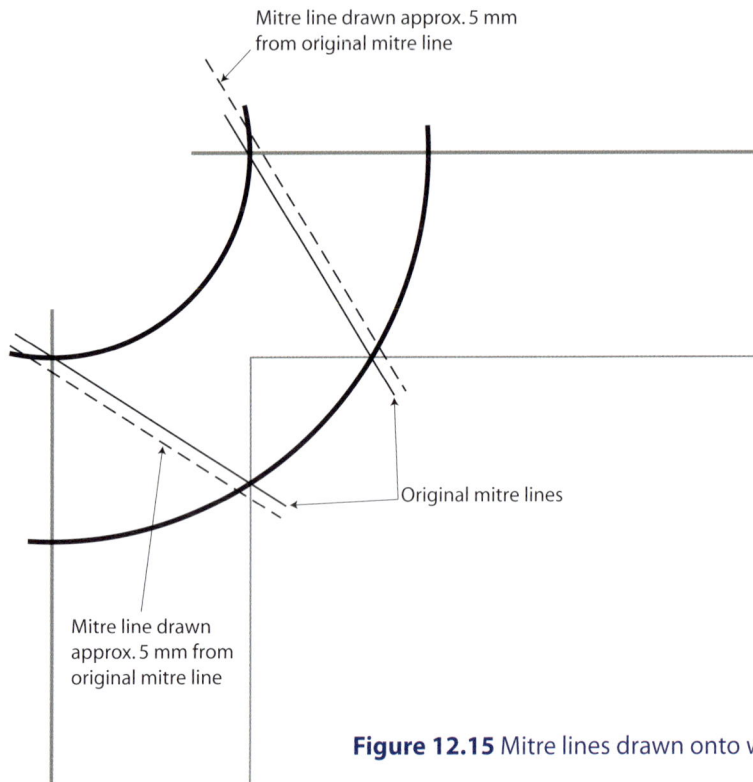

Figure 12.15 Mitre lines drawn onto working surface

Now extend (draw longer) the line of the mitre through the mitre and beyond the inner and outer moulding lines.

Now move the mitre line back about 5 mm away from the curved mitred line.

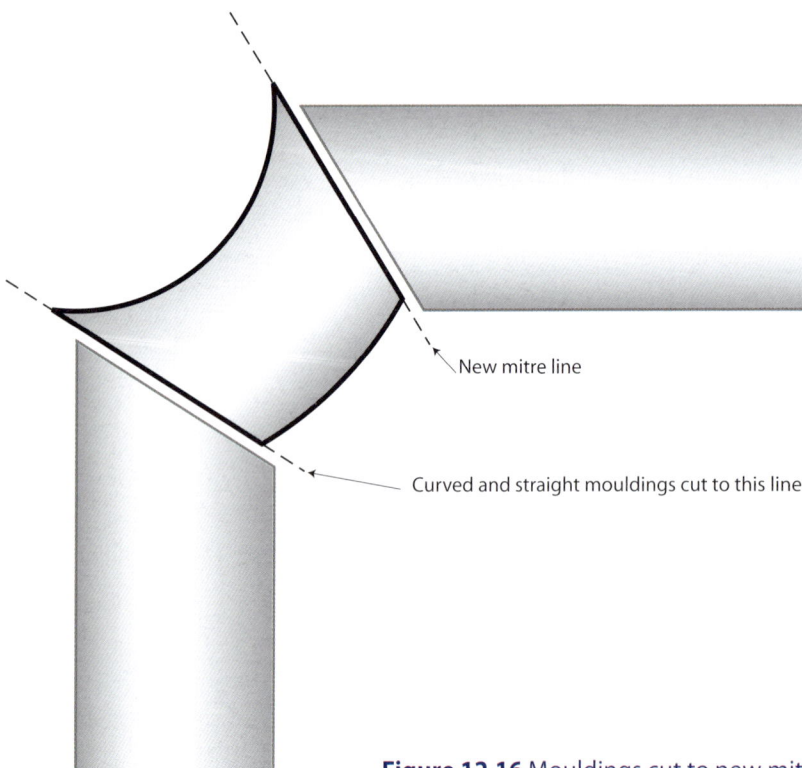

New mitre line

Curved and straight mouldings cut to this line

Then hold your straight panel moulding between the two lines and mark the new 5 mm reduced mitre line on the moulding.

Next take the curved moulding and again hold it between the lines and mark it to the extended 5 mm mitre line.

Now cut the mitres as marked on the straight and curved mouldings.

The mouldings are then fixed in position.

Figure 12.16 Mouldings cut to new mitre lines and secured (fixed in position to new mitre lines)

The mitre may look strange but what you are going to do now is to scribe the curve mitre in by using your joint rule and, resting on the straight moulding, carve back the curved moulding until it lines up with the straight one.

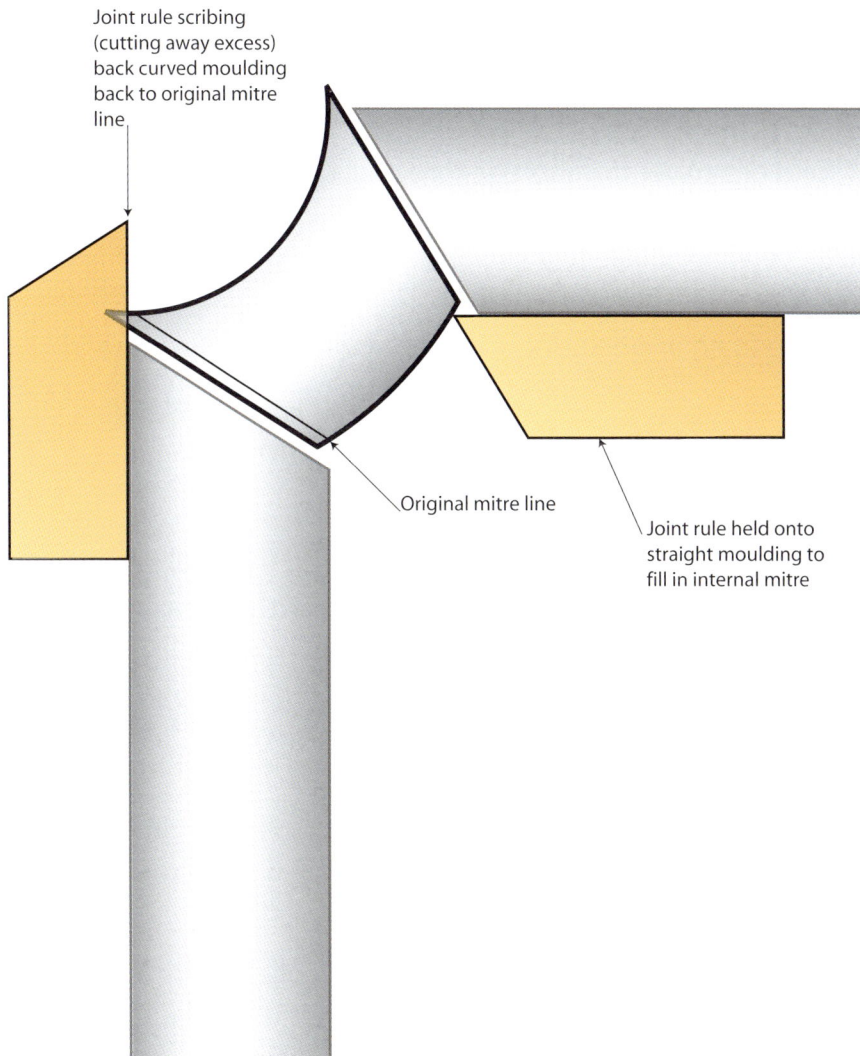

Joint rule scribing (cutting away excess) back curved moulding back to original mitre line

Original mitre line

Joint rule held onto straight moulding to fill in internal mitre

Figure 12.17 Moulding cut back on external mitre to line up to original mitre line

You will now see the mitre line showing on the curved moulding. This will allow you to work your mitring from the straight and you do not have to touch the curved moulding.

Fixing plain face slabs to ceilings

The method used for fixing plain face slabs to a ceiling will depend on the type of ceiling.

Fixing to a timber ceiling

Setting out

When fixing to a solid or timber framed background, the line of the finished ceiling would have already been established from a datum line.

Centre lines are set out, and the position of the plain face slabs marked. A string line can then be fixed in position to work out where the first line of slabs is to be fixed.

Fixing

Using two 'tee struts' (or dead men) to support the slabs while fixing, the slabs can be adjusted to the line, and the face checked with a straight edge. The first slab is then fixed through the face of the slab into the timber joists.

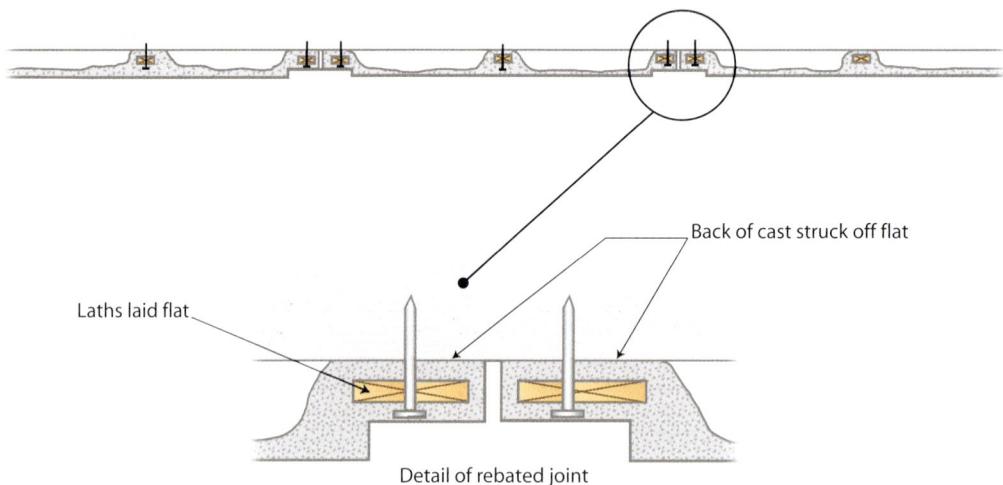

Back of cast struck off flat

Laths laid flat

Detail of rebated joint

Figure 12.18 Fixing to timber ceiling joists

The next slab is then fixed up to the line and adjusted with a straight edge and wedges across the joint until it lines up with the first cast and the line. The rest of the casts are then fixed.

Fixing to a suspended ceiling

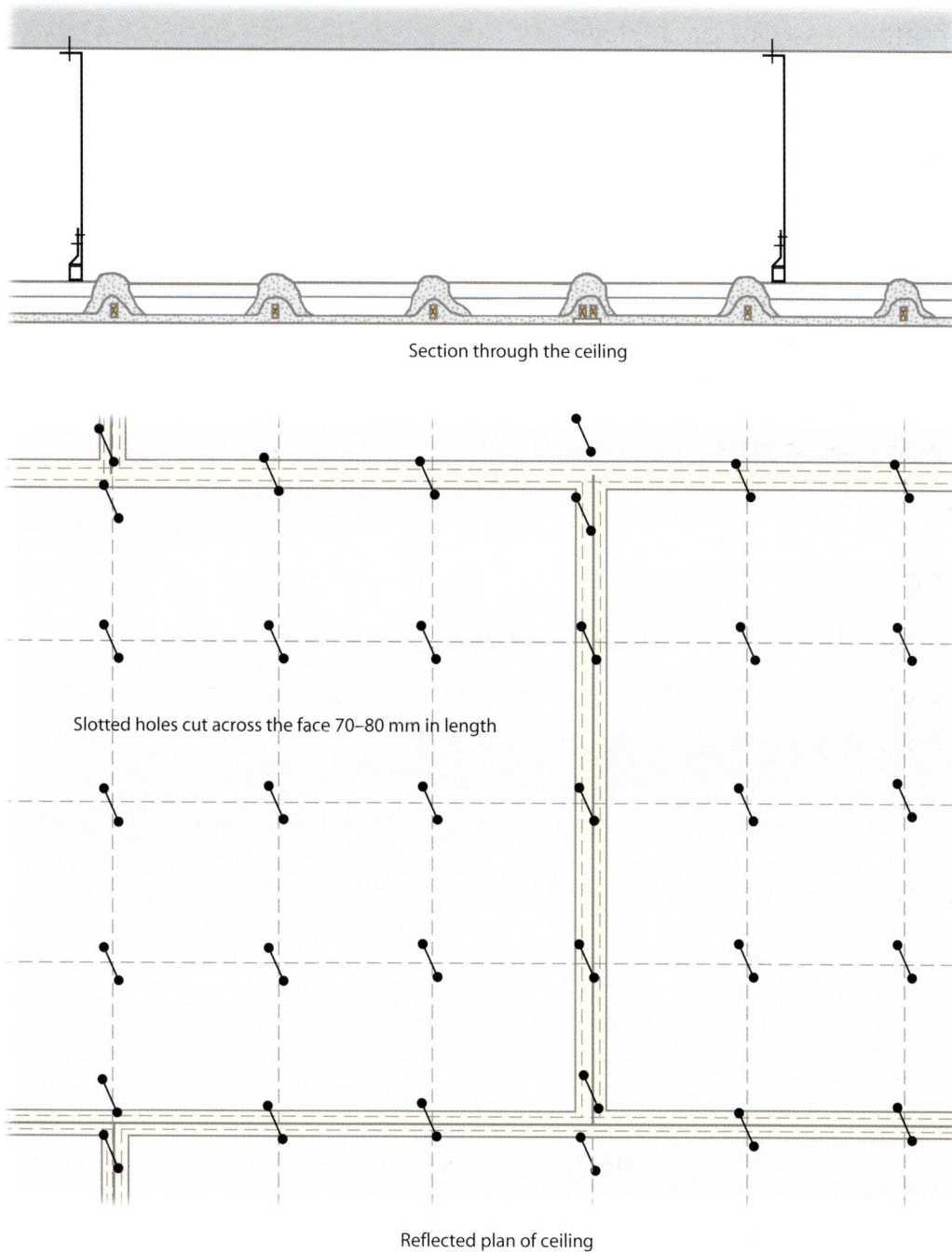

Section through the ceiling

Slotted holes cut across the face 70–80 mm in length

Reflected plan of ceiling

Figure 12.19 Fixing plain face slabs to a suspended ceiling

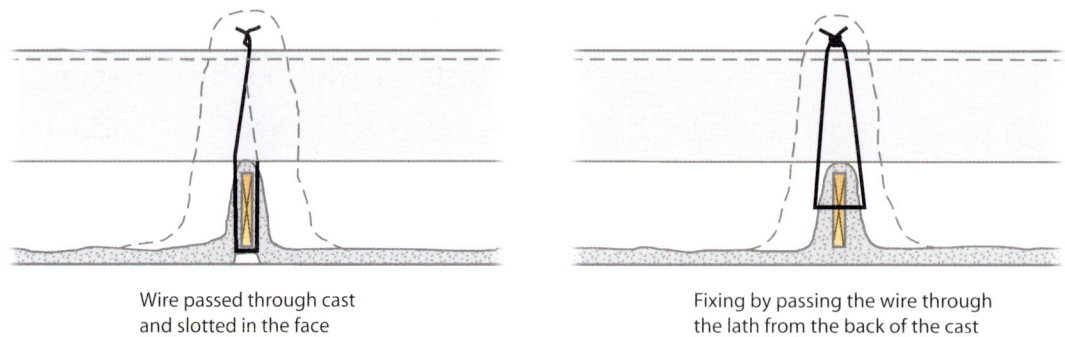

Wire passed through cast and slotted in the face

Fixing by passing the wire through the lath from the back of the cast

Figure 12.20 Fixing plain face slabs to a suspended ceiling (continued)

1. Set out centre lines and mark the position of the slabs.

2. Fix a string line through the first line of slabs.

3. Drill holes each side of the lath diagonally at 70–80 mm centres to line up with the fixing points of the grid.

4. Form slotted grooves between the holes below the surface of the slabs.

5. Support the first slab in position by struts (dead men).

6. Wire through the slab with 18 SWG wire.

7. Adjust the wires using top cutters until the slab is level and in line.

8. Wad up the slab from behind the back of the cast.

9. Repeat the operation for the other slabs in the line.

10. Reposition the string for the second row of slabs.

11. Fix the second line and keep repeating until the ceiling is complete.

You may need to cut holes in some of the slabs to get a fixing, as for fixing to timber backgrounds.

Finishing the ceiling

Stopping in

Rebates and holes are wetted, and canvas wads are soaked in plaster and laid along the length of the rebate joint (a gauging trowel can be used for this). The joints are then finished off with a small tool and joint rule or busk. No canvas should show on the face. Holes and slots are filled in with a creamy mix of plaster and finished with a joint rule or busk. A tool brush will help with the finishing as it stops the old plaster sucking out the water from the new mix. A weak solution of PVA will also stop the water being sucked out of the mix.

When the ceilings are finished, the standard should be flat to within 3 mm in a 1.8 m rule and level overall.

Mitring and stopping in

Wads or strings of canvas should be soaked in plaster and worked into the mitres and joints. The mitres should be well soaked in water and a soft mix of plaster is then worked into the mitre or joints using a small tool. A joint rule is then used to follow the moulding outline either side of the mitre until all moulding sections are complete, with no misses. The use of a tool brush helps in the finishing of the mitre. Fresh mixes of plaster are used until a finish has been achieved. Try not to work on the same mitre, but move around and let the plaster you have put on harden up a little: this way you will not remove the plaster you have already put on. Always stop in the ceiling and wall lines.

Always take time to stand back and look at your work, viewing from the ground, because how you fix and stop in is what people will see for many years to come.

Repairs to fibrous plasterwork

First we will cover the method of forming simple repairs to the damaged face of fibrous plasterwork. This may be either a cornice or a plain face slab ceiling. This method is for slight accidental knocks to the finished face.

Simple damage repair

1. Look at the damage to the casts to see whether it is only facial damage. If there has been no damage to the body of the casts, it can be easily repaired.

Remember

Do not over-wet the moulding because it becomes soft, and your joint rule can damage the surface of the moulding. Keep all mitring tools clean as you work

Did you know?

One method of making plaster last longer when stopping in is to put water into the bowl, add your plaster but do not mix up. Take the wet plaster from the bottom of the bowl and slowly the plaster will start to set. A second method is to use size water, but be careful that you do not over-size the water as it will weaken the plaster

2. Gently remove the damaged area, by using either a small tool or a sharp knife. Do not hit the plaster with a hammer, or hammer and bolster, because you will create more damage than you started with.

3. Get your tools, equipment and materials for repairing ready. For this you will need small tools, joint rules or busk, and fitch brush (tool brush) or small paintbrush, small bowls for mixing and water, plus a bucket for water. The materials you need are casting plaster and PVA glue.

4. Protect the area that you are working in because it may be an occupied house. Put down sheets on the floor and on any furniture that is close to where you are working. Protect, as much as you can, any decoration (wallpaper, etc.) that is around the area where you are working.

5. Remove any damaged areas and brush down loose bits of plasterwork. Trim off any strings of canvas that may show after making good.

6. Either wet in the old plaster by using a brush or, better still, put some diluted (wetted down) PVA glue in a bowl and brush it onto the surface.

7. Now mix up your plaster in a small bowl; do not make it too stiff or too wet. While the PVA is still tacky, small tool the plaster onto the damaged area. Using either your joint rule (this is the best tool for the job and gets the best match) or a busk, follow the shape of the existing moulding either side of the small damaged area until you have completely matched the existing cornice or slab. Only use a tool brush if the plaster is drying out too quickly. Too much water brushing will leave lines behind.

8. Stand back and look at the repair: does it match the existing or not?

Heavy damage to basic fibrous plaster casts

In cases of repair where a cast has suffered severe damage such as water damage, fire or age decay, and in rooms that have had a change of use, a more substantial repair may be needed.

Remember

You are really a guest in the person's house, so act correctly: work cleanly, protect the people's possessions and watch your language

Did you know?

You can mix up your casting plaster in the PVA water as it can give extra strength to the plaster

In most of these situations, some of the original cornice would still be available and so a repair could be made. If the fibre has suffered so much damage that all of it needs replacing, it can be said that it no longer becomes a repair but a complete replacement.

With any repair, it must match the existing. A good repair should never be seen, so the work of a good 'making-good hand' should never be noticed.

So what do you do to replace, say, a 3-metre length of plain cornice? There are four methods of getting the information needed to make a new length of cornice.

Method 1

1. A piece of the existing cornice can be removed very carefully and made ready for transporting to the workshop.

2. Take a measurement of the projection of the cornice, and the depth, and record it on paper (Figure 12.21).

3. Take a photograph of the cornice and note the amount of cornice that is needed to replace the damaged area.

4. Square off the end of the cornice that you have taken down.

5. Draw a ceiling and wall line at 90° to each other on a piece of paper and place the cornice onto the paper, marking which is the ceiling line and which is the wall line.

6. Now draw around the cornice line onto the paper.

7. Tidy up the moulding outline, but not too much because you want it to match the existing cornice.

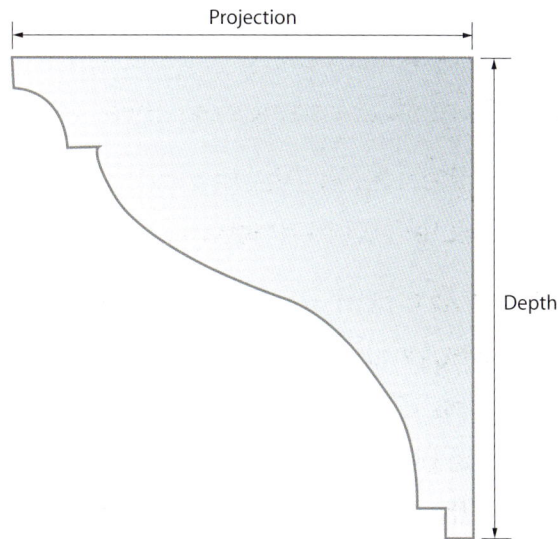

Figure 12.21 Recording the **girth** of the cornice

Safety tip

When checking the look of your work, do not stand *too* far back if working on scaffolding of any type – you could fall and do yourself a lot of harm

Definition

Girth – the measurement right around the cornice's outline

8. Now extend the ceiling and wall line (shown as a dotted line in Figure 12.22) and put in the bench line. This will now give you your template that needs filing and horsing up.

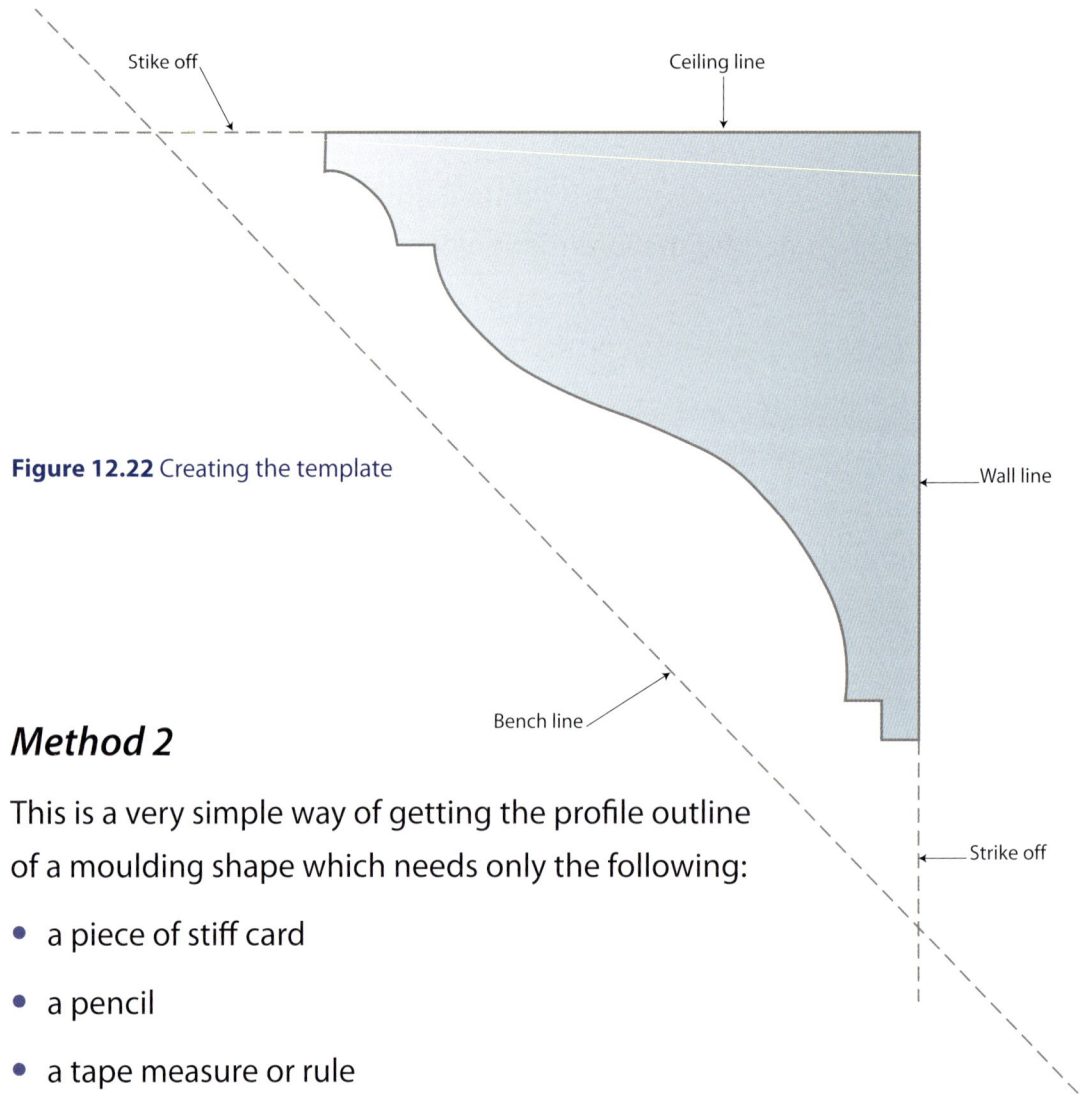

Figure 12.22 Creating the template

Method 2

This is a very simple way of getting the profile outline of a moulding shape which needs only the following:

- a piece of stiff card

- a pencil

- a tape measure or rule

- a square

- a fine-tooth saw.

This method is more suitable for getting the profile outline if a section cannot be removed or if you're using a section of the same cornice that is in another room.

1. Find a good section of the cornice in an area that will not be noticed in the future, such as above a door.

2. Make a fine saw cut into the cornice wide enough to slide the card into.

3. Slide the card into the cut and draw the outline of the cornice. Cut the card along this outline.

4. Now repeat steps 5–8 in Method 1, using the card outline to create the template.

Method 3

If it is impossible to remove a section of cornice or put a saw cut into the cornice, you can draw the section in one other way. For this method, you will need an extra pair of hands and work in a team with your mate, using the following:

- a level
- a metal rule
- a piece of paper
- a digital camera
- a drawing set.

1. Complete a rough sketch of the shape of the cornice on the paper.

2. Hold the level vertical with the end of the level on the ceiling.

3. Measure from the level to the moulding outline and record the measurements onto the rough sketched outline of the cornice.

4. Now hold the level horizontal with one end against the wall.

5. Take further measurements from the level edge to the cornice and record the measurements.

6. With the drawing set, draw the cornice outline onto the paper.

7. Cut out the cornice shape and hold it up to the original cornice as a check. Any adjustments can then be made to the paper outline.

8. Take a photograph to check back on the original cornice outline.

9. Create the template as before using this outline.

Method 4

This method involves taking a cast of the original cornice but, before using it, contact the client and, after explaining what you intend to do, check whether they are in agreement. This method can only be used on a plain cornice and not one with an **undercut**.

1. Find an undamaged section of plain cornice.

2. Apply three thin coats of shellac about 150 mm wide.

3. Grease up the shellacked area.

4. Take a cast of the greased and shellacked area using the same method as described in the casting section of the book (pages 315–325).

5. When the plaster has set, take it down and square off one edge of the cast.

6. Follow steps 5–8 in Method 1, using the squared off cast to create the template.

Repairing hairline cracks

Small **hairline cracks** can be simply repaired by removing any loose plaster around the cracks and very carefully opening them up a little using a bottle top opener. Wet in the crack and apply a watered down coat of PVA adhesive and make good with plaster.

FAQ

What happens if the fibrous plaster cast that arrives on site does not have the same projection and depth as the existing one?

Try the cast up against the original and see if there is much difference. Is it in a position that you can still fix it and lose the difference in the mitre? Does it line up with an existing cornice or is it a stand-alone repair? If you cannot hide the fact that the mouldings do not match, you must contact the workshop and get them to make a new cornice.

On the job: Unloading fibrous casts

Lewis has been told by his supervisor to go to a site and unload the plaster casts and store them in the rooms where the casts are to be fitted. Lewis needs to go to the site office and read the drawings to find out in which room the different casts are to be fitted.

When he is in the site office, he realises that he cannot read the drawings and so cannot understand which cast goes into which room. What should he do now?

- Should Lewis just store them in a storage cabin and walk away?
- Should he store them all in one room and wait until his supervisor turns up in a couple of days' time?
- Should Lewis ask for help from the site agent on site?
- Or should he just phone up the company office and tell them the truth?

Knowledge check

1. What can be used to help fixing on a high-suction background?

2. What is the projection of a cornice?

3. Is an external mitre longer on the wall line or on the ceiling line?

4. Should cornice mitres be cut with the wall line or the ceiling line on the bench?

5. Name the equipment that will help you to cut mitres accurately and easily.

6. Name two tools used to form a mitre.

7. What angle should be cut for a moulding to form a 90° angle?

8. What should be added to a mitre to stop it from cracking out?

9. Name two ways of preventing plaster from setting too quickly during mitring.

10. What is a self-return mitre?

11. What is a leader hole?

12. When fixing mouldings to a wall, what should the setting out be done from?

13. When fixing two lengths of moulding together on a straight run, how can you best hide the joint between the two?

14. Name three materials used for fixing casts.

15. What is a 'dead man' used for?

Glossary

Acoustic performance
controlling and reducing the noise levels within buildings

Adhesion
the ability of the plaster coat to stick to the surface

Adhesive
glue

Air hole
a hole cut into a case mould to allow air to escape as the compound is poured in

Architrave
a decorative moulding, usually made from timber, that is fitted around door and window frames to hide the gap between the frame and the wall

Arris
a sharp edge or internal corner on a cornice

Balling
when the sand and cement mix does not have enough water, it will bind together in small balls, which will make it extremely difficult to lay the floor

Barrier cream
a cream used to protect the skin from damage or infection

Bearers
pieces of timber placed on the ground to stack material on to keep it away from the ground

Bellcast
a curve built into the bottom edge of a roof or wall surface designed to throw off water. It looks like the edge of a bell, hence bellcast

Building Regulations
a set of rules for various products relating to fire safety, sound insulation, drainage, ventilation and electrical safety, dictating how and where they should be installed. The regulations aim to ensure the health and safety of people in and around buildings

Bulking
the increase in volume of sand caused by it being wet

Carded scaffolder
someone who holds a recognised certificate showing competence in scaffold erection

Cast
piece of manufactured plasterwork that is ready to be fixed

Chattering
small ridges caused by the template vibrating as it slides along the face of the mould

Cockling
where the first coat expands and breaks up into the second coat

Conservation
preservation of the environment and wildlife

Consolidate
compact or pack down hard

Contamination
when harmful chemicals or substances pollute something (e.g. water)

Corrosive
describes a substance that can damage things it comes into contact with (e.g. material, skin)

Coving
a decorative moulding that is fitted to the top of a wall where it meets the ceiling

Dab
a trowel length of adhesive that is applied to the wall. It should be raised up and then tapered down to smear into the wall. This raised part of the dab is what holds the plasterboard to the wall, and the smeared part is what holds the dab to the wall

Damp proof course
a waterproof layer placed above ground level in a brick, block or stone wall to stop moisture coming up into the building

Daywork joint
the finish of the floor at the end of the day, especially used in larger floor areas

Dermatitis
a skin condition where the affected area is red, itchy and sore

Double shank
a trowel with two pieces of metal holding the handle to the metal face, not just one

DPM
a layer of waterproof material placed under the screed to stop moisture coming up from the ground into the building

Dressing
smoothing the surface of masonry or timber

Egress	an exit or way out		**Model**	the original moulding that is to be reproduced
Employer	the person or company you work for		**Muffle**	a false template that stands in front of the template by about 6 mm. It can be made from plaster, metal or hardboard and formed in the same shape as the profile, then temporarily nailed to the template face
Enforce	make sure a law is obeyed			
Enriched work	any plasterwork that has a pattern or design			
FIFO	first in first out: a system of using stock whereby the oldest material is used first so that it doesn't perish			
			Nosing	the curved central strip of the bead to which the wings are attached
Fines	the small bits of sand that help to hold in the water		**Noxious**	harmful or poisonous
			Part E	the regulations dealing with the transmission of sound
Fixing blocks	blocks of wood which are nailed onto the wall to help support the cornice or moulding when working on your own		**Pick up**	another term used to describe the process of a material setting or 'going off'
			Plain face	a flat plaster cast used for forming suspended ceilings or walls, or for use as a temporary bench to which to fix a model
French chalk	a very fine powder			
Gauge	measure the correct proportions of materials in a render mix to achieve full strength when set			
			Plant	in the context of the construction industry, industrial machinery
Girth	the measurement right around the cornice's outline		**Plaster skim**	a thin layer of plaster that is put onto walls to give a smooth and even finish
Grid lines	equally spaced parallel horizontal or vertical lines drawn on the wall or ceiling, from which the setting out can be completed			
			Plinth	render applied below the damp-proof course to ground level
			Pour hole	a hole cut into a case mould through which the moulding compound is poured
Hairline crack	a very narrow crack which can show on the face of plaster			
Hazard	a danger or risk		**Proactive**	taking action *before* something happens (e.g. an accident)
Induction	a formal introduction you will receive when you start any new job, where you will be shown around, shown where the toilets and canteen, etc. are, and told what to do if there is a fire		**Projection**	how far something sticks out
			Proportionately	when one thing increases in step with something else
			Proportioning	dividing into parts
			Prosecute	accuse someone of committing a crime, which usually results in them being taken to court and, if found guilty, punished
Jeweller's snips	small delicate snips, which have straight or curved blades			
Joggle	a location point used to prevent movement between the moulding compound and the plaster case			
			PVA	polyvinyl acetate, a water-based adhesive
Jointing sequence	taping plasterboard joints and applying material to seal the tape and joints		**Quoin**	brick or large stone, set in an external corner of a wall
Knocking back	the dubious practice of adding extra water to plaster and working it with the trowel so that it can continue to be used even after it has begun to set		**RCD (residual current device)**	is used as a safety cut-out when using electrical equipment, to protect you from electric shock
			Reactive	taking action *after* something happens
Leader hole	a small pilot hole drilled into the cast so that the nail or screw can be fixed through the hole without damaging the plaster face		**Reveal**	the side of a window opening or doorway which is at right angles to the face of the work
Making good hand	a plasterer who is employed to make good damaged areas			

Rope	in casting, a strip of canvas about 150 mm wide soaked in plaster, rolled and lightly passed through the hand
Rubbing up	the process of closing in the surface, rubbing out any small imperfections on the surface and providing a key for the finishing coat of plaster to adhere to
Run	how much cornice needs to be fixed – the continuous length of cornice running along one wall
Safety edge	some square edge files have one edge that is smooth, so that you do not cut into the side against which you are
Sand down	use sandpaper to smooth down an area of wall in order to erase a bump or rough area in dry lining
Shelf life	the length of time that materials can be stored before they deteriorate
Silt	very fine particles of sand which help with the ability to work the sand with the trowel. Too much silt is not good as it does not have a lot of strength and this can lead to cracking
Size	a gelatine-based material (gelatine as used in jellies which is made from animal bones)
Skirting	a decorative moulding that is fitted at the bottom of a wall to hide the gap between the wall and the floor
Slaking	the process of mixing calcium oxide (lime) with water
Slipper	part of the running mould that runs against the running rule. The running mould is used to form the shape of plasterwork, such as a dado. It is made using timber
Snot	a lump of aggregate stuck on a wall, left over from bricklaying, which often needs to be removed before plastering can commence
Specification	a document giving information that is too detailed to be contained on a drawing
Stiles	the side pieces of a stepladder into which the steps are set
Stopping in	using casting plaster for filling in the gap between the cornices or mouldings and ceiling and wall lines
Suction or absorption	the ability of the material to soak up water. The more water soaked up, the greater the suction
Symptom	a sign of illness or disease (e.g. difficulty in breathing, a sore hand, or a lump under the skin)
Tampering back	adding water to the mixed plaster on the spot board and remixing
Tie-rods	metal rods underneath the rungs of a wooden ladder that give extra support to the rungs
Togged	nailed at an angle
Toxic	poisonous
Truss	a prefabricated component of a roof that spreads the load of a roof over the outer walls and forms its shape
Undercut	an overhang that ties in the cast and so stops easy removal. An example is a re-entry curve, which is found on cornices that have been run in situ and which hug the wall and ceiling line
Vial	the glass tube containing liquid plus an air bubble
Vibration white finger	a condition that can be caused by using vibrating machinery (usually for very long periods of time). The blood supply to the fingers is reduced, which causes pain, tingling and sometimes spasms (shaking)
Wad	a piece of canvas soaked in plaster which forms an extremely strong fixing
Well	in the mixing process, the sand and cement is spread out and a hole is made in the middle for putting in the water; this is called the well
Work short	where the water runs out of the mix because there are no fines
Worn in	refers to a trowel that has been used mainly for floating, which makes it less rigid. A worn-in trowel reduces the lines left in the finishing coat of plaster, making it more suitable for skimming to produce a good finish

Index